A Korean War Captive in Japan, 1597–1600

A Korean War Captive in Japan, 1597–1600

The Writings of Kang Hang

EDITED AND TRANSLATED BY

JAHYUN KIM HABOUSH AND KENNETH R. ROBINSON

COLUMBIA UNIVERSITY PRESS   New York

COLUMBIA UNIVERSITY PRESS
Publishers Since 1893
NEW YORK   CHICHESTER, WEST SUSSEX
cup.columbia.edu
Copyright © 2013 Columbia University Press
Paperback edition, 2016
All rights reserved

This project was supported by the Academy of Korean Studies (Korean Studies Promotion Service) Grant funded by the Government of the Republic of Korea (Ministry of Education) (AKS-2007-AC-3001).

Library of Congress Cataloging-in-Publication Data
Kang, Hang, 1567–1618.
  [Kanyangnok. English]
  A Korean war captive in Japan, 1597–1600 : the writings of Kang Hang / edited and translated by
    JaHyun Kim Haboush and Kenneth R. Robinson.
      pages   cm.
  Includes bibliographical references and index.
  ISBN 978-0-231-16370-5 (cloth)—ISBN 978-0-231-16371-2 (pbk.)—ISBN 978-0-231-53511-3 (e-book)
  1. Korea—History—Japanese Invasions, 1592–1598—Prisoners and prisons, Japanese. 2. Korea—History—Japanese Invasions, 1592–1598—Personal narratives, Korean. 3. Prisoners of war—Japan—Biography. 4. Prisoners of war—Korea—Biography. 5. Japan—Description and travel—Early works to 1800. I. Haboush, JaHyun Kim editor, translator. II. Robinson, Kenneth R., 1962– editor, translator. III. Title.

  DS913.45.K36A313   2013
  951.9′02—dc23

                                                            2012039687

BOOK AND COVER DESIGN: CHANG JAE LEE
COVER IMAGE: PHOTOGRAPHY BY FUJITA SEIICHI, PROVIDED BY NHK PUBLISHING, INC.
  © TMHM (TOKIWA MUSEUM OF HISTORICAL MATERIALS).

Contents

Acknowledgments   vii
Introduction   ix

1. Encounters with the Adversities of War   1
2. An Exhortation to Koreans Still Held Prisoner in Japan   23
3. A Report to the Royal Secretariat on Japanese Social Practices   29
4. A Memorial Sent from Captivity   41

    Appendix 1. Japanese Daimyo in the Invasion of Chosŏn and Other Information   47
    Appendix 2. Suggestions for Military Reform and War Strategies   54
    Appendix 3. Japanese Generals Who Participated in the Imjin and Chŏngyu Invasions   71

5. Postscript   99

    Appendix 1. The Eight Circuits and Sixty-six Provinces of Japan   101
    Appendix 2. Japanese Government Offices   129
    Notes   133
    Bibliography   213
    Index   225

Acknowledgments

JAHYUN KIM HABOUSH SUGGESTED A JOINT TRANSLATION OF Kang Hang's *Kanyangnok* (The Record of a Shepherd) after seeing the list of titles for the Academy of Korean Studies Korean Classics Library 100 translation project. We submitted a proposal and were grateful to receive approval and funding. Sadly, she passed away before this translation could be published. I thank The Academy of Korean Studies for its continued support of this translation. And I thank her husband, William Haboush, for his constant encouragement.

In completing the translation we benefited from numerous library collections and the assistance of staff there. These include the Changsŏgak at The Academy of Korean Studies, the National Library of Korea (K. *Kungnip chungang tosŏgwan*), the Korea University Library (K. *Koryŏ taehakkyo tosŏgwan*), the National Archives of Japan Cabinet Library (J. *Kokuritsu kōbunshokan Naikaku bunko*), the National Diet Library (J. *Kokuritsu kokkai toshokan*), the University of Tokyo Institute for Advanced Studies on Asia Library (J. *Tōkyō daigaku Tōyō bunka kenkyūjo toshoshitsu*), the Tōyō Bunko, and the International Christian University Library (J. *Kokusai kirisutokyō daigaku toshokan*). We also learned from members of the PMJS: Premodern Japan Studies listserve. In particular, Brian Steininger, now Assistant Professor at Bates College, helped us to identify and study a Chinese poem. And the anonymous readers for Columbia University Press provided numerous suggestions for improving the text.

All of the administrative duties associated with The Academy of Korean Studies translation grant were handled by the International Christian

University Research Support Group. The staff expertly and patiently worked with documents in three languages, navigated financial systems in three countries, explained details in two languages, and managed numerous other bureaucratic matters. I am grateful to all of the Research Support Group staff for their assistance, and am very pleased to thank them here.

Introduction

THE RECORD OF A SHEPHERD (K. *KANYANGNOK*) CONSISTS OF the writings of Kang Hang (1567–1618) while he was a war captive in Japan during the Imjin War of 1592 to 1598 and for many months after. He and his family were captured by Japanese forces off the coast of Chŏlla Province, near his hometown, in the ninth month of 1597. They were taken to Japan, from which they made a number of attempts to escape, finally succeeding and returning to Chosŏn Korea (1392–1910) in the fifth month of 1600. Kang and his family were held by Tōdō Takatora (1556–1630) in Ōzu, in Shikoku, for about 10 months, were moved to Osaka in the ninth month of 1598, and then moved to Fushimi, from where they escaped to Chosŏn. Kang was one of a huge number of people taken captive and brought to Japan. It is not possible to ascertain the exact figure, but scholarly estimates range from 20,000 to 100,000.[1] Nor is it possible to determine how many of those taken to Japan returned to Chosŏn. After the war ended, the Chosŏn government insisted, as a condition for peace, on the repatriation of all Korean prisoners of war, but records show that about 7,500 people went back to Chosŏn.[2] Kang, one of the fortunate who returned home, would not have been counted in this number since he had escaped.

The war in which Kang was taken to Japan is known by various names, including the Imjin War (K. *Imjin Waeran*), the Campaigns of 1592 and 1597 (J. *Bunroku-Keichō no eki*), and the Rescue of Chosŏn (C. *Yuan Chaoxian*). It consisted of two parts: the first from the initial Japanese invasion that started in the fourth month of 1592 until a quasi-truce in the summer of 1593, after Ming China came to Chosŏn's assistance; and the second from the second month in 1597 until the Japanese retreat in 1598, following Toyotomi

Hideyoshi's (1537–98) death in the late summer. The two invasions are viewed as having been differently motivated. The first was launched by the self-assured Hideyoshi, who had recently unified Japan, to pursue his dream of establishing an Asian empire.[3] The second was carried out by a humiliated Hideyoshi, who belatedly realized that he had been duped into false terms of peace. He was intent on punishing the arrogant Ming and occupying the southern half of the Korean peninsula. He could not accomplish this either, but the second invasion is considered to have been more cruel, the damage to property and lives in Chosŏn greater, and the number of Koreans captured and taken to Japan larger.

The Imjin War, a rare event in which the three countries of East Asia, Japan, Korea, and China, were fully engaged at the state level,[4] had an immense impact on the region. The first effect in these three countries was from its sheer magnitude. More than 300,000 soldiers fought over the course of the war, by far the largest number fighting in the sixteenth century anywhere in the world. More crucially, both the invader and the aider changed political regimes after the war: Japan's government transformed into the Edo shogunate (1603–1868) and the Ming government was replaced by the Qing government (1644–1911), a Manchu-led multiethnic empire in China. The conventional wisdom that Ming China's participation in the war in Chosŏn had depleted the state treasury and thereby weakened it, hastening the empire's demise, has been contested. It has been proposed instead that Ming China was, in the first and second decades of the sixteenth century, much stronger and richer than previously estimated.[5] Whether or not Ming China's participation in the Imjin War led directly to its downfall, clearly, in the late sixteenth and the early seventeenth centuries, the region was caught up in a whirlwind of change both conceptually and phenomenally. Japan, an island country on the margin of the continent, claimed its own centrality, attempting to build a pan-Asian empire. Qing China was the Manchus' fulfillment of centuries-old dreams of ruling the whole of China. It is interesting that the new dream failed whereas the old one succeeded. Still, Japan also came to be seen differently. Viewed with fear, if not respect, it earned reluctant recognition as a power. East Asia fifty years after the Imjin War was a different place, measured either by the traditional concept of a central empire or by the relations among its constituent polities.

Negative encounters with "the other" are believed to engender and deepen a sense of identity.[6] In Chosŏn, where no one could avoid the brutalities of war, this became a conspicuous phenomenon. Movement by a great number of people caused by war also contributed to new conceptions of place. Many who lived through the war left some kind of writing, and although these texts differ in genre, content, and objective, they offer wide-ranging reactions to the mayhem, the discovery of the other, the reconsideration of self, and the emergence of a concept of home.

Prisoners of war occupied a special position in defining and articulating the emergent sense of identity. While they were hopeless outsiders, they also could be made into insiders. In a position of powerlessness, often subjected to torture and threats on their lives, they could be coerced into betraying their home country and swearing oaths of fealty to the new state. Some, however, endured threats and coercion and remained loyal, even seeking opportunities to spy for their home country. Others chose both alternatives. By their home country and by their captive one, prisoners of war were presented with delicate problems of "loyalty."

Protestations of loyalty by returned prisoners, thus were expressed in tropes embedded in the cultural logic of place. *The Record of a Shepherd* is regarded as a master tale of Confucian loyalty, narrated in familiar cultural symbols and icons. The Chinese, long in contention with the "barbarians" outside the Great Wall, from early on produced two opposite icons: one of loyalty, including those who remained faithful to civilization and the Chinese state, and one of traitors, including those who succumbed to barbarians, thus betraying civilizational values and the Chinese state. Of many, Su Wu (140–60 B.C.E.) and Li Ling (d. 74 B.C.E.) of the Han dynasty served as primary historical models. On a diplomatic mission, Su Wu's party was trapped by the Xiongnu and told to surrender under threat of death. Su Wu alone refused. After torture, Su was sent into distant exile to tend sheep; despite constant pressure to surrender, he persisted in his loyalty. In 81 B.C.E., a Han envoy, upon discovering that Su was alive, tricked the Xiongnu into admitting his existence. Su was repatriated to China, where he was honored and given high office. He had been a captive for nineteen years. Su Wu and shepherding became emblems of loyalty for prisoners of war. At the opposite stood Li Ling, a famous general, who, when he was nearly defeated, defected to the Xiongnu and accepted the riches and power that they offered. At some point, he even attempted to persuade Su Wu to accept the Xiongnu's offer. In the narrative of the encounter between Li and Su, their choices are portrayed as the result of an attachment to personal riches and power or a determination to live and die in whatever the circumstances might be, maintaining civilizational values including loyalty and seeking to be remembered in history.

That *The Record of a Shepherd* is written in the cultural trope of Su Wu is obvious. Both the text and paratext place Kang in a historical framework of unswervingly loyal heroes in the larger national tragedy. Kang himself makes numerous references to Su Wu. In "An Exhortation to Koreans Still Held Prisoner in Japan" (chapter 2), he recalls the nineteen long years that Su Wu spent in remote Xiongnu lands to encourage his fellow Korean captives. In renaming the text *Kanyangnok*, or *The Record of a Shepherd*, Kang's students were clearly drawing a parallel to this famed cultural icon of loyalty. Taking a cue from Su, Kang not once expresses ambivalence about his intentions. From the outset, there is no question of compromise. When Kang and his family felt that they could not escape being captured by the enemy, they all jumped into the sea. But because the water was shallow, they did not drown. This may have been an obligatory gesture of loyalty, and afterward Kang did not try to kill himself again. There is much death in the family—aside from various members who were taken away and never seen again, Kang's young son and daughter, who had been left on a beach when the adults jumped into the sea, were swallowed by the tides. When his eight-year-old nephew became ill, the Japanese threw the boy into the sea to drown. Two more children, a niece and a nephew, died of illness. One of the duties of a Confucian man in the patriarchal system was to preserve his line, and Kang, leading his family, might have felt compelled to abide by this. He certainly decided that dying was a waste. Even under the extreme circumstances, it was better to preserve his life, as Su Wu did, and find some way to display his loyalty.

Kang's responses to Japan and his activities there were construed with this objective in mind. When he first saw Tsushima, he realized that he had come to a different world. When he saw Kamigaseki, he admired its beauty but did not neglect to comment, "how lamentable that this place was a den of devils." Several failed attempts to escape from Japan seem either unprepared or ill-considered, but this did not affect him or his family. They took every chance they could, sometimes at great peril. On one occasion, Kang and a compatriot were threatened that in punishment for their escape attempt they would be drawn and quartered. Notably, Kang spied for his country, an ultimate expression of loyalty. During his captivity, he was able to gather information on Japan and copied voluminous quantities of material. "A Memorial Sent from Captivity" (chapter 4) is accompanied by a number of pieces he gathered and copied. Some are straightforward copies of such things as a gazetteer of Japan, and others are policy suggestions based on his observations and analyses of Japanese practices in comparison with Korean ones. He offered a prodigious amount. Chosŏn was in dire need of information about

Japan, and though some of these materials were not current or useful, others were. Whether the material was accurate was not as crucial as the very fact of Kang's assiduous endeavors to amass and relay information.

How did he procure the material that he passed on to Chosŏn? Some news Kang received by talking to other Korean captives. As for the written materials that he copied, such as a map, a gazetteer (appendix 1), and a list of Japanese government offices (appendix 2), he seems to have borrowed these from a Japanese monk or found them in an encyclopedia. It is not clear why the Japanese monk would have lent this material to a Korean captive, but it is plausible that Kang asked and the monk did not see much harm in doing so. However we interpret the process, we can see a different relationship between captor and captive, and with this change we witness a different concept of civilization.

On the one hand, civilization is defined as geographical and cultural distinctiveness that separate a region from barbarian areas. On the other hand, civilization is shared and sustained by all civilized persons, transcending regional and ethnic barriers. Though contradictory, these exclusive and inclusive definitions coexist. Kang's life as a captive straddled the two: while he was actively copying information on Japan, he was also making acquaintances and engaging in discourse on Confucian philosophy with Japanese scholars. Of particular note is his friendly relationship with Fujiwara Seika (1561–1619), an early Edo-period scholar of Neo-Confucianism, who appears in this narrative under his Buddhist name of Myōsuin Sōshun. In Kang's narrative, Seika appears friendly and supportive, if somewhat elusive. They seem to have spent time together enjoying aesthetic and scholarly activities. On one occasion, for instance, they wrote poems together on painted screens. Seika also seems to have helped Kang to escape—first by finding a way for him to accumulate money by selling his calligraphy, and then by helping him to procure passage home. It appears they did forge a respectful and trusting friendship that transcended the adversarial relationship their countries imposed on them and that opened an inclusive civilizational space.

It is interesting that Kang's devotion to the exclusive notion of civilization could be fulfilled only when he embraced an inclusive idea of civilization. His spying as well as his safe return home were made possible through friendly relations with Japanese. *The Record of a Shepherd*'s historical importance can also be attributed to his dual position. Many historians, including Abe Yoshio, believe that Kang played a crucial role in transmitting the Zhu Xi school of Neo-Confucianism to Japan. That is, the T'oegye school of Zhu Xi (1130–1200) scholarship, developed by Yi Hwang (pen name T'oegye; 1501–70), was transmitted to Seika through Kang.[7] Seika, in turn, had a decisive influence on Hayashi Razan (1583–1657), who established a Neo-Confucian school based on Zhu Xi scholarship and served as an adviser to Tokugawa shoguns. Kang's work does not highlight his relationship with Seika, but does not hide it either. It is just part of the background to his activities. In the collected works of Seika, Kang's written conversation (K. *p'ildam*, J. *hitsudan*) with Seika on philosophy occupies a prominent place.[8] Although this piece does not reveal much—the text is short and formal—it is noteworthy that a work devoted to Kang is in a place of honor. Today, Kang's importance is understood to lie in the intellectual connection he made with Japan at a time of suspicion and distrust between Chosŏn and Japan. It is ironic that while *The Record of a Shepherd* professes to be devoted to the most exclusive notion of civilization, its value lies in its opening and practicing a more inclusive idea of civilization. This expressed the tensions and contradictions of East Asia at the time.

The Main Texts

When Kang returned to Chosŏn, he brought along what he had copied and written in Japan. His former students edited and compiled these writings into a cohesive book, titling it *Kanyangnok*. Intent on establishing Kang's unswerving loyalty to Chosŏn, they highlighted political pieces, placing them first in the book. We have translated all of *The Record of a Shepherd*, but we have changed the order in which the pieces are presented. We start with personal and individual pieces. The first, "Encounters with the Adversities of War," is Kang's account of his experience as a prisoner of war, from the time that he and his family were captured by the Japanese and taken to Japan until he escaped and returned to Chosŏn. Though narrated in a simple manner, it is an extraordinary story, both complex and revealing. It gives an account of the sufferings of prisoners of war. As an official, Kang was treated better than others, but even he and his family could not escape the cruelty of the Japanese toward the old and the sick. The account exhibits Kang's sense of self—the degree to which his sense of identity was informed by the Confucian concept of loyalty, which drove his unflagging determination to return home and his repeated attempts to escape from captivity. It also points to encounters with others, the way the barrier between the self and the other was perceived, shifted, and, occasionally, transcended. The account also documents Kang's friendship with Seika—their periodic get-togethers, their discourse, and their aesthetic enjoyment of calligraphy, poetry, and painting.

The second piece, "An Exhortation to Koreans Still Held Prisoner in Japan," is an open letter Kang wrote to the Koreans held in Japan. As befitting an exhortation, a genre directed against the other and expounding on a shared objective of maintaining a distinct community, it is a rousing anti-Japanese and antibarbarian piece. Following the logic of the civilized interior and the barbarous exterior, Japan is condemned for barbarity, inhumanity, and cruelty to the Korean state and people. Kang wrote that the only way to recover humanity and restore civilization to Chosŏn was to persevere, just as Su Wu and countless others had done. This is, of course, a familiar trope, but this letter articulates most clearly and vociferously the notion of an exclusive civilization, without ambiguity. Apparently, Kang's students included it in the collection to demonstrate his total, unsullied loyalty.

The third piece, "A Report to the Royal Secretariat on Japanese Social Practices," is the only text in the collection that Kang wrote after he returned to Chosŏn. He wrote it at the explicit request of King Sŏnjo (1552–1608, r. 1567–1608), who wished for more information on Japan, especially on the question of whether Japan might again invade Chosŏn. Kang begins with a long account of his conversations with Japanese friends and Koreans in the Japanese capital area and their views of the likelihood of Japan's reinvasion. He even relates a conversation in Tsushima with Yanagawa Shigenobu (1539–1605), who was one of the island province's top officials. Yanagawa spoke of the difficulties that Hideyoshi's push for war had brought to the islanders and of their desire to revive relations with Chosŏn. This is the only time in *The Record of a Shepherd* that Kang presents the voice of a Japanese man who fought in the war. As this memorial includes Kang's passage through Tsushima, it seems to have also been based on notes that Kang carried (perhaps "smuggled" is a more appropriate word) with him from Japan. In particular, he quotes or paraphrases conversations about the possibility of future conflict.

He also discusses a number of topics, such as the poor quality of Japanese practitioners of divination and fortune-telling because of their lack of knowledge, Japanese construction and residences, swords and social position, religion, and personal relations. He writes of Japanese interest in visits by foreigners and notes the presence of Chinese residing in the capital area. Having begun this section with a brief comment about his arrival in Pusan, Kang describes the route by which his boat sailed there from Fushimi, in Japan. He closes by noting the prevalence of natural disasters in Japan, which he sarcastically attributes to the "barbarian virtue" of the Japanese. This piece shows how broadly Kang ranged in collecting information about Japanese culture, society, and politics; speaks of the wealth of written and vocal conversations he engaged in with Japanese and Koreans; and hints at the volume of the notes that he wrote in Ōzu and Fushimi.

The fourth piece, "A Memorial Sent from Captivity," is what Kang sent to King Sŏnjo from Fushimi. It was written as a cover letter to a number of pieces on Japan that he had copied or written and secretly compiled for the benefit of the Chosŏn court. The memorial is dated the tenth day of the fourth month in the twenty-seventh year of Wanli (1599). The narrative is similar in structure to "Encounters with the Adversities of War," but it is less than half as long and is entirely informed by a Confucian political sense of self. At the beginning, Kang confesses that in the course of his being captured the Board of Taxation documents that recorded army provisions disappeared into the water, that he may have been seriously derelict in his duty, and that he deserves severe punishment. He says that the Japanese recognized him as an official, placed him and his family on a ship, and took them to Japan. He focuses on several themes in his memorial. The first is Korean captives. At the beginning of the journey, he saw six or seven hundred ships, half of which were filled with Korean captives. At Ōzu, the first place his group was made to stay, there were about 1,000 Koreans. Koreans appear constantly as co-conspirators for escape and as sources of information with whom he exchanged news.

The second theme is Kang's continuous efforts to escape from Japan. He made several attempts. There were only limited ways to earn money to procure a ship: by eating less and selling the remaining provisions, and, in the case of Kang, who apparently was recognized for his erudition, by selling calligraphy. The repeated failures at escape plunged him into deep despair at times, but he concluded that if he were to die, it would make him "unable to repay the state by acts of loyalty and integrity, and make it impossible to leave an honorable name by choosing the right moment to die." In his situation, the way to show loyalty would be by spying and offering information on Japan, and this is his third theme. He copied a gazetteer and a text regarding the administrative offices of Japan from texts borrowed from a Japanese monk; he also copied a map of Japan that he had encountered. In addition to these documents, he offers his own policy opinions. Kang says that he is aware that this is an inappropriate act for a criminal, but he could not but speak up for the benefit of his country.

Kang's memorial ends with fervent protestations of his loyalty. He mentions several historical personages who had been taken captive but who persevered. Kang confesses he is not as worthy as they, but as far as loyalty or concern for the country's welfare is concerned, he concedes nothing to these paragons:

> Even though my life is worth no more than the life of an insect, as long as I have even one breath remaining, my loyalty is like that of a dog or a horse that cannot be broken even after ten thousand blows. It would be much better, even if having escaped to my country by using my wiles, I were to be punished by death, my head and body sliced in half at the middle in the courtyard of the Royal Court, than to be buried in this barbarian land.

Kang's memorial is a tour de force display of the Confucian rhetoric of loyalty; it also articulates a sense of Korean ethnicity and of Chosŏn as homeland. For example, when he saw thousands of Korean captives held in ships, they all wailed and cried. He met with them, sympathized with them, and unceasingly schemed for ways to escape from Japan. When he writes, "As long as I live, I can never resume the dignity of an official at our royal court; but if I could pass Tsushima to see Pusan even but once again in the morning to die that evening, I would have no regret," one cannot but be moved by his heartfelt longing for his homeland. This poignant expression of his sense of Korean ethnicity and his concept of home as the locus of a civilized people are repeated and expressed in other writings, where they are in fact the foundation of his narrative. In this starkly political document, however, the sharp expression of sympathy and kinship with his compatriots, and longing for his home, emerge vividly and jolt the reader.

The memorial arrived safely at the Chosŏn court on the fifteenth day of the fourth month of 1599, a mere five days after it was dated.[9] It is quite remarkable that, sent as it was through a secret courier—a Chinese man by the name of He Yingchao (d.u.), it reached its destination so swiftly. It is not clear, however, that the copy that arrived at the Chosŏn court was given to He on the tenth day of the fourth month. To make certain that the memorial and the information it contained were authentic, the Chosŏn court conducted a careful investigation. Three months later, in the seventh month, the findings were reported to the throne. What He reported to the court was that Kang had made copies and given one to He and one to another person.[10]

Moreover, within the memorial, Kang mentions that he is giving a copy to a Korean captive who was planning an escape to Chosŏn.

The memorial must have been considered quite significant, as the greater part of it was transcribed into *Sŏnjo sillok*. The text in the *Veritable Records*, however, is not a truncated version of that in *The Record of a Shepherd*. The two versions are quite similar—indeed, almost identical—but each includes passages not found in the other.

What distinguished the memorial were the informative reports on Japan that accompanied it. There were six extra items, four of which are translated in the main section of the text here; the other two appear as appendices. In *The Record of a Shepherd*, the items are presented under the heading, "What I Have Seen and Heard in My Captivity." The first item, "Japanese Daimyo in the Invasion of Chosŏn and Other Information," is a broad selection of contradictory information about Japan that is introductory but that Kang thought was of interest to the Korean government.

He begins with a historical overview of the rulers of Japan, from the ancient emperors to Oda Nobunaga (1534–82) and Hideyoshi. Expanding on military rule, he discusses landholding by warrior elites in the provinces. This topic provided the text's intended readers in Chosŏn with a comparison to the stipend land grants that the Korean government extended to officials who had passed the higher civil service examination (K. *munkwa*).

Kang then discusses travel and travelers in Japan and those from Japan to the continent, including Kōbō Daishi (774–835), better known as Kūkai. This leads to a consideration of the ninth-century monk's statistics on religious institutions, population, and other metrics of Japanese society. Then Kang provides two lists of Japanese generals who fought in Chosŏn. The first identifies men who participated in the first invasion, and the second identifies men active in the second invasion and occasionally includes their activities in Chosŏn. He also profiles three monks who assisted in the war.

The last topic he discusses is the military: how soldiers and resources were mobilized for battle, including logistical support such as weapons and food accumulated through a local chain of command in the provinces. This discussion was also no doubt intended for comparison with the Korean government's system of recruitment and training. As the worry of another invasion from Japan had not been quelled, this discussion might have been of considerable interest to the Korean government.

The second piece accompanying the memorial, "Suggestions for Military Reform and War Strategies," is more specifically on military matters. It begins with a sharp criticism of the Korean military system and its practices. Kang says that there was neither recruitment nor systematic military training in Chosŏn. Appointment was indiscriminate and tenure was arbitrary. Dismissals were irrational, for example, that of Admiral Yi Sunsin (1545–98), which led to the loss of Hansan Island. Kang then argues for the construction of fortifications and the recruitment of permanent personnel to staff them, and mentions the consequent desirability of offering salary land and making associated posts heritable. He also argues for a consolidation of ramparts and towns. Many of these suggestions seem to have been based on his acquaintance with the Japanese system. Further, he points out the advantages of embracing and using Japanese who surrendered to Chosŏn.

In shifting his focus to how to end the war, Kang begins with Hideyoshi's illness and death. Here Kang talks of the order that Hideyoshi is said to have made at the time of the second invasion: soldiers were instructed not to sever the heads of Koreans after killing them but to cut off their noses, salt them, and send them to Japan. It is interesting that the nose mound in Kyoto was already known. Kang ends this report with the acerbic remark about Hideyoshi: "Within a year, his own stomach was salted!" In any event, the situation in Japan became rather complex after Hideyoshi's death, and Kang discusses in detail three options to end the war.

The third piece accompanying the memorial is "Japanese Generals Who Participated in the Imjin and Chŏngyu Invasions." Kang's survey of Japanese generals and their activities, which he wrote after returning to Chosŏn, describes how complicated and unstable Japanese politics became after Hideyoshi's death. In providing background on many of the most powerful generals in the late 1590s, Kang introduces his readers to men maneuvering for power in Japan. He also offers historical background, notes on the generals' activities during the invasion, and comments on the future.

Kang begins with a biography of Hideyoshi, clearly a leader of interest to Korean officials. It describes Hideyoshi's skill at negotiation and relates reports of his determination before the 1592 invasion to confront the Korean military and then the Chinese military at their best. Profiles of several generals and their conflicts convey a sense of complicated political and familial relationships, rivalries, and alliances.

Kang concludes by writing about two Japanese, Seika and Akamatsu Hiromichi (1562–1600), who befriended him during his residence in Fushimi. Kang recalls how Seika and others helped him, his family, and other Koreans to escape Fushimi and to reach Chosŏn in 1600. The section contains many details that overlap with information provided in other texts in *The Record of a Shepherd*. Reading the section with the earlier texts in mind only enhances its importance.

The memorial is followed by a "Map of Japan" (Waeguk chido), which will be discussed below. The "Postscript," which completes the book, was written by Kang's student Yun Sun'gŏ (1596–1668). A student panegyric, it reverentially places Kang beside historical icons of loyalty. It is one of the first paratexts on this theme, and many followed.

Appendices

The gazetteer "The Eight Circuits and Sixty-six Provinces of Japan" is probably the text Kang reproduced in Ōzu in late 1597 or early 1598. It divides Japan into circuits and then introduces the provinces in each circuit. The profiles of the provinces follow a set pattern. They begin with the province's official name and a second name by which it also was known. Next is the province's rank within the ancient hierarchy and the number of districts, and their names. Following this is information about agriculture and other forms of production. The size of the province and the quality of its land also are ranked. Information about topography and weather are provided for some provinces, and special features are noted. The profile ends with names of men holding domains in that province.

If this gazetteer is the one Kang reproduced in Ōzu, he must have added information after his relocation to Fushimi, including names of landholders in each province. Landholders are not identified elsewhere in *The Record of a Shepherd*. While the provincial profile provides information originally structured for a Japanese audience, the landholders were added probably because they would have been of interest to the Chosŏn king and government officials.

The title of the second appendix, "Japanese Government Offices," suggests that in this text Kang describes the central government of Japan. He concentrates, rather, on the titles of offices and posts, most of which had been introduced in and after 645 and used by the Heian court. While the Kamakura *bakufu* governed from the Kantō area, the Heian court continued to exercise power. In 1392, the Northern Court supported by the Muromachi *bakufu* defeated the Southern Court in a war fought from 1336. Established in Kyoto in 1336, the Muromachi *bakufu* utilized Heian government posts as court titles with few or no significant administrative duties in its government.

Aristocratic families whose ancestors had held posts in the Heian court continued to receive those appointments, but their efforts focused on landholdings or the imperial family.

This list of offices and posts may be that which Kang had reproduced from a Japanese text in Ōzu in late 1597 and early 1598. He provides most of the highest-ranking posts in the court's hierarchy but does not include every bureau, office, and agency. Kang offers two types of information for each entry. In *The Record of a Shepherd*, the Japanese term is in regular font size. Printed in a smaller font size is an explanatory term or the office's or post's equivalent in Tang China's (618–907) bureaucracy, which the Japanese government adopted and adapted from the seventh century. It is not clear what text or texts Kang used in compiling this list. The inclusion of Chinese government equivalents suggests that his source(s) provided that information too.

Various Editions of *Kanyangnok*

The oldest extant printed edition of *The Record of a Shepherd* is in *Suŭn chip* (The Collected Writings of Suŭn), or Kang's collected writings compiled by former students. Suŭn was Kang's pen name. Yun Sun'gŏ and his fourth uterine younger brother, Yun Sŏn'gŏ (1610–69), completed this compilation in the fourth month of 1658.[11] *The Record of a Shepherd* ends with a postscript written by Sun'gŏ and dated to 1654. The collected writings conclude with a postscript written by Yu Kye (1607–64) in 1656.[12] Song Siyŏl (1607–89) wrote the preface for *Suŭn chip* in 1658.

Various relationships linked the authors of the postscripts for *The Record of a Shepherd* and *Suŭn chip* and the preface for *Suŭn chip*. These men and their families were connected by education and marriage ties. Yun Sun'gŏ had accompanied his father, Yun Hwang (1571–1639), to Yŏnggwang County on his assignment as magistrate in 1609. The father served there until the second half of 1613.[13] While in Yŏnggwang, Sun'gŏ studied poetry under Kang and the classics under Sŏng Munjun (1559–1626). The first son of Sun'gŏ's second uterine younger brother, Mun'gŏ, married the daughter of Song Siyŏl.[14] And Sun'gŏ, Yu Kye (1607–64), and Song Siyŏl (1607–89) studied under Kim Changsaeng (1548–1631), who had studied under Yi I (pen name Yulgok; 1536–84). Kang had studied under Sŏng Hon (1535–98), and Yun Hwang married Sŏng Hon's second daughter.[15]

Locally, members of the Kang and Yun families cooperated in the establishment of Yonggye Shrine for Kang in Yubong Village, Pulgap District,

Yŏnggwang County in 1635. Fire destroyed the shrine before the year ended, and it was rebuilt in 1636. Song Siyŏl contributed by writing the shrine name on the shrine tablet (K. *p'yŏnaek*).[16] In 1682, Sun'gŏ, who had died in 1668, was added to Yonggye Shrine. It also had a school with an enrollment of fifteen students.[17] Naesan Sŏwŏn, an academy, was opened in Pulgap in 1635 to commemorate Kang. The earlier, manuscript edition of *The Record of a Shepherd* is preserved there today.

Suŭn chip begins with Song Siyŏl's preface. The table of contents and the collected writings, including poems, memorials, and other texts, follow. *The Record of a Shepherd*, a distinct text within *Suŭn chip*, is followed by a biography (K. *haengjang*) of Kang written by Sun'gŏ, an appendix (K. *purok*) of writings by others about Kang, and an addendum (K. *pyŏlchip*) to Kang's collected writings. Thus, there are multiple sets of pagination in *Suŭn chip*: for Kang's poetry and other writings (volumes 1 through 4); for *The Record of a Shepherd* (1a–92b); for the biography (1a–15b); for the appendix (1a–11b); and for the addendum (1a–42a).

The earliest confirmed printing of *The Record of a Shepherd* is believed to have been based upon a manuscript text that bears the date 1605 and is thought to be similar to Kang's text.[18] It includes a note presumed to have been written by the copyist, who identified himself as an official dispatched to the southern part of the country. While performing his duties, he met Kang in Yŏnggwang County. This individual probably was Min Yŏim (1559–1627), whom King Sŏnjo appointed as the Secret Censor of Inspection for Chŏlla Province on the first day of the third month of 1605.[19] If Min was the copyist, he must have completed his work in Yŏnggwang before the twenty-third day of the sixth month, when he sent a memorial to the throne. Three days earlier, King Sŏnjo had appointed him to the Office of the Inspector-General as Fourth Inspector.[20] Considering the time needed to travel from Yŏnggwang County to Seoul, Min probably completed the reproduction by early in the sixth month. The 1605 Naesan Sŏwŏn manuscript text may have been completed between the first of the third month and the middle of the sixth month.

The 1605 manuscript text varies from the 1658 printing. First, the order of sections in the table of contents for the 1658 *Suŭn chip* follows the order in the Naesan Sŏwŏn text, but the actual order of sections in *The Record of a Shepherd* in the 1658 *Suŭn chip* does not match the table of contents. The manuscript text does not include the map of Japan in *The Record of a Shepherd* in *Suŭn chip*. And the postscript written by Yun Sun'gŏ in the Naesan Sŏwŏn text is reported to be shorter than that in the 1658 printing.[21] This third point is intriguing, because Sun'gŏ, having been born in 1596, would have been but ten years old when Min Yŏim completed the Naesan Sŏwŏn text in 1605. To speculate, Sun'gŏ's postscript may have been appended to the manuscript edition later and subsequently revised for the printed edition.

As noted, the 1605 Naesan Sŏwŏn text is believed to have been the source for the 1658 printing. In a detailed comparison of the 1605 manuscript text and the 1658 printed text, Song Ilgi and An Hyŏnju identified 176 differences between these two editions. They grouped the changes into nine categories, which include the addition of a section title (*Chŏkchung pongso*; "A Memorial Sent from Captivity"), the "correction" (K. *kyojŏng*) of Chinese characters, edits such as the addition or deletion of characters, and the movement of text. Among the corrections are those for Japanese court titles held by individuals, personal names (for example, "Shimazu Hidehiro" became "Shimazu Yoshihiro"), place names, and numbers. In one instance, the term "King of Japan" (K. *kugwang*)—the formal title for diplomatic purposes by which the Chosŏn government had referred to the sitting shogun or the retired shogun, with whom the King of Chosŏn had engaged in diplomatic relations of equality within Ming China's tribute system—was changed to "Emperor" (K. *ch'ŏnhwang*, J. *tennō*).[22] How incorrect characters for Japanese terms were identified and appropriate characters known is an important issue for understanding the preparation of the 1658 printing.

Korean government officials had access to Kang's writings on Japan from the first decades of the seventeenth century. Both direct references to the text and transcriptions that do not name the source are numerous. An early example of the latter is found in the writings of the government official Yi Sugwang (pen name Chibong; 1563–1628). He included material about Japan in his survey of foreign countries in *Chibong yusŏl* (Classified Essays of Chibong), completed in 1614.[23]

A much later example is from Yi Chihang (d.u.), whose ship sailed off course to the island now known as Hokkaido in 1756. Yi noted at the end of his account that Kang had been taken to Japan in 1597 and had compiled *The Record of a Shepherd*. He then repeated information about the island of Kinzan in Mutsu Province and people residing there from Kang's treatment of Mutsu Province in the gazetteer. And he wrote, "The printing blocks for Lord Kang's *Suŭn chip* are in Yŏnggwang."[24] Further, references to Kang, *Kanyangnok*, and *Suŭn chip* by Korean officials who visited Japan in the embassies of the seventeenth and eighteenth centuries may have derived from *Haehaeng ch'ongjae*, a collection of Korean writings on Japan that included *Kanyangnok*.

The Record of a Shepherd was available even in Japan in the early eighteenth century. Sin Yuhan (b. 1681), the Secretary (K. *Chesulgwan*) in the 1719 Communication Embassy, expressed concern that *The Record of a Shepherd* and other Korean texts conveying information about Chosŏn that should be kept from the Japanese were available for purchase in Osaka.[25] No extant printings are reported, however.

The Record of a Shepherd was later printed as a single text; several examples are extant in South Korea.[26] Though this is speculation, they may have been printed as early as 1805. A manuscript text held in the Changsŏgak library at the Academy of Korean Studies suggests this. On the cover is the phrase "presented to the King in the fifth year." Im Ch'igyun combines that date with other information in the manuscript to argue that a text presented to King Sunjo (r. 1800–34) in 1805, or the fifth full year of his reign, served as the manuscript edition's base text. The Changsŏgak manuscript text, which has only the sections of *The Record of a Shepherd* that directly relate to Japan and writings on foreign relations found elsewhere in *Suŭn chip*, is dated to the spring of 1812.[27]

Another printing of *Suŭn chip* appeared in 1868. *The Record of a Shepherd* in this edition of Kang's collected writings varies from the 1658 printing. First, the pagination of the 1868 printing proceeds without break through folio 89. The next folio is also numbered 89, though its contents differ from the preceding folio 89. Following the second folio 89 are folios 91 and 92. That is, there is no folio numbered 90. Following folio 92 is the map of Japan. Folio 93 closes *The Record of a Shepherd* with Yun Sun'gŏ's postscript.[28]

Second, the title that appears in the middle of the folio (K. *pansimje*; folding mark title), where it is folded in half for binding, is not consistent between the versions. In the 1658 printing, the title in the middle of the folio has a space of two characters between the word "Suŭn" and the word "Kanyangnok." This space was closed in the 1868 printing.

A third distinction is the number of characters per column. The 1658 printing and the 1868 printing are consistent through folio 6b, column 8. Each folio has ten columns, and each column has twenty characters. From folio 6b, column 9, the number of characters in each column in the 1658 printing becomes inconsistent; column 9 has 19 characters, for example. In the 1868 printing, column 9 has 20 characters. Fourth, the font of the characters varies. The earlier printing alternates between two fonts. The 1868 printing has one font throughout. These features result in text not being on the same folio side (recto or verso) in the two printings.

Two further differences are found in the map of Japan. One is the shape of the island of Tsushima. In the 1658 edition, the island was carved with an indentation that resembles a bay on the right side. In the 1868 edition, the island was carved in a circular shape. The other is the way the name of the island called "Tsushima" in Japan was printed. In the 1658 printing, the island's name is "Tsushima," or "Taema" in Korean. The two characters are printed vertically in the island cartouche. In the 1868 printing, however, the name is "Tsushima-tō," or "Taema-do" in Korean. That is, a third character, K. *to* (J. *shima, tō*; island), was added. The name was printed in two rows, each read from right to left. The third character is in the second row and below the first character in the first row, *tae*. Other distinctions may perhaps be added, but those noted here provide means for distinguishing between the 1658 printing and the 1868 printing.

Collecting Information in Japan

The Record of a Shepherd relates opportunities for Kang to gather information in Japan, including from written texts. Soon after arriving in Ōzu, he met a Japanese monk who subsequently showed him "various documents relating to his country, among them a geographical gazetteer and a table of the administrative offices of Japan." Kang copied these. He may have learned one or both of the Japanese *katakana* and *hiragana* syllabaries while in Ōzu, for he wrote, "When I copied those documents of the Japanese monk, I translated those portions written in Japanese *kana* into Korean so that they may be used in interrogating and acquiring information from Japanese who have surrendered to Chosŏn." Or perhaps he asked one or more Koreans who had been in Japan longer and who were more familiar with the Japanese language to assist in preparing the translations.

The gazetteer in *The Record of a Shepherd* may have derived from that in an edition of the Japanese dictionary *Setsuyōshū* (Collection of Words for Everyday Use).[29] This dictionary is in the traditional *iroha* order of the syllabary, with words arranged by category under each *kana* entry. A gazetteer follows the dictionary in the 1597 printing of *Setsuyōshū*, which is referred to as the Ekirin text, after the Buddhist monk who edited this edition.

Kang's profiles of provinces contain data found in the Ekirin text's gazetteer. These include a second name by which each province was known, the province's administrative rank, the number of its districts and their names, the province's size, and comments on its land. Kang's order of information differs from the Ekirin text, though. In *The Record of a Shepherd*, the lists of districts precede descriptive notes on the size and quality of the land. And as noted, he added further information, such as who were the important landholders and what was grown in the province.

The source for the information about the government bureaucracy may have been an encyclopedia then in wide circulation in Japan. *Shūgaishō* (Collection of Oddments), compiled in the first half of the fourteenth century and extant in manuscript editions completed in the sixteenth century, contains a list of government offices and posts and their equivalents in the Tang bureaucracy.[30] The order of government offices and posts in *The Record of a Shepherd* does not match it, but this may perhaps reflect consultation with Japanese acquaintances about, for example, which offices and posts had been entrusted with guarding the imperial palace and policing the capital. Nor do the Tang equivalents match in all instances. It is not clear, however, to what extent Kang understood that administration in Japan in the late 1590s did not follow the outline he was reproducing. This information in *Shūgaishō* may have derived from *Shokugenshō* (Treatise on the Origins of Government Offices), a more detailed description that was completed in the fourteenth century and widely known.[31]

Kang mentions a map of Japan twice in *The Record of a Shepherd*. In the first instance, he states that he learned of "an extremely detailed map of Japan" that the father of Tōdō Takatora possessed. The father showed the map to an "interpreter," probably a Korean captive who had been in Japan some time and had achieved some fluency in Japanese. Later, Kang refers to the same map in the context of reporting statistics for population, temples, shrines, fields, and other items in Japan. He introduces those figures by stating, "Earlier, someone showed me a text that Kōbō Daishi is said to have written." A similar list accompanies the sixteenth-century manuscript map of Japan entitled "Nansenbushū Dai Nihon-koku shōtōzu" (Orthodox Map of Great Japan in Jambūdvīpa) that is held by Tōshōdaiji temple, near Nara. Interestingly, the Ekirin text's gazetteer bears the same title as this map.

Mapping Japan

A model for the map of Japan in *The Record of a Shepherd* may have been "Nansenbushū Dai Nihon-koku shōtōzu" or a similar handwritten image. Kang's description of Japan matches the orientation in this map. His "Map of

Japan" too is set with north at the bottom of the frame and west to the viewer's right. In this arrangement of space, Tsushima is in the lower right corner.³²

Kang's map depicts foremost the administrative geography of Japan. Beginning with Kyoto, the emperor's capital, it extends downward through the circuits (J. *dō*) to the provinces (J. *shū*). Other features of the political landscape include Osaka, Fushimi, and Edo. Kang identifies Osaka as the "western capital" (K. *sŏgyŏng*) and Fushimi as the "new capital" (K. *singyŏng*) elsewhere in *The Record of a Shepherd*.³³ Kyoto (as J. *kukto*; the capital of the country), Fushimi, and Edo are marked in double-line, circular cartouches and Osaka in a single-line, circular cartouche. The identification of Edo in a double-line cartouche must have occurred after the establishment of the new government there in 1603, meaning that this cartouche must have entered the map after Kang's return to Chosŏn. And the marking of Osaka with a single-line cartouche suggests that the map was completed after the defeat of Hideyoshi's son Toyotomi Hideyori (1593–1615) at his base of Osaka Castle in 1615 and the elimination of Osaka as a capital (in this case, of Hideyori and his claims as successor to Hideyoshi) in Japan. That is, this image does not reflect Japan during the period of Kang's captivity; it is an updated representation.

Two other cartouche forms identify levels of administration introduced nearly one millennium earlier. The single-line, eight-sided cartouche is for the circuits, and the single-line, rectangular cartouche is for the provinces. Among the terms marked in the latter style is "Yama." This is an abbreviation of "Yamatai," the name of an ancient country in Japan that Kang writes was situated in what became Yamato Province. (In "Map of Japan," the first character in "Yamato" is written not as "big" 大 [K. *tae*, J. *dai*] but as "broad" 太 [K. *t'ae*, J. *tai*].)³⁴

Tsushima and Iki were not identified by the cartouche for provinces because Kang, following his source, classified them as "islands."³⁵ These two place names were written in island icons. Kang also identified an area in northern Honshu and an island north of Honshu as "Ezochi" and "Ezogashima," respectively.

There are thirty-seven landforms in the image that Kang presumably intended as representing islands. Three of these were provinces (Awaji, Oki, and Sado), but Shima Province, although depicted as an island and despite sharing the same pronunciation as the Japanese word for "island," was not an island. Also, the map historian Unno Kazutaka suggested that Kang had read district names in the Ekirin text's gazetteer ending with the character for "island" as identifying islands, although they sometimes did not, and included several in his map.³⁶

Following the gazetteer and a discussion of Hideyoshi and Japanese politics in *The Record of a Shepherd* is a sentence that identifies several Japanese islands: "In addition, there also are Erabu, Hirado-jima, Gotō, Shichijima, Tanegashima, Isshujima, Koshikijima, and Hachijōjima."[37] Of these eight island names, Erabu, Gotō, Shichijima, Isshujima, and Hachijōjima are not in Kang's gazetteer. But all eight names are in "Map of Japan."

Four mountains are marked on the map. These are "Atago-san," "Kumano-san," "Atsuta-san," and "Fuji-san." A mountain icon marks each site, and clouds cap Mount Fuji.[38] According to a Japanese monk cited by Kang, Mount Atsuta and Mount Fuji were two of the three heavenly mountains where immortals reside (J. *sanshinsan*). Mount Kumano was the third. Kang describes Mount Fuji as being visible from the sea, according to merchants visiting from foreign countries. These polite comments by foreigners reflect the cultural significance of Mount Fuji even then in Japan.[39] Most of the place names in "Map of Japan" are mentioned elsewhere in *The Record of a Shepherd*. This underscores the importance of reading the map together with the written text.

Koreans frequently reproduced Kang's image of Japan in private writings and in state mapping projects in the late Chosŏn period. His map was a standard reference from the early seventeenth century. An early reproduction was printed in *Kŭmgyerok* (The Account of Kŭmgye) by No In (1566–1622).[40] Like Kang, No had been taken to Japan during the second invasion. In the third month of 1599, he escaped from Satsuma Province, in southernmost Kyushu, and reached Ming China. He returned to Chosŏn by late in the twelfth month of 1599, having traveled overland from southern China.[41] The map in *Kŭmgyerok* is attributed to Kang and *The Record of a Shepherd*. Next in the collection is a discussion of Japan that includes a geographic survey following Kang's order of circuits and provinces and repeated written text from *The Record of a Shepherd*. No also provides details not in Kang's province profiles.[42]

No's map is not, however, an exact replication of "Map of Japan." For example, the cartouches for several provinces are not in the same places. Kang did not mark the island name of Iki in a province cartouche, but No's map has this place name in such a frame. The words "*kukto*" and "Fushimi" are in single-line, rectangular cartouches. And only "Edo" is in a double-line, circular cartouche, which likely signified that Edo, the shogun's capital, was also the country's administrative capital.

Other Korean mapmakers removed Kang's map from its setting in *The Record of a Shepherd*. His "Map of Japan" appears in single-frame images of

Japan, in state atlases, in privately produced atlases (K. *yŏjido*) as the image of Japan, and in single maps showing two or more countries. These uses detached Kang's map from the expressions of loyalty and the gathering of information that had informed his writing on contemporary politics and geography in Japan and postwar reforms in Chosŏn. The images became representations used for purposes unrelated to explaining the Japanese invaders to Korean government officials. And separated from the written text in *The Record of a Shepherd*, information in the maps could not be so readily understood.

As the Chosŏn government produced the *Haedong chido* (Atlas of the Eastern Country) in the mid-eighteenth century, state cartographers prepared maps of foreign countries as well as images of districts and counties in each of Chosŏn's provinces. Officials constructed the map of Japan from Kang's image, added colors, and gave it the same title.[43] This image of Japan is quite similar to Kang's in its use of place names and icons.

Kyoto, here too identified as the country's capital, is distinct from other city names by having been marked in red. Fushimi and Edo are set in double-line, circular cartouches, and Osaka is in a single-line, circular cartouche. This depiction of Fushimi in the state atlas's representation of Japan retained the anachronism in Kang's map as printed in the mid-seventeenth century, for Fushimi no longer could be considered a capital. Further, written text accompanying the image in *Haedong chido* states that Fushimi is the "new capital" and Osaka is the "western capital," and that both Osaka and Fushimi "belong to the Kanpaku Regent," that is, to Hideyoshi. This written text also identifies "Yama" as Yamatai, the "southern capital." Government officials imparted outdated knowledge to the users of this atlas. Kang had sought to provide his king with a deep, broad, and current description of Japan. The compiler(s) of this map of Japan in *Haedong chido* did not do likewise.

Kang's map also appeared in the eighteenth century as part of a sheet that may have been in a privately produced atlas. In addition, the compiler(s) transcribed the gazetteer in *The Record of a Shepherd* on that sheet. The provinces in the map are separated by color, and Kyoto, Edo, Fushimi, Osaka, and Yama[tai] are each marked with a double-line cartouche as capitals. The sheet has the title "Ilbon chŏndo" (Complete Map of Japan).[44] Anachronism appeared here too.

The private work separated the map and the gazetteer from the contexts and intratextual connections in *The Record of a Shepherd*. That is clear in the attempt to correct the gazetteer text. Someone crossed out the first character in the Japanese term "Atago-san" (愛), thinking it to be incorrect, and wrote

K. *wi* (馬) next to that character. Kang's "Map of Japan" likely circulated more widely as reproductions in manuscript atlases than in printed versions of *The Record of a Shepherd*.

After the war, Kang Hang's writings on Japan and his map of the island country provided Korean government officials and other elites with their newest information on Japan. But Tokugawa Ieyasu's victory at the Battle of Sekigahara in the ninth month of 1600 and his establishment of a new government in Edo in 1603 rendered much of the former captive's information outdated. Nevertheless, *The Record of a Shepherd* remains a valuable source of details and impressions about Japan of the late sixteenth century, and is an enduring statement on civilization and loyalty.

Notes on the Translation Text

It may be helpful to explain practices used in the translation and the notes. These include the use of blank lines, parentheses, brackets, dating styles, and years of age. In a chapter, a blank line between two paragraphs indicates a new section in Kang Hang's text.

Parentheses present two types of information. First, the printed *Kanyangnok* includes text printed in a smaller type size. That text is marked by placement in parentheses. Second, parentheses identify terms translated from Korean, Chinese, and Japanese.

Brackets surround words that we have introduced to enhance clarity and precision in the sentence. Another practice is the addition of elements of a person's name and broader social identity. Kang frequently refers to Japanese by combinations of surname, adult given name, title, and other names. However, he does not present an individual's identifiers in a consistent manner. Ishida Mitsunari is an example. In *Kanyangnok*, his full identity is as Ishida Jibu no shō Mitsunari. "Jibu no shō" was the title by which he was commonly known in Japan. However, Kang identifies him inconsistently, as Ishida Jibu no shō, Jibu, and Ishida Jibu. The missing piece or pieces have been added in brackets in each instance.

Dates in the text and in the notes present different problems. The calendar in Japan differed from that in Ming China and Chosŏn. The Japanese used the Tang-period Chinese calendar, while the Chinese and Koreans used the newer Ming-period Chinese calendar. We have not converted dates to the respective Julian calendar or Gregorian calendar. Rather, we have preserved the month or the month and day in the original text and converted the reign year into the Western calendar year. For example, Sŏnjo 30 (in Chosŏn, the thirtieth year of the reign of King Sŏnjo), Wanli 25 (in Ming China, the twenty-fifth year of the reign of the Wanli Emperor, who is also known by his posthumous temple name, Shenzong), and Keichō 2 (in Japan, the second year under the reign name Keichō) are rendered here as 1597. This practice for dating the year poses the possibility of dating events in the second half of the twelfth month to the wrong Gregorian calendar year, that is, to 1597 rather than to 1598. However, it does not invite confusion by using a Western-style date such as January 1, 1597, for the Chinese, Korean, and Japanese calendars. And it enables readers to readily find materials and information in sources of this period. For specific dates, in the translation of the original text is, as an example, "the seventeenth day of the fifth month," with the year following the month or known by context. In citations that date is rendered as "1597.5.17." In the latter format, the order is year, month, and day of the month. Readers wishing to convert dates in the Chinese and Korean calendars between 1341 and 1661 are encouraged to consult the second printing, revised edition of Keith Hazelton, *A Synchronic Chinese-Western Daily Calendar 1341–1661 A.D.* (Minneapolis: Ming Studies, 1985).

Regarding age, we have followed the practice in Chosŏn, Japan, and Ming China at that time. The year of birth was the child's first year. The child became two years of age at the turn of the next year. That is, born in 1579, the child was two years old in 1580.

A Korean War Captive in Japan, 1597–1600

1

Encounters with the Adversities of War

ON THE EIGHTH DAY OF THE SECOND MONTH OF THE CHŎNGYU year [1597], I was granted leave from my post of Assistant Section Chief in the Board of Punishments.¹ I returned home and was looking after my farm in my hometown, Yubong.² On the seventeenth day of the fifth month, Commander Yang [Yuan],³ the Ming general, leading 3,000 soldiers, left Seoul and pressed south to defend Namwŏn against a Japanese attack.⁴ Yi Kwangjŏng, after receiving an order to become the Second Minister of a branch office of the Board of Taxation, was placed in charge of transporting army provisions in Chŏlla Province.⁵ He petitioned the court for personnel. The court assigned the task [of recruiting them] to me and Yun Sŏn,⁶ an Assistant Section Chief in the Board of Rites who lived in Samga [County].⁷ Toward the end of the fifth month, I reported for duty, sending out letters of exhortation [to join the army] (K. *kyŏksŏ*)⁸ as I went to my post. Lord Yi was busy overseeing food operations at Namwŏn, and he ordered me to hasten the transport [of provisions]. Toward the end of the seventh month, Regional Navy Commander Wŏn Kyun suffered total defeat at Hansan Island,⁹ and the island fell to the enemy.¹⁰ In the middle of the eighth month, enemy troops attacked Namwŏn, and after three days under siege Commander Yang broke through the blockade and escaped to the north. Namwŏn fell.

I was an assistant to the Deputy Minister [Yi Kwangjŏng], and I realized that I did not know the whereabouts of my superior. I ran all day and all night from Hamp'yŏng to Sunch'ang,¹¹ where I learned that Lord Yi had left for the north. I returned to the county and, together with Kim Sangjun, the former magistrate [of Yŏnggwang County] and attendant to the governor, traveled through many towns to distribute letters of exhortation to raise volunteers for the army.¹² Several hundred patriotic scholars came forward. However, a battalion of the enemy already had crossed the Noryŏng mountains,¹³ and there was nowhere along the coastline that they had not infiltrated. The volunteer army of untrained civilians dispersed rapidly. Upon leaving the fort, Master Kim went north, and I returned home. With my elderly parent and children,¹⁴ I went to Nonjap Port.¹⁵ I was in the midst of negotiations to procure a boat when the new governor, Hwang Sin,¹⁶ summoned me to be his assistant. Land routes were already blocked, and I was unable to go.

On the fourteenth day of the ninth month, the enemy was already burning Yŏnggwang, searching every cranny of the mountains and the seas, indiscriminately killing anyone they found. Around ten at night, I boarded a boat. I thought that since my father suffered from seasickness¹⁷ he would have more difficulty in a smaller boat, so I had him go with my uncle's family. That boat did not have enough room, so my cousins could not board it.¹⁸ They boarded our boat, which already had my family—three sisters-in-law, including the widow of my eldest brother;¹⁹ my wife's parents and grandparents;²⁰ my wife; and my concubine. My brother-in-law's father, Sim Anp'yŏng,²¹ and his family were in a desperate situation with nowhere to go, and so, unable to leave them behind, we asked them to come on board. Since the boat was small, with many people aboard, it moved extremely slowly.

On the fifteenth, both of our boats docked at Myodu. There were many hundreds of boats with refugees. We stayed the night there, and the night of the sixteenth, but reached Piroch'o for the night of the seventeenth.²² On the eighteenth, my cousin Hyŏp, serving as a royal messenger, delivered a royal appointment to Yi Sunsin to serve as the new Regional Navy Commander,²³ and he hurriedly left the Right Naval Headquarters to come join us.

On the twentieth, we heard that an enemy fleet of 1,000 ships had come to the Right Naval Headquarters, and Regional Navy Commander Yi, deciding that it was impossible to fight so many with only a few ships, made a strategic move to the west coast. My family—all the men of my father's and my generations—discussed our destination. Some suggested that we abandon ship and go by land, while some argued that we should go to Hŭksan Island.²⁴ I and two of my cousins, Hyŏp and Hong, forcefully argued: "There are about forty strong men among us in these two boats. We should join Admiral Yi. There is no guarantee that we will be successful in battle, but neither is it true that we will all die." Thus, we decided [to go to Admiral Yi].

The boatman Mun'gi heard our discussion and decided to take along his four children, who were on Ŏŭi Island at the time.²⁵ In the middle of the night of the twenty-first, while we were sound asleep, taking advantage of a strong wind, he untied the boat. In a split second, our boat separated from my father's boat. When the boat arrived at Chinwŏl Island,[26] we heard that more than ten ships under Admiral Yi had passed by Kakssi Island. We sternly ordered the boatman to turn the ship around to head west. The north wind was so fierce that we could not go up the coast. With the enemy encroaching, father and son were separated from each other. In this desperate situation, we had only boatmen to rely upon. Scolding them was not possible.

On the twenty-second, having heard that my father's boat had headed toward the salt fields—wrong information, as it turned out—we went to Tangdu in the salt fields,[27] but it was not there. Sim Anp'yŏng's family, thinking that the boat was too crowded, disembarked. Manch'un, a male slave whom I had cared for and relied upon, said that he would fetch water, but ran away.

On the twenty-third, in broad daylight, we headed toward Nonjap Port in the hope of finding my father's boat. In the fog, a strange-looking ship appeared and approached. The boatman shouted in panic that it was a Japanese ship. Thinking that I had no chance to avoid capture, I threw off my clothes and leaped into the sea. More than half of my family—siblings and their spouses—jumped into the sea with me.

The water was shallow, however. The enemy scooped us all up with hooks, tied us [with rope], and made us stand up. Only two of my maternal cousins, Kim Chuch'ŏn and his brother, and several slaves climbed up a hill, thus managing to escape. When he jumped into the sea, my second eldest brother had on his back the spirit tablets of our deceased mother and eldest brother,[28] but when the enemy scooped him up, the tablets were not saved. We had lost our living father and the tablets of our deceased, failing in all our filial duties!

This was not all. We left my young son Yong and my daughter by my concubine, Aesaeng, on the sand at the beach, but they were swallowed by the returning tides. Their cries lasted a while and then went silent. Yong was a child that I had at the late age of thirty. When he was conceived, I had dreamt of a dragon child floating in the water and so named him "Dragon" (K. *Yong*). Who could have known that he would drown? Everything in this floating life has been destined. It is simply that we do not know.

Attaching our boat to theirs, the Japanese enemy headed south. The wind was strong, and we seemed to be moving as fast as an arrow.

On the twenty-fourth, we arrived at a bay called Naktu, in Muan County.[29] Enemy ships in the thousands filled the port, and flags of white and red fluttered in the sun.³⁰ The ships were filled with men and women of my country. On the coast in both directions, dead bodies were piled high as mountains. Weeping and wailing reached the heavens, and the sound of the waves seemed to be cries. What was life; for what crime were people dying? All my life, I was the most cowardly and fearful of persons, but on this occasion I had no desire to live.

When the ship sailed out to sea, a Japanese man asked me through a translator, "Where is the commander of your navy now?" I replied, "There is a place called Anhaeng Strait in T'aean [County]. Its original name was Nanhaeng Strait; every year, passing ships either went astray or shipwrecked there. The present name, Anhaeng, meaning 'safe passage,' was given with a wish to pacify the strait.³¹ It is indeed a natural blockade in seafaring. The two Ming generals, Ming and Gu, leading a fleet of 10,000 battleships, crossed this strait in the upper and lower channels, and the fleet has already arrived at Kunsan Port.³² Our Regional Navy Commander strategically retreated and joined the Chinese navy." The enemy sailors looked at each other, visibly dejected. I asked the translator the name of the person who had captured us and was told that he was Nobushichirō, an underling of [Tōdō] Sado no kami [Takatora].³³

Around the second hour [10:00 P.M.], having freed himself from the rope, my father-in-law took off his clothes and jumped into the sea. The Japanese rose in pandemonium and quickly retrieved him. They bound us even more tightly, the ropes cutting into our skin. The backs of my hands were torn, and eventually large warts grew on those spots. For three years, I could not close my hands or open them, and the right hand still bears a scar. I asked the translator, "Why don't they kill us?" He replied, "You are wearing scholars' hats and silk clothes. They believe that you are an official family. They want to dispatch you to Japan, bound in rope. That is why they guard you." When the Qin discarded propriety, Lu Zhonglian attempted to drown himself in the Eastern Sea;³⁴ though King Wu subjugated the tyrant, Bo Yi went to the Western Mountain and starved himself to death.³⁵ How much worse was my situation! These thieves are the most despicable and ugly of barbarians, unforgivable enemies of my people. To live one minute in their custody was worse than ten thousand deaths, but bound as I was, I had no freedom to die!

After three days, the enemy came with a translator, asking who the legal wives were. When they came forward, they were put on the Japanese ship. The enemy made my brothers and cousin board a separate ship and threatened to kill us all. Then the enemy placed our concubines, the grandfather of my wife, my eldest sister-in-law, approximately ten remaining female servants, and the half-sister of my wife's father on separate boats and may even have killed some of them. How sad! On his deathbed, my eldest brother wrote, "Since you are there, my wife has someone to rely upon," and entrusted her to me. Who could have known that she would encounter this today! When I would think of life and death, I could not but be deeply stirred. I simply did not know if I myself would die. Those slaves who deserted and ran away survived; those who could not tear themselves away from their master were all massacred. Pitiful! Sad!

Soon, many Japanese ships headed south, passing the Yŏngsan storehouse[36] and the Right Naval Commandery headquarters,[37] and arrived at Waegyo, in Sunch'ŏn [County].[38] The enemy was already in the process of constructing a fort, building high walls along the coast. Many ships were allowed to dock, but about a hundred ships with prisoners of war on board were made to strike anchor offshore. For nine days after our capture, we had eaten nothing but were still alive. How tenacious is human life. The captives who arrived later than we did were families of friends. We heard that Yang Usang's entire family was exterminated.

On this day, a Japanese woman distributed a bowl of rice to each of us. Not only was it full of yellow husks, it seemed half sand and bore a strong odor of fish. So starved were we that we ate it.

In the middle of the night, a woman in the adjoining ship stopped crying and began to sing. It was so heartrending as to split jade. After the disasters that befell my family, my eyes remained dry. On this night, however, tears fell, completely wetting my sleeves. I composed a poem:

Whence this sad song to an old tune?
So bright the midnight moon.
All those on nearby ships shed tears;
Wettest were my sleeves.

On the following day, a Japanese ship passed by and a woman on it called out desperately, "Anyone from Yŏnggwang? Anyone from Yŏnggwang?" My second sister-in-law got up and responded.[39] It turned out that she was the mother of Aesaeng! When she was made to board a separate ship, I had assumed that she would be killed, but there she was alive. Her plaintive pleas were too sad to hear. Later, I learned that every night she wailed and was beaten for it. Still, she could not restrain herself from crying. She refused to eat, and died. I wrote a poem:

The vast, blue sea is still, the moon about to drop into it.
My tears fall like dew, drop by drop soaking the collar of my robe.
Do the full waves long for my love?
The Herd Boy and the Weaving Maiden will understand the heart of this night.[40]

My second brother's son Karyŏn was only eight years old. Seized by thirst, he drank salt water and became ill with nausea and diarrhea. Weakened, he lay on the ground. Suddenly, a Japanese man burst upon us, seized him, and threw him into the sea. He called out to his father for a long time. How incredibly pitiful! The old saying, "Child! You cannot even look to your father," must refer to such a situation as this!

Several days later, my father-in-law and my two brothers attempted to escape on a small boat that they had stealthily procured,[41] but they were discovered. The enemy reported this to [Tōdō] Sado no kami [Takatora]. That evening, they put all of my family onto another large ship. There were also nine women of scholarly families who had been moved from other ships. One turned out to be the daughter of Hong Kunok.[42] We talked of the past and were profoundly affected. Uyŏng, my father-in-law's half-sister, was a very pretty thirteen-year-old girl. We did not know what had happened to her after she was separated from us. She came on board at this time, and from her we learned that my wife's grandfather and all the female slaves had been killed. The ship embarked in the evening. We docked at An'gol Port for the night.

The next day, we left An'gol Port. Navigating to the south and then to the east, the ship traversed the vast sea all day, continuing deep into the night. Suddenly, at a distance, we heard a cock crow. Through the fog of early dawn, a great mass of land came into view. This was Tsushima Island. The way the houses were built and the way the clothes and headgear were made were truly peculiar, and made me realize we were in fact in a different world. There is a custom that when a boy is born, one celebrates by shooting arrows from a mulberry bow into the four directions, wishing for vastness of his sphere of activity. But who would have wished that I come to Japan this way!

Because of wind and rain we stayed two days at Tsushima. We crossed another vast sea and arrived at Iki Island. The following day we crossed another sea and arrived at a large trading port beneath a long mountain. This was Shimonoseki, in Nagato Province. The following day we crossed another sea, and, circling a slope, came to another big trading port. This was Kaminoseki, in Suō Province. The sea and the mountains were picturesque: persimmons and oranges shone brilliantly beneath the sun. How lamentable that this place was a den of devils. The following day we crossed yet another sea, pulling in at Nagasaki in Iyo Province. We disembarked, placing our feet on solid ground. When I walked, I faltered nine of ten steps. My little daughter, aged six, could not walk on her own, and so my wife and my wife's mother carried her on their backs by turns. Crossing a stream with my daughter on her back, my mother-in-law fell. Completely exhausted, she could not get up. On the bank of the stream, a Japanese man watched this, and, in tears, helped her up. He said, "This is too much. What does His Excellency intend to do with all these captives? Doesn't Heaven see?" He quickly went into his home and brought out cooked grain and tea, feeding us. Only then could I hear and see. There were good Japanese! Their fondness for killing arose from particular laws and rules. The Japanese call [Toyotomi] Hideyoshi[43] "Retired Imperial Regent,"[44] and so this person also referred to him as Retired Imperial Regent.

We walked about 10 *ri* to Ōzu Castle, where we were made to stay.[45] I, my two brothers, and my father-in-law and his family were put into the same house, though in separate rooms. Every morning and evening, a Japanese soldier and a small Japanese woman delivered us a meal consisting of a bowl of rice, a bowl of soup, and fish. It was fortunate that brothers could be together in this distant barbarian land at the edge of the earth. At the year's end [1597], I gathered ancient phrases to express my frustration and sadness:

At last year's passing, we offered our king
A full glass of wine, wishing for peace the coming year.
This year, we shed only tears of devotion.
Each day, in my heart despair deepens.

The twenty-sixth year of Wanli,[46] the *musul* year [1598] (since I am confined in this cave of demons, I dated it this way to display my respect for the king) ended and a new year began. Fireworks were displayed to drive away evil ghosts; lanterns were lit throughout the night to keep vigil on the passing year. The festivities resembled those described in *The Annual Festivities and Celebrations of the Chu* (K. *Hyŏng Ch'o sesigi*, C. *Jing Chu suishiji*).[47] These people had the faces of human beings, but hearts of beasts. On such occasions of merrymaking and festivity, one grew even sadder. I gazed toward my king and my father, a vast ocean of 10,000 *ri* separating us. When balmy spring came, plants and trees and all living things rejoiced; our family gazed at one another with tearful eyes. Our ancestral grave site must have been burned under fires of battle; who would have offered even one bowl of barley to the graves? Everything we saw made us grieve; on all occasions we grew despondent anew. It was not only the fragrant spring of the third month or the clear autumn moon of the ninth that plunged us into mournful desolation.

On the fifth, Yewŏn, my third brother's daughter,[48] died of illness.

On the ninth, Kahŭi, my second brother's son, died of illness. We brothers carried them and buried them by the sea. Of six children born of us, three drowned and two died in Japan, leaving only one, a little girl. This is exactly what a poem by Sandu[49] describes:

I have killed you; it is all my fault.
My shame and pain will last a hundred years; will tears ever dry?

How pitiful! We deeply grieved but also envied their oblivion.

Toward the end of the first month [of 1599], we heard news that the large Chinese army had arrived to aid [our country] and, together with our army, had reaped victories; that more than half the enemy troops at Ulsan were killed; and that all their remaining camps in Chŏlla but the one at Sunch'ŏn were destroyed. Even in our sadness, we were elated at such wonderful news. I wrote a five-character poem:

Oh, joy that Master Wang has come,
Half Honam has been pacified.
Can it be my king remains without illness,
My aged father still in good health?
The wrath of Heaven bestirred great seas,
On hornet's nests moon's halo shines its light.
Oh, happy news to deepest sorrow comes,
My joyous tears as mighty rivers flow.

On the fifth day of the second month, we heard from a translator that about 100 soldiers under Sō Yoshitoshi[50] had surrendered to Chosŏn and that more were following suit. I wrote another five-character poem:

Sharp enemy swords are rendered dull,
Surrendering foes each day appear in rows.
No more does Honam house wandering multitudes,
But scattered lonely troops are seen beyond the pass.

Eternal waves becalm the Eastern Sea,
Star Sirius bows to its polar counterpart.
Even if this soul dies yet a hundred deaths,
My whitened bones will be inscribed with joy.

In the spring rain, I added a quatrain:

The rains of spring arrive and pass,
My thirst for home each spring redoubled.
When will I gaze again upon the blooms
I planted there beneath the garden walls?

The twenty-seventh day of the fourth month was the anniversary of my mother's death. Under normal circumstances, one could not perform a sacrificial rite unless properly attired and the offerings were of unblemished and spotless materials. It was unimaginable to express our sincerity in a ritual addressing the dead with offerings of leftovers given to us by Japanese thieves. It was, however, equally unbearable to pass it over. We decided to perform a simple rite and prepared offerings purchased with money obtained by selling our possessions. Our address read:

Your unworthy children have failed to preserve the ancestral mantle: the whole family is plunged into ruin. We have been taken to a barbarian land at the far edge of the earth. Our ancestral grave, left unattended, must be in thorny thickets; the wooden tablets have sunk into the sea. Thinking of our dead, pain and sorrow strike sharply. In autumn frost or spring dew, where can we satisfy our longings for you? Days have passed; then months flowed, and the anniversary [of your death] has arrived. Abducted to this strange land, we have meager offerings. Relentlessly watched by beasts, we cannot even wail to our hearts' content. When we look at the sky, even plants and trees seem to quiver with emotion. Spirit! If you can see this situation, please understand!

A temple called Kinzan Shussekiji[51] was located about 30 *ri* south of Iyo Province. A monk there told me that he was from Hizen Province and that he had visited our capital as a member of a Japanese diplomatic mission. He had received a title in the Board of Censors,[52] but had retired and was given a plot of land beneath the temple, and lived from the rents provided by farmers working the land. He treated me with courtesy and asked me to write a poem on a fan. I wrote a seven-character poem:

> The silk-recorded name fell east beyond the sea,
> From a land beyond 1,000 *ri*, windblown tidings fly.
> Tidings of that Palace Royal far beyond great waves;
> Dim faces of my parents as in a butterfly dream.
> Shamed so my eyes avoid both sun and moon,
> With swollen heart, I only long for the old lord.
> In brilliant Jiangnan where flowers dazzle and birds do fly,
> Where lies a boat to bear this captive home?

He looked at the poem, and nodded his head sympathetically and said, "I understand it very well. However, there is no boat. Moreover, you are under arrest. What can be done?"

Ōzu Castle was on a high mountain, beneath which a long river wound by. The river was always blue and clear. Every time I went up to the empty castle, I gazed west and wailed. Afterward, I came down slowly. Later, I wrote a five-character poem:

> I dreamt this road,
> East of the vast blue sea.
> Mountaintop castle towering over,
> Men at water's edge.
> Murmuring the Buddha's teachings,
> They daily train for war.
> Neither beauty nor custom are like my land,
> Mount Nam beyond what many-numbered obstacles.

There was a Korean man from Chuksa, in Seoul, who had been captured and brought to Japan in the *imjin* year [1592]. He ran away from the Japanese capital to Iyo Province. He came to me and asked, "Do you think we can help each other to escape and return home?" I replied, "If you can arrange it so that I may see the sky of my homeland again, I will be indebted to you for the rest of my life." He had money and was fluent in Japanese, and so I entreated him. Finally, on the twenty-fifth day of the fifth month [of 1598], under cover of night, we left on our westward journey. We walked all night long about 80 *ri*. My feet bled. By day we hid in bamboo groves. When night came we passed Itajima,[53] and we put up a poster in big letters that read:

To the ruler and the people of Japan! With no legitimate cause, you invaded a blameless country. You defiled the Temple of Royal Ancestors,[54] disinterred and defiled the royal tombs, slaughtered young and old, and took away sons and brothers. Nothing escaped your harm: all—seedlings, chickens, dogs, and pigs, even insects, plants, and trees—were poisoned. Since the dawn of humanity, never has there been such cruel devastation in war as that your ruler and your people have visited upon Chosŏn! You sacrifice to the sun and moon seeking good fortune, and you honor Buddha hoping for blessing. The sun and moon are my eyes that shine upon the earth, telling of good and evil, guiding me to bestow blessing or misfortune. I sent Shakyamuni Buddha as a model to prohibit killing, to make a world where my wish that life be honored and preserved could be known. I preside far beyond the sea. The people of Chosŏn are also my children. Your ruler and the people of this region massacred them, determined to exterminate them till not a trace was left. How can the sun and moon have mercy on you; how can Shakyamuni Buddha bless the unrighteous? Last year, the castle in the capital crumbled, crushing your people and your domestic animals. Yet you did not recognize this sign of retribution! This year, a great flood in the southeast destroyed the entire barley crop and much rice. Again, you did not take warning. Can blindness and deafness reach this extreme? By the power of Shakyamuni Buddha who presides over the Eastern region, I warn the ruler and the people of your country. To protect what remains of the Chosŏn people, I order you: acknowledge your crime. If not, I will mercilessly rain calamities of unimagined magnitude upon your country! Beware! I will not speak twice. Do not regret!

The Japanese, fearing ghosts, always sacrifice offerings of food to the sun and the moon. Awake and asleep, they incessantly invoke Buddha. Hoping that they might realize their crime, invoking the power of Heaven's works and Buddha's word, I warned them. In a short period, in the sixth month [of 1598], that evil ruler of the thieving Japanese [Hideyoshi] took to his bed. When the season changed to autumn, he died! Could it be that our words had some effect?

Ten *ri* west of Itajima, a bamboo forest appeared, and we decided to rest. We noticed a man of about sixty years of age bathing under a waterfall. Then he cooked rice and made an offering to the sun. Afterward, he seemed to fall asleep on a rock. Our translator stealthily approached and conveyed to him our plan of going west. The monk agreed to take us to Bungo Province by boat. We happily followed him, the monk first, followed by the translator, and then us. In ten steps, however, a Japanese man appeared accompanied by two soldiers. Looking at us, he shouted, "You Korean runaways! Take this sword!" We stretched out our necks to receive their swords. The Japanese ordered the soldiers to bind and take us. When we reached the gates of Itajima, we saw that there were about ten long wooden poles bearing severed heads. This was none other than the place the enemy designated to exhibit the heads of the executed.

They made us kneel and were about to cut off our heads. A Japanese man stopped them, turning the blades away, and sent us into the city. As soon as we passed through the gate, a man came from the city and dragged us. It was none other than Nobushichirō, the thug who had first captured our family. He gave us tea, wine, soup, and rice. After three days, we were sent back to Ōzu Castle.

After this incident, we were allowed even less movement, and I idled with little to do. I often went to the monks' quarters beneath the wall. One day a monk, greeting me with extreme courtesy, recited a poem:

> A sage appears; I know not if I dream or wake.
> How deep my sorrow that our guest wanders in a distant land.
> The bright moon and lovely flowers must deepen sadness
> In this land of endless war.

I composed a poem in the same rhyme:

> Can he of frosty hair and snowy eyebrow
> Reincarnate a sage of distant India?
> A pristine poem lays out the sadness of my deepest plight.
> From those who bear those swords, by how many lives am I separated?

I saw an old crane at the home of Hakuun [Kōsetsu], the father of [Tōdō] Sado no kami [Takatora].[55] I was moved by the sight and composed a poem:

> A celestial crane descended to the world of men,
> When will you return to the fragrant fields of yore?
> Paused a thousand years upon a road sign,[56]
> And several more at Shimonoseki.
> Unable to depart this world of dust,
> Ever longing for yon mountains far beyond the sea.

When will you take your proper form,
To touch again that white tree?

Sŏ Kuk, a local functionary in the Muan County office, had been captured and brought to Ōzu. He visited me frequently, and asked for a poem. So I wrote one for him:

Once a guest in the Western Capital,
Today a wanderer in the Eastern Sea.
As time flows and the world yet again transforms,
Heaven's Way cannot be one that ends in defeat.
Longing for the Royal Palace, [I] gaze upon the sun,
Recalling parents, [I] behold the passing clouds.
Feigned merriment begets tears;
Cold smiles turn to frowns.

In the sixth month of that year [1598], [Tōdō] Sado no kami [Takatora] retreated from Kosŏng and returned to the capital of Japan.[57] He sent his underling, ordering that all my family be relocated to Osaka, their western capital. We were forced to board a boat. Deeply saddened, I wrote another poem:

Outside my country, I am 1,000 *ri* away.
Against my hopes, I am brought yet farther east.
Brought to the place from which the sun does rise,[58]
A place where tidings are sent only by wind.
It was the Yellow Emperor who first waged war,[59]
This evil place begun by many wise in magic herbs.[60]
Though as a man I sought to know the way of the four directions,
Who could have known that I would come so far to live among
    Japanese!

I also wrote a poem on the voyage:

Ten thousand worries, a thousand thoughts swirl as bees in a hive;
At thirty, my hair turned white beneath the ears.
It is not poor appetite that saps body and soul,
It is that I cannot gaze upon my king.

All my life I have read books and understand the gravity of names and righteousness;
When later generations view history, right and wrong will be disputed.
A captive is not a crane from Liaodong;
Awaiting death, I must look for sheep over the sea.

On the eighth day, sailing, at dawn, as I lay deeply asleep, a compatriot on the same boat announced, "We approach the capital." I arose as in a dream, and through the mist a ten-storied pagoda suddenly appeared, so high that half seemed hung from the sky. Shaking, I felt faint. For a long time, I could not control myself. Afterward, I wrote a poem:

Thus, we near their capital;
It is but a place of ghosts.
I do not seek to search the tiger's cave,
It is that I cannot behold my king.
At the new year, I dreamt of drinking to my heart's content.[61]
What must this lonely captive endure to return?
In despair, I daydream,
And suddenly I see Mount Nam.

I noticed a warship of our country, obviously taken by the enemy, at the mouth of the Uji River.[62] Saddened, I wrote a poem:

Alas, Yellow-Dragon Ship,
What brought you here east of the blue sea?
Oh, sturdy construct,
It is your general who must have failed.
Rain soaks a broken oar,
The tiger flag does not fly.
I exist as a wooden figure;[63]
At your sight, tears flow.

We were moved again, from Osaka to Fushimi Castle, in a small ship. At night in the boat, I tried to calm my despair. I wrote a seven-character quatrain:

Beneath a bright moon, a boat glides by a field of reeds;
Seagulls sleep upon a sandy bank, too early they awake in fright.

For many years a boat upon the sea has been my shelter,
Where I rested to the sound of a white-haired boatman's rowing.

Once we arrived at Fushimi, the Japanese placed us in a great storehouse attached to an empty house and left an old Japanese man, Ichimura, to guard us. Among the captives from our country were Kim Ujŏng of Tongnae, Kang Sajun,[64] Kang Ch'ŏnch'u and Chŏng Ch'angse of Hadong,[65] Pak Yŏjip of Hamyang, Chŏn Sisŭp of T'aean, and Sŏ Kyŏngch'un of Muan,[66] all scholars. We met almost daily. Ujŏng told us the story of Yi Yŏp, an officer in the Left Battalion of Chŏlla Province. [Katō] Kiyomasa, who captured Yi, sent him to Hideyoshi. Hideyoshi treated Yi with extreme courtesy, arranging that his living quarters and food were not different from those of Japanese generals. Yŏp distributed silk and other valuables that he received from the enemy, and in alliance with other captives of the *imjin* year [1592], procured a boat and escaped westward. When the boat arrived at Shimonoseki, pursuers were already waiting for them. When he saw this, Yŏp stabbed himself, and his body fell into the sea. Those Japanese thugs retrieved his body, and, in a thoroughfare, they hung it and his compatriots' bodies on a great chariot, and all, living and dead, were torn to pieces. Yŏp, versed in literature, had written a poem when he boarded the ship:

Spring arrives from the east, deepening my regret;
The wind blows west, leading my thoughts astray.
Losing the night, my parents wail at the moon of dawn;
My wife weeps dripping tears like a midday candle in the morning sun.
Flowers must have fallen at the ancient, centuries-old academy;
The graves of my ancestors are overgrown by weeds.
Descended from families of the Three Hans,
How can I mix with cows and sheep in foreign lands!

When I heard the story, I sweated [with shame], thinking, "Could there have been such a person among military men? Am I not a scholar of learning, and yet I am in this situation!" I wrote a poem to rhyme with Yi's poem:

A general's courage reaches Heaven;
Who can describe it as a hasty escape?
Your righteous bones rest deep in the Eastern Sea;[67]
Clear wind takes your thought to Mount Shouyang.[68]
Heads on poles will be washed clean by the rain,

A buried body will not be covered but by overgrown grass.
As a scholar who should know principle, I hang my head in shame,
For I have spent two years in this desolate land![69]

I wrote another poem in the same rhyme:

My longing for the king makes the sea vast as Heaven;
My wandering in the east flows on and on.
The heliotropic sunflower makes me blush with shame;
A flock of geese pursuing the sun drives envious longing.
My soul looks into rain from distant skies;
My heart pursues the wind to remote mountaintops.
How kind the intentions of him deceased;
With wine, he consoles the one who shepherds sheep.

I composed yet another poem in the same rhyme:

How far the Green Hills beyond the sea of 10,000 *ri*;[70]
In dreams, can souls return and leave so freely?
Farewell's regrets begin beyond Penglai, the mountain home of
    immortals;
My heart longs so for that place below the River Han.
Though life is short,
Heaven's Way is not so vague.
My family's creed: achieve benevolence, choose the righteous;
Even children know there's shame for those who bow to dogs and sheep.

I gave a poem to Kang Sajun, Chŏng Ch'angse, and Ha Taein. They were of the three great descent groups of Chinju, the Kang, the Ha, and the Chŏng. I wrote a poem because I was truly moved to see them at the edge of the world:

To Pangjang Mountain came a man exceptional;
Three surnames live in Chinju side by side.
Many-generationed offspring of illustrious lines,
Sad captives in the wasteland at earth's end.
By now the plums of Tansoksa temple must have bloomed;[71]
Old family homes are green with grass of spring.

Should the Eastern Emperor let you fly on eastward wind,
In fields of green with crystal dew, again you'll join as neighbors there.

(My ancestor T'ongjŏng planted a plum tree at Tansoksa.[72] A temple monk named the tree the "Assistant Executive Plum Tree" [K. *Chŏngdangmae*]. When the tree withered, he planted a new one there.)

I wrote another poem to rhyme with the first one:

Finding one from home, a fellow captive in a foreign land,
Saddened so are we, we cannot speak of how we came.
So shamed am I, three years staying upon this island far,
Though imprisoned in this land, so far your great figure stands tall.
Tough grass will not bend or lose its green beneath the frozen snow;
The noble plum seeks cold, blossoming before spring's warmth.
With cups of wine, let's turn our tears into smiles;
In base captivity, I will cherish virtuous comradeship.

Kim Hŭngdal and his brother Hŭngmae,[73] grandsons of the [former] Headmaster of the State Academy[74] Kim Sik,[75] the famous scholar who was involved in the purge of the *kimyo* year [1519], and also nephews of the scholar Kim Kwŏn,[76] knowing that I had been acquainted with their uncle, called upon me frequently. They brought rice and cloth, rescuing us from cold and hunger. In gratitude, I responded with a poem, using the same rhyme as the previous poem:

Here amid tattooed barbarians, I am amazed
To meet one with whom I share a special bond.
Inheritor of proud scholar's ways,
Embodiment of sages' principle and spirit.
In this deep frost, your gift of cloth warms me to the heart;
Empty-pocketed, we knew not where to find spring rice.
Today's encounter drew tears from me,
In yet another year, will we again meet with happy smiles?

I wrote another poem using the same rhyme:

Yesteryear, a denizen of scholars' halls;
Today, a prisoner of war; what caused that fate?

18 ENCOUNTERS WITH THE ADVERSITIES OF WAR

Seeking life, he cast aside the principles of the three bonds;
Once dedicated to my country, in its abandonment I live.
Hoping for great fortune, in vain I clung to a dream of a thousand-*ri* return.
But then, I greet yet one more spring in this accursed land.
Great principles sustained humanity through all of its history;
Can I be one closer to the beasts and birds?

Yet another poem in the same rhyme:

Captives from Chu trembled in the frosty land of Yan;[77]
Three years as wanderers must be our destiny.
Rituals and music, studying the Classics, we fulfilled life's duties
Of manly physique and clear intelligence born.
In our next life, we will not be born to an age of war!
Voided are happy times: peaches and plums of happy spring no more.
Who planned these trials and plotted troubles for our dynasty?
Can such a question asked in blood be answered from a palace?

On the new year's day of the *kihae* year [1599], I wrote a poem in fullness of emotion:

The delicacy of frost cannot be dulled by coarse dust;
Sorrow that hangs on the moon is refreshed each night.
The horse's horn grows not;[78] it is only one more spring that comes:
This recognition troubles this alien captive heart.

A Japanese monk called Tonsured Prince Kōi was the uncle of the emperor. He had left the secular world and resided at the Daibutsuji temple.[79] Sending ten fans, he requested a poem from me:

The kindness sent through these beautiful fans
Will be cherished by my grateful heart.
For much time, this miserable life could not face the sun;
Now I have something that can cover my shamed face.

When that evil ruler of the thieving Japanese, Hideyoshi, died and was buried in the northern suburb, a shrine of yellow gold was built over the grave.⁸⁰ The monk Nanka Genkō⁸¹ composed the following inscription in large characters:

Big, bright Japan! He has shaken the world.
He opened the road of great peace; the sea is vast, the mountain high.

Lingering there, and putting ink to brush, I wrote a poem next to the inscription:

A half-life's work leaves but a handful of dust;
A ten-story gold pavilion will deceive no one.
Those arms will yet fall to another hand;
What gain in taking the Land of Green Hills?

The Japanese monk Myōsuin Chief Seat [Sō]shun came to see me later and chided me: "The writing posted on the gate of the burial shrine of His Excellency was unmistakably in your own hand. Why don't you take better care of yourself?"⁸²

The chief guard, Ichimura, came and said, "You are all in the same family, brothers, uncles, and nephews. I can let an elder brother go because a younger brother remains, and allow a nephew to leave if an uncle stays." I also heard that the Ming envoys Mao Guoke and Wang Jiangong were staying at a lodging in Sakai.⁸³ I went there with a fellow compatriot, Sin Kyeri. We knocked at the door, and the doorkeeper, receiving a generous bribe, allowed us in. The two envoys sat in chairs facing west and offered me a chair in the west, and so we sat facing each other. They treated me with extreme warmth and courtesy, offering tea and wine. In tears, I pleaded with them, "I hear that the Japanese are making an arrangement to sail soon to send freight. Please take me on your boat as a servant, so that I can receive proper punishment in my homeland." They pitied me and asked, "To which Japanese general does Your Lordship belong?" I replied that it was [Tōdō] Sado no kami [Takatora]. The Chinese general said, "We will send our recommendation to [Tokugawa] Ieyasu⁸⁴ that he have [Tōdō] Sado no kami [Takatora] free you."

Sin Kyeri, imprudent by nature, blurted out in a loud voice, "Now that Hideyoshi is dead, Japan will fall into great turmoil. Japanese thugs and generals will die." The translator from Tsushima understood our language and hurriedly went to Nagauemon, the person in charge of us. Nagauemon was the elder brother of Yukinaga. They were waiting for us when we came out of the envoy's residence, and they tied us up and locked us in a room. Sin Kyeri, also bound, was placed in a separate room.

That evening, we were to be executed by being drawn and quartered by chariots. The Chinese general repeatedly pleaded for mercy, saying, "The reason that person called upon us is to inquire for news of his father. There was absolutely nothing else." Nagauemon could not refuse these entreaties and released us. Because we had passed the point of being bound by life or death, though we were in danger, we had not been afraid. Upon my return, I saw my two brothers, and just smiled.

Ever since I entered the land of my enemy, not for a second did my determination to return home flag, a determination to return even in death. Japanese mores were such that if you had money you could command ghosts. Following [the advice of] the Japanese monk Chief Seat [Sō]shun, I sold my calligraphy and writing to amass silver. Secretly, I planned with Sin Kyeri, Im Taehŭng, and a few others who had been captured in the *imjin* year [1592]. My second brother, in alliance with Kyeri, bought a boat for 80 *mon* of silver. We planned, as soon as repairs to the boat were completed, that we would all go together. Then Kyeri, once again imprudent, revealed the plan to the Japanese. [Tōdō] Sado no kami [Takatora] arrested my brother and Kyeri, locking them up in Osaka, and was going to kill one person a day. However, since my brother did not speak Japanese, he surmised that it was Kyeri who had instigated the escape, and after three days, sent my brother to Fushimi Castle.

My compatriot Kang Sajun came with drink and comforted me. I wrote a poem releasing my frustration:

I gaze upon a different vista,
Reawakening captive sorrows.
If one asks where is it that we meet,
I'd say beneath Mount Atago, by the River Uji.

The Japanese monk Kako Sōryū brought a screen painted with yellow and white chrysanthemums, magnolias, and morning glories, and asked for a poem:[85]

The midnight winter wind brought frost,
Blanketing the world in white with yellow bits.

Deepening autumn urges the gathering of flowers,
But, oh, take not morning glories or magnolias!

On another panel there was a painting of beautiful flowers and plants that I did not know the names of, and so I wrote the following poem:

Beautiful flowers, fragrant grasses, I know not their names;
How glorious, though they do not bloom in the spring.
If I could but send them to that moonlit pavilion,
The beautiful one will understand my devotion from afar.

Chief Seat [Sō]shun wrote a poem on a different panel:

Many-colored chrysanthemums wondrously blended;
Our guest's new poems exceed their beauty.
Faithfulness and righteousness are lofty even beneath autumn frost;
These flowers are indeed my teacher.

On the eve of the second invasion of our country, Hideyoshi is said to have told his generals, "A person has two ears, but only one nose." He ordered that soldiers sever the noses of our people, to be used in place of severed heads. When they transported the severed noses to the Japanese capital and piled them up, they formed a small hill. They buried them in front of Daibutsuji, and the mound was as high as the waist of Mount Atago. One can deduce from this the savagery of the killings! The people of our country collected rice so as to offer a sacrifice to the mound, and asked me to write a eulogy. I wrote:

Noses and ears heaped in a western hill,
Men vicious as great snakes lurking in the east.
Severed bodies piled on salt,
Can flesh be salted thus to fragrance?

In the second month of the *kyŏngja* year [1600], [Tōdō] Sado no kami [Takatora] summoned the head guard and ordered him to relax the watch upon my family. The head guard told us to leave at once. I went to see Chief Seat [Sō]shun and asked him to find a suitable way to return home (the details are in my memorial to the throne). On the second day of the fourth month, we finally departed the Japanese capital. Once on board, I wrote a poem:

> The beneficence of my king reached even prisoners in the enemy cave;
> The sail that left the edge of the earth nears the season of our barley harvest.
> So distant are the enemy islands, so vast the sea;
> My eternal heart swells to fill the lonely ship.

At Iki Island, we were delayed by wind and rain for ten days. We climbed up the mountain and prayed to Heaven. On the following dawn, stars shone, the moon was bright, and the wind hastened us as we sailed speedily home. It was the fifth day of the fifth month.

2

An Exhortation to Koreans Still Held Prisoner in Japan

AH, SAD! I, WHO LIVE ONLY BECAUSE I WAS UNABLE TO DIE, wish to say a few words to my compatriots of a similar outlook. Though miserably incarcerated in isolation, we hail from a country of civilization, a place where the ideas of Confucius and Mencius infused government academies, village schools, and family beliefs.[1] All of us were born and raised in this culture. There is none who has not heard and learned the way of kings Yu, Tang, Wen, and Wu, and of the Duke of Zhou, and of Confucius.[2] The distinction between the civilized interior and the barbarous exterior is something we have spoken of and heard of innumerable times. Respect for the ruler and attention to our elders guide our behavior and fill our hearts. Most sharply felt is our sense of indebtedness to our state; it is lodged so deeply in our hearts that it cannot be blotted out. By our grandfathers' and fathers' generations, we had been graced by six or seven sage-kings. If we consider our children and grandchildren, thirty more years of royal grace are accrued. Even in a thousand or ten thousand generations, we will not be able to forget the royal grace showered upon us over two hundred long years.

How could we have known that we were fated for such trouble and that our country would be visited by such immense misfortune? Is it that we cannot have pervasive abundance and great joy any longer, and must accept that peace and harmony are being replaced by stagnation and obstruction?[3] Taking advantage of this time of uncertainty, groups of people hatched evil plans; we have already witnessed the disaster wrought by these thieves. We met this calamity because our civil government sought only a comfortable existence while our army trained as if on a playing field, using neither weapons nor armor.

Look at this repugnant place where teeth are blackened! These slit-eyed ones are genuinely of a different race! This is a place not yet graced by King Yu's influence, where even the cart wheel is different from that of the Zhou. [It is a place so far from civilization that] Yan Shigu left it out of the *Diagram of the Civilized and the Barbarous* (C. *Huaidu*),[4] and Liu Zongyuan did not include it in his *Record of the Various Customs* (C. *Fengtuji*).[5]

Blasphemously claiming that their emperor came from the sun, they stealthily occupied the land beyond the sea. They slight their ruler as if he were a stone on a *Go* board, and treacherous officials and scheming scoundrels rub shoulders. They regard their people as if they are as insignificant as weeds and insects and inflict upon them excessively cruel punishments. The evil ruler of the thieving Japanese, Hideyoshi, is a repulsive insectlike thing full of the evil designs of a panther or a wolf. Exploiting his lazy old master, he transformed himself from insect to tumbler pigeon.[6] Then, "like the praying mantis that waved its arms angrily in front of an approaching carriage,"[7] he dared shoot a poisoned arrow into the sun. Consumed by an ocean of insatiable desire, his beastly heart was not satisfied. He took advantage of the fact that we have enjoyed long years of peace, and that our men have not engaged in military training. He also thought it was opportune that our country had experienced several years of poor harvest and that many roamed the streets suffering from famine. They devised a tactic of first attacking Yuan to invade Gong,[8] and destroying Guo by taking Yu.[9] Thus, in our country, all is destroyed. Chickens, dogs, even pigs were decimated without issue; plants and insects were annihilated by poison.

Let us enumerate the deeds they did to make them the enemy of our state. They burned the Temple of Grain[10] and the Temple of Royal Ancestors; they defiled our capital and other regions; they forced themselves into our office of government; they occupied the sacred quarters of our kings and queens. How unbearable was it to watch the red flames that for three long months consumed the palace of our ruler! The graves of ten generations of our kings were defiled and reduced to a handful of dust. Able men at our Board of Military Affairs, young and old, disappeared, becoming the aggrieved ghosts of blood-drenched battlefields. Roaming in white clothes, our ruler sang the sorrowful song of the wanderer. Oh! Too painful for his subjects; no one of spirit could hear it without being stirred.

Let us speak of what they did to earn the undying enmity of our own people. They burned our family shrines and disinterred our ancestors; they raped and assaulted our women, old and young, and bound and seized our brothers and children. Those bodies cut in two at the waist, those were our parents who gave birth to us and raised us; those bodies that fell from their spears as if in a dance troupe, those were our beautiful and lovely young children. We could not keep our betrothal pledges to our spouses, nor could we aid our brothers in need. This was a disaster to common humanity! This was what the affections of kin suffered! Those who escaped murder were taken captive.

The heirs of elite families became the errand boys of the enemy; women of distinguished families were made servants of thieves. Their comely eyes and shapely brows are not adorned by the clothes of Xuanhe,[11] their attire and wide waistbands no longer recall the dignity and elegance of yore.

There are, however, different ways of coping with captivity. Some followed the footsteps of King Che of Wei, speaking the dialect of barbarians,[12] and some, as did Zhongyong, cut their hair in the barbarian style.[13] Others passed years in miserable incarceration, and some grieved the fate of the Chu prisoner.[14] Aggrieved wails pierced through to Heaven, and spirits fell to Earth. We must remind ourselves of the beautiful phrase of Weizi: "I cannot be someone else's official or servant."[15] How can we possibly become barbarian ghosts as Li Ling did, who said that when he died, he would be buried in barbarian lands?[16] Thinking of home is a natural inclination for all beings. The birds of Chu are anxious to return home, while those of Yue gather to the south. Foxes turn their heads toward the hills, while horses follow the northern winds. Winged or four-legged, all creatures are thus.

How much more determination must we have to return to our roots, we humans verily made of benevolence. Climbing this hill or that mountain, we recall our parents' loving gaze; standing by this stream or that embankment transports us to where we played and fished as children. Such sights as a cold rain or a deep fog sadden us; the rooster's crow or the dog's bark plunges us into grief. Our ancestors' weed-covered graves would be empty of an offering even of barley; our villages under tall trees would be desolate, overgrown by three-year-old millet. Ah! Frustration! How can we sit and endure? Cool autumn comes to this land beyond the borders, and hearing people sing in groups makes it even harder to endure. We long for the southern spring, imagining trees covered with flowers. How can we, isolated and incarcerated, not fall into sorrow and resentment, however unworthy we be?

Speaking of myself, I hail from an old family; I am a student of Confucianism. From the time I was a child in braids I studied the Six Classics and understood the principle of the relationship between the ruler and the ministers. I took the civil service examinations, wrote an essay on the three strategies, and basked in the shining light of the Royal Grace.[17] I am, completely and totally, indebted to my king; every strand of my hair, every part of my body from head to foot, all is owed to my ruler. Within four years, I came to serve in a post of the sixth grade. Can I ever forget my country? Can I ever forget my king? I will not fear riding the tiger, seizing the snake. Life I desire, and righteousness I also desire. But I discerned for myself that I would discard the fish and take the bear's palm.[18] Though my power to assist in restoring our country is small, my desire to do it has been sincere, constant, and urgent. Like Zu Ti, I beat the boat in determination;[19] who could have known that I would be captured! That I lived in shame was not because I begrudged dying. I felt regret that the eight days of starvation did not extinguish my life. That I did not die, however, is because there is something yet for me to do. Dying meaninglessly will not wash away shame. There are other ways: wait beneath a bridge, dagger in hand, to take revenge on Zhao Meng;[20] vent the wrath of Zhang Liang with an iron hammer in the sandy land;[21] shout behind the lines to help defeat Qin to facilitate the return of the governor of Xiangyang;[22] beg the Xia army in the west in the spirit of the great general Pu.[23] All of these have been constantly in my mind. You can ask the spirits and gods about the veracity of this statement.

The jade of Zhao is still intact,[24] and the faithfulness of Han persists.[25] Since a ram cannot give birth to a lamb, it is possible to become Lord Su.[26] How could you bear to be Wei Lu even if the horses and beasts of the mountain and multitudes would be yours for the asking?[27] I have always dreamt of returning to my homeland white-haired. Returning with black hair would shame me. People's lives are not like those of chickens or of pigs; the human body is not wood or stone. To point toward our country from the land beyond the sea makes mountains and rivers look distant. Gazing at the white clouds on the horizon sets one's heart in turmoil.

The sounds of the edict of pain and sorrow at Fengtian still ring in my ears;[28] gazing on the noble countenance of Jinyang makes me feel as if in the presence of the Royal Majesty.[29] I raise my head to ask Heaven; I strike Earth with my fist. The strategy that leads righteousness to triumph will succeed, as multitudes put all their might into saving themselves. Money can let us employ even ghosts; why should we be concerned that there is no bridge across the Eastern Sea? To navigate the waves is not too difficult; the west wind will surely help us through. Why should there not be a seaman who can handle a ship as a horseman handles a horse?

Some say that to catch thieves, you should catch their ruler first. This is not a difficult thing, either. Only a few bared the right shoulder in support of Lu,[30] because everyone knew the distinction between legitimacy and illegitimacy. The statement that "if it weren't for him [Guan Zhong], we'd still button our robes to the left"[31] means that everyone should adhere to the principle of "respect the civilized and reject the barbarous." We have not pledged ourselves to a foreign country, because we value the rightness of the bond of three lives [between the ruler and the subject]. Success or failure depends on Heaven. Though one cannot know the future, since our sincerity pierces through the sun, we will succeed. I will not say any more. Bring your forces together!

King Wu pacified the empire with benevolence; still, Bo Yi starved himself to death in the Western Mountains.[32] When the emperor of Qin discarded propriety and valued accomplishment, Lu Zhonglian attempted to die in the Eastern Sea.[33] Sunflowers are heliocentric; can a human being be less so? The *ji liao* bird will not perch on a mountain in barbarian lands because it regards it as shameful to turn barbarous. This writing does not fully express my intentions. Still, I send this exhortation.

3

A Report to the Royal Secretariat on Japanese Social Practices

(ON THE NINETEENTH DAY OF THE FIFTH MONTH OF THE KYŎNGJA year [1600], I arrived at Pusan and there spent the night. My return was reported to the central government. As King Sŏnjo had ordered that I be summoned to the court, I went to the capital. Because the king inquired about conditions in Japan, I submitted this memorial. The king presented me with alcohol outside the gate to the royal residential compound, and upon his command a horse was provided for me. He then urged me to return home and greet my elderly father. This day was an auspicious day in the eighth month.)

On the day I departed from the Japanese capital, the Japanese monk Chief Seat [Sō]shun brought a translator for me, a captive from Taegu named Kim Kyŏnghaeng. [Sō]shun then secretly told me the following. "Yesterday I met [Kobayakawa] Chikuzen Chūnagon Kingo [Hideaki].[1] He said, 'The Daifu [Tokugawa Ieyasu] will launch a second attack on Chosŏn. If this happens, I too will have to go [to Chosŏn] again.' While Hideyoshi was alive, Ieyasu argued for stopping the war. That there is such a discussion now is because of Ieyasu's bad relationships with [Maeda] Hizen [no kami Toshinaga][2] and [Ukita] Bizen [no kami Hideie].[3] They feel that no incidents will occur if we leave that land in peace, and that their power will be exhausted by sending troops to Chosŏn. Within this year, if Ieyasu does not restore good relations with Hizen, the basic policy will not be decided, and thus there will be no reason for Chosŏn to worry. If the two men restore good relations, there is no doubt that armies will be mobilized. The attack would likely happen next year. Chosŏn should prepare for war. After you have returned home, I want you to not forget what I have told you. Although the Korean people are guilty of nothing, they have suffered the ravages of Hideyoshi's invasions. My feelings have always been occupied by that war. Therefore I have told you of this."

And Rian, the doctor, came from the home of [Kobayakawa] Kingo [Hideaki] and said this: "I have heard that there will be an attack next year and that the Daifu will appoint his first son, [Yūki] Mikawa no kami [Hideyasu],[4] as general."[5]

I could not repress my surprise and doubts. I delayed my departure for several days and asked around for more information. Someone told me the following: "During this year's New Year period, the Daifu decided to take as hostages the children and younger brothers of men holding lands of 50,000 *koku* or more and ordered that they be sent to the Kantō. Several men sent their adopted son or their younger brother. However, he requested that only [Katō] Kiyomasa, [Hosokawa] Etchū no kami [Tadaoki],[6] and others send their uterine mother or their biological sons.

"In addition, when, on New Year's Day, the Daifu tried to greet the emperor in the capital, Kiyomasa and others led troops into Fushimi and tried to meet Ieyasu there. Hearing of this, the Daifu said that he had been taken ill and did not go to the capital. Japanese laughed and said that the Daifu was a coward. [Kinoshita] Wakasa Province [Palace Guard] Lieutenant Katsutoshi was at that time serving Hideyoshi's principal wife [Nene].[7] It is said that, hearing that Ieyasu would come to the capital, Katsutoshi spent more than 40 *jō* of gold and prepared his residence for receiving Ieyasu. Upon hearing that Ieyasu was ill, he was quite disappointed. Because what Kiyomasa and others desired was not in Chosŏn, Ieyasu did not forget about them for even one day.

"Japan for several hundred years has been divided into four and cut into five. The Kantō is one region, Mutsu Province is one region, the Chūgoku area is one region, Shikoku is one region, and Kyushu is one region.[8] [Oda] Nobunaga became the most powerful man in the country and for a time controlled Japan. In his last years, Japan returned to the earlier situation and again became divided.

"After Hideyoshi became the leader, he too controlled Japan for a time. Now, however, he has passed away, and the country seems as if it will again become divided. If it falls apart, someone like Hideyoshi will be born, and perhaps Chosŏn will again suffer the ravages of war. However, in this world things change in the morning and change again in the evening, or they are unchanging from beginning to end. This we cannot know.

"Ieyasu possesses a great amount of land, and many commoners live there. He is in an advantageous situation between the two capitals and is giving orders to many elites. Even if his loyal followers are few, those who follow him are the majority. For the time being, for your country, keeping distance from Ieyasu and observing what is happening in Japan would be advisable."

(These were the words of the Japanese man, Sagain Yoichi.[9])

[Mōri] Terumoto's[10] chief adviser, the monk Ankokuji [Ekei],[11] has usually been in charge of the government. Those around him are all people from our land, and they have not forgotten their country. As I passed by, I asked about inside secrets. All of them told me, "For the next several decades, there is probably no worry of an invasion. Currently, they are arguing about staples for their horses. If one is to worry, it is about civil war. As they are consumed by this, could they also invade a foreign country?"

Because I also heard comments that differed from this, I am reporting all views.[12]

[Yanagawa] Taira Shigenobu[13] is an elder adviser of [Sō] Yoshitoshi.[14] In the governing of Tsushima, the elder advisers hold the power and Yoshitoshi only approves decisions after they have been made.

When we tried to sail past Tsushima, Yoshitoshi was at that time traveling to the Japanese capital. Shigenobu was governing the island in his absence. Shigenobu dispatched a small boat toward us, and we were asked where we were headed. Having no choice [but to reply], we reported that we were returning to Chosŏn. Shigenobu sent food, including vegetables, to our boat, and through a translator said that he wanted to meet with us two or three times. Having no choice, we alighted from our boat and met with him. On the surface, Shigenobu was respectful and warm and in gentle words spoke through the translator.

"That Hideyoshi was born in Japan was Heaven's timing, and that Chosŏn received the ravages of war also was Heaven's timing. On the contrary, you of Chosŏn, from the events of the *imjin* year [1592], direct blame to this island. On our island, we have always thought of approaching Chosŏn directly and happily, and before and after the war we dispatched men there. However, no one has returned, and thus there is no way for us to inform Chosŏn of conditions here. Our island is between the two countries, and after Hideyoshi attacked Chosŏn, we too wondered how we could have prevented the war. Thus, before the armies moved, we informed Chosŏn that war was coming and hoped that your country would strengthen defenses beforehand. That the great army conquered everything, though, was for our island something about which we had no choice but to follow commands. In this world of people, matters are repeated. Someday, Japan will be weak and Chosŏn will be strong, and should a great army cross the sea and attack the east, our island will have no choice but to follow commands. Some two hundred years ago, ships secretly sailed to Chosŏn. Even though [pirate] ships attacked Chŏlla Province from the great sea, [pirate] ships have never reached the southern coast of Kyŏngsang Province until now because they were blocked by this island.[15] From now, should Chosŏn forbid interaction completely, even if our island does not attack Chosŏn, what shall we say to other Japanese that will prevent them from sailing past this island?

"Commands utterly impossible to disobey all came from Hideyoshi. Nowadays, there will be no such demands. We do not think of receiving the rice that your country once provided us. And regarding the sending of envoys, we do not seek to receive a high-ranking official. If the Pusan official will send someone [to our island] who will bring an official document from the Board of Rites, we will first repatriate the captives on this island."[16]

We left [the meeting], and then tried to ask questions of countrymen who were captives.

[They stated,] "Since the beginning of the war in the *imjin* year [1592], the Japanese who passed through Tsushima [en route to Chosŏn] as a rule took lodging and requisitioned firewood and vegetables. Or, even if they did not request these items, there was not one occasion when they did not receive provisions. In addition to being boisterously troublesome, they also cost unreasonable expenses. From our bone marrow we have learned from experience. Because it is now the second year since the Japanese armies withdrew and finally the situation is returning to normal, Tsushima is trying various ways to request permission for [trade] ships to again sail. Each time our people cross the sea [back to Chosŏn], as a common practice the Tsushima islanders greet them and ask that their request be delivered [to our government]."

In Japanese customs, regarding personal matters and skills, they always evaluate people and rate someone as the best in Japan. Once something has been produced by the best in Japan, regardless of whether the object is extremely crude or extremely dull, it will be bought at a high price with gold or silver. If an object is not produced by the best in Japan, it will not attract the same price even if it is very refined.

Even for such uninteresting skills as binding wood, painting walls, and roofing, there is a best in Japan. And, remarkably, even for the writing of one's name, one's style of clothing, and one's monogram there are bests in Japan. Once a person receives that appraisal, if someone leisurely looks at their creation, it will be worth thirty or forty *jō* of gold and silver.

There is a man named Hotta Oribe who determines the best in Japan in everything.[17] For planting flowers and bamboo or furnishing a tearoom, for example, if one pays 100 *jō* of gold, one will be appraised by him as the best in Japan. Even for a broken gourd to fill with charcoal and a bucket for drawing water, if one were to be praised by Oribe, the evaluation could not be disputed. Because this custom is well established in Japan, though craftsmen may occasionally laugh derisively, the practice cannot be prevented. The richness of Oribe's residence compares with Ieyasu's residence. Others who are the best in Japan are similar to Oribe.

The people of our country [who are in Japan] say that recently the Japanese pirates have improved at incantations and fortune-telling, and observe the heavens well, divine geography well, and tell one's fortune well. I have looked into these deeply, but regarding their so-called incantations, I have never heard one. And a so-called fortune-teller only matched the birth year to a particular divination sign in *Book of Changes* (C. *Zhouyi*), copied the hexagram (C. *gua*), the explanation of the horizontal lines (C. *xiao*), the explanation of the divination (C. *tuan*), and the illustration (C. *xiangci*), and then passed that text to the customer.[18] The customer paid in gold and silver and asked about the fortune. The fortune-teller replied that the information was in the text just handed to him. The customer replied, "Oh, I see," and left. He placed the paper carefully in his satchel so that no one else would see it. (However, if that text were written by the best fortune-teller in Japan, it would fetch a great amount for him. But if another fortune-teller wrote exactly the same text, there would be a significant difference in the fee charged.)

The divination of the heavens, geography, and people has not been passed down from ancient times [in Japan]. Ankokuji [Ekei] is said to have some skill at reading the heavens. But divination too is nothing more than deluding the masses through nonsense. The doctor-monk [Yoshida] Ian constructed a device for measuring the sun's shadow and a brass armillary sphere for surveying the heavens, and he also has calculated the circumference of the earth.[19] But this does not equal measuring astronomical phenomena or examining human affairs.

People from Ming China [who are in Japan], including Huang Youxian, are all licentiates from prefectural schools.[20] They came to the Japanese capital by boat. They state that they are skilled at fortune-telling and that their medical skills are good, as is their reading of horoscopes. The Japanese eventually recognized them as the best in Japan. Generals visited them seemingly every day by palanquin or by horse. Because of the generals' payments of gold and silver or of brocades and silk-filled boxes, these Chinese have been in this barbarian country for more than ten years and have forgotten about returning to their home country. They are not lawless. Rather, the Japanese pirates are fools, and because they can be easily deluded, the Chinese are still living here.

Among those so-called Japanese generals there is not one who can read Chinese. The writing system that they use is similar to our *idu*. When I asked people about the original meaning of characters, they replied vaguely that they did not know.

Seven Military Classics (C. *Wujing qishu*) is owned by many people, but there is no one who can read even half a line.[21] The Japanese disperse and fight one-on-one; thus, even if they are satisfied with a temporary victory, they do not ask how the battle could have been better fought.

What I have written here is what I have learned from other captives with whom I have spoken, and I do not know if this information will break the delusions of our country's foolish peasants and defeated soldiers.

While under construction, Fushimi Castle was tall, clear, bright, and beautiful. The lumber had been finely prepared and was easily transported, but in terms of the structure being strong but finely finished, it does not reach even one one-hundredth of the quality of structures built in our country for the ruler. When I asked why there was such a difference, I was told, "Fires started by armies flare often, and because we do not know if the evening will be like the morning, we simply work in high spirits and good moods. We do not worry much about [the building's] strength and perfection."

In their rear gardens everyone plants pine, bamboo, rare flowers, and unusual grasses, and it does not matter to them from how far away these must be transported. In [the garden] they construct a tearoom, which is about the size of a boat. They cover the roof with hemp and reeds, apply yellow ocher to the walls, and furnish the *yokomon* with bamboo and a fan.[22] The tearoom is arranged in an extremely austere style. They open a small door in the wall, and finally people can enter and leave.[23] If a person of high rank comes, they open the door, greet him, and invite him to enter. In the tearoom, they drink tea.

In general, their mind is not to show someone simplicity. Even if they are to share a conversation while drinking tea, they avoid unexpected situations by having their attendants wait outside, for incidents sometimes occur suddenly.

Japanese men always wear a sword at the waist. Beyond the wearing of the sword, its only other uses are for military matters and related duties. Monks, however, are not the only people who do not wear swords. Those who are studying medicine, who are engaged in merchant activities, who practice divination, and who clean the tearooms in the homes of the generals also do not bear swords. These men all have a wife and children, drink alcohol, eat meat, and live in the cities. Other men teach students, or reverently chant prayers, or recite texts written by Confucius, or escape into the mountains and while reflecting upon the weal and the woe of life subsist by begging. These men do not have a wife and children, do not eat meat, and live apart from human communities. If there are ten Japanese men, then four or five of them will have taken the tonsure. This is because those who dislike military matters and the related duties, and wish to perfect their bodies and avoid harm, become monks.

Men who once served as monks but later became generals are called by their administrative post in the temple, or by the name of their temple, or by the name of their monastery.[24] Or, they are known as His Holiness (J. *hōin*). Monks who do not become generals are promoted through the following series of posts: first they are Sutra Repository Prefect (J. *zōsu*), then they are Chief Seat (J. *shuso*), Eastern Hall (J. *tōdō*), Western Hall (J. *seidō*), Venerable (J. *oshō*), and Abbot (J. *chōrō*), which is the highest rank.[25]

Those who are monks and are studying Buddhist sutras emphasize either the Nenbutsu (J. *Namu Amida Butsu*) or the *Lotus Sutra* (J. *Myōhō rengekyō*). They are divided into different temples, they debate and denounce, and they are precisely like bitter enemies. Those who study Confucianism emphasize either the commentaries of Kong Anguo[26] and Zheng Xuan[27] or the commentaries of Zhu Huian,[28] are divided into different schools, and have established factions. The enjoyment of battles over manners is as above. The way of the monk too cannot escape.

There is Shōkōin Tonsured Prince Kōi. He is the Brahma (J. *bonō*) of Daibutsuji temple and the uncle of the emperor [Go-Yōzei]. He holds lands valued at 10,000 *koku* and oversees the monks in temples in six provinces. On New Year's Day, monks visit him to offer greetings.[29]

There is Taichōrō Seishō Shōtai.[30] He boasts of his abilities in reading and writing Chinese.

There are Sanchōrō Hayashi Razan[31] and Tetchōrō Ikyō Eitetsu.[32] They are famous for their skills in poetry.

There is Gakkō [Kanshitsu Sanyō].[33] He teaches *Analects* (C. *Lunyu*) and *Confucius's Family Teachings* (C. *Kongzi jiayu*),[34] and he has become Ieyasu's tutor. However, it is said that actually, he does not know the difference between the characters 魚 [fish] and 魯 [foolish].

There are doctor-monks who are very skilled at reading Chinese. At times, they have served generals, and a large number of them went to our country [during the war]. However, monks consider these men to be monks. (The temple posts of abbot, venerable, and others all are assigned by the emperor.)

In Japanese customs, people believe strongly in demon spirits, and service to the gods is like service to one's father and mother. Those who were revered by people in a previous life will be revered by people after their death. Even if one does not fast or eat vegetarian meals on the anniversaries of the deaths of one's father and mother, one is forbidden to eat fish or meat on the death anniversary of a god. From generals and their wives and concubines to commoners, on each celebratory day and death anniversary, those who solemnly wear nice clothing and go to the temple's gate and throw coins look at the road with saddened eyes.

Shinto shrines are spacious and luxurious and are illumined by gold-colored walls. There is the Amaterasu Shrine; the ancestor of the Japanese is a female god.[35] There is the protective deity (J. *gongen*) of Mount Kumano, which is Xu Fu. There is the protective deity of Mount Atago, which is Illa, a man of Silla. And there is the tutelary deity (J. *daimyōjin*) of Kasuga [Shrine], the bodhisattva (J. *bosatsu*) of Hachiman [Shrine], and the *Tarōbō* and *Shōrōbō*.[36] The number of gods in Japan cannot be counted. In their pledges and commandments, they always vow to pray to these spirits. I have heard that at times, even if one is in a trial that is like burning the elbow and cutting a muscle, those who find it difficult to transgress against the commandments say, "The way of Heaven is fearful and thunder and lightning is frightening [if one transgresses]."

The Japanese call each other *sama*, and also *tono*. When writing, they always attach the honorific prefix 御, and this honorific is used for everyone from the emperor to commoners.[37] Presenting from one above to one below is called bestowing "tribute." And one above being seen by one below is "to be seen by a superior."[38] The absence of status distinctions is like this. At times, even while engaged in battle, if a counterpart treats one with respect and proper behavior, after one has left he will calmly abide by graces while coldly laughing to himself. The coarseness and laxness of their conduct is like this.

The nature of the Japanese slaves is to enjoy the great and to take pleasure in skill. The arrival of ships from faraway countries is normally considered a grand event, and if merchant ships or trade ships arrive, they are treated as diplomatic envoy ships, it is said. I heard the following while in the Japanese capital. The Japanese pirates frequently reported that European envoys had arrived. The country would become very excited, and these visits became quite the topic of discussion. So I asked my countrymen about this. They said that about ten people carrying one white parrot had come.

When people from faraway countries arrive, Japanese sometimes inflict harm upon them. Officials fear that the road to be followed [by the foreigners] might not be safe, and they will kill all the relatives of anyone who harms the foreigners.

In the eighth month of last year [1599], when ships from Fujian approached Satsuma Province, Japanese along the coast gathered their own ships and sent armed men aboard the Chinese boats. Leaving only the merchants, they stole the valuable items and cargo. The merchants were extremely angry and, eventually reaching Satsuma Province, they informed subordinates of [Shimazu] Yoshihiro[39] of what had occurred. Yoshihiro reported this to Ieyasu, and, arresting the men, brought them alive to the Japanese capital. The men all were sentenced to the punishment of being torn apart by carts pulling in opposite directions,[40] and all of the treasures and cargo were returned to the merchants.

Ch'ŏnch'uk and other countries are great distances from Japan.[41] And Japanese do not try to go there. The merchant ships from Fujian as well as the trade ships of Europe, Ryukyu, and Luzon [that come to Japan] are overseen by [Shimazu] Yoshihiro and Ryūzōji.[42] [Terazawa Shima no kami] Masanari and [Sō Tsushima no kami] Yoshitoshi oversee ships sailing from our country.[43]

Year after year, donkeys, mules, camels, elephants, peacocks, and parrots are carried to Japan.[44] Ieyasu and others, following common practice, pay high prices [for them] with gold and silver or with spears and swords. Because they engage in the exchange of things with no benefit whatsoever and in the exchange of profitable things, those merchants gladly visit Japan. Chinese goods and European products are on display in Japanese markets. As for goods that seem to have been produced in Japan, excluding gold and silver, there is little that could be called rare, it is said.

From the capital of Japan to Fushimi is 10 *ri* overland. (Below, all distances will be calculated by the Japanese measure. Three *ri* is equal to 30 *ri* in our measure.) From Fushimi to Osaka by water is 10 *ri* and by land is 10 *ri*. From Osaka to Hyōgo, in Settsu Province, is 10 *ri* by sea. To the left is Awaji [Province] and to the right is Settsu Province; boats sail between these places. From Hyōgo to Murotsu, in Harima [Province], is 20 *ri*. To the left is Awaji and to the right is Harima; boats sail between these places. From Murotsu to Ushimado, in Bizen [Province], is 10 *ri*. To the left is Shikoku and to the right is Bizen; boats sail between these places. From Ushimado to Tomo, in Bingo [Province], is 23 *ri*. To the left is Shikoku and to the right is Bingo; boats sail between these places. From Tomo to Kamigaseki, in Suō [Province], is 35 *ri*. To the left, one has already passed Shikoku and can now see Kyushu's Bungo [Province]. To the right, one passes through Aki [Province] and arrives in Suō. Boats pass between these places. The passage into the sea [between Honshu and Kyushu] is extremely narrow, and because the flow of the saltwater current is exceptionally fast, this place is called a toll barrier (J. *seki*). From Kamigaseki to Shimonoseki, in Nagato [Province], is 35 *ri*. To the left, one passes Bungo and reaches Buzen [Province]. To the right, one leaves Suō and arrives at Shimonoseki. Boats pass between these places. The coastlines [of Honshu and Kyushu] face each other, and their breadth and narrowness resemble the mouth of the Kŭm River in our country. Handling boats is extremely difficult. From Shimonoseki to [the island of] Ainoshima is 25 *ri*. Because Ainoshima is between Shimonoseki, Hakata, and Iki [island], it is called by that name [meaning "the island among"]. The land on the right side ends here, and it is said that the sea stretches to the left circuit of Yŏngnam.[45] A broad expanse, there are no harbors or islands, and one proceeds by following the provinces of Buzen and Chikuzen. If one sails from Ainoshima straight to Iki, the distance is 48 *ri*. If one goes to Karatsu, in Hizen [Province], the distance is 21 *ri*. From Karatsu to Nagoya is 3 *ri*.[46] From Nagoya to Iki is 15 *ri*. From Iki to Yoshizu, in Tsushima, is 48 *ri*. (Yoshizu is also called Fuchū.) From Yoshizu to Toyosaki is 35 *ri*. From Toyosaki to Pusan is 38 *ri*. It is said that when the wind is blowing from the east, south, or north, one may raise sail at any time.

From Toyosaki, if one gazes toward Pusan, Kimhae, Ungch'ŏn, Ch'angwŏn, Kŏje, and other places, one may easily count them. From Kijang northward, the sea is far too broad, and if the strength of the wind is slightly unmanageable, there is fear of losing one's boat. From Hansan island to the west, the sea route extends quite far, and crossing is not easy.

Natural disasters occur frequently in Japan. During the daytime, there is a rouge-red mist as far as one can see. When there is dirt rain or hair rain, it does not stop for several days. Japanese consider the hair rain as a sign to celebrate and place the rain in their pockets or wear the hairs on their waists.[47] Only learned Japanese monks said, "During the reign of Emperor Wu of Han China, hair rain fell because there was construction, and conquest frequently flourished. In Japan, even from ancient times there was no period when construction and forced labor on government projects was more common. Thus, Heaven made hair rain down."

Since 1595 and 1596, great earthquakes have occurred over this period of four to five years. And sometimes the aftershocks have continued for several days. On the twenty-fourth day of the twelfth month of 1599, there was a fire in Fushimi. The house of Ōta Hida no kami [Kazuyoshi],[48] the house of Konishi Settsu no kami Yukinaga, the houses above and below that of Mashita [U]emon no shō[jō Nagamori],[49] and the house of Hijikata Kanpei[ei Katsuhisa] all burned at the same time, and the flames reached the outer ramparts of Ieyasu's residence.[50] As the north wind was blowing extremely fast and the strength of the fire was very great, people raised sheets in the air atop the inner ramparts and thereby slowed the winds. Thus the flames did not reach the inner area of Ieyasu's mansion.

On the tenth day of the second month of 1600, there was a fire at the house of [Ukita] Bizen Chūnagon [Hideie]. On the second day of the fourth month, a fire blazed at the house of Miyabe Hyōbu [no shō] Nagahiro.[51] Why is it that the insincere barbarian virtue of the Japanese does not last long? This is likely because the leader of the thieving Japanese, in intensifying his brutality and carrying his tyranny to extremes, acted contrary to the spirit of Heaven and Earth.

4

A Memorial Sent from Captivity

YOUR SERVANT KANG HANG, THE FORMER ASSISTANT SECTION Chief in the Board of Punishments, ranked junior sixth grade, after purifying myself, having bowed one hundred times facing west and wailing, respectfully sends this memorial to Your Majesty, the Great King of Correct Principle, Established Perfection, Great Virtue, and Far-Reaching Brilliance.[1]

In the *chŏngyu* year [1597], your servant, a lower-ranking official, was assigned to Yi Kwangjŏng, Deputy Minister of a branch office of the Board of Taxation, to help amass food provisions in Honam [Chŏlla Province], to transport them to troops under Commander Yang.[2] By the time provisions were ready, the enemy's vanguard army had already reached Namwŏn,[3] and Kwangjŏng had left for Seoul. I and Kim Sangjun,[4] the assistant to the governor, sent out open letters of exhortation to many villages to raise a Righteous Army (K. *ŭibyŏng*) of volunteers.[5] Patriotic scholars responded to the call and came forward, but they numbered only several hundred; even this group, fearing for their families, soon disbanded.[6]

Reluctantly, I placed my father, elder brother, younger brother, and my wife and children on a boat. We intended to go north to Seoul by way of the West Sea. The boatman was unskilled, and while he lingered by the coast, we were overtaken by an enemy ship. Realizing that we could not escape, I and all the members of my family jumped into the sea. The boat was in shallow water, however, and everyone except my father, who escaped by boarding another boat, was captured by the Japanese. Moreover, several hundred appointment documents that [showed the means by which] the Board of Taxation had amassed army provisions sank into the water.[7] I have committed a serious dereliction of duty, bringing dishonor to the government. There is no way I can avoid receiving severe punishment.

The enemy immediately recognized us as an official and an official's family. They tied me and my elder and younger brothers to the ship planks, turned the ship around, and took us to the edge of the sea in Muan County.[8] In that space stretching about 2 *ri*, there were about six or seven hundred enemy ships docked closely together. About half of the people on board were men and women of our country and half were Japanese, but they were mingled together. Loud wailing was heard from each ship, and it echoed through the seas and mountains. Upon our arrival at the headquarters of the Left Province Navy Commander in Sunch'ŏn County,[9] a general of the enemy army, [Tōdō] Sado no kami [Takatora], put me; my brothers, Chun and Hwan; my father-in-law, Kim Pong;[10] and all our families on a ship and took us to his country.

A week after the ship left Sunch'ŏn, it arrived at An'gol Port,[11] and a day later at Tsushima, where the ship docked for two days because of a storm. When the ship sailed, it arrived at Iki Island in the evening of that day; Hizen Province the following evening; Shimonoseki, in Nagato Province, the evening after; the evening after that, Kaminoseki, which is also called Akamagaseki, in Suō Province;[12] and, a day later toward evening, finally at Ōzu, in Iyo Province.[13] They kept us in this town. Ōzu was one of the three castle towns that belonged to [Tōdō] Sado no kami [Takatora].[14]

I discovered that this town had more than 1,000 Korean men and women who had been taken captive and brought from our country. Newly arrived people formed themselves into throngs that roamed the streets from morning till night, crying and wailing loudly. Those who had been captured earlier, however, their paths to return completely blocked, were halfway to being acculturated as Japanese. When your servant stealthily suggested to them that we plot an escape, no one responded. Then, toward the end of the fourth month the following year [1598], one man, a former resident of the Chuksŏ district in Seoul, who was captured and brought in 1592, fled the Japanese capital and went to Iyo Province. He spoke Japanese fluently. When I floated to him the idea that we plan our escape westward together, he responded positively. I did not know a word of Japanese, so unless I was accompanied by an interpreter, I could not move around at all.

On the twenty-fifth day of the fifth month, under cover of darkness of night, we escaped and walked west for three days. We rested hidden in the bamboo forest by the seashore, and we noticed a Japanese monk of about sixty years of age bathing in a waterfall. Afterward, he sat on a rock and appeared to be dozing. My companion approached him and cautiously told him the reason we had arrived there. He lamented sympathetically a couple of times and then offered to take us to Bungo Province.[15] We were deliriously happy. Before we took ten steps descending the slope after the monk, suddenly, a man named Dōhei, an underling of [Tōdō] Sado no kami [Takatora], appeared before us. He was leading a number of soldiers. Our escape had been discovered. We were forcibly returned to Ōzu and placed under much stricter surveillance.

There was a monk named Kōjin, from Kinzan Shussekiji temple, who was quite learned. He pitied me and treated me with particular respect. He showed me various documents relating to his country, among them a geographical gazetteer and a table of the administrative offices of Japan with no omission. As soon as I returned [to my residence], I copied them. I also heard that [Tōdō] Sado no kami [Takatora]'s father, Hakuun, possessed an extremely detailed map of Japan, and so I had an interpreter examine it. I wrote what I had learned [from these records] and what I had observed with my own eyes, placing this information in the context of the long-term defense strategy of our country. On occasion, I inserted my own ideas, although I am afraid that only one of one thousand might be useful.

Alas! A general who has been defeated in battle cannot speak of courage. How dare I, captured by the enemy and living shamefully in the enemy's cave, discuss national policies or the gains and losses of the state? I am painfully aware that this is utterly ludicrous, and [I] cannot escape being severely punished. On the contrary, we are told that there was in olden days a person who remonstrated with his corpse,[16] and another who did not forget on his deathbed to send his ideas on national policy. Thus, I feel that it is not right not to speak up, even though I am a criminal, if there is any chance of benefiting our country.

Since this place is separated from our country by an expanse of 10,000 *ri* of open sea, and since things are planned within the closed gates of the palace of these beasts, Your Majesty might not have been able to penetrate into the cunning schemes of these thieves. Envoys came and went on a fixed schedule and moreover, because of tight surveillance and prohibitions, the information they could obtain cannot have been detailed or extensive. As for those captives who managed to escape, most were from the lower orders. Illiterate and unlearned, they had a limited sense of what was important and what was not, and thus what they saw and heard was likely to have been diffuse and fragmentary. In consideration of these facts, in shame, I record this. When I copied those documents of the Japanese monk, I translated those portions written in Japanese *kana* into Korean so that they may be used in interrogating and acquiring information from Japanese who have surrendered to Chosŏn.

I met a Korean captive named Kim Sŏkpok, who was from Ulsan.[17] He told us that he had been a slave belonging to the family of Commander Kwŏn Yul and had been captured and brought to Iyo Province in the fall of the *kyesa* year [1593].[18] He also said that he had been planning to lease a Japanese ship at a high price and go westward to home. I immediately entrusted him with the copy that I had made. If he does not meet misfortune on the way and this writing reaches Your Majesty's penetrating gaze, even though Japan is located far across the sea, all the secrets of these Japanese thieves will vividly appear to Your Majesty. [If this were to happen,] although these thieves are despicable creatures who engage in hundreds of deceptions and tricks, they will be awed by Your Majesty's prescience and will regard Your Majesty as a god. I also hope that this memorial, even in the smallest degree, will help in planning national defense policy and handling [the outside threat].

On the eighth day of the eighth month of that year [1598], the Japanese relocated me and my family, and we arrived at Osaka on the eleventh day of the ninth month. The evil ruler of these Japanese thieves, [Toyotomi] Hideyoshi, had already died, on the seventeenth day of the seventh month.[19] Osaka is Japan's western capital, and after several days there we were again moved, to Fushimi Castle. Fushimi is the new capital of Japan.[20] As soon as the head of the Japanese thieves died, the politics and the situation of Japan changed drastically. Lest our government miss this golden opportunity, I and Kim Ujŏng from Tongnae and Kang Sajun from Chinju, both scholar-captives who were in the capital of Japan, bought one silver coin every day with what we saved from food [rations]. We hired a Korean interpreter who spoke Japanese fluently enough not to reveal his foreign origin, providing him with travel expenses and funds to hire a boat, and he was able to reach beyond the border area. Before he could dispatch a letter [to Chosŏn], however, many Japanese had already retreated [from Chosŏn].

I searched for and schemed many different ways to escape. I had no money, so reluctantly, I decided to sell my calligraphy to Japanese monks and in this way amassed fifty silver coins, with which I was able to secretly purchase a ship. Several of us, including Kim Ujŏng, Sin Tŏkki from Seoul, and Chŏng Yŏnsu from Chinju, a boatman, planned an escape to the west. One day, before I, my brother Hwan, and my father-in-law, Kim Pong, were ready, my brother Chun, along with the boatman and interpreters, went ahead to the place where we were supposed to board. Someone near the seashore must have informed [Tōdō] Sado no kami [Takatora]. He immediately dispatched soldiers, who searched and arrested everyone present. They imprisoned them and, after twenty days, killed all the interpreters. The rest were released, but after a long while. Thus, a thousand ideas of mine and a hundred schemes I devised came to naught. Must it not have been because my devotion [to you] was insufficient and thus incapable of moving Heaven and Earth that I met so many obstacles?

When the Qin state discarded ritual and upheld efficiency, Lu Zhonglian wished to go to the Eastern Sea.[21] Although King Wu, with his benevolence, subjugated the tyrant [Zhou],[22] Bo Yi still went to the Western Mountain and starved himself to death there. How much worse the present situation is! The filthiness of these thieves and the remoteness of this godforsaken place from our country are beyond compare. These thieves are the worst enemies of our people ever! Moreover, as a humble man from the south, I passed the higher civil service examination and, despite lowness of rank and brevity of experience, I was appointed a temporary recorder in the Royal Secretariat during the autumn and winter of the *kabo* year [1594], and thus had the honor of attending to Your Majesty about twenty times. The brightness of the sun and moon [the king's countenance] shone near me, and, in that warm Heavenly voice, Your Majesty even inquired after your servant's name. In the *pyŏngsin* year [1596], I was even promoted to Assistant Section Chief in the Board of Punishments.[23] From the top of my forehead to the soles of my feet, I am completely indebted to Your Majesty's boundless grace. Yet, without being able to repay it in the smallest degree, I fell into this den of beastly barbarians in a distant land beyond the pale. For living so shamelessly even for one day, I deserve death ten thousand times over.

It is not because I value my life, which I hold as lightly as goose feathers, or because I cannot bear the momentary pain of dying that I am alive. It is because dying now would be like strangling myself in a dark abyss to vanish without trace, thus annihilating my name. It would make me unable to repay the state by acts of loyalty and integrity and make it impossible to leave an honorable name by choosing the right moment to die. I would be merely a skeleton felled by an enemy sword, like illiterate women and small children—who remembers their deaths? As for being taken captive and having to plan for the future, it was [a fate that] even such a famous loyal minister as Wen Tianxiang and such a brave general as Zhu Xu could not avoid.[24] Yet historians did not judge them to be at fault and awarded them the verdict of absolute integrity (K. *chŏnjŏl*). This is because even though their bodies were captured, they did not allow their integrity to be compromised.

Your servant is shallow and stupid and is not worth one ten-thousandth of these ancients. When it comes to having a loyal heart that desires to do good for the country, however, I cannot concede to them an inch. Even though my life is worth no more than the life of an insect, as long as I have even one breath remaining, my loyalty is like that of a dog or a horse that cannot be broken even after ten thousand blows. It would be much better, even if having escaped to my country by using my wiles, I were to be punished by death, my head and body sliced in half at the middle in the courtyard of the Royal Court, than to be buried in this barbarian land.

Now, with my understanding of the conditions of this den of thieves, if Heaven turned the situation to our favor and we could seize an opportunity, even with this meager body, I would at once place myself at the vanguard of our royal army. Under [the protection of] the awesome spirit of our royal ancestors, I will, above all, wipe away the humiliations inflicted upon the royal graves and the Temple of Royal Ancestors,[25] and after that avenge the unbearable shame of those years in captivity. Then, I would like to receive the punishment of our royal court to pay for the crime of having lived shamefully amid the enemy. This is why your servant arises in the middle of the night to stroke the sword, and this is why his intestines twist nine times a day.

To quote the old saying that even the ancients lamented being held in a distant land is simply platitudinous. As long as I live, I will not be able to resume the dignity of an official at our royal court; but if I could pass Tsushima and have one look at Pusan, even to see it in the morning and die that evening, I would have no regret.

What follows are the report on the state of things in Japan and the cunning schemes that erupted after the death of the enemy head [Hideyoshi]. I sincerely hope that Your Majesty will not discard my words just because I am living shamefully. I believe that, if Your Majesty reads these documents occasionally, when the sun dispels the shadows, or when the lightning strikes and the wind arises, they will not be completely useless in charting policies and recalibrating plans. In prostration, I beg that Your Majesty test this and give them some attention.

Hardly able to bear the extreme awe, the profound sorrow, and my desperation, your servant hereby respectfully submits this memorial.

The tenth day of the fourth month in the twenty-seventh year of Wanli [1599]

Appendix 1

Japanese Daimyo in the Invasion of Chosŏn and Other Information

(See below. Because this list will be repeated and the treatment below provides greater detail, I will not also place that text here.)

In ancient times, there was a person called Fukiaezu no mikoto.[1] He was also called Tenjin. It is said that he descended to Hyūga Province bearing one sword, one jewel, and one mirror. He made Hyūga his capital, and later moved the capital to Yamato. He also moved the capital to Toyora in Nagato Province and to Yamashiro Province. The capital of Japan today is in Yamashiro Province. Since the time of his establishment of the capital, the rulers have inherited one family name, and this has not changed even today.

When I read this chronology of Japan's history and acquired *Azuma kagami* [Mirror of the East] (It is said that one's own good points and bad points are soon seen in one's wife. If one observes one's wife, one can know his good points and bad points. For this reason, the history book was titled thus), I realized that 400 years earlier the so-called Emperor of Japan had not lost his majesty. From earlier generations, the emperor has appointed a Minister (J. *daijin*) and entrusted him with governing the country. (The Senior Counselor [J. *Dainagon*], Prime Minister [J. *Dajo Daijin*], Shogun [J. (*Sei-i*) *Taishōgun*], Imperial Regent, and other officials carried out the policies.) The minister also oversaw the execution of the commands of the emperor. (The emperor [J. *tennō*] was also called *tenson*.[2])

Since the Kantō Shogun Minamoto no Yoritomo, governance has been entrusted to the Imperial Regent, and the emperor has conducted state rites. After Hideyoshi, the evil ruler of the thieving Japanese, succeeded [Oda] Nobunaga, the overthrow of those above by those below (J. *gekokujō*) became extreme. The emperor's lands in the Kinai provinces were all taken by the leader of the thieving Japanese. Hideyoshi divided those lands and distributed them among his retainers. (The stipends [J. *hōroku*] of the emperor's supporters are quite low, and even those with larger stipends receive but a few thousand *koku*. As with [Tokugawa] Ieyasu and [Mōri] Terumoto,[3] the prebends of those with larger stipends reach eight or nine provinces, and their stipends exceed 5,000,000 or 6,000,000 *koku*.)

Numerous lands for deputies (K. *taegwan*, J. *daikan*) have been established in the provinces. The generals who possess those lands are forced to jointly administer the deputies' lands. And the generals are forced to forward to the capital the silver cash obtained through the trade of the yield from those lands. The silver cash is used for state purposes. If a deputy's land is valued at 30,000 *koku*, the person who manages that land takes 10,000 *koku* for himself. Thus, a person who manages many lands of deputies becomes extremely wealthy. There are many examples of this. In earlier times, men who possessed lands considered it shameful to take the entire yield from the farmers. Because they left half the yield and gave it to the farmers, the farmers were not exceptionally poor and the generals were not exceedingly wealthy.

Upon the leader of the thieving Japanese Hideyoshi's succession of Nobunaga, the collection of yield changed in the extreme. Because nothing produced in the fields, even straw, belonged any longer to the farmers, even if the wealth of the generals could be compared to that of Hideyoshi, the farmers were poor and had not even enough rice for the next day.[4]

The so-called Regent in earlier times was appointed from among the four great descent groups of the Fuji[wara], the Tachibana, the Minamoto, and the Taira.[5] Because men born to high status succeed to high status and men born to mean status succeed to mean status, Japanese who held positions of power prized names and did not stray as they wished from the way. Nobunaga was killed by his retainer Akechi.[6] Hideyoshi rose from base status, attacked and killed many high-ranking officials, and called himself the Imperial Regent. He then tried to request of the King of Japan the surname of one of the four Regent families,[7] but all the king's close advisers said, "We will follow your orders in other matters, but we will not permit him to be granted [such] a surname." Hideyoshi became angry and left, and on his own [he] took the surname Taira. Later, he changed his surname to Toyotomi.[8]

The men in positions of power today all are of ordinary background and sons of merchants (men of slavelike status or criminals), and relying upon Hideyoshi, [they] have quickly become wealthy and successful. And among monks, they say no matter their position, "Since the founding of Japan, Japan has never been turned upside down as it is now." (The leader of the thieving Japanese was first called the Imperial Regent but later rose higher and was called *Taikō*. He adopted his nephew [Toyotomi Hidetsugu], who later was called the Imperial Regent. But in the *ŭlmi* year [1595], Hideyoshi heard an untruthful secret report and ordered Hidetsugu and his retainers to kill themselves, it is said.[9])

During the reign of the first Emperor of Qin, Shi Huangdi, Xu Fu took to the sea with young boys and girls in boats and reached Mount Kumano, in Japan's Kii Province.[10] Still today there is a shrine for Xu Fu on Mount Kumano. His descendants are today's Hata family, who over the many generations have referred to themselves as Xu Fu's descendants.[11] It is not true that Xu Fu's descendants became the emperors of Japan. During the Hongwu period,[12] the Japanese monk Zekkai Chūshin entered Ming China to deliver tribute [from the Muromachi *bakufu*].[13] The Hongwu emperor ordered Zekkai Chūshin to compose a poem. Zekkai Chūshin wrote:

Before the peak of Kumano stands Xu Fu's shrine;
The mountains abound in herbs thanks to the rains.
Now the billowing waves of the sea are calm;
A favorable wind blows ten thousand miles—it's time he went home.[14]

The Hongwu emperor bestowed upon Zekkai Chūshin a poem:

At Kumano's soaring craggy tines, a shrine that descendants will so nourish
At roots of clinging gnarled pines, the precious amber will so flourish
That year Xu Fu had but one urge, of finding that Immortal Potion
From then 'til now the present verge, of returning there is no notion.[15]

There was a monk called Kōbō Daishi.[16] He was from Sanuki Province.[17] Traveling through [Tang] China, he reached India, where he studied the Buddhist law, and upon completion of his studies [he] returned to Japan.[18] People called him the living Buddha. Because Japanese could not understand Chinese characters, he divided spoken Japanese into forty-eight sounds and created *kana* for writing. That script is similar to our vulgar script (K. *ŏnmun*).[19] When *kana* are mixed with Chinese characters, at its worst it resembles our *idu*.[20] When *kana* are not mixed with Chinese characters, at its worst it resembles our vulgar script. Those people in Japan with a reputation for skill in reading Chinese are used only for translation. Japanese do not understand Chinese characters well.

However, among Japanese who read Chinese well, their nature is rather different from typical Japanese, and they are amused by the generals.

Earlier, someone showed me a text that Kōbō Daishi is said to have written. When I saw the postscript to that map, I read that Japan is composed of eight circuits, that there are 66 provinces, and that Iki and Tsushima are not counted as provinces. There are two islands, 92,000 districts (J. *gō*) (a place that has a fort and a pond is called a district), 109,856 villages, rice fields totaling 899,160 *chō*, and other fields totaling 112,148 *chō*. (In Japanese measure, our country's 5 *ch'ŏk* is 1 Japanese *ken*, 55 *ken* is 1 *chō*, and 36 *chō* is 1 *ri*.[21] The

Japanese *ri* is exactly 10 *ri* in our country's measure. However, in the Kantō area, only 6 *chō* equals 1 *ri*. Wet rice paddies are called *den*, and mountain fields are called *hatake*.) There are 2,958 Buddhist temples, 27,612 Shinto shrines, 1,994,828 males, and 2,904,820 females. Even if the increase and decrease of the population over time is not equal in each period, in general, the population can be estimated.²²

Further, it is said that at the far east of Japan is Mutsu Province and at the far west is Hizen Province. From eastern Mutsu to western Hizen is 415 *ri*. At the far south is Kii Province and at the far north is Wakasa Province. From southern Kii to northern Wakasa is 88 *ri*. From Hiraizumi, in Mutsu, to Ezo is 30 *ri* by sea.²³ The Bandō road is 180 *ri*.

Previously, I thought that Japan was not as large as our country. I met a Japanese monk named Ian.²⁴ He is from the capital of Japan. His grandfather and father had studied in China,²⁵ and by Ian's generation the family knew mathematics, astronomy, and geography well. Earlier, Ian had built a clock for measuring the sun's shadow, and he knew more or less the circumference of the earth and the distance to a mountain or to a river, it is said.²⁶

As was said earlier, "During the Imjin invasion, Japanese brought all of the land registers from the Board of Taxation to Japan. I have heard that half of those land registers do not surpass Japan's land registers." The person who said that is honest, thus he can probably be believed. This comment may be considered not unfounded. Moreover, if we were to calculate the size of Japan based upon the distance from the Kantō to Mutsu Province, compared to our country it is extremely large.

Illa, a man from Silla, came to Japan.²⁷ The Japanese respected him and made him the Great Tengu Tarōbō.²⁸ After his death, Illa was revered and enshrined as a protective spirit for the protective deity of the Mount Atago avatar (J. *gongen*).²⁹ Even today, there are people who throw coins and rice and pray for good fortune.

In general, Japanese are sharp at reading lesser things and know little of important things. People intently follow what is praised without examining it carefully, and once they are fooled they will never realize it until they die. The vulgarity of the barbarians is like this.

The three circuits of Tōkaidō, Tōsandō, and Hokurikudō are far from our country. For this reason, they were not involved in the invasion of our country from the *imjin* year [1592]. The four circuits of Kinai, Sanyōdō, Sanindō, and Nankaidō were forced to send troops in rotation to our country. The

Seikaidō circuit is extremely close. For this reason, it[s generals] continually stationed troops in our country from 1592. The number of Japanese troops in the *imjin* invasion was 165,000. (This figure includes soldiers but does not include sailors.) The Japanese generals were:

[Mōri] Aki Chūnagon Terumoto[30] (He was in Sangju.)
His adopted son [Mōri] Aki Saishō Hidemoto[31]
[Ukita] Bizen Chūnagon Hideie[32] (He intruded into the Southern Detached Palace.[33])
[Kobayakawa] Chikuzen Chūnagon Kingo [Takakage][34]
Mashita [U]emon[no jō] Nagamori[35] (He intruded into the capital.)
[Date] Chūjō Masamune[36] (He intruded first into Chinju. He had only one eye and was brave but rough.)
Wakisaka Nakatsukasa [no shō Yasuharu][37]
Nagaoka Etchū no kami [Hosokawa Tadaoki][38]
Toda Jibu no taifu [Katsutaka] (He intruded into Hwanghae Province. After the invasion ended, he returned to Japan and died there.)[39]
Ishida Jibu no shō [Mitsunari][40]
Satsuma no kami Shimazu Hyōgo no kami Yoshihiro[41]
Hizen Province *jinushi* Ryūzōji [Masaie][42]
Asano Danjō [Nagamasa][43]
His son Asano Sakyō no daibu [Yukinaga][44]
Ikoma Uta no kami [Chikamasa][45]
His son [Ikoma] Sanuki no kami [Kazumasa][46]
Chōsokabe Tosa no kami Morichika[47]
Hachisuka Awa no kami Iemasa[48]
Ikeda Iyo no kami Hideo[49]
Tōdō Sado no kami [Takatora][50]
Ōtani Gyōbu no shō [Yoshitsugu][51]
Katō Sama no suke [Yoshiaki][52]
Ogawa Sama no suke [Suketada][53]
Miyabe Hyōbu no shō [Nagahiro][54]
Fukutaka Uma no suke [Naotaka] ("Fukutaka" might also be written as "Fukuhara.")[55]
Nakagawa Shūri no daibu Hidenari[56]
Katō Kazue [no kami] Kiyomasa[57] (Another name [for Kiyomasa] was Toranosuke. He intruded into Hamgyŏng Province.)
Konishi Settsu no kami Yukinaga[58]
Kuroda Kai no kami [Nagamasa][59]

Mōri Iki no kami [Katsunobu][60]
Mōri Minbu no taifu [Takamasa][61]
Matsura Hōin [Shigenobu][62]
Takenaka Gensuke [Takashige][63]
[Ko]bayakawa Shume no kami Nagamasa[64]
Yanagawa Tachibana Sakon [no e Shōgen Muneshige][65]
Terazawa Shima no kami Hirotaka[66]
Hashiba Tsushima no kami [Sō] Yoshitoshi[67]

The number of soldiers in the *chŏngyu* invasion was less than half [the number in the *imjin* invasion]. They totaled 104,500 men. The Japanese generals were:

Aki Saishō [Mōri] Hidemoto
[Ukita] Bizen Chūnagon Hideie (He intruded into Nŭngsŏng and Hwasun.)
[Kobayakawa] Chikuzen Chūnagon Kingo [Hideaki][68]
Asano Sakyō no daibu [Yukinaga]
Shimazu Hyōgo [no kami] Yoshihiro (He established a base at Sach'ŏn.)
Hizen Ryūzōji [Masaie][69] (His retainer Nabeshima Kaga no kami [Naoshige] served in his stead.[70])
Katō Kazue [no kami] Kiyomasa[71]
Konishi Settsu no kami Yukinaga (He established a base at Sunch'ŏn.)
Kuroda Kai no kami [Nagamasa][72]
[Hachisuka] Awa no kami Iemasa (He reached Muan by boat.)
Ikoma Sanuki no kami Kazumasa
[Chōsokabe] Tosa no kami Morichika (He intruded into Naju.)
Katō Sama no suke [Yoshiaki] (He reached Muan by boat.)
Fukutaka Uma no suke [Naotaka] (He reached Muan by boat.)
Hayakawa Shume no kami Nagamasa
Mōri Iki no kami [Katsunobu][73]
Mōri Minbu no daiu [Takamasa][74] (He reached Muan by boat.)
Yanagawa Tachibana Sakon [Muneshige][75]
Tōdō Sado no kami [Takatora] (He reached Muan by boat.)
Terazawa Shima no kami Masanari[76]
[Ikeda] Iyo no kami Hideo (He intruded into Kwangju; the killings were most extreme there. He died aboard ship after reaching Chindo.)

Kakimi Izumi no kami Kazunao[77]
Matsura Hōin [Shigenobu]
Kumagai [Ō]kura no jō Naoshige[78]
Hashiba Tsushima no kami [Sō] Yoshitoshi
Kurushima [Izumo] no kami [Michifusa][79] (He died by an arrow shot by Yi Sunsin.[80])

There is Ankokuji Ekei.[81] He is a Japanese monk. He first served [Mōri] Terumoto. Traveling back and forth between Terumoto and the leader of the thieving Japanese, Ekei ended the fighting between these two armies and eventually brought about a truce between the two men [in 1582]. Ekei did not take many of the lands that the leader of the thieving Japanese had provided as his reward and accepted only 20,000 *koku*. At the second invasion, Ekei became a commander, and he bragged greatly about his resources. All of the Japanese monks were good at the beginning, but later they became bad, he said, laughing. He has endeavored to achieve peace and from the beginning until now has done so.

There is the Taichōrō Saishō Shōtai. He brags of his skill in written Chinese. He curried favor with, and served, the leader of the thieving Japanese, and even received more than 10,000 *koku* of lands. Through Japanese monks I obtained and read *Gakumon ki*, which Saishō Shōtai had prepared for the leader of the thieving Japanese,[82] and the record of the conversation with Shen Weijing.[83] But these texts are greatly exaggerated. A particularly terrible example is: "The Great Ming heard the wind and came to Japan. Chosŏn, being immoral, we attacked." Truly, my heart hurt and my bones felt as if they had been cut.

And there is Ankokuji Saidō. (In our country, we call him Genso.[84]) He became an assistant to [Sō] Yoshitoshi. It is said that he writes Chinese very well, and that many of the letters that slander and express scorn for our country come from his hand.

In Japan, those who have gained merit in battle receive rewards of land. The largest extend across eight or nine provinces, or across several provinces. The next levels of reward are to govern a province, to govern several castles, and to govern one castle. The smallest reward is several divided villages. Or, they sometimes receive a few provinces or districts from another general. If one does not gain merit in battle, then one's social position is reduced, one's lands are reduced, and one may even be ignored. If one loses in battle, one commits suicide without waiting for punishment.

A military leader who dies in battle is succeeded in his position by a son or younger brother. When Ikeda Iyo no kami Hideo died of illness at Chindo, his son Magoshirō immediately received his father's position in the army.[85] And when Kurushima [Izumo] no kami [Michifusa] died in battle at the Chŏlla Province Right Naval Commandery, his younger brother went to Kurushima's fort.

If a dispute occurs and it expands into a decisive battle, after killing the enemy, the victor will cut off his own head or cut open his own stomach. People will say, "He is a true man," be impressed, and spare no regret. People will point to his descendant and say, "He is the descendant of a samurai who killed himself." That person will be able to marry well.

People who possess lands divide those lands and give plots to retainers who have earned merit. The retainers will recruit specially picked soldiers and support them with the yield from those lands. The retainers will recruit those who are brave and strong, those who have practiced sword fighting, those who shoot arquebuses, those who fire arrows, those who swim well, those thoroughly versed in military strategy, those who run fast, that is, those who have one skill or one talent. In the case of generals holding several provinces, their soldiers will be in the tens of thousands. In the case of lesser generals, their soldiers will number in the thousands. If there is an attack, the leader will immediately send commands to his generals, who will then send commands to their retainers, and the retainers will send commands to the various units. The organization of the army, even if only the necessary select and stalwart soldiers are chosen, has flexibility. The peasants cling fast to their wet fields and dry fields and supply military provisions.

Because the retainers of a general will be his officers and soldiers, there is no difficulty in securing men and weapons. Because the storehouses of a province supply the military provisions, there is no worry of exhausting food. This is the situation of the villages of the barbarians. Because the military units have already been decided and training is conducted regularly, they are successful.

Appendix 2

Suggestions for Military Reform and War Strategies

Your servant, in prostration, dares say that our country neither has trained officers nor has instructed civilians [in warfare]. When the war broke out, the government rounded up peasants and placed them on the battlefields. Those possessing a modicum of influence or money managed to escape either by bribery or through connections; only the poor with no connections were sent to fight. Moreover, a general does not have a group of soldiers assigned to him, nor does a common soldier follow a particular leader. Half the villagers belong to the Mobile Inspector and the other half belong to the Army Commander.[1] The same soldier is under the Mobile Inspector in the morning and under the Supreme Field Commander in the evening.[2] Since the positions of generals and solders are shifted constantly, there is no time to check and organize matters and no established line of command. Nor can a semblance of hierarchy be preserved. Under these conditions, how is it possible to send troops into battle and to expect them to kill the enemy?

We have so many different offices; orders and ordinances issued from one do not coincide with those issued by another. The officers and soldiers of a county are sent away, and provisions in the village storehouse are moved elsewhere. When the enemy arrives, no one but the magistrate remains guarding the empty fort. Even if Zhang Liang, Han Shin, Liu Bei, and Yue Fei could be brought back to life today, they could not but take flight.[3]

That Yi Pongnam was the magistrate of Namwŏn [County] in the morning,[4] the magistrate of Naju [County] in the evening, a Defense Commander one day, and an Army Commander the next makes no sense.[5] If he was thought unsuitable as a Defense Commander, how could he be made an Army Commander? If he was deemed suitable to be an Army Commander, then why relieve him of the post of Defense Commander? Frequent shifts in military leadership leave soldiers undisciplined; their general will be like an empty fort to them. In the event of a sudden encounter with the enemy, will the general command obedience?

Yi Sunsin used the sea as a long defense wall. With no indication of a crime, he was abruptly jailed and replaced with Wŏn Kyun.[6] This was truly an error. Those who had become prisoners of war during the first invasion in the *imjin* year [1592] and been forced to fight in the enemy army all spoke of the battle of the fifteenth day of the seventh month of the *chŏngyu* year [1597].[7] The Japanese general chose several gunners and placed them on a boat to spy on our warships. Every boat seemed full of dozing soldiers, and snoring filled the area. The enemy fired two empty shots into the air. A spectacular commotion ensued—soldiers ran around in frenzy, some of them cutting down sails and some rowing. The enemy moved swiftly, advancing all their warships as one. We lost Hansan Island.[8] The enemy pushed ahead directly to the Western Sea. But when they arrived at the Right Naval Headquarters of Chŏlla Province,[9] Yi Sunsin lay in wait with a dozen or so ships. With indomitable will, this small navy destroyed the Japanese fleet.[10] In this battle, the Japanese general Kurushima [Izumo] no kami [Michifusa] was killed.[11] [Mōri] Minbu no kami [Takamasa] was thrown into the sea, barely escaping death, while lesser generals and officers died in numbers. By this account, one can readily compare Wŏn Kyun's senseless leadership with Yi Sunsin's remarkable strategy by which he destroyed the enemy with such a small fleet.

Once the Hansan defense broke, the enemy came to Honam. It was an error to replace Mobile Inspector Pak Hongno with Hwang Sin at this time.[12] In the interval between Hongno's replacement and Hwang Sin's arrival, military units fell into disarray; there was no way to maintain order. Of the fifty-three counties,[13] not one summoned soldiers. Thus, the enemy's unchecked rapacity reached an unprecedented extreme.[14] That Honam among all the provinces suffered incomparable damage was due to the fact that not even the governor was in charge.[15]

Another error was that only when Hansan was broken and the enemy had surrounded Namwŏn did the government appoint O Ŭngt'ae as Chŏlla Province Defense Commander[16] and Kim Kyŏngno as Chŏlla Province Auxiliary Defense Officer.[17] At the time, your servant served in Tamyang County,[18] and thus witnessed Kyŏngno's assumption of his post. There was not one soldier under his command. The imminence of the enemy attack did not allow time to assemble a force. On horseback, he had to gallop to the governor and borrow two assistants from him; then he managed to join with soldiers who had been in hiding.

In such conditions, even a great general of the caliber of Guo Ziyi would not have found a way.[19] From the point of view of the government, replacing an official or appointing an agent may not seem a matter of significance. However, it is an exceedingly serious affair. Many in the three southern provinces might perish by the sword of a vicious enemy, and the very safety of the dynasty stands exposed. In prostration, I beg Your Majesty to be extremely cautious in appointing or replacing a general in the provinces. Your Majesty should not evaluate candidates by such measures as whether they are civil officials or military officials or whether their status is adequate. Nor should You look for someone whose conduct is as correct as that of Weisheng or as filial as that of Xiaoji,[20] or whose familial prestige is as great as that of Zui, Lu, Wang, or Xie.[21] Choose those with boldness and vision, who have displayed this in actual battles with the Japanese. They should be appointed as the generals of Honam and Yŏngnam.

Along the coasts, choose places that would be most suitable as points of defense and construct large fortifications (K. *chin*) about every one hundred *ri*. Relocate some families from outlying areas and have them surround the fortification. Permit sons to inherit the posts of their fathers. Place them in charge for a long time, just as Emperor Taizu of Song China entrusted Xishan to Guo Jin for twelve years and Yanmen to Pan Mi for fifteen years.[22] If they achieve merit, raise their rank, and if they make errors, lower their rank. However, even if You receive a stream of slanders and accusations against them, punish them only if they are defeated in battle and lose their fort. If they accomplish great merit, they will advance in rank and prestige. Just as certain posts of Tang China and Song China were administered, do not allow these generals to leave their forts. Let them be in charge of educating and training those in the fort, and, beyond the tax required by the central government, military expenses should be assigned priority in disbursements made from local taxes.

It is essential that other offices or units be prohibited from taking soldiers or provisions from these fortifications. Generals in the provinces must train soldiers, purchase necessary equipment, refurbish warships, care for forts, and faithfully carry out their day-to-day duties. When an emergency occurs, generals in charge lead the army under their command, helping and coordinating the entire unit. In this way, there will be enough provisions, generals and soldiers will trust each other, and order will be naturally established. Generals will have power in their own hands, and thus there will be no scrambling for leadership.

Then there is the matter of the needs of these generals. They would wish for comfortable living quarters and abundant clothing and food, and they would like to enjoy the attendance of wives and concubines. This is a natural human inclination. Even those with great knowledge cannot escape it. How much more so must it be with military men? Under our current system, generals in the provinces depend on the officers and soldiers beneath them for their livelihoods. How can they not exhort and pressure them?

The soil of numerous small islands off the southern coast is incredibly rich. Furthermore, the profits of the fisheries and of salt mining even exceed the profits from crops on land. For this reason, control of these areas is sought by the powerful. One can see this by something that happened after the war broke out. During the war, villages grew empty, and fertile fields and beautiful houses fell into ruin and were overgrown by weeds. Powerful local families, by coaxing and threatening the magistrate, obtained rights to these lands, gathered peasants and runaway soldiers, and had them till the land. During the investigation and survey of these lands, officials had their hands tied. They did not dare inform on the powerful families. When the enemy approached, the powerful families filled cart upon cart with their wares and escaped. Who among our people create more trouble?

In prostration, I dare suggest that Your Majesty clearly send messages to the officials in charge. Choose islands with profitable fisheries and salt mines, and fertile, cultivable lands, and join them with fertile coastal lands that have fallen to waste. Distribute them among deserving generals as salary lands (K. *sigŭp*). Hire people wandering about after having lost their homes and have them cultivate the land. The young and strong among them can be trained as soldiers, while the income from the land can be used for military expenditures. If these grants are made heritable and sons can inherit their fathers' grants, not only will the wealth and power of a general depend on his doing a good job, so will the wealth of his descendants. Thus, he will regard guarding and fighting for the fort as his own affair. Officers and soldiers will increase in number, provisions for them will grow, warships will be maintained, the people's livelihood will be secured, and the state will not have to worry about transporting provisions to them by boat. Only after these matters are settled for them can the state hold them responsible to guard their forts and to defend them from enemy attack. If they can be depended upon to hold their forts, why scrimp on their share of land? If they can defend against the enemy, why begrudge their accumulation of riches?

Your servant hears that in times of peace most of the crops taken in taxes from the Yŏngnam region are transported to Tongnae and Pusan, where they are used to provide for the needs of visiting Japanese envoys. After I came here as a prisoner of war, I heard a detailed explanation [of envoys] from a Japanese monk. The so-called Japanese envoys were all private individuals sent by the Governor of Tsushima, and their so-called state letters (K. *kuksŏ*) were all fabrications written by him. Not only did other Japanese not know about them, even military men in Iki and Hizen Province had not heard of them. There is not even an acre of cultivable land in Tsushima. With the rice they acquired by deceiving us, they funded public and private expenditures. There is a rumor that when Kim Sŏng'il's diplomatic mission was in Japan,[23] a Japanese monk, hearing of the situation from our translator, was about to enlighten us, but a Tsushima translator, fearing that the truth might be revealed, stopped the monk by waving his hand and silencing him.

The war originated with [Sō] Yoshitoshi's scheming. [Konishi] Settsu no kami Yukinaga is Yoshitoshi's father-in-law.[24] Yoshitoshi could not communicate directly with Hideyoshi, so he sent a detailed report on the defenses of our country through Yukinaga, who also volunteered to take charge [of the invasion]. The war resulted. Because a great many Japanese also died, Japanese resentment toward him runs bone deep. They say that it was Yukinaga who started the war. Even that frightful [Katō] Kiyomasa is said to have declared that it was Yukinaga who stirred up the war.[25] While Yukinaga understands that there is no hope for an ending favorable to Japan, he is afraid that, should Japan withdraw precipitously from Chosŏn, we would punish Yoshitoshi and not permit [Tsushima] to engage in trade. He exerts himself strenuously to conclude peace negotiations to benefit Yoshitoshi.

Is this not truly infuriating? The crop of a whole province produced by the sweat and blood of our people was spent to indulge the greed of an ugly, evil thief. We suffered such calamity from his schemes and betrayals. It would be much better to reduce the tax and add it to the expenses of local generals.

Regarding castles, [in Japan] they are constructed thus. They are invariably on the peak of a lone mountain with a river or sea on one side. The four sides of the peak are cut and polished smooth so that even one with the skills of a monkey could not climb them. The top of the castle is pointed; its grounds are broad. A tall house of three stories is built on the four-cornered base. The lord of the castle resides here. Military provisions and weapons are all stored in this house. There is one gate, and one roadway through which people enter and exit. Inside the gate are piles of sand and stones. Outside the castle, there is a long wall about one jō high surrounding it,[26] but every two steps there is a hole through which cannonballs can be fired. Outside the wall, a moat eight or nine jō deep is dug and filled with water drawn from the river.[27] Beyond the moat is a wooden gate. In the adjoining river or sea, many boats and ships are moored, and people and workers are encouraged to engage in aquatic recreation. Well-trained and brave soldiers live around the castle.

When I asked why castles were constructed in this way, this was the answer. A lone mountain peak allows you to look down and survey what goes on below but does not allow the enemy to climb up. You can shoot down, but they cannot shoot up. Because of the river or sea, you need not worry about [defending from] that direction. Thus, with half the forces you can accomplish twice the tasks. The base is broad so that it would be difficult to destroy or collapse it, while the top is tall and pointed to make it easier to survey below. Allowing only one entrance and one path permits an undivided defense, and piling stones inside the gate makes them accessible to the old or the young so that they might throw them. Placing the boats in rows in the water beside the castle defends the water passage, and encouraging water play prepares the populace for sea battles. Having well-trained soldiers live around the castle makes them available for defense in case of sudden attack.

Our fort structure, however, is very different from that of the thieves. In the invasion of the *chŏngyu* year [1597], the thieves looked at forts in Chŏlla Province and laughed at them, thinking them poorly constructed. They thought them fragmented. Only when they saw Kŭmsŏng, in Tamyang [County],[28] and Kŭmsŏng, in Naju [County],[29] were they alleged to have said that had the people of Chosŏn defended these forts to the last, they would not have been able to take them. These are the stories I have heard directly from the interpreters who had accompanied Japanese [to the war].

In your servant's view, our mountain forts are well situated, but because they are distant from towns, residents of towns can be led into the forts only when they have been forewarned of emergency. When the situation has eased somewhat, ordinary people wish to tend to their livelihoods and are reluctant to stay in a distant and inaccessible fort. When the arrival of the enemy is imminent, unwilling to listen to orders, these people flee to mountains and fields, helping the old and carrying the young in search of hiding places. How much less chance is there for residents of adjoining towns to enter the fort?

Now, forts and towns in Honam and Yŏngnam have been razed and destroyed. It would be wise to take advantage of this destruction and transfer the Tamyang County office to the mountain fort of Kŭmsŏng, relocate several towns into the fort to make it larger, and make the residents and officials of the adjoining area live in the fort. Adopt the ancient system that placed half the population in the fields and half in the town. Men would leave their families inside the fort in the growing season and go out to the fields to tend to crops. During the harvest, they would gather what was grown in the fields and bring it to the fort. The commanding general should repair the fort during the slack season, but should it be attacked, utilizing the fort and its residents, he should defend it against the enemy. The official in charge of the fort should be a person versed in civil and military arts, someone who has the leadership to care for the people [in the fort]. He should be entrusted with the responsibility of [managing the fort] for a long period, and he should be treated in the same way as generals. It may be beneficial to send governors or army commanders to forts from time to time and to let them handle their affairs in connection with the local officials on site.[30]

I suggest that Chŏngŭp and Changsŏng be moved to Imam,[31] and that the model of Kŭmsŏng be followed. Move Tongbok and Ch'angp'yŏng to Ongsŏng in the same manner.[32] If the mountain forts of Yŏngnam were to be constructed and governed in this way, then they would be able to keep watch upon and assist one another. If this were done, the enemy would not dare to encroach upon us as they did. Some might say that because the roads to forts are long and hazardous, it is exceedingly inconvenient to gather and distribute crops. We could consider revising the old system of storehouses. Let the crops in the nearby towns go directly to a fort, but let the crops from distant places be secured in storehouses. Use the crops inside the fort as provisions for the military; the crops in the storehouses could be distributed to the people.

Regarding Honam, two forts, Hŭngdŏk and Kobu, are in good shape, but the magistrates of both counties and their residents display a strong distaste for guarding them. They desert their forts and evacuate to mountain forts. Should an emergency occur, chances are they will desert their forts. Is this situation not terrible?

The objective of the construction of ramparts at regular intervals along the coast, like that of surveillance of the sea from high places, was to be prepared for naval battles. However, these ramparts have turned into children's playthings and create nothing but problems. Those officials in charge of them receive payments [for taking care of them], but they use the money to support their families. Since the war broke out, almost all the sailors in the navy have been killed, and what remains are unattended ramparts. To make matters worse, the residents of Yŏng'am are sent to defend Haenam Port,[33] while the residents of Posŏng are transported to guard the ramparts in Sunch'ŏn.[34] The difficulties these people experience in going back and forth are tremendous. What is worse, however, is that many of them desert and are dispersed, and it is exceedingly difficult to track down runaways and return them to their posts.

One way to solve this problem is to demolish small and sundry ramparts along the coast and to centralize the coastal structure. Assign the villages along the coast to important, strategically located towns. Soldiers of associated ramparts should be expected to reside in the towns, with the understanding that it is the people of these towns—residents and soldiers—who should guard their own fort. Aside from military training, soldiers should not be subject to other demands, such as corvée labor. And apart from training in naval warfare, they should not be assigned to grooming horses or other miscellaneous tasks.

During peace, construct warships and have them stay at sea. Count both civilian males and soldiers, organize them into units, and, by turns, train them in the use of weapons and in naval warfare. At the time of a military attack, place them all under the Regional Navy Commander, each with his own task. Then the defense of forts and victory in naval warfare will both be accomplished.

Referring to others, Japanese use such terms as *sama* or *tono*. They apply these terms indiscriminately to everyone from the shogun to commoners, which displays their barbarian insensitivity in refinement and hierarchy. From generals to their underlings, they carry two swords, one long and one short. Sitting or lying down, they do not let go of them. This shows that the whole country is a battlefield. The so-called regents of the government seldom live long lives.[35] Everywhere in all four directions, they attacked and seized from one another; hence, only force was viewed as supreme. Then, the leader of the Japanese [Hideyoshi], employing schemes and manipulation, succeeded in forcing his contenders to succumb to him. He summoned a number of generals from the east to Fushimi and gave them the project of constructing a new castle, while the generals in the west were ordered to invade our country by turns. This was all part of his scheme of making it impossible for other generals to challenge him.

I hear that by the sixth month of the *chŏngyu* year [1597], many Japanese forces had left [our country], but about ten armies led by [Katō] Kiyomasa, [Konishi] Yukinaga, [Kuroda] Kai no kami [Nagamasa], [Shimazu] Yoshihiro, [Nabeshima Naoshige], that is, the replacement for Ryūzōji Hizen no kami, [Sō] Tsushima no kami [Yoshitoshi], and others still remain in our country. Kiyomasa and Yukinaga disliked each other from the start, and after the war their hostilities deepened. Though Hideyoshi availed himself of every means to bring about reconciliation between them, he could not dissolve their antagonism. It is said that when Kiyomasa meets Yukinaga, he invariably shouts in anger, but Yukinaga responds outwardly in a calm and polite manner.

Ancient strategists aimed to create fissures between trusting lords and their vassals and among equally devoted generals of the enemy camp. In a situation in which two enemy generals are actually at each other's throat, one wonders why we have not been able to exploit it by fanning their animosity and using it with the dexterity of Bian Zhuangzi.[36] We cannot credit our generals for excellence in strategy or clever ideas.

[In Japan], peasants are not permitted to carry swords. Though peasants are given land to till, there is not even an inch of it that does not belong to officials. From land into which one *to* of seeds is sown,[37] they invariably take one *koku* of rice.[38] Their one *koku* is about 25 of our *mal*. Even though they work hard, they cannot produce enough to pay their rent. When they cannot pay rent, they borrow. But if it is still insufficient, they send their children to work as servants. If this is still not enough, they are thrown into prison, and they are tortured. Only after their amount is fully collected are they released. Thus, even during a good harvest year, peasants eat husks. They climb mountains and gather ferns and roots for their morning and evening meals. They still have to attend to their masters by turns, gathering firewood and drawing water for them. Among the Japanese, the most pitiful are powerless peasants.

When they treat their own people in this [cruel] way, what can be expected for how they treat the subjects of another country? It is difficult to live even one day [under them]. Our people along the coast in Yŏngnam are living a terrible nightmare.

Because castles and towns are filled with trained soldiers while peasants have only hoes or shovels, peasants bear the situation, but once in a while they arise as a mob and attack and destroy the main office of the local government. This is why, when the Japanese invaded our country, they had to leave half their troops to guard castles. Their fear of their own people is shown by this.

Japanese spears, armor, helmets, flags, tents, and ships are constructed simply but luxuriously. Tiger skin and chicken feathers are used to ornament military uniforms, while gold and silver are inlaid on wooden masks and the masks placed on the heads of horses or the faces of people to bedazzle others. When your servant first saw the masks, I could not help but laugh at them.[39] However, when our troops retreated in the *imjin* year [1592], they all said that because tigers and ghosts suddenly appeared everywhere at once, they were dazed and dispirited. Is it not incredible? How could it be that tiger pelts and chicken tails can kill people, and that wooden masks on people or horses can kill people? Does it not say that our military rank and file carries less authority than a dead tiger, a dead chicken, or wooden masks on people or horses? The Japanese are small and weak. If men of our country wrestle with Japanese men, the Japanese will invariably succumb. It should also be noted that the idea that Japanese regard life lightly and do not fear death does not apply to all of them. From the autumn of the *chŏngyu* year [1597] to the spring of the *musul* year [1598], a great many Japanese died or were wounded in fighting the Chinese army. In order to supplement the army, they conscripted men, and those called up for military service departed crying. Some of them left their families and ran away. Their mothers and wives were taken until they returned and joined the army. Of ten soldiers, only two or three were familiar with guns, and good shots were extremely rare.

Is it not lamentable that our elite forces who were masters of archery were humiliated by inept enemy troops? Will we really leave the enemies of our ruler-father undisturbed, and will we really throw our children to Japanese thieves rather than fight to the death? People such as me who live as prisoners of war deserve ten thousand deaths.

In the summer of the *musul* year [1598], the enemy withdrew from the coast of Yŏngnam. They all said, "Japanese swords are effective at a distance of a few steps, but Korean arrows reach a distance of several hundred steps. If Chosŏn soldiers had really fought hard, they would not have been our match."[40] Your servant is one of the most incomparably weak, witless, and incompetent men in the whole world. Nevertheless, even I felt that if I could command a well-trained army of several thousand men, I could defend a fort and a smaller, detached fort.

It is unwise policy to kill Japanese who surrender. It is not merely that it is against humanity to kill those who have already surrendered. As soon as they are out of diapers, these [Japanese] were handed over to the general's household [to work]. They grew up seldom seeing their parents or visiting their hometowns. They follow their general to distant and near battlefields, moving from place to place. Even if they have a wife and children, they rarely get to see them. In fact, only generals and peasants have wives and children; most common soldiers do not. For this reason, they do not entertain a longing for their hometown, parents, wives, or children. They only wish for a comfortable life with good food and clothing. They see that our land is fertile and productive, and we have a plentitude of food and clothing. They are aware that the laws and regulations of their own country are severe and cruel, and that there has been endless warfare and conflict. When these soldiers gather, they often say to one another, "Chosŏn is a utopia! Japan is truly a vile country." One or another [of us] may rejoin with, "Our government treats Japanese who have surrendered with kindness and generosity. It provides them with food and clothing worthy of a general. I even heard of a case of someone receiving a high official post of the third rank." They could not help being amazed by the story and would sincerely wish to surrender.

Your servant observes that since the *kyegap* years [1593 and 1594], our country has killed many Japanese who surrendered. Since they have already surrendered, if we accommodate them to our leadership, there is absolutely no reason that they should run away. Your servant sincerely wishes that, from this time, all generals be clearly instructed to provide Japanese who have surrendered with generous grants and to bind them to us with kindness and trust. If they are stealthily sent to battlefields accompanied by interpreters to induce other Japanese to surrender, they will be able to lure tens or hundreds of them daily. Thus, not only by plucking the feathers and fur will [their strength] gradually decrease to a nadir, but also in daily encounters we can attack their weakness with what we plucked from them and with our own strength. We will surely triumph. When the Chinese say the best strategy is to attack barbarians with barbarians, they refer to this method. Moreover, Japanese thieves captured many of our men, and they fill their rank and file with them. Why should we kill Japanese who are surrendering of their own accord, and make the enemy thugs feel good?

(From the section on the structure of the Japanese military to the above was recorded while Kang Hang was in Iyo Province. It was sent to Chosŏn in the *musul* year [1598] via Kim Sŏkpok.)[41]

The evil ruler of the thieving Japanese, Hideyoshi, became ill toward the end of the third month of the *musul* year [1598], and his condition grew critical in the summer. His son was only eight years old.[42] Aware of his impending death, Hideyoshi summoned his generals and entrusted them with future tasks. After completing this, he died on the seventeenth day of the seventh month. Some generals, including Ieyasu, were reluctant to announce his death. They cut open his belly and filled it with salt, dressed the corpse in his official robes, and sat him in a wooden stand. Many generals did not know that Hideyoshi had died. By the end of the eighth month, however, it was no longer possible to conceal his death. They were afraid that there might be some unforeseen upheaval, and to prevent possible disturbances they very quietly performed funeral rites. Some speculated that because several generals, including [Katō] Kiyomasa, had not participated in a meeting in which the generals pledged fealty [to Hideyoshi], they feared those generals might become turncoats. I heard that they summoned this group and, telling them that Hideyoshi's condition was very critical, watched their reactions.

During the invasion of the *chŏngyu* year [1597], Hideyoshi is said to have ordered his departing generals: "A person has two ears, but only one nose. Cut off the noses of the Chosŏn people and send them to Japan instead of severed heads. Each soldier is responsible for one *masu* of noses."[43] The generals salted noses and sent them to him. Only after every soldier had filled his quota was permission granted to capture [Koreans] alive. Can suffering worse than this have been inflicted upon us? After inspecting the noses sent, the chief then allowed them to be buried about 10 *ri* outside [of Kyoto]. The burial place of the noses looks like a grave mound. Within a year, his own stomach was salted!

After the death of Hideyoshi, [Tōdō] Sado no kami [Takatora] took us to their capital. Only then did we hear that Ieyasu's men went with a fleet of ships to Chosŏn, where they took possession of military provisions from Kŏje Island, abducted the residents, and looted every possible ware they found in the marketplaces of our coastal areas; secured them on board their ships; and carried them all back to Japan. After they retreated [from Chosŏn], they ordered Ishida Jibu [no shō Mitsunari] to summon back Kiyomasa. Not long after that, a flying messenger (they call a messenger bearing urgent news a flying messenger) arrived in a fast boat that had reached the capital in seven days. He brought a message from Kiyomasa, which said, "Chinese and Korean warships cover the Western Sea, bearing toward us. Japanese forts, all sixteen that we built [in Chosŏn], are under siege. I do not know even when I will die. If relief troops do not arrive soon, I will have to commit suicide. I cannot die by someone else's sword." [Ishida] Jibu [no shō Mitsunari] lingered in the Hizen area, not daring to cross the sea. Ieyasu summoned generals to discuss the matter, but they could not reach a decision.

Your servant has been living in the abyss of a long dark night and has not heard news from the bright outside world for several years. I could not possibly fathom the intricacies of the changing military situation. Nevertheless, with fellow prisoners of war, I devised three strategies. Those strategies are:

1. Before the relief troops arrive, send orders to all military headquarters. Bring together all the Chinese troops that are scattered at different points in

our country. Gather together all of our troops of every category as well. At a distance of 3 miles (10 *ri*) from the enemy camp, surround barracks and fortifications and attack them by taking turns, not allowing the enemy any rest. The navy should blockade the rear of the enemy camp, and warships should cruise the sea beyond. However, they should not advance too closely in range of the Japanese fort, and should be careful not to inadvertently fall into a position where they might be overrun by the desperate Japanese. Wait until they lose their position and move about. At this point close in on them, and let not even a vessel with but one sail return. Thus, we will vindicate the humiliating offense to the Temple of Royal Ancestors and the royal tombs. We all agree that this is the best strategy.

2. Your servant clearly heard that Kiyomasa's army is no more than several thousand men. Moreover, though [Shimazu] Yoshihiro leads eight thousand, a majority is said to have died and to have been wounded from years of battles. It is clear that we have numerical superiority, and that our strength relative to the enemy has completely turned. It is not possible that we be defeated now.

Some might say that Kiyomasa is great in battle, but his troops are isolated far from home. Their strength will not last. Moreover, the lands of Kiyomasa and other generals are all in Hizen Province, Higo Province, and elsewhere in Kyushu. Their castles, subjects, storehouses, and gold and silver are all there. These are their bases. Ulsan and Sunch'ŏn would seem mere stone fields. Kiyomasa is deeply concerned with internal discord and the possibility of unforeseen dangers. He is aware that if he advances, he has nothing to gain, but if he retreats, he has no place to fall back upon. He must be very eager to return [to Japan], but it is not good to retreat without a legitimate pretext. He also worries that he might not be able to safely retreat—our troops might set off in pursuit of his men. There are generals who would send relief forces, but these generals must consider their own safety. By helping someone else, they might be exposed to danger. Eventually, they will have to retreat. As a way to help [Sō] Yoshitoshi, however, [Konishi] Yukinaga is determined to retreat only after a truce is signed. We should not accept his peace envoy. We should divide our land forces and place them at critical positions to harry the Japanese to exhaustion and pursue them in retreat to Tsushima to destroy them in the water. This is the second strategy to prevent the Japanese generals from harboring any further ambitions.

3. Warfare is the Japanese specialty. Since the war broke out, however, from generals to the lowliest commoners, eight or nine of every ten of those who went back and forth to our country have become familiar with such details as the strong and weak points of different forts, the origins of different

products, and so forth. They have developed a keen desire for them, which they have not forgotten even for a moment. The fact that our country is so close entices them. Previously, the Governor of Tsushima, greedy for sweet official emoluments [from us], would tell them that the distance was great, the winds and waves high and perilous. To ingratiate himself to Hideyoshi, however, Yoshitoshi told him the truth. It takes one day by ship from Pusan to Tsushima, another day from Tsushima to Iki, and less than one day from Iki to Hizen. Even if the Japanese retreat now, their ambition will be rekindled in several decades.

The Japanese take their pledges very seriously. If we enter into a security agreement, we may be able to ensure peace for one hundred years. Now, since the enemy leader Hideyoshi has perished, struck down by Heaven's wrath, Ieyasu and [Mōri] Terumoto sincerely wish for peace. In reply to their request for peace, Your Majesty might say, "If your request for peace is a genuine expression of the intentions of the ruler and the ministers of your country, then have all your army stationed in our country retreat to Tsushima and elsewhere. Then, send an envoy. It does not make sense to seek peace while you station your army in our country. When you send an envoy, we will greet him." These thieves are very eager for peace, and it stands to reason that they will agree to the proposed terms. If this were to happen, not only would our people be freed of the sufferings of war, but also common subjects, not to mention officials, of our two-hundred-year-old dynasty taken captive would be released from the tiger's mouth to return to their loving mother [country]. This is the third strategy.

What I have said is based on what your servant has heard and seen in person, not rumors or hearsay that would but insult Your Majesty's clear intelligence. In prostration, your servant suggests that Your Majesty discuss with the Ming court, consult the officials of your court, and, in consideration of the constantly shifting international situation, choose one of the three proposals described herein.

Yi Yŏp, an officer in a regional military unit, was captured by Kiyomasa, who then sent him to the leader of the enemy thieves.[44] Hideyoshi summoned Yŏp frequently, complimenting him on his beard, stroking it, or patting him on the back, or running around vigorously showing off his own prowess. He arranged for Yŏp to stay at the house of [Natsuka] Ōkura [no shō Masaie][45] and provided him with beautiful silk clothes. Yŏp would say, "Do you think you can buy me with silk?" After about four months, plotting with several men who spoke Japanese, he bought a ship with silver that he had received from Hideyoshi and fled westward. Several days later, Ōkura discovered his escape. He pursued Yŏp on land and sea and caught up with him at Habu,[46] in Bingo Province. Yŏp took out his sword and plunged it into his chest. The sword went through his body and out his back. Then, Yŏp threw himself into the sea.

Of those in that boat, some killed themselves with swords, some were captured. Japanese retrieved Yŏp's body and, along with those captured alive, transported all to the Japanese capital. They punished them by tying the limbs of their bodies, including those of Yŏp's dead body, to the wheels of carts and tearing them apart. All among the men and women of our country shed tears for him. Some even composed a eulogy. I heard about Yŏp only after I arrived in the Japanese capital. One can say that he was a man of true courage.

Konishi Yukinaga took the Envoy from Ming China and had him stay at Sakai, in Izumi Province. (Because this was the border separating Izumi, Settsu, and Kawachi provinces, it was called Sakai. Foreign envoys are usually lodged here.) Nagauemon, the son of the older brother of Yukinaga,[47] guarded the place. At night, I stealthily left my lodging. I, Sin Kyeri, Im Taehŭng, and others captured during the *imjin* year [1592] decided to go to see the envoys. We bribed the gatekeeper and were let in. The envoys took great sympathy upon us. They summoned an interpreter and asked for details of my capture. They even served us a meal. After we had talked a while, one of the guards caught on to what was happening and barged in, bound me with rope, and placed me in a dark and isolated room. He also bound Kyeri and the others and took them elsewhere. He probably suspected that we had informed the envoys of secrets of their country.

Paek Suhoe was from Yangsan.[48] He was captured in the *imjin* year [1592] and was made to stay at Nagauemon's house. He heard the rumor that the Japanese were planning to execute us at dusk on that day by having us drawn and quartered. With the help of monks at the temple, he made strenuous entreaties to spare us. The envoys also vouchsafed for our innocence and pleaded for us two or three times. The Japanese untied us and sent us back to Fushimi. Afterward, people from our country were forbidden to enter the envoys' residence. Envoys themselves also made it known that they would only permit those [Korean] persons whom the Japanese had examined and cleared, and whom they were allowed to take to Chosŏn, to stay at their residence.[49]

After the Governor of Tsushima, [Sō] Yoshitoshi, concocted a pretext for a military invasion against us, Hideyoshi rewarded him with lands valued at 20,000 *koku* in Hakata, in Chikuzen Province. Aside from Tsushima, he did not have additional lands. The Japanese regard Iki and Tsushima as being like foreign countries and do not view them in the same way as the sixty-six provinces. In the third month of the *kihae* year [1599], rumors circulated widely that the Ming armies and our armies would in coalition make a punitive raid on Tsushima. People gathered at every street corner talking about it, but no one expressed a desire to save Tsushima. Yoshitoshi himself holed up in the Japanese capital, not seeking a way [to defend it], either. It was quite amazing, but this shows how things are. In the *kabo* year [1594], Konishi Hida [no kami Joan] came to our country as the envoy of Japan, but in fact he was sent by Yukinaga, not by Hideyoshi. (Konishi is his surname. Hida is the name of a province, and he took it as his official name. He is Yukinaga's cousin. Yukinaga's surname is also Konishi.)[50] Though the Ming envoy is kept at the Japanese residence, he maintains his dignified manner and does not bend his will at all. Thus, Yukinaga wishes to send him back, but he is concerned that Ieyasu may not agree. Most Japanese generals are tired of the question of war or peace with our country. Only Yukinaga, on behalf of Yoshitoshi, insists on a peace agreement before ending the war. In prostration, your servant wishes that Your Majesty issue clear instructions to all generals that they not relax defenses just because the enemy retreats, and that a hundred times more attention than even during the war be paid to the upkeep of the military and their suitable placement at crucial locations. This will bring true fortune to our country.

According to the laws of military strategy, using dull weapons is like giving your soldiers to the enemy. While living among Japanese for three years, your servant has observed that they devote a great deal of attention to the maintenance of their weapons, swords, and spears. They prize thousand-year-old swords as superior. Ranked below them are swords that are six hundred or seven hundred years old, which are viewed as adequate. Those swords made recently are regarded as useless; they are left around but not used. When the Japanese do not use newly made swords, what can we say about swords made in our country? This is indeed giving away our soldiers to the enemy. Among the Japanese who have surrendered to us, there must be people who can discern the quality of swords, how to cast them, and how to sharpen them to the right edge. Buy their loyalty and trust by treating them generously. Thereupon, let them daily devote themselves to casting swords. When the

Japan House market (K. *hosi*) reopens in Pusan,[51] have a translator and an expert in swords go there carrying huge amounts of good-quality products, and [with them] buy many [swords], and store them for emergency. This has to be carried out by generals of the local areas, and they should find good makers of swords.

Ah! The old saying has it that hearing [something] a hundred times is not as good as seeing it once. What I have recorded here is based on what I have observed myself. I composed this putting all my heart and soul into it and sealed it with my blood. I can say that it is a rare document. Taking advantage of the Ming envoy's return entourage, I made two copies, giving one to the Ming envoy and entrusting the other to Sin Chŏngnam, my compatriot. This was because I was afraid of possible mishap on the way. If Your Majesty does not discard this writing on account of its author's meager character, it may be able to contribute to the fortune of our dynasty and our people.

(This, along with what Kang Hang previously sent through Kim Sŏkpok, constitutes what he wrote in Fushimi and sent through Wang Jiangong in the *kihae* year [1599], and which arrived at the court. There are three copies of the memorial and the attached writings. One copy is that which he sent through Kim Sŏkpok in the *musul* year [1598], when he was in Iyo Province; a second copy was that sent via Wang Jiangong from Fushimi in the *kihae* year;[52] and the last is that which Kang copied again and sent through Sin Chŏngnam. The copy carried by Sin did not arrive, and only that held by Wang Jiangong reached the court. His Majesty was extremely pleased with the memorial and prized it highly. He sent it to the Border Defense Command (K. *Pibyŏnsa*) [for officials to read]. Only in the fall of the *sinch'uk* year [1601] was Kim Sŏkpok able to show his copy to Yi Tŏkhyŏng,[53] who advised him that since Kang had already returned alive, it would be better to send the memorial to him rather than to submit it to the court. Hence, Kim returned the memorial to Kang.)

Appendix 3

Japanese Generals Who Participated in the Imjin and Chŏngyu Invasions

(See above. Generals who participated in the invasions have appeared frequently above, and those references are detailed. Here, the descriptions will be abbreviated.)

There is [Tokugawa] Ieyasu. He is a great general in the Kantō area. Currently, he is called the Daifu.[1] He is the eleventh-generation grandson of Fuji[wara] Minamoto no Yoshisada. Yoshisada was appointed Imperial Regent in the past, and his descendants have lived for generations in the Kantō.[2] Ieyasu now holds eight provinces. Because men in the Kantō are fearless and cruel, and skilled at battle, others have not challenged them in war.

In Ieyasu's time, [Toyotomi] Hideyoshi followed [Oda] Nobunaga first. Because Ieyasu remained in his castle and did not submit [to Hideyoshi], Hideyoshi attacked him. Ieyasu met Hideyoshi in battle in Sagami Province with 18,000 select troops. Hideyoshi's forces were defeated; in the end, he accepted peace with Ieyasu. Ieyasu too explained his bitterness and submitted to Hideyoshi, and has not forgotten the proprieties of a lifelong retainer.[3]

The intelligence and bravery of Ieyasu's first son, [Yūki] Mikawa no kami [Hideyasu],[4] exceeded those of his father. However, Ieyasu loved his second son, [Tokugawa] Edo Chūnagon [Hidetada],[5] and sought to name him as successor. His youngest son is the Iki no kami; he is but ten years old, it is said.[6] At this time, Ieyasu is sixty-three years old.[7] His domains are valued at 2,500,000 *koku*, though the actual yield is more than double the *koku* assessment.

(According to the record of fields that Ieyasu submitted to Hideyoshi, the assessment is stated as "2,500,000 *koku*." From the time of his ancestors, and during his father's and his own generations, new lands have been opened. The additional yield from those lands is not included in the *koku* figure. It is said that the yield is twice that number.)

Ieyasu is cautious and a man of few words. He is heavy-set in build. His castle's walls are extremely steep. While he was alive, Hideyoshi gained the hearts of the people, but since his death the wishes of Japanese no longer are met.

(Even when Hideyoshi attacked a castle and defeated an enemy, if the enemies submitted, he would forget his spite at their having been enemies. He never seized even one castle or source of water, or even farmers or lords. In some instances, he combined villages so to increase their wealth. Ieyasu, however, buries mercy and grudges deep in his heart. If someone looks at him even one time with a cross glance, he will pursue that person until he is dead and buried, and then feel satisfaction. Many generals thus fear Ieyasu's strength. On the surface they behave as if they have submitted, but not one of them has submitted in his heart, it is said.)

There is [Mōri] Terumoto. He is a great general in the region west of the capital. In the *imjin* invasion he became the commander of an army.[8] He is called the Aki Chūnagon, and also Mōri Chūnagon. ("Aki" is the name of a province. "Mōri" is his surname.)

Long ago, when Paekche was falling, Prince Imjŏng sailed to Japan and became Ōuchi Sakyō no daibu. (The Japanese call their king "Ōuchi."[9] For this reason, even today there is in Suō Province the title "Ōuchi-dono."). He governed Suō Province. Over forty-seven generations, his descendants served as Japanese officials and inherited lands.

Terumoto's ancestors were retainers of the Ōuchi. Prince Imjŏng's descendants became the Tatara descent group; Terumoto's ancestors became the Ōe descent group. Later, the surname became Mōri. After Prince Imjŏng's line of descendants ended, Terumoto's ancestors came to succeed to those lands. Terumoto governs from Hiroshima, in Aki Province.

Terumoto surpasses in material wealth, and his riches compare to those in the Japanese capital. His manners are, among Japanese, discreet. His disposition is extremely calm and magnanimous. His temperament is quite similar to that of the people of our country, it is said.

Terumoto is forty-eight years old at this time.[10] His lands extend from west of the capital into Kyushu, and they are valued at 1,500,000 *koku*. The actual yield exceeds that figure. He and Ukita Hideie both detested the commands of the leader of the thieving Japanese but could only obey. They felt great pity when cutting off the noses of our country's people, it is said.

There is Maeda Hizen no kami [Toshinaga].[11] He is the son of the Kaga Dainagon Maeda Toshiie.[12] ("Maeda" is the surname.) Toshiie originally was equal in rank and in power to Ieyasu. As he lay dying, Hideyoshi entrusted [his son] Hideyori to Toshinaga, saying, "You together with [Ukita] Bizen Chūnagon Hideie will support Hideyori and live in Osaka. I entrust you with managing his affairs."[13]

After Hideyoshi's passing, Toshiie died in the winter of the *musul* year [1598].[14] Toshinaga succeeded to the three provinces of Etchū, Kaga, and Noto, and [he] supports Hideyori in Osaka. His power is not inferior to Ieyasu's.

(Toshiie built the gate tower quite tall; it was as high as the keep of Osaka Castle.[15] Secretly, he, [Uesugi] Kagekatsu, [Date] Masamune, Satake [Yoshinobu],[16] [Ukita] Hideie, [Katō] Kiyomasa, [Nagaoka] Etchū no kami [Hosokawa Tadaoki], and others made a blood pact to plan to kill Ieyasu and divide his lands among themselves. After this agreement had been reached, Toshinaga returned to Etchū [Province].

By chance, Ishida Jibu no shō [Mitsunari] was reproached by Ieyasu. While withdrawing to his domain of Ōmi Province, Ishida learned of this plan and secretly informed Ieyasu in writing. On the ninth day of the ninth month of the *kihae* year [1599], on the pretext of paying his respects to Hideyori, Ieyasu entered Osaka Castle riding upon a lie. He summoned Toshinaga's retainers and tried to make them demolish the gate tower. The retainers said, "Our lord is away, and we have heard of no such command. Death occurs only once. Even if we were to die mistakenly following Ieyasu's command, there is no dying mistakenly following our lord's command." Ieyasu's anger grew increasingly violent. Hideie, who was the nephew of [Maeda] Toshinaga's wife, came, admonished Toshinaga's retainers, and forced the dismantling of the gate tower. He said to Toshinaga's retainers, "Your lord has said to me, 'I will take responsibility.'"

Ieyasu eventually commanded the Kantō generals to block the road to the Japanese capital that Toshinaga would follow. And he ordered Ishida Jibu no shō [Mitsunari] to defend strategic positions in Ōmi Province. Toshinaga strengthened his castle and moat and designed plans for defense. When, with time, on the pretext of going hunting, he passed through Etchū and Echigo provinces leading several tens of thousands of select troops, he secretly pledged with [Uesugi] Kagekatsu to assist each other. Many Japanese are encouraging Ieyasu to reach an accommodation, but Ieyasu probably will not listen to them.

With this momentum, if they do not go to war, they may reach an accommodation. If they do not reach an accommodation, then only war is left. If they resolve this without accommodation, then the country of the vile slaves will likely from here on be one battlefield. For our country, this would be fortunate.)

There is [Uesugi] Kagekatsu. He is now called the Echigo Nagon.[17] His family has lived for many generations in the three provinces of Echizen, Etchū, and Echigo. After Hideyoshi followed Nobunaga, Kagekatsu was defeated in battle by Hideyoshi and pledged submission. Hideyoshi relocated Kagekatsu to the provinces of Dewa and Sado and assigned those lands to him, but took Echigo and bestowed that province upon Hori Kyūtarō [Hideharu].[18] Kagekatsu was not satisfied, and the people of Echigo wished for Kagekatsu to be their lord.

After Ieyasu followed Hideyoshi, Toshinaga and Ieyasu fell into discord. Kagekatsu returned to his own territory without permission and, joining armies with Toshinaga, tried to attack an area of Echigo [Province]. [Hori] Kyūtarō [Hidemasa] was quite fearful and frequently sent reports to Ieyasu. Ieyasu himself came to fear for his base in the Kantō. He frequently sent letters to Kagekatsu and endeavored to encourage him to return to the capital. Kagekatsu did not abide by this request, however.

(All Japanese say that Kagekatsu has indeed joined armies with Toshinaga and will soon attempt to attack Ieyasu in the Kantō. If Ieyasu tries to return and reinforce the Kantō, then, perhaps, because [Katō] Kiyomasa and others might all take to the field, Osaka will be lost as Ieyasu's holding. Should he return to the Kantō and first lose the base that he must defend, he will then likely be attacked from the front and from the rear by enemies. If Kagekatsu and others mobilize, there is no reason they will not succeed, but, who knows? Kagekatsu and others are foolish and cowardly. They will not necessarily make the effort by themselves, it is said.)

There is [Date] Masamune. The Date family has lived in Mutsu Province for several generations. After Hideyoshi followed Nobunaga, Masamune warred with Hideyoshi, but he was defeated and pledged submission.

His riches from gold and grains double those of other Japanese, but the road to the capital is endlessly long. The winds from the northern sea are strong, and ships frequently capsize. And the laborers and supplies in his capital do not reach even one-half of those of [Mōri] Terumoto and others.

(Masamune's depravity, compared to other Japanese, is most extreme, and extends to having killed his own elder brother and son.[19] Gifted and excelling at strategy, when there was no more water inside Fushimi Castle, Masamune devised a plan to draw water from a river outside the castle. He made a long contraption, and water flowed directly into the area of the castle where Hideyoshi resided. The men and women in the castle to this day still rely upon that device, it is said.)

There are the Satake.[20] Generation after generation they have held Hitachi and other provinces.[21] This continued as in the past while Hideyoshi ruled.

There is Mogami [Yoshiaki].[22] Generation after generation his family has lived in an area of Mutsu Province. This continued while Hideyoshi ruled.

There is [Kobayakawa] Chikuzen Chūnagon Kingo [Hideaki]. He is the nephew of Hideyoshi's principal wife and the son-in-law of [Mōri] Terumoto. The surname that Hideyoshi used in the past was Kinoshita, and the Kingo too assumed that surname.

The Kingo was one of four brothers, the others being [Kinoshita] Wakasa Province [Palace Guard] Lieutenant Katsutoshi,[23] the Himeji Castle lord [Kinoshita] Uemon no taifu Nobutoshi,[24] and [Kinoshita] Kunai no shō [Toshifusa].[25] He was the youngest of the four. Because he was loved as a child, his territory was twice the size of those of his elder brothers.

In the *kyŏngja* year [1600], [the Kingo] was nineteen years old. In the invasion of the *chŏngyu* year [1597], he served as a general and was based at Pusan. Hideyoshi, however, strongly reprimanded him for his many failures in maintaining discipline.

(In general, his personality is insincere, and the undulations of his emotions are severe and far beyond those of his brothers. Fujiwara Seika has taught the Kingo in the past and knows him extremely well. The Kingo's lands are valued at 990,000 *koku*.)

There is [Ukita] Bizen Chūnagon Toyo[tomi] Hideie. He is the son-in-law of Hideyoshi through marriage to Hideyoshi's adopted daughter.[26] At first Hideie served Hideyoshi under the command of Akamatsu Harima no kami [Hiromichi],[27] and later rose to success. His ancestors are from our country. His lands include all of Bizen Province, one half of Bitchū Province, and half of the villages in Mimasaka Province. He governs from Okayama, in Bizen Province. He excels with weapons, and his soldiers are highly skilled with weapons. His lands are fertile, the goods there abundant.

During the invasion in the *imjin* year [1592], he broke into the Southern Detached Palace in the capital. Although he strictly prohibited killing and looting, he captured large numbers of our country's youthful males and took them to Japan.[28] (He and Ieyasu are gradually growing jealous of each other. During the invasion in the *chŏngyu* year [1597] Hideie made many mistakes and lost the respect of his soldiers.)

In the second month of the *kyŏngja* year [1600], retainers of Hideie became angered by his actions. All of them put on their swords and carried their spears and went to him. They threatened Hideie, saying, "If you do not reform your conduct, you do not know what kind of calamity will befall you." Hideie fell into a panic and did not know what to do. Ōtani Gyōbu no shō [Yoshitsugu] heard of this and went to Hideie. Together, they rode in a boat to Osaka. With that, Hideie's problems were resolved. Among those who had protested to Hideie, some committed suicide, some fled, and the remaining men were not questioned about their conduct.[29]

Ieyasu, thanks to Hideie's carelessness, did not conduct an investigation of the crimes of those who had killed people. Many Japanese began to say that Ieyasu was a lesser man for not having done so, it is said. Hideie's landholdings are assessed at 690,000 *koku*.

There is [Shimazu] Yoshihiro. (Shimazu is the surname. The Hyōgo no kami is in charge of the weapons storehouse.[30]) For generations the Shimazu have governed the provinces of Satsuma, Hyūga, and Ōsumi [in southern

Kyushu]. These provinces are near to China, Ryukyu, Luzon, and other countries. Chinese ships and Western ships come and go without cease. When Japanese sail to and from China and Southeast Asia, they always pass through this area. Chinese and Southeast Asian goods spill out of the shops here.

Yoshihiro's military prowess is peerless compared to other Japanese. Japanese have said, "Were Yoshihiro in a place where he could display his prowess, that he would also annex Japan would cause trouble." His retainers too are strong and brave. Further, their families have been retainers of the Shimazu for many generations.

In the last years of Nobunaga's life, the Shimazu took all of Kyushu. (The Seikaidō Circuit is composed of all nine provinces of Kyushu. Iki and Tsushima are not counted among those provinces.) After Hideyoshi succeeded Nobunaga, Yoshihiro fought against him but in the end was not victorious. Yoshihiro ceded six provinces and held on to the three provinces that he possessed.[31]

(In the invasion in the *chŏngyu* year [1597], his retainers camped at Sach'ŏn. At that time, the pirate slaves declared, "In the spring of the *musul* year [1598], the Chinese army surrounded the Japanese base at Sach'ŏn but were roundly defeated. The saying 'strongly attack the enemy and break it down' refers to exactly this situation."

In the spring of the *kihae* year [1599], one of his retainers, a man who held lands assessed at 80,000 *koku*, plotted a rebellion. Yoshihiro responded and killed the man. That man's son was in Hyūga Province at that time; he was seventeen years old. He repaired forts and moats at twelve places and launched a rebellion.[32] Yoshihiro immediately rode to meet the rebellion and, attacking the leader, surrounded his forces. The bones were piled like mountains, and in the end Yoshihiro defeated three forts. [Kobayakawa] Kingo [Hideaki] and [Katō] Kiyomasa said that they would send troops in support, but Yoshihiro declined their offers. "Because my soldiers have rebelled, I must kill them. Why should I trouble someone to send assistance?" he said. The rebels used large amounts of bribe money from Ieyasu to encourage a settlement. Saying that they had gone crazy, they asked not to be killed, it is said. It also is said that Ieyasu and others were secretly elated by the deaths and injuries that a great majority of the elite units [of Yoshihiro] had suffered over the past year.

There are other Japanese generals. Horio-shi [Horio Yoshiharu];[33] Hori-shi [Hori Hidemasa];[34] Tsutsui-shi [Tsutsui Sadatsugu]; Sanada-shi [Sanada Masayuki]; Masuda Emon no suke [Nagamori]; Ishida Jibu [no shō Mitsunari]; Fukushima Taifu [Masanori]; Tanaka Hyōbu [Yoshimasa]; Miyabe

Hyōbu [no shō Nagahiro]; Ōtani Gyōbu [Yoshitsugu]; Ryūzōji [Masaie];[35] Ikuta Sanzaemon [Ikeda Terumasa]; [Katō] Kazue Kiyomasa; [Konishi] Settsu no kami Yukinaga; Asano Danjō father and son [Asano Nagamasa and Asano Yukinaga]; [Oda] Gifu Chūnagon [Hidenobu]; [Mogami] Hashiba Dewa no kami [Yoshimitsu]; [Kinoshita] Shōshō Katsutoshi; Sano Shūri [Nobuyoshi]; [Hasuka] Awa no kami Iemasa; Ikoma Uta father and son [Ikoma Chikamasa and Ikoma Kazumasa]; [Chōsakabe] Tosa no kami [Motochika] and [Chōsakabe] Morichika, who are father and son; Kuroda Kai no kami [Masanaga]; Tōdō Sado no kami [Takatora]; Katō Sama no suke [Yoshiaki]; Nagaoka Etchū no kami [Hosokawa Tadaoki]; and others.

The landholdings of generals reach 400,000 and 500,000 *koku*, and landholdings at their smallest are not less than 100,000 *koku*. One cannot argue that there are generals whose landholdings do not exceed 100,000 *koku*, it is said.

Toyotomi Hideyoshi was from Nakamura District in Owari Province. He was born in the *pyŏngsin* year [1536].[36] He was ugly and short, and because he looked like a monkey that description became his nickname. (At his birth, Hideyoshi had six fingers on his right hand.[37] As he grew older, he noted, "People have five fingers. There is no use for a sixth finger." He cut off the sixth finger with a sword.)

His father's family was poor and of low status. Hired by a farming family, his father somehow made a living. In the prime of his youth, Hideyoshi worked hard and became a slave of the former Imperial Regent, [Oda] Nobunaga.[38] Excelling at nothing, he fled to the Kantō area and lived there for several years. Upon returning, he surrendered himself to Nobunaga, who overlooked his offenses and employed Hideyoshi as in the past. Hideyoshi devoted himself to serving Nobunaga and spared no effort in any weather and at any time of the day or night.

Although Nobunaga always made many of his subordinates purchase goods at the market, he always made them buy at high prices. If the price did not quite fit the item, he made them return without buying it. After Nobunaga started having Hideyoshi purchase goods at the market, he had him buy valuable items at low prices. Hideyoshi quickly accomplished this too. Nobunaga was greatly puzzled. (Actually, Hideyoshi, seeking Nobunaga's favor, added some of his own money. Other people did not know of this, however.)

Nobunaga attacked even the rebels in a northern province. Hideyoshi swung his spear as he charged and was able to kill many of the enemy.[39] Nobunaga took Himeji Castle in Harima Province and rewarded Hideyoshi for his contributions. A short time later, he issued to Hideyoshi the title Chikuzen no kami.[40]

At first, Hideyoshi's surname was Kinoshita and his given name was Tōkichi 藤吉 (or it was Tōkichi 藤橘).[41] After taking this surname, Hideyoshi changed it to Hashiba and thus was called Hashiba Chikuzen no kami.[42] (The Japanese slaves typically take the name of their birth village as their surname. When of higher position, they will always change that surname used when they were of lower status. If they fall to lower status, they will always change the surname held when of higher position.)

In his later years, Nobunaga dispensed punishments and death penalties as he pleased, and [he] envied and hated people. The daimyō could not feel safe, and many of them repaired their castles and improved their moats. They prepared for self-defense.

(There was a man named Bessho Shōzaburō [Nagaharu].[43] He led a rebellion in Harima and Inaba provinces. Nobunaga dispatched troops there and tried to kill him. Hideyoshi requested permission to visit Bessho and convince him to desist, and Nobunaga granted approval. Hideyoshi personally led just 1,000 men. Upon arriving at Bessho's base, he halted his troops outside the castle. He said to the soldiers, "There is no reason for you to be worried. I will enter alone." Crying, Hideyoshi's soldiers asked him, "We do not know what will happen if you enter the castle alone. Please allow us to enter together with you and live or die together with you." Laughing, Hideyoshi said, "Were one to compare victory and defeat, how different is only 1,000 soldiers from throwing meat to a starving tiger? If you disregard victory or defeat, then there is nothing to be worried about when offering your body and entering alone."

Riding alone, Hideyoshi removed his sword and spear, disguised himself as a merchant, and entered the castle through the gate. The guards did not stop him either. Hideyoshi proceeded toward the curtain behind which Bessho sat. He advanced toward Bessho and, taking his hand in his own, said, "Although Lord Nobunaga treats you well, you have rebelled against him—why? Now, as a plan, nothing will be better than removing your armor, throwing aside your weapons, coming before Nobunaga, and apologizing. If you do so, Lord Nobunaga will accept your actions, and you might not lose your riches."

Bessho replied, "The differences have grown deep. There is nothing that I can do." His retainers wanted to kill Hideyoshi, but Bessho said, "He has designed a plan for me. Why do you wish to be able to kill him?" He then escorted Hideyoshi to the castle gate and bade him return to his camp. Because

Hideyoshi's soldiers thought that Hideyoshi had already died, they were surprised when he emerged from the castle gate, and there was not one man who did not go gladly to greet him.

When Hideyoshi informed Nobunaga of what had happened at Bessho's castle, Nobunaga ordered Hideyoshi to attack. Bessho's army was routed, and his soldiers fled along the west road.)

[Mōri] Terumoto held eleven provinces in the Sanyōdō and Sanindō circuits at that time and did not follow Nobunaga's commands. Nobunaga again dispatched Hideyoshi with troops and ordered him to attack Terumoto. (Terumoto's lieutenant defended Takamatsu Castle and protected Terumoto against attack by Hideyoshi's army.[44] In order to lay siege to the castle, Hideyoshi built an embankment around it, poured water on the castle side of the embankment, and attacked. The embankment grew taller and taller, and the water rapidly grew deeper and deeper. All but one *jō* of the castle was under water. However, the will of the soldiers defending the castle grew stronger and stronger.)

Unexpectedly, the Hyūga no kami Akechi [Mitsuhide] murdered Nobunaga.[45] He who informed Hideyoshi of Nobunaga's death rode day and night. Upon unfolding and reading the report, Hideyoshi wanted no one else to learn of its contents.[46] He killed the messenger. He then heightened his attack upon Takamatsu Castle and acted as if Nobunaga had not been killed.

(There is a man named Ankokuji [Ekei]. He is a monk who served the castle lord as an adviser. Hideyoshi sent a letter to Ankokuji asking to meet him. Ankokuji heard of the command to meet Hideyoshi and immediately departed. Hideyoshi called him into the room and said, "It is a matter of time before your castle falls. However, as for me, I do not desire to sacrifice the lives of tens of thousands of men. If your lord will commit seppuku, I would be willing to halt my army and negotiate." Ankokuji returned to the castle and reported. The castle lord immediately climbed aboard a boat and committed suicide in the middle of the river.[47])

Hideyoshi soon explained his regret and reached an agreement with Terumoto, withdrew his army, and headed east. Leading several armies, the Hyūga no kami Akechi [Mitsuhide] met and attacked Hideyoshi at Yamazaki (between Osaka and Fushimi, at the mouth of the Uji River) in Settsu Province. Because the level of fatigue in the two armies already varied and the number of soldiers in each army was so different, Hideyoshi's spirit grew more and more vigorous. He fought strenuously during the battle, and, among the many thousands of soldiers on the battlefield, he himself took Akechi's head.[48] The Hyūga no kami's army did not fight further. They were routed and fled.

Hideyoshi embraced his army and entered the castle. He asked where Nobunaga's corpse could be found. Carrying Akechi's head, he climbed to a mountain temple, and there conducted a Buddhist memorial service for thirty-seven days.[49]

At this time, there was no leader in Japan. The people's hearts were full of disquiet and fear. But Hideyoshi, who was quietly calm, took control of the government, exhibiting no sign of hesitation. There were none even among the daimyō too who dared speak. And for Hideyoshi there was not even a day of rest as he attacked and killed those who did not join him.

(The people of Kii [Province] joined together and rebelled. Their base camp extended across several tens of *ri*. Hideyoshi himself led an army that crushed the rebellion.[50]

Shimazu Hyōgo no kami Yoshihiro, whose family has governed the three provinces [of Satsuma, Hyūga, and Ōsumi] for many generations, was in Satsuma. Taking advantage of the events in Japan, he sought to unify all of Kyushu. Hideyoshi then went to Kyushu and attacked him [in 1587]. Yoshihiro returned to the three provinces that he held and presented the rest of the island to Hideyoshi.[51]

Ieyasu was in his eight provinces in the Kantō area. There he observed what was happening elsewhere in the country. Hideyoshi led an army and attacked Ieyasu, but this ended in defeat. In the end, he accepted peace with Ieyasu. Ieyasu too again fell to the floor in a bow toward Hideyoshi, behaving just like a subject of the ruler. Terumoto heard of this and presented Bizen and another province to Hideyoshi.)

The sixty-six provinces had already been pacified. [Sō] Tsushima no kami Yoshitoshi, speaking through [Konishi] Settsu no kami Yukinaga, volunteered to Hideyoshi to guide the invasion of our country. Yukinaga introduced his daughter to Yoshitoshi and introduced Yoshitoshi to Hideyoshi. Hideyoshi was greatly pleased and bestowed upon Yoshitoshi his surname, Hashiba.[52]

(When the envoys from our country came to Japan[from 1590 to 1591], Hideyoshi had the two Japanese monks Saishō Shūtai and Ikyō Eitetsu write the letter of reply. He had them state clearly the conditions for dispatching troops. His retainers all said, "It is probably best to send a reply with vague language and then shock them." Hideyoshi replied, "How is such a method different from cutting off the head of a sleeping person? Now, it is best to write the reply clearly, make them prepare in advance, send our troops, and determine which will be the winner and which the loser."

The Chinese man Xu Yihou was a castaway who landed in Satsuma Province. He made his living there selling medicine. He also wrote down secrets about Japan and reported these to the Ming China government. Another Chinese person secretly stole his letters and delivered them to Asano Danjō [Shōhitsu Nagamasa]. Asano informed Hideyoshi of this, and captured Xu alive and sent him to the Japanese capital. Hideyoshi's advisers all tried to have Xu boiled to death, but Hideyoshi said, "He is from Ming China. That he informed the Great Ming about Japan for the sake of the Great Ming is appropriate. Further, to catch people unawares is not my intention. Making the Great Ming prepare in advance is not necessarily a bad thing. Moreover, from ancient times, emperors and kings all have emerged from the lower classes of society. Even if the Great Ming was told that I am of base origin, this will cause no damage." He did not inquire into Xu's crimes. On the contrary, he told the informant, "Although you too are a person from the Great Ming, you accused a person from the Great Ming. You, especially, are an evil person.")[53]

In the *imjin* year [1592], Hideyoshi dispatched his armies to attack our country. In his mind, he thought that the absorption of Chosŏn would not take long. [Konishi] Yukinaga was defeated at P'yŏngyang, and the Japanese thieves retreated to Yŏngnam.[54] The leader of the thieves was greatly incensed and, leading his troops, proceeded to Kyushu in the third month of the *kyemi* year [1593]. He established his base at Nagoya, in Hizen Province, and decided to stay at Nagoya for a long period of time and direct the war from there. He declared, "I will wait for Honam and Yŏngnam to be secured, and then I will cross to Pusan."[55]

He then learned that his mother had passed away from illness, and [he] returned to the east in a great hurry.[56] It is said that at that time, among the Japanese generals, one who held great power plotted to kill Hideyoshi and install a new leader. Unfortunately, Hideyoshi quickly returned to Nagoya, and the plot could not be achieved.

(The country of Ryukyu is near Satsuma Province. Its islands are scattered and numerous, and convenient for sea routes. Hideyoshi wanted to send troops and attack Ryukyu. [Shimazu] Satsuma no kami Yoshihiro greatly feared this and presented large bribes to Hideyoshi's favorite retainer, Ishida Jibu no shō [Mitsunari]. Yoshihiro said, "As a country, Ryukyu is composed of just two small islands, and it has no rare objects or treasures of cash to be levied. There is no reason to mobilize the people and put them to labor for an attack on Ryukyu." He thus persuaded Hideyoshi, who dropped this idea after Yoshihiro brought several Ryukyuans, gave them a letter, forced them to present gifts, and made them apologize to Hideyoshi.)

Japanese living west of the capital were already exhausted from fighting in our country. Hideyoshi also considered trying to weaken the military power of families east of the capital. He gathered soldiers serving under leaders based east of the capital near the Uji River, which is close to Fushimi, 10 *ri* from the capital. There they constructed a new castle. It was built as tall as the summit of a high mountain. But soon after the castle was completed, an earthquake destroyed it.[57] It was decided to rebuild the castle east of the original site and to rebuild it exactly like the first one. Houses were constructed around the castle's outer wall, and Hideyoshi made his trusted retainers live there. Mashita [U]emon no shō[jō Nagamori][58] resided to the south; Ishida Jibu no shō [Mitsunari], Asano Danjō [Shōhitsu Nagamasa], and others to the west; Natsuka Ōkura no kami [Masaie], Tokuzenin [Maeda Gen'i],[59] and others to the north; and Ōno Shūri no daibu [Harunaga][60] to the east. The residences of various daimyō serving under [Tokugawa] Ieyasu and [Mōri] Terumoto in turn surrounded the homes of Hideyoshi's trusted retainers.

Water drawn from the river was poured into the moat at the east gate, and was more than 20 *jō* deep. In the open space in all directions, pine and cypress trees were planted in rows. In but a few months' time, the trees had grown so well as to resemble the luxuriance of Nanshan. As if moving mountains, filling in rivers, making rocks run, and making water fly, they labored to complete this construction project in a very short time. Not destroying several tens of immense mansions, these residences were carried on people's shoulders, moved to the east, and placed in the west.[61] Seemingly every day, Hideyoshi carried a cane and shouldered a plow, directly supervised the construction, and did not complain about the severe winter or the hot summer. Ieyasu and others bustled about working, and their loud voices encouraging the laborers made them seem like laborers.

(After Hideyoshi's death, when Fushimi Castle became empty, I secretly entered the castle guided by a Japanese monk. It was written that there was one temple every five steps, and one palace every ten steps. The temples extended in all directions, causing one to lose one's way. Whether gods or demons carried the construction materials, it did not seem that the work would be finished quickly. But the construction was completed in less than one year. Hideyoshi made the Japanese work that hard. That Japanese can endure such strenuous labor may be readily imagined.)

Prior to this, as Hideyoshi had no son, he adopted the son of his younger sister. He called himself the Retired Imperial Regent, and, making his adopted son [Toyotomi Hidetsugu] the Imperial Regent, he divided Ise, Owari, and other provinces and made the Imperial Regent a holder of lands there.

In the winter of the *imjin* year [1592], Hideyoshi's beloved concubine [Yodo-dono] gave birth to a boy named Hideyori. (According to one person, Ōno Shūri no daifu [Harunaga] gained Hideyoshi's favor, and from that time on entered the sleeping quarters and with Hideyoshi's beloved wife secretly sired Hideyori.[62]) After Hideyori's birth, the Imperial Regent [Hidetsugu] naturally felt doubt and worry in his heart and tacitly embraced rebellion. Although Ishida Jibu [no shō Mitsunari] was loyal to the Imperial Regent, he turned against Hidetsugu. Hideyoshi tried to make the Imperial Regent commit suicide, but the Imperial Regent fled to Mount Kōya, in Kii Province, took the tonsure, and became a Buddhist monk. Hideyoshi immediately ordered that the Imperial Regent commit suicide on Mount Kōya. (In Japanese law, even for people who are sentenced to death, if they dispose of their lands and become monks, in common practice the sentence will be ignored. Only Hideyoshi was satisfied by killing the Imperial Regent.) Hideyoshi surrounded the Imperial Regent's residence and killed his retainers, leaving not even one man alive. He then took possession of the residence and gave it to [Maeda] Kaga Dainagon [Toshinaga].

Although the family troubles were resolved, the armies invading our country showed no results. Ieyasu and others stated that a second invasion would be a mistake. Ishida Jibu [no shō Mitsunari] said, "The sixty-six provinces are sufficient. Why must we use our soldiers, who are in difficult straits, in a foreign country?" However, only [Katō] Kiyomasa urged that a second invasion was appropriate.

Hideyoshi said, "If we send troops every year, and kill all the Koreans and render Chosŏn an empty land, and then move Japanese from the western provinces to Chosŏn and make them live there, and move Japanese from the eastern provinces to the western provinces and make them live there, we will without doubt meet with success."

It was eventually decided to proceed with a second invasion, and Hideyoshi issued orders to those Japanese who would participate. "People have two ears, but they have only one nose. Cut off the noses of the Koreans and inform me of the totals. (Each soldier will collect one *masu* of noses.[63] After that amount has been reached, you have permission to capture Koreans alive.)" The Japanese followed the order to cut off the noses of our people and sent them to Hideyoshi preserved in salt. (After the completion of the examination of the noses, Hideyoshi interred them near Daibutsuji temple,[64] which was just 10 *ri* from the northern precincts of Fushimi, and constructed a small mound there.[65] The horrors of blood and flesh may be known through this.)

In the fifth month of the *musul* year [1598], Japanese armies retreated from their bases along the coast. However, [Katō] Kiyomasa, [Konishi] Yukinaga, [Shimazu] Yoshihiro, [Sō] Yoshitoshi, and [Kuroda] Kai no kami [Nagamasa], and others, or ten armies, remained in our country. The evil ruler of the thieving Japanese assembled his generals and asked, "Why has the war in Chosŏn still not yet resulted in victory?" Ieyasu and others replied, "Chosŏn is a great country. If we attack to the east, we must defend in the west. If we hit to the left, we must assemble to the right. Even if we fight for ten years, we cannot expect victory." The leader of the thieving Japanese cried, saying, "You all see me as an old man. My first wish is not a difficult one in this realm. Now I have grown old. I do not know when I will die. What if we were to suspend fighting and negotiate for peace?" His generals replied, "We would be pleased."

The arrogance in Hideyoshi's appearance and words pains one's heart and cuts one's bones when one merely imagines the scene. However, discussion of negotiations had begun before his death.

Hideyoshi's character was truly cunning. Playing the fool entirely, he sported with his underlings, and his contemptuous treatment of Ieyasu and others was like one playing with an infant. Further, imitating a water seller or a rice-cake seller and tailoring Ieyasu and others as wayfarers, he made them take on the appearance of buyers of things and made them compete in trivial tests of strength that were his pranks. Moreover, he controlled many generals completely through trickery. Many times he issued the order, "Tonight we will attack to the east," and then attacked to the west that evening. He was exactly like an imitator of the false burial mounds of Cao Cao.[66] On one occasion, he went hunting and for a time pretended to be dead. His retainers, thrown into a panic, did not know what to do. His ministers calmly did nothing. Finally they realized that this was a trick. After a while, Hideyoshi presented himself as having returned to life.

Hideyoshi fell ill on the first day of the third month of the *musul* year [1598]. He probably realized that he would die soon and summoned his generals to give them instructions for after his passing. Hideyoshi made Ieyasu accept that [Toyotomi] Hideyori's mother [Yodo-dono], as the wife of Hideyoshi, would oversee governance, and that after Hideyori became an adult, governance would transfer to Hideyori. And Hideyoshi made [Maeda] Hizen no kami [Toshinaga], who was the son of [Maeda] Kaga Dainagon [Toshiie], accept that he would become the fictional father of Hideyori and together with [Ukita] Bizen Chūnagon Hideie that they would from beginning to end support Hideyori and live in Osaka.

(Further, Hideyoshi forced other men to send him their daughters, and he treated the girls as his own daughters. He enticed men with even a small amount of power to be married to an adopted daughter. He gave them gold, silver, and lands as rewards. By gaining their gratitude, Hideyoshi suppressed their later ambitions. He made the daughter [Senhime][67] of [Tokugawa] Edo Chūnagon [Hidetada], who was the son of Ieyasu, become the wife of Hideyori.

Osaka is the western capital and is in Settsu Province. Fushimi is the eastern capital and is in Yamashiro Province.)

Compared to Fushimi, Osaka's topography is far superior. Therefore, Ieyasu led generals from the east to live in Osaka and in so doing pressured those western generals who might plot rebellion. And he made [Mōri] Terumoto lead generals from the west to live in Fushimi. Ieyasu thus prepared for incidents that might be caused by eastern generals. He then ordered that the stores in Osaka be cleared away, and he undertook great repairs of the castle's moats.

(In general, the disposition of the Japanese slaves is excitable, and they enjoy causing incidents. If they are still for two months, they feel that they should incite a disturbance. Thus, they do not rest while doing heavy labor, and by exerting their physical strength they release feelings that are like sharp poison, it is said.)

The leader of the thieving Japanese had died, but a civil war did not break out because several Japanese began exchanging blood oaths of alliance and together agreed to support Hideyoshi's young son [Hideyori].

The corpse of the leader of the thieving Japanese was placed [in the hills] above Daibutsuji and a gold mausoleum was constructed for his body. It truly was an imposing shrine.[68] (People in Kumano, in Kii Province, rebelled, but Ieyasu and others sent troops and quelled the disturbance.[69] Undoubtedly, the menace of the leader of the thieving Japanese continued to be felt throughout Japan, probably because he had tricked the people through his enticements. However, how could he bind people's hands and feet through trickery? The evils concealed in the tricks will over time come to the surface, it is said.)

Ieyasu ordered Ishida Jibu no shō [Mitsunari] to go to Chosŏn and tell [Shimazu] Yoshihiro, [Katō] Kiyomasa, and [Konishi] Yukinaga to return to Japan. Several days later, Kiyomasa's urgently dispatched representative arrived and reported difficulties in Chosŏn. [Ishida] Jibu [no shō Mitsunari] remained in Hizen, not daring to cross to Chosŏn. Ieyasu tried to send reinforcements, but there was no one who would agree to go. That Ieyasu did not in the end send reinforcements expressed his worry about defeat. However, because only Tōdō Sado no kami [Takatora] wished to go to Chosŏn, Ieyasu gladly approved.

(Just a few days later, there was another urgent report. According to the information, the Ming army had surrounded [Shimazu] Yoshihiro's forces at Sach'ŏn. Yoshihiro feigned defeat and entered the Sach'ŏn fort but did not close its gate. When the Chinese troops rushed into the fort, Yoshihiro unleashed his soldiers. There was not a single survivor among the Chinese inside the fort. The Japanese regained their spirit upon hearing of this victory. However, because the Japanese slaves exaggerate their feats, I cannot judge the accuracy of this information.)

I thought that I should observe conditions in Japan and discern the actual situation here, and determine how to adapt to changing circumstances in order to design policies toward Japan in the future. At this time, I am recording the situation in Japan and, though presumptuous, have devised three policies toward Japan. I and others intended to entrust this memorial to someone aboard a Japanese ship carrying translators to Chosŏn and have it delivered to the king. However, before that ship could depart, the Japanese armies withdrew from Chosŏn.

After the fifteenth day of the twelfth month of the *musul* year [1598], [Katō] Kiyomasa and [Kuroda] Kai no kami [Nagamasa] arrived at the Japanese capital ahead of others. [Konishi] Yukinaga and [Shimazu] Yoshihiro arrived at the end of the twelfth month. (Kiyomasa, having reached the capital earlier, laughed at Yukinaga's cowardice. Yukinaga, upon returning to the capital, said, "Kiyomasa did not hold on to the royal princes whom he had taken as prisoners of war, burned his camp, and hurriedly left Chosŏn. He destroyed the opportunity for peace negotiations just when it was at hand. Shimazu and I led the Chinese hostages and, calmly serving as the rear guard, returned to Japan after everyone else.[70] Did I exhibit cowardice, or did Kiyomasa exhibit cowardice?" [Mōri] Terumoto and others blamed Kiyomasa for the failure to begin peace negotiations. Kiyomasa, as expected, of course blamed Yukinaga, saying that Yukinaga was of two minds regarding negotiations with our country. The discussion grew ever more entangled, and the enmity grew deeper and deeper.)

Ishida Jibu no shō [Mitsunari] is a high-ranking supporter of the leader of the thieving Japanese. He holds lands in Ōmi Province, and the fertility of those lands surpasses other lands throughout Japan. Ishida together with Mashita [Sa]uemon no shō[jō Nagamori], Asano Danjō [Shōhitsu Nagamasa], Tokuzenin [Maeda] Gen'i, and Natsuka Ōkura no kami [Masaie] became the five commissioners, and they chiefly govern Japan.

Fukuhara Uma no suke [Nagataka], who had returned to Japan from the invasion in the *chŏngyu* year [1597], complained through [Ishida] Jibu [no shō Mitsunari] that several armies in Chosŏn had stopped in their tracks and had not pushed forward with the attack.[71] [Nagasuka] Awa no kami [Iemasa], [Kuroda] Kai no kami [Nagamasa], [Tōdō] Sado no kami [Takatora], [Katō] Kiyomasa, [Hayakawa] Shume no kami Nagamasa, Takenaka Gensuke [Shigetaka], and others all were reprimanded. The leader of the thieving Japanese confiscated 60,000 *koku* of lands in Bungo Province from Hayakawa Shume no kami [Nagamasa] and [Takenaka] Gensuke [Shigetaka] and awarded them to [Fukuhara] Uma no suke [Naotaka].

Because Hideyoshi had passed away by the time Kiyomasa and others had withdrawn from Chosŏn and returned to Japan, they wanted to kill [Fukuhara] Uma no suke [Nagataka]. As [Ishida] Jibu [no shō Mitsunari]'s group had helped Uma no suke, the generals soon split into two groups. (Ieyasu formed one group with [Katō] Kiyomasa, Nagaoka Etchū no kami [Hosokawa Tadaoki], Fukushima Taifu [Masanori], [Kuroda] Kai no kami [Nagamasa], [Hachisuka] Awa no kami [Iemasa], [Tōdō] Sado no kami [Takatora], and the father and son Asano Danjō [Shōhitsu Nagamasa and Yukinaga]. Innumerable lesser daimyō also joined this group. [Mōri] Terumoto formed another group with [Ukita] Bizen Chūnagon [Hideie], [Kobayakawa] Chikuzen Chūnagon [Hideaki], Ishida Jibu [no shō Mitsunari], Mashita [Sa]uemon no shō[jō Nagamori], Satake [Yoshinobu] of Hitachi Province, [Date] Masamune and [Mogami] Yoshimitsu of Mutsu Province, and [Uesugi] Kagekatsu of Dewa Province. Also in the group were Natsuka Ōkura [no kami Masaie], Shimazu Yoshihiro, and [Konishi] Yukinaga. The groups met morning and night, concentrating on plots, almost as if they were treacherous people.)

On the twelfth day of the first month of the *kihae* year [1599], Ieyasu, calling it the dying instruction of the leader of the thieving Japanese, moved Hideyori to Osaka, and he resided in Fushimi.[72] It seemed as if something might happen; people were constantly worried, and half of the shops closed. On the ninth day of the intercalary third month (there is an intercalary third month in the Japanese calendar, thus, "intercalary third month"[73]), Kiyomasa led troops to Fushimi intending to attack [Ishida] Jibu [no shō Mitsunari]. Ankokuji [Ekei], who was [Mōri] Terumoto's top adviser and a monk, explained to Terumoto, "There is only one Imperial Regent and Regent. Even if one is rich with subjects, one does not transgress against the public good. If you make war with Ieyasu, what, then, will you do?" Terumoto understood in his heart that Ankokuji Ekei was correct. He sent Ekei to Ieyasu, and the monk persuaded Ieyasu too.

Natsuka Ōkura [no kami Masaie], who is related to [Ishida] Jibu [no shō Mitsunari] by marriage, convinced Terumoto and sent him to Ieyasu to apologize. In the end, Terumoto supported Ieyasu, entered into an alliance with him, and acceded to his move to Fushimi Castle.

[Ishida] Jibu [no shō Mitsunari], the main plotter, sent his own son to Ieyasu as a hostage. Ieyasu then removed Mitsunari from his lands. [Fukuhara] Uma no suke [Nagataka] lost his lands because he was the perpetrator. [Hayakawa] Shume no kami [Nagamasa] received those lands. The Uma no suke took the tonsure, became a monk, changed his name to Ryokuun, and lived in a mountain temple that he constructed. The political climate is just like that of the Spring and Autumn period and the Warring States period in ancient China.

("Jibu" is the equivalent of the Ministry of Rites [C. *Libu*], and "shō" is the equivalent of Vice Director [C. *Yuanwai lang*].)

[Katō] Kiyomasa's disposition is wicked and violent. He supported Ieyasu in attacking [Ishida] Jibu [no shō Mitsunari] and wanted to thus provoke a disturbance. He went so far as to explain that Ieyasu and Mitsunari hated each other. In the end, he could not successfully carry out that treachery. He made many indignant comments and turned against Ieyasu. He entered into blood alliances with Maeda Hizen no kami [Toshinaga], [Ukita] Bizen Chūnagon [Hideie], [Date] Chūshō Masamune, Nagaoka Etchū no kami [Hosokawa Tadaoki], Kuroda Kai no kami [Nagamasa], and the father and son Asano Danjō [Shōhitsu Nagamasa and Yukinaga]. Together, they promised that they would remove Ieyasu from power and divide his lands among themselves.

(Only five or six men, including [Mōri] Terumoto and [Kobayakawa] Kingo [Hideaki], did not participate in this plot. Although that group had formed an alliance, they all were men who wanted an equal share of Ieyasu's lands, and because no one among them wanted to lead the action, more than half of them, including [Maeda] Hizen no kami [Toshinaga] and [Katō] Kiyomasa, returned to their home lands.)

On the ninth day of the ninth month of the *kihae* year [1599], Ieyasu paid a call on Hideyori in Osaka. The Hizen group led by Maeda Toshinaga knew beforehand of this visit and hid soldiers along the road so as to meet Ieyasu. Hijikata Kanpei[ei Katsuhisa] requested that he be permitted to stab Ieyasu.[74] Ishida Jibu [no shō Mitsunari] had already had a falling out with Kiyomasa and others, and he intended to flatter Ieyasu. He secretly informed him by letter of the plan to attack him along the road to Osaka. Ieyasu inquired of [Asano] Danjō [Shōhitsu Nagamasa] about this information, but the Danjō flatly denied the report.

(When the Imperial Regent [Toyotomi Hidetsugu], who was Hideyoshi's adopted son, was killed by Hideyoshi, [Asano] Danjō [Shōhitsu Nagamasa] was arrested for being a retainer of the Imperial Regent. But he was saved through Ieyasu's assistance just at the time when it seemed that he was in most danger of being killed. Ieyasu thus treated the Danjō as a trusted retainer and immediately asked him whenever something happened. But because the Danjō had entered into an alliance with [Maeda] Hizen [no kami Toshinaga], he did not tell Ieyasu of the plan.)

When Ieyasu next asked [Mashita U]emon no shō[jō Nagamori], Nagamori replied, "I too have heard of that plan." (Other information about that plan is found in the entry for [Maeda] Hizen no kami [Toshinaga] above.) Ieyasu was incensed and tried to force [Asano] Danjō [Shōhitsu Nagamasa] to commit suicide. The Danjō said, "Hideyori is a young ruler, and if he were to bestow death upon me, I would obey his command. Even though the Daifu [Ieyasu] is one of the most powerful daimyō, if you were to bestow death upon me, I would not be able to obey." Eventually, Ieyasu banished [Asano] Danjō [Shōhitsu Nagamasa], forcing him to return to his lands in Kai Province.

Ieyasu, again claiming to know Hideyoshi's dying wishes, tried to take Hideyori's mother [Yodo-dono] as his wife. Because she had already become pregnant by Ōno Shūri [no suke Harunaga], his plan failed.[75] Becoming ever angrier, Ieyasu arrested [Ōno] Shūri [no suke Harunaga] and banished him to the Kantō. Moreover, he had [Ōno] Shūri [no suke Harunaga] killed en route.[76] He also arrested Hijikata Kanpei[ei Katsuhisa] and banished him to the Kantō.

Ieyasu forced daimyō in the Kantō area to send troops to central Japan and to protect the road that the Hizen [no kami] [Maeda Toshinaga] would follow. Ieyasu stayed in Osaka, where he calmed unease and suspicion.

(Ieyasu entrusted the protection of Fushimi Castle to his first son, [Yūki] Mikawa no kami [Hideyasu], and his youngest son, the Iki no kami.[77] He entrusted the protection of their base in the Kantō to his middle son, [Tokugawa] Edo Chūnagon [Hidetada].)

Ieyasu then hurriedly summoned the daimyō who had returned to their lands and examined their attitudes. He tried to flatter those who sought to join him and tried to make those who opposed him clarify their situation. He made some temporary progress. However, only [Katō] Kiyomasa stayed put after receiving the summons. He finally came three months later. [Nagaoka] Etchū no kami [Hosokawa Tadaoki] repaired his castle in Tango Province. He said, "Protecting this castle is fine for me. Why is it necessary for me to make plans for the sake of the Daifu [Ieyasu]?"

At precisely this time, if [Mōri] Terumoto were to have moved even one step, he would have been faced with fighting for victory or defeat. However, because he and Ieyasu had already reconciled, other Japanese generals made no particular moves.

Ieyasu then tried to make [Ukita] Bizen Chūnagon [Hideie] and [Kobayakawa] Chikuzen Chūnagon [Hideaki] live in Fushimi. The former refused, saying, "The Taikō as his dying wish entrusted [Maeda] Hizen no kami [Toshinaga] and me with Hideyori and defending Osaka. I can still hear his voice delivering these commands. I am sorry, but I cannot accept your command." However, Ieyasu strongly rejected this reply, and eventually Ukita Hideie had no choice but to relocate to Fushimi.

(In the beginning, Ieyasu gave the Japanese leaders residences in Kyoto, Fushimi, and Osaka and made them travel among the three places. With Ieyasu living in Osaka, most returned to their lands, leaving Fushimi empty.)

Ieyasu's lands are in the Kantō. (From a distant area in the Kantō to Kyoto, travel takes less than twenty days. From a closer place, travel consumes fifteen days.) [Mōri] Terumoto's lands are in the Sanyōdō and Sanindō circuits. (From distant areas in the Sanyōdō and Sanindō circuits to Kyoto, travel takes less than fifteen days. From closer places, travel takes seven or eight days.) As Japanese say, "Ieyasu could build a road from the Kantō to Kyoto from his rice revenues. And Terumoto could build a bridge in the sea from the Sanyōdō and Sanindō circuits to the Japanese capital from silver coins." (This is how wealthy they are.)

In ancient times, "The riches of Yan and Zhao, and the administrations of Mr. Han and Mr. Wei" too probably did not extend widely. Other Japanese considered it difficult to fight against Ieyasu or Terumoto, and one after another supported either leader. The general outline can be imagined from the above.

(Lands valued at 1,000 *koku* will feed 50 soldiers. Lands valued at 10,000 *koku* will feed 500 soldiers. One can know the number of soldiers a general has based upon the amount of rice available to him.)

The lands of [Tokugawa] Ieyasu, [Mōri] Terumoto, [Uesugi] Kagekatsu, [Satake] Yoshinobu, [Date] Masamune, Mogami [Yoshimitsu], [Shimazu] Yoshihiro, Ryūzōji, Ikuta [Sanzaemon],[78] Horio [Horikawa Yoshiharu], Hori [Hidemasa], Tsutsui [Sadatsugu], Sanada [Masayuki], [Chōsokabe] Morichika of Tosa, [Ikoma] Uta [no kami Chikamasa] of Sanuki, and others all have been inherited over generations. And all of their subordinates have served as retainers for many generations.

If a general loses a battle and commits suicide, his retainers too will commit suicide. "To die together with the 500 loyal soldiers of Tian Heng" is not an unreasonable act.[79] (The so-called self-restraint of Lord Huan and Lord Wen and the "martial skills of the men of Qi and Chu" in ancient times do not surpass this.)

Other Japanese are either workers for hire or people of base status, but, serving Hideyoshi, they became successful, and through physical strength and bravery they became wealthy and of high status. They received land for the first time, and their retainers are itinerants. Their landholdings are as large as those of [Ukita] Hideie and [Kobayakawa] Kingo [Hideaki]. Even if they are as courageous as [Katō] Kiyomasa and Nagaoka [Etchū no kami Hosokawa Tadaoki], if the general dies in battle or commits suicide, those retainers will either disappear or surrender, it is said.

Earlier I wrote that I had asked Japanese generals and soldiers, "To love life and to hate death is a feeling shared by humans and animals. Why do only Japanese look forward to death and hate life?" When I asked them this question, they all responded, "Japanese military officials monopolize the profits of the commoners, and there are no animals that belong to commoners. Thus, if they do not visit the home of a military official, there is no place for them to receive clothing or food. If people only visit the house of a military official, their body too is not their own body. If they show even slightly that they lack fortitude, there is no place where they may live. If one is not strong, he is not treated as a human. If one bears the scar of a sword cut on his face, he is considered to be a brave man and will receive a high stipend. If one bears such a scar behind the ear, he will be considered merely as someone who runs away and will be rejected. Thus, rather than dying from lack of clothing and food, it is better to face the enemy and expend all of one's strength. Fighting strongly truly is scheming for oneself, and is not at all planning for one's lord."

In short, the heart that enjoys the poison of snakes, the desires of wild animals, reliance upon military power, the endurance of tragedy, and thunderous war not only bears this as his innate disposition, his ears and eyes have become accustomed to this. The heart is similarly restrained by laws and ordinances, and is encouraged by rewards and punishments. Thus, even if the great majority of Japanese generals are without talent, they are able to gain the power of death over their retainers. And even if the great majority of their soldiers are fragile and weak, all of them can face the enemy and fight until death. The saying "If an army reaches 10,000 men, it cannot be fought" probably refers to such people. Among several tens of thousands of people, this cannot be helped.

The troubles of the realm usually are born of that which one neglects. In our country, to defend against Jurchens we appointed two army commanders, one for the southern area and one for the northern area [of Hamgyŏng Province]. We gave that post the second grade [in the bureaucracy]. We also appointed two Army Aides, one for the western area and one for the northern area [of Hamgyŏng Province].[80] To these [four military] posts we have appointed civil officials of high reputation. The appointment of military officials to Chŏlla Province and in Kyŏngsang Province usually follows routine practice. The high rank of second grade and well-respected civil officials do not contribute to defense. We can know this too from raising the point of having turned away from the south and emphasized the north.

Something I have thought about in the back of my mind is that even one million Jurchens are not the enemy that is 100,000 Japanese soldiers. Despite that fact, our kings turned away from the south and emphasized the north. I still do not understand why.

When I have tried to enter into the hearts of others or have asked Japanese [about why the invasion occurred], they have given me generally consistent answers, which are as follows. The Japanese laws and codes from several hundred years past were almost no different from those of Ming China and our country. Aristocratic families held slaves, and commoners possessed private land. The rotation of government officials and the selection of personnel by state examination also were nearly identical. In a word, the many thousands of *ri* of Japan was a country at peace.

However, after the wars of the Kantō shogun [Minamoto no] Yoritomo, Japan eventually became one country at war. The so-called riflemen had not existed in the past; men improved their skills with spear and sword. Some fifty years ago, a Portuguese ship washed ashore. It was loaded with muskets, arrows, gunpowder, and other items.[81] The Japanese then learned how to fire muskets. They are intelligent and study well, and in the space of forty or fifty years experts in gunnery could be found throughout the country. Today's Japanese slaves thus are not the Japanese slaves of the past. Further, our country's defense too cannot be the defense of the past. In other words, the guarding of our country's border areas must improve one hundredfold over that of yesterday.

I respectfully ask that if Your Majesty were from now to make officials work toward firmly revising the evil practice of turning away from the south and emphasizing the north, unifying the hearts and minds of the people, strengthening border defense, selecting military officials, repairing forts and moats, distributing navy ships [among the ports], valuing the beacon system, training soldiers, and readying weapons, this would bring me unending happiness.

In general, avoiding war and providing relief from famine are similar. In providing relief from famine, there are only two approaches. One approach is to invite favorable weather from the heavens and bring forth years of abundant crops. The other is to build up stores of grain. Even if one were to wait for another famine and then learn another approach, today what other policy might there be?

In avoiding war too, there are two approaches. In one approach, as is written in *Spring and Autumn Annals* (C. *Chunqiu*), "If there is a Way, it is in defense against the barbarians of the four directions."[82] The other approach is simply to prepare a strong border defense. Even if there later were to be a clash with another enemy and one were to learn another approach, today what other kind of strategy might there be?

After having been brought to the Japanese capital, and from before, I wanted to learn about the domestic situation in Japan. I occasionally met with Buddhist monks. Among them, there were many who could read Chinese characters and who understood principle. Among the doctors are Ian and Rian.[83] They visited me regularly while I was detained [at the residence of Tōdō Takatora].[84]

There also is Myōsuin Chief Seat [Sō]shun [Fujiwara Seika]. He is a descendant of Kyōgoku Kōmon [Fujiwara no] Sadaie[85] and the teacher of Tajima no kami Akamatsu Sahei[ei] Hiromichi. He is extremely wise and understands ancient texts, and there is nothing about which he is not versed regarding the classics. His personality is strong and strict, and in Japan there is no setting in which he does not fit. The Daifu [Tokugawa] Ieyasu heard of Seika's talent and virtue and built a house for him in Kyoto, giving him an annual stipend of 2,000 *koku* of rice. Chief Seat [Sō]shun discarded the house and did not live there, and refused the stipend. He spent time only with the Wakasa Province Lieutenant [Kinoshita] Katsutoshi and Sahei Hiromichi.

(Hiromichi is the ninth-generation descendant of Emperor Kanmu.[86] He very much enjoys reading the Six Classics and has never let go of a text in wind or in rain, or when on horseback. He is dull-witted and slow, and is said to be unable to read even one column if there is not also a translation into the vernacular.)

In the past, Chief Seat [Sō]shun said, "There has not been a time when the anxiety of Japanese people was as terrible as it is now. Were Chosŏn to join with the Chinese army and attempt to console the people and punish the rebellious, first, it should give to the Japanese who defected to Chosŏn and to translators an announcement written in *kana*. In that announcement, express in detail that the people will be saved from the trauma of fire and water, and that, if the armies do not inflict even slight damage in the areas through which they pass, they may even go as far as Shirakawa. As the Japanese killed Koreans and destroyed things, were the Koreans to behave similarly here, they would not be able to pass through even Tsushima."

(He also said the following. "The military officials of Japan all are thieves, but only [Akamatsu] Hiromichi has a heart like a human. In Japan there were no Confucian-style mourning rites. Only Hiromichi has done the three years of mourning, and he greatly enjoys the institutions of Tang China and the rites of Chosŏn. Even for trivial matters such as clothing and food is he trying to learn from Tang China and Chosŏn. Hiromichi is in Japan, but he is not Japanese.")

At long last, I spoke to Hiromichi about myself. He occasionally visited me, and we engaged in conversation. He said that because he is not on good terms with [Katō] Kiyomasa and [Tōdō] Sado [no kami Takatora], the Tōdō family absolutely cannot learn that we know each other.

Also, on one occasion, he requested of *yangban* captives from our country and of my elder and younger brothers that they prepare a manuscript copy of the Six Classics with annotations and commentary. As payment, he secretly bore the expenses in silver cash for our travel and assisted with the preparation for our return home to Chosŏn.

(On another occasion, Hiromichi acquired *Oryeŭi sŏ* [The Five Rites of the State] and *Kunhak sŏkch'ae ŭimok*.[87] And he built a temple for Confucius on his land in Tajima Province. Further, he introduced our country's ritual clothing and ritual caps and often had his retainers learn rites.)

On the ninth day of the second month of this year [*kyŏngja*; 1600] [Tōdō] Sado [no kami Takatora] came from his lands to Fushimi upon Ieyasu's order. Kim Kyŏnghaeng, who had been taken captive in Taegu, had learned the Japanese *kana*. We had him write the following letter for us in *kana*, and the letter was delivered to [Tōdō] Sado no kami [Takatora]. "Although you futilely provide for ten people, there is no benefit for you. Imprisoned across four years, we have not died. If you do not wish to kill us, then we request that you permit us to leave your residence. If you do not permit us to leave, then we do not wish to live." The Japanese monk Keian strongly recommended the following to [Tōdō] Sado [no kami Takatora].[88] "Thinking of one's parents and longing for one's home village is the same for them and for us. If you permit them to leave, this will also be convenient for their return home." And thus, [Tōdō] Sado [no kami Takatora] freed my family.

I gathered the *yangban* from our country that I had previously contacted and summoned people living in Japanese houses to be deckhands, collected the silver cash that had been gained here and there, and secretly bought one boat and foodstuffs. As we people from another country were to sail 1,000 *ri* through the tiger's lair ourselves, I worried that unexpected situations would arise. I went to meet Chief Seat [Sō]shun and [Akamatsu] Hiromichi and asked them to lend us their strength for our departure. Hiromichi requested a letter from Terazawa Shima no kami [Masanari], who prepared a document for the inspections at toll barriers (J. *seki*) and cities. Chief Seat [Sō]shun added another deckhand, having him guide the boat through the waters, and asked us to allow him to return upon our arrival in Tsushima.[89]

I brought my family of ten people and *yangban* who had been taken as captives and also the deckhands and their wives and children. There were thirty-eight people on the same ship. We left the Japanese capital on the second day of the fourth month [of 1600]. Because of problems steering the boat and the winds blowing in the wrong direction, finally, we arrived in Pusan on the nineteenth day of the fifth month.

People who had been taken as prisoners of war and who tried to return home called Tsushima the end of the Demon's Gate, for example. Thus, I wrote a public letter to awaken Tsushima and make it listen, explained the righteousness in permitting one to return to one's country, and argued that there should be no obstructions in Tsushima.

(From "A Memorial Sent from Captivity" to here I forwarded to the court on the day of my return to Chosŏn in the *kyŏngja* year [1600].)

5

Postscript

THE ORIGINAL TITLE OF THIS BOOK WAS *KŎNCH'AROK* 巾車錄 (The Record of a Criminal), named thus by the Master himself. A *kŏnch'a* is what criminals ride. The Master took this title out of humility—he considered himself a criminal. However, even though he thought that, others cannot. How much more is it impossible for his students to refer to this book by that name, thus debasing him, without thinking of retitling the book?

Our Master's plight was arduous in the extreme, indeed unprecedented in history, but the Master conducted himself unequivocally and veered not from the correct path. He threw himself into the sea twice, did not take food for nine days, and memorialized the throne three times. For the entire four years [of captivity], the Master abided by faithfulness (K. *chŏl*), remaining dignified and calm. His utmost sincerity and great principle glowed brightly from beginning to end, overcoming frost and snow and reaching the sun and the moon. Ask the shades and deities of Heaven and Earth, any of them—none would gainsay this. Even those strange black-toothed ones admired the Master's righteousness (K. *ŭi*),[1] praising its loftiness and comparing him to Lord Su.[2] When he returned home, though, instead of clamoring that he be rewarded with honor and tribute, the people maligned him and pelted him with stones. This is behavior completely lacking in humanity, lower than that of barbarians.

When the Master left the Japanese capital by sea, he wrote a poem:

> All my life I have read books and understand the gravity of names and righteousness.

When later generations view history, right and wrong will be disputed.
A captive is not a crane from Liaodong.
Awaiting death, I must look for sheep over the sea.³

Another of the Master's poems written as a rejoinder to someone else's has the line: "With a bottle of wine I console the one who shepherds sheep."⁴ It appears that the Master had already foreseen his future.

A poem by Kwŏn Sŏkchu has the phrase:⁵

Faithfulness lowers itself for the sake of [he who] shepherds sheep;
A letter is transmitted by a goose.⁶

This extols the Master by referring to praise for Su Wu, who chose not to die, and comparing the Master's faithfulness to Su's.

Thus, after consulting others, we retitled the book *Kanyangnok* (The Record of a Shepherd) to signify the Master's unswerving faithfulness. As for the task of publicizing to the world the as yet unrevealed loftiness of our Master's faithfulness, we will await a principled and articulate gentleman.

Summer of the *kabo* year after the *chongzhen* year [1654], the Master's disciple Yun Sun'gŏ⁷ of P'ap'yŏng⁸

Appendix 1
The Eight Circuits and Sixty-six Provinces of Japan

Translators' note: The printed edition of *Kanyangnok* in the *Han'guk munjip ch'onggan* series provides three pieces of information regarding the province name. The first word is the heading for that individual entry, that is, the official name of the province. The second word, which is in parentheses here, is another name or names by which that province was also known in Japan. This second name is printed in smaller-size type in the text. The third name is a Korean-language rendering of the official Japanese-language province name spelled in *han'gŭl*. These Korean spellings appear to have been written either on the printed folio or on a small piece of paper affixed to the printed folio. The source of these spellings is not known. Also, the readings of Japanese place names are difficult to confirm. There may be incorrect romanizations below.

(During the reign of Emperor Yōmei,[1] the government established the five provinces of the Kinai area and the seven circuits. And during the reign of Emperor Monmu,[2] the government divided the country into sixty-six provinces.)

(The text provided by the Japanese monk is unclear in some places. Because I was concerned that facts would be lost if I did not follow the text, I copied the information in the older text. Further, I have appended to the end of each province's entry additional information that I have heard and seen in the hope that the data will be useful for reference.)

KINAI: FIVE PROVINCES

YAMASHIRO (YŌJIN, KISHŪ) YAMASIRO

Major province rank (J. *jōkan*)[3]

There are eight districts: Otokuni-fu, Kadono, Atagi,[4] Kii, Uji, Kuze, Tsuzuki, Sagara (the [first] character 捨 is also written as 相).

The province is more than 100 *ri* from south to north. There are numerous ancient sites, and medicinal plants also are plentiful. If one sows seeds, the yield is one hundredfold, and the taste is good. The province is vast in size and the land is excellent in quality (K. *taesangsangguk*).

(The term "second" [K. *sang*] in "second rank" [K. *sanggwan*] refers to the quality of the land. The term "vast" [K. *tae* in *taesang*] refers to the size of the province. The term "excellent" [K. *sang* in *sangsangguk*] also indicates the quality of the land. The designations in province entries below all follow this format.)[5]

(The capital [K. *wanggyŏng*] of the King of Japan and the new capital constructed by the leader of the thieving Japanese [Toyotomi Hideyoshi] at Fushimi are in this province.)

YAMATO (WASHŪ) YAMADO

Superior province rank (J. *taikan*)

There are fifteen districts: Sofunokami, Sofunoshimo, Heguri,[6] Hirose, Katsujō, Katsuge, Oshinomi, Uchi, Yoshino, Uda, Shikinoagata, Shikinoshimo,[7] Takachi,[8] Toichi-fu, Yamanobe.

The province is more than 200 *ri* from south to north. It is surrounded by mountains, and its land yields ten times the crops of other provinces. The famous places and historical remains are truly numerous. The province is vast in size and the land is excellent in quality.

The southern capital of Japan is here, and the ancient capital of Japan's rulers was here. The country was called Wa-koku. Another name for the country was Yamatai. The name "Yamatai" derives from a command by Emperor Wu of Liang.[9] He named the capital Yamatai because the insincerity of Japanese people toward truthfulness resembled that of wild horses. Japanese people today still refer to Yamato as Yamatai.[10] There are 480 temples in the province, and their magnificence is remarkable.

(Mashita Emon no kami [Nagamori] holds lands valued at 300,000 *koku* in this province as a commissioner [J. *bugyō*].[11] Shinjō Suruga no kami [Naoyori] holds lands valued at 30,000 *koku*,[12] and Ikeda Magoshirō holds lands valued at 20,000 *koku*.)

(The land is fertile, and the rice is extremely white.)

KAWACHI (KASHŪ) KAWAUJI

Superior province rank

There are fifteen districts: Nishikori, Ishikawa, Furuichi, Asukae-fu,[13] Ōgata, Takayasu, Kawachi, Sara,[14] Mamuta, Katano, Wakae, Shibukawa, Shiki, Tanboku-fu, Tannan.

The province is more than two days in each direction. There are many embankments, swamps, ponds, and wells, and if one sows seeds, the yield is fivefold. Merchants' shops are numerous. The province is vast in size and the land is average in quality (K. *taejungguk*). In 716, the government divided Kawachi and Ōtori-gun. In 770, the government closed Kawachijima Province.

(Several of Hideyoshi's lesser generals divide this province as domain lands.)

Izumi (Senshū)[15]

Minor province rank (J. *gekan*)

There are three districts: Ōtori, Izumi-fu, Hine.

The province is more than 100 *ri* south to north. Because the province carries mountains on its back and embraces the sea, grains are affected by the cold climate and they lack taste. The province is broad, and soy sauce, vinegar, and varieties of fish are plentiful. The province is vast in size and the land is poor in quality (K. *taehaguk*).

(Koide Harima no kami Hidemasa[16] and Ishida Moku no kami [Masazumi][17] hold lands in this province.)

Settsu (Sesshū) Soetchu

Major province rank

There are thirteen districts: Sumiyoshi, Kutara, Higashinari,[18] Nishinari-fu, Yatabe,[19] Shimashimo, Shimakami, Teshima,[20] Kawabe, Muko, Ubara, Arima, Nose.

The province is more than two and one-half days [in size]. The province borders the emperor's capital and embraces the sea to the west.[21] Because the south is warm and the north is cold, grains ripen early. Fishing and salt production are common. The province is vast in size and the land is excellent in quality (K. *taesangguk*).

(Osaka, the western capital of Japan, is here. Three rivers flow into the inland sea. The topography is superior to Fushimi. All of the lands in this province are held by the Imperial Regent.)

Tōkaidō: Fifteen Provinces

Iga (Ishū) Ingga

Minor province rank

There are four districts: Ae-fu,[22] Yamada, Iga, Nabari.

The province is more than one day in each direction. To the southeast is the sea and to the north are many mountains. Accordingly, warm air forms, and trees, plants, and varieties of bamboo are numerous. The province is limited in size and the land is excellent in quality (K. *sosangguk*).

(The Tsutsui hold this province as a domain. They are a powerful family in Yamato [Province]. There was a man named Tsutsui Junkei who was extremely fearless and cruel. Hideyoshi killed Junkei by poisoning,[23] and Junkei's son moved to Iga Province, making that his domain.[24] [Tsutsui] Iga no kami [Sadatsugu], who is the younger brother of Natsuka Ōkura [no daibu Masaie],[25] divided the province and has his domain there.)

ISE (SEISHŪ) ISHYŎ

Superior province rank

There are sixteen districts: Kuwana, Asake, Suzuka, Kawano, Ichishi, Anki, Tado, Nishikijima, Gozashima, Inabe, Mie, Ano, Iitaka, Iino, Watarai, Take.

The province is more than three days south to north. The mountains and the sea are in good balance, and the province is superior to other provinces in this respect. For this reason, the people are respectful. The soil is rich and the taxes submitted are many. If one seed is planted, one gains one hundredfold. The province is vast in size and the land is excellent in quality (K. *taedaesangguk*).

(The Kyōgoku hold this province as a domain. The Ise Daimyō[ji] Shrine is in this province. Local people serve this shrine as if they are serving their parents.)

(A local product is gold [J. *hakkin*].)

SHIMA (SHISHŪ) SIMA

Minor province rank

There are two districts: Tōshi-Ago-fu, Kamejima.[26]

Of these districts, one belongs to Ise Province. Shima Province is more than one-half day in each direction. This province is formed from one district. Marine plants are numerous. The province is small in size and the land is poor in quality (K. *hahaguk*).

(The father and son Kuki Ōsumi no kami [Yoshitaka and Kuki Moritaka] hold lands in this province.[27])

OWARI (BISHŪ) OWARI

Minor province rank[28]

There are nine districts: Ama-fu, Nakashima, Haguri, Niwa, Kasukabe, Yamada, Aichi,[29] Chita, Tōshinoshima.

APPENDIX 1. THE EIGHT CIRCUITS AND SIXTY-SIX PROVINCES OF JAPAN 105

The province is more than three days south to north. The land is deep, the soil fertile. Merely by sowing seeds, one reaps one thousandfold. The large number of villages is unsurpassed by any other province in Japan. The province is vast in size and the land is excellent in quality.

(Fukushima [Saemon no] taifu [Masanori] holds a domain in this province.[30] Several lesser generals also hold lands here.)

MIKAWA (SANSHŪ) MIGAWA

Major province rank

There are eight districts: Ōmi, Kamo, Nukata, Hatsu, Hoi-fu, Yana, Shitara, Atsumi.[31]

The province is more than one and one-half days east to west. Mountains and rivers are numerous, but because the soil is shallow at one *shaku*, grains do not flourish. This province is small in size and the land is meager in quality (K. *hahasoguk*).

(Ikuta Sanzaemon[32] and Tanaka Hyōbu [no taifu Yoshimasa][33] hold lands in this province.)

TŌTŌMI (ENSHŪ) TODOUMI

Major province rank

There are thirteen districts:[34] Hamana, Fuchi, Inasa,[35] Aratama, Naganokami,[36] Naganoshimo, Iwata-fu, Suchi, Yamana, Sano, Kikō, Haibara, Yamaka.

Mountains and rivers, villages and hamlets mix together. The land is seven *shaku* deep, and if seeds are sown, one gains one thousandfold or several ten thousandfold. The province is vast in size and the land is excellent in quality.

(Horio Tatewaki [Yoshiharu] holds this province as a domain.[37])

SURUGA (SHUNSHŪ) SURUNGGAWA

Major province rank

There are seven districts: Shita, Mashizu, Udo, Abe-fu, Ihara,[38] Fuji, Suruga (Kami-, Shimo-). (These district names are the same as the province name.)

The province is more than two days east to west. Mountains, plains, wild lands, and villages are equal in area. The province embraces the sea and encircles the mountains. The land is fertile and the products are many. The province is vast in size and the land is average in quality.

(Nakamura Shikibu no shō [Kazuuji] holds this province as a domain.[39])

In this province is Mount Fuji. Its shape resembles a jar turned upside down. At its summit is a large hole that is deep and without bottom. Warm air rises directly from the base to the top and is like clouds and fog. Even in the sixth month there is usually snow [on the mountain]. Grand Astrologer (C. *taishi*) Song Jinglian[40] wrote a poem:

> Mount Fuji is like ten thousand lotuses,
> Its tangled roots pressed to the earth of the three provinces.
> Its crowning summer snowflakes shimmer like the feathers of a bird;
> In which deep forest can I find a white pheasant?[41]

(Among the Japanese slaves, those who have traded with Fujian, with the Nanban, and with other countries will raise their sails after seeing the summit of Mount Fuji from the sea. Japanese monks say that Atsuta in Ise Province,[42] Kumano in Kii Province, and Fuji are the three sacred mountains in Japan. They also say that the waters of Lake Biwa, in Ōmi Province, were created naturally in one day. Mount Fuji, in Suruga Province, also appeared naturally in one day. It became a mountain from the accumulated sands of the lake. It is said that if people who come from the four directions to enjoy the view of Mount Fuji stay ten days there, they will not encounter disasters. And in the case of people from Ōmi Province, if they stay even one day, then there is no concern that their feet will slip and they will fall to their deaths. These are the kinds of strange stories that Japanese enjoy.)

Izu[43] (Tōshū) Iju

Minor province rank

There are three districts: Takata, Naka, Kamo.

In addition, there are Ōshima and Hirugashima.

The province is more than one day east to west. Fields are numerous, but rice paddies are few. The mountains are tall, and the sea is wide. Salt and varieties of fish are many, and these are used as taxes. The province is vast in size and the land is average in quality.

(The Daifu [Tokugawa] Ieyasu and his son [Tokugawa] Edo Chūnagon [Hidetada] hold lands in this province.)[44]

Kai (Kōshū) Kii

Major province rank

There are four districts: Yamanashi, Yamashiro-fu, Yatsushiro-jō, Koma.[45]

The province is more than two days south to north. The wet rice paddies are shallow, and the fields are deep. It is cold throughout the province, and there is no warm weather. Grasses grow luxuriantly, and cattle and horses are innumerable. The province is average in size and the land is average in quality (K. *chungjungguk*).

(Asano Danjō [no shōhitsu Shōsuke Nagamasa] and his son [Asano] Sakyō no taifu [Yukinaga] hold lands in this province.)[46]

Sagami (Sesshū) Sanggami

Major province rank

There are nine districts: Ashigarakami, Ashigarashimo, Ōsumi, Yurugi, Aikō, Takakura,[47] Kamakura (a famous site in Japan; there have been many artisans who cast famous swords in Kamakura[48]), Miura, Enoshima.

The province is more than three days in each direction. The soil is more than nine feet (K. *iljang*, J. *ichijō*) deep, the land is fertile, and the products are numerous. The mountains are low, and there is no timber. However, there are many marine plants and varieties of fish. The province is average in size and the land is poor in quality (K. *chunghaguk*).

(The Daifu [Tokugawa] Ieyasu holds this province.)

Musashi (Bushū) Musasi

Superior province rank

There are twenty-one districts: Kuraki, Tsuzuki, Tama-fu, Tachibana, Niikura, Iruma, Koma, Hiki, Yokomi, Saitama, Kodama, Obusuma, Hatara, Hanzawa, Naka, Kami, Adachi, Chichibu, Ebara, Toshima, Ōsato.

The province is five and one-half days in each direction. Because the open fields are wide and there are no mountains, the province is lacking in good timber. There are abundant wet rice paddies and fields and numerous varieties of vegetables. The province is vast in size and the land is excellent in quality.

(The Daifu [Tokugawa] Ieyasu holds this province.)

Awa (Bōshū) Io

Middle province rank (J. *chūkan*)

There are four districts: Hei-fu, Awa, Asai, Nagasa.

The province is one and one-half days south to north. The mountains, rivers, plains, wet rice paddies, and villages are in good balance. Fish and shells are many, and these also are used for fertilizer in the wet rice paddies and in the fields. The province is vast in size and the land is average in quality.

(The Daifu [Tokugawa] Ieyasu and Satomi [Yoshiyasu] hold lands in this province.)[49]

Kazusa (Sōshū) Kanjusa

Superior province rank

There are eleven districts: Susu, Amaha, Ichihara, Unakami, Ahiru, Mōta, Ishimi, Habu, Nagara, Yamabe, Mushiya.

The province is more than three days south to north. The coastline is long, and there is much green-colored seaweed. The province is known for silk cloth, stirrups, and long-blade hoes (J. *kuwa*). The province is vast in size and the land is average in quality.

(The Daifu [Tokugawa] Ieyasu holds this province.)

Shimōsa (Sōshū) Samoosa

Superior province rank

There are twelve districts: Katsushika-fu, Chiba, Inba, Samuma, Sashima, Yūki, Toyota, Sōsa, Unakami, Katori, Habu, Okada.

The province is more than three days south to north. Products from both the mountains and the seas are extremely numerous. Although birds and animals are everywhere, they do not taste good. The province is vast in size and the land is average in quality.

(The Daifu [Tokugawa] Ieyasu holds this province.)

Hitachi (Jōjin) Sdidi

Superior province rank

There are eleven districts: Niibari, Makabe, Tsukuba, Kawachi, Shida, Ibaraki-fu, Namekata, Kashima, Naka, Kuji, Taka.

To the right is Tōtōmi Province.

The province is approximately four days in each direction. Farms and shops extend in all directions. Cattle and horses fill the pastures, silkworms are numerous, and cotton is abundant. The province is vast in size and the land is average in quality (K. *taedaejungguk*).

(Satake [Yoshinobu] holds this province.[50])

Tōsandō: Eight Provinces

Ōmi (Kōshū) Uumi

Superior province rank

There are thirteen districts: Shiga (the [first] character 滋 is also written as 志), Kurimoto, Yasu, Gamō, Kanzaki, Inukami, Sakata, Echi (jō-ge), Asai, Ikako,[51] Takashima, Kōka, Yoshizumo (Kami-, Shimo-).

The province is three and one-half days in each direction. Mountains, rivers, wet rice paddies, and fields protect the borders. The soil is rich, and if seeds are sown, one gains one thousandfold. The province is near the capital. The sense of the spring season arrives early. This province is the number four province in Japan. ("Number four" means that in order from the number one province, Ōmi Province is number four.)

(Kyōgoku Jijū [Takatsugu],[52] Ishida Jibu no shō [Mitsunari],[53] and Natsuka Ōkura no kami [Masaie][54] divide the lands in this province.)

Mino (Jōshū) Mino

Major province rank

There are eighteen districts: Ishizu, Fuwa-fu, Anhachi, Ikeda, Ōno, Motosu, Mushiroda, Katagata, Atsumi, Kagami, Yamagata, Mugi, Gujō, Kamo, Kani, Toki, Ena, Tagi.

To the right is Ōmi Province.

The province is more than three days south to north. Mountains, plains, and rice fields are numerous. Cotton is abundant, and grains grow ten thousandfold. The province is vast in size and the land is excellent in quality.

([Oda] Gifu Chūnagon [Hidenobu][55] and other generals divide the lands in this province.)

(The local product is paper of the seventh grade in quality.)

Hida (Hishū) Hinda

Minor province rank

There are four districts: Ōatsu, Mashida, Amano (the [first] character 天 is also written as 大[56]), Araki.

The province is more than two days south to north. The mountains are deep and the timber, which is presented as taxes, plentiful. Brushwood and firewood (charred wood) are numerous, but fish and salt are scarce. Crops too are not abundant. The province is small in size and the land is poor in quality.

(Kanamori Hōin [Nagachika][57] and his adopted son [Kanamori] Izumo no kami [Yoshishige][58] hold lands in this province. "Hōin" is the name of an administrative post for monks.)

(A local product is gold.)

Shinano (Shinshū) Sinano

Major province rank

There are ten districts: Minochi, Takai, Hashina, Chiisagata, Saku, Ina, Suwa, Chikuma-fu, Azumi (the [second] character 裏 is also written as 雲), Sarashina.

To the right is the Chūgoku region.

The province is more than five days south to north. The *yin* is deep, and grasses grow long. The sea is blocked by mountains; thus, fish and salt are scarce. The land is one *shaku* deep, mulberry and hemp grow well, and cloth and cotton are plentiful. The province is vast in size and the land is poor in quality (K. *taedaehaguk*).

(Sanada holds this province. His name is Sengoku Echizen no kami [Hidehisa].[59])

Kōzuke (Yashū)[60] Kamijugye[61]

Superior province rank

There are fourteen districts: Usui, Agatsuma, Tone, Seta (the [second] character 田 is also written as 多), Sai, Nitta, Kataoka, Ōra, Gunma-fu, Kanra (the [second] character 羅 is also written as 楽), Tako, Mitono, Nawa, Yamada.

The province is more than four days east to west. The temperature is warm. Mulberry is plentiful, silk and cotton are abundant. Sulphur is presented for taxes. The province is vast in size and the land is excellent in quality.

(The Daifu [Tokugawa] Ieyasu and Sano Shūri no daibu [Nobuyoshi] hold lands in this province.)[62]

Shimotsuke (Yashū) Simojugye

Major province rank

There are nine districts: Ashikaga, Yanada, Aso, Tsuga-fu, Haga, Samukawa, Shioya, Nasu, Makabe.

The province is three and one-half days east to west. There are few mountains, and the plains are broad. The soil is fertile, and grasses and trees are plentiful. If seeds are sown, the yield is one hundredfold. The country is average in size and the land is excellent in quality (K. *chungsangguk*).

(The Daifu [Tokugawa] Ieyasu holds this province.)

Mutsu (Ōshū) Mujunoogu[63]

Superior province rank

There are forty-nine districts:[64] Shirakawa (where Shirakawa barrier is located; "Kantō" means "to the east of Shirakawa"), Kurokawa, Iwase, Miyagi-fu, Aizu, Yama, Oda, Asaka, Adachi, Shibata, Karita, Tōda, Natori, Shinobu, Kikuta ([the place name] 菊多 is also written as 菊田[65]), Shibane, Kawanuma,[66] Namekata, Iwate, Waga, Kawachi, Hienuki, Takano, Watari (the [second] character 理 is also written as 利), Esori, Isawa, Nagaoka, Toyone, Mohara,[67] Mashika, Gungi,

Katsuno, Hashigami, Tsugaru, Uta, Iku, Motoyoshi, Ishikawa, Taiji, Shikama, Inaga, Shitewa, Iwasaki, Kinbara, Katsuta (the [first] character 葛 is also written as 新), Date, Tsuka, Hei, Kesen.

The province is more than sixty days east to west. Long ago, this province and Dewa Province formed one province. Markets and forts, and palaces, are unsurpassed in number. Birds and animals are extremely numerous. Lacquer ware is presented as taxes. The province is vast in size and the land is excellent in quality (K. *taedaesangsangguk*).

([Date] Chūshō Masamune,[68] [Uesugi] Echigo Nagon Kagekatsu,[69] and Nanbu Shōgen [Nobunao][70] hold lands in this province.)

In the sea is Kinzan. The island's protector performed purifications and ablutions and requested a quantity of gold from the island. However, he later went to the island by boat to collect the gold and was told that the boat would sink if he stole even a little.

Mutsu borders Ezo and is vast and without end. This province is larger than any other province in Japan. The circuit road passes through fifty-four districts. The mountain barbarians build their own villages, and, beyond imperial commands and control, their lands are beyond the fifty-four districts. They are tall and large of build, and hirsute. The Japanese call this land Ezo.

From Hiraizumi in Mutsu Province to Ezo is but 30 *ri* by sea (in the Japanese measure of distance). According to one person, Ezo is held by Jurchens who live in our country. I have heard that this land produces octopus, sable fur, and other items in abundance. This may be believable.

According to what the Japanese slaves always say, if one crosses in a straight line from Mutsu Province to northeast Chosŏn, the distance is extremely short. However, because the winds are high in the northern waters, it is doubtful that people do cross. What they say is questionable, and I will stop writing for the time being. Although I have doubts about this information, I have written what I have heard.

Dewa (Ushū) Tewa

Major province rank

There are thirteen districts:[71] Akumi, Kawabe, Murayama, Oitama, Tsūkachi, Hiraga, Tagawa, Dewa-fu, Akita, Yuri, Sanboku, Mogami, Yamamoto.

The province is more than fifty days east to west. Warm weather has a short season, and the soil for cultivation is deep. The province is vast in size and the land is excellent in quality.

([Uesugi] Echigo Nagon Kagekatsu, Mogami Hashiba Dewa no kami [Yoshiaki],[72] Akita Fujitarō [Sanesue],[73] and others hold lands in this province.)

Hokurikudō: Seven Provinces

(This area is extremely cold, and the snowfall every winter reaches several feet.)

WAKASA (JAKUSHŪ) WAKASA

Middle province rank

There are three districts: Onyū, Ōi, Mikata.

The province is more than one and one-half days south to north. The sea is nearby, and warmth is felt. Fishing is profitable, and there is much iron. Lacquer ware is presented as taxes. The province is small in size and the land is excellent in quality.

([Kinoshita] Shōshō Katsutoshi and his younger brother [Kinoshita] Kunai no shō [Toshifusa] hold lands in this province.[74] Katsutoshi is the elder brother of [Kobayakawa] Chikuzen Chūnagon Kingo [Hideaki] and the nephew of the wife of Hideyoshi, the leader of the thieving Japanese.)

KAGA[75] (KASHŪ) KANGGA

Middle province rank[76]

There are four districts.[77] [Text has been blacked out here.][78] The province is more than two and one-half days south to north. [Text has been blacked out here.][79] The province is average in size and the land is excellent in quality.

(The Chikuzen Dainagon [Maeda Toshiie] held this province. He died in the twelfth month of the *musul* year [1598].[80] His son [Maeda] Saishō Hizen no kami [Toshinaga][81] and his younger son Magoshirō[82] hold this province.)

ECHIZEN (ESSHŪ) YEJIJYŎN

Superior province rank[83]

There are twelve districts: Tsuruga, Niu-fu, Imatachi, Ashiwa, Ōno, Sakai, Kuroda, Ikegami, Sakakida, Yoshida, Sakakita, Nanjō.

The province is more than three and one-half days south to north. Mountains are located in the south, and in the north the province is embraced by the sea. Grains do not flourish. Mulberry and hemp are plentiful. (In one book it is written that grains, if planted, will grow ten thousandfold.) The province is vast in size and the land is excellent in quality.

([Oda] Nobuo, who is the son of the former Imperial Regent [Oda]Nobunaga,[84] and Ōtani Gyōbu no shō [Yoshitsugu][85] hold lands in this province.)

ETCHŪ (ESSHŪ) YŎNJYU

Major province rank

There are four districts: Tonami, Imizu, Nei, Niikawa.

To the right is the Chūgoku region.

The province is more than three days in each direction. Salt, varieties of marine plants, and varieties of fish are numerous, grains are plentiful, and implements are many. Lacquer ware is presented as taxes. The province is vast in size and the land is of average quality.

(Maeda Hizen no kami [Toshinaga] and his younger brother Magoshirō hold lands in this province.)

ECHIGO (ESSHŪ) YEJINGGO

Major province rank

There are seven districts: Kubiki (also called Ihono), Koshi, Mishima, Uoji (the [second] character 治 is also written as 沼[86]), Kanbara, Nutari, Iwafune.

The province is more than six days in each direction. In the north, the province is embraced by the sea, and grains do not flourish. Mulberry and hemp are plentiful. The province is vast in size and the land is average in quality.

(Hori Kyūtarō [Hidemasa] holds this province.[87])

(A local product is fine white linen. The fine white linen is laid out in the snow and glossed.[88])

NOTO (NŌSHŪ) NOTO

Middle province rank

There are four districts: Hakui, Noto-fu, Hōshi, Suzu.

The province is more than two and one-half days east to west. The area is cold, and crops ripen late. There is much good iron, and when it is melted, large tools are made. Mulberry is plentiful, and the varieties of clothing are numerous. The province is small in size and the land is excellent in quality.

(Maeda Hizen no kami [Toshinaga] holds this province.)

SADO (SASHŪ) SANDO

Middle province rank

There are three districts: Umo, Sawada-fu, Kamo.

To the right is Tōtōmi Province.

The province is more than three and one-half days in each direction. The area has many grasses and trees, but I do not know the value of the cattle and horses that are raised there. The varieties of fish and the grains are plentiful. The province is average in size and the land is excellent in quality.

([Uesugi] Echigo Nagon Kagekatsu holds this province.[89])

Sanindō: Eight Provinces

Tanba (Tanjin) Tamba

Major province rank

There are six districts: Kuwada-fu, Funai, Taki, Amata, Higami, Ikaruga.

The province is more than two days in each direction. It is a province upon which capital labor taxes are assessed. Grains and rice, brushwood, and firewood are plentiful. The province is average in size and the land is excellent in quality.

(Tokuzenin [Maeda] Gen'i and his son [Maeda Sui] hold lands in this province.[90])

Tango (Tanshū) Tanggo

Middle province rank

There are five districts: Kasa, Yosa,[91] Tango, Katano (the [first] character 片 is also written as 竹[92]), Kumano.

The province is more than one and one-half days south to north. It is abundant in varieties of fish, mulberry, and hemp. The province's special product is fine textiles. The province is average in size and the land is excellent in quality.

([Hosokawa] Yūsai Fujitaka and his son [Hosokawa] Chōkō Etchū no kami [Tadaoki] hold lands in this province.[93])

(Local products are thick cotton and pongee. These are said to be strong and sturdy and to last for some ten years.)

Tajima (Tanshū) Tanjima

Major province rank

There are eight districts: Asago, Yabu, Izushi, Keta-fu, Kinosaki, Futakata, Shitsumi, Mikumi (the [second] character 舎 is also written as 念).

The province is more than two days east to west. The wet rice paddies are deep and broad. Chestnuts and deccan grass are extremely plentiful, and brushwood is abundant. The province is average in size and the land is excellent in quality.

(Koide Yamato no kami [Yoshimasa],[94] Niimura Saheiei, and Bessho Bungo no kami [Yoshiharu][95] hold lands in this province.)

(The local product is gold.)

Inaba (Inshū) Inaba

Major province rank

There are seven districts: Hōmi, Yakami, Chizu, Ōmi, Takakusa, Keta, Kono.

The province is more than two days south to north. To the north is the sea, and the numerous mountains are high. Also, marine plants and the production of silk cloth both are plentiful. The province is average in size and the land is average in quality.

(Miyabe Hyōbu [no shō Nagahiro] holds this province.[96] Himeji Castle is held by the Ue no taifu.[97] He is the older brother of [Kobayakawa Chikuzen Chūnagon] Kingo [Hideaki].[98])

Hōki (Hakushū) Hoki

Major province rank

There are six districts: Kawamura, Kume, Yabashi, Aseri, Aimi (the [second] character 見 is also written as 美), Hino.

The province is more than two and one-half days south to north. The mountains are high and the land fertile. Grains and silk for clothing can be grown in rotation. The province is average in size and the land is average in quality.

([Mōri] Aki Chūnagon Terumoto holds this province.[99])

Izumo (Unshū) Injumu

Major province rank

There are five districts:[100] Iu-fu, Nogi, Shimane, Aika, Tate[blank].[101]

The province is more than two and one-half days east to west. Trees and shrubs, as well as melons, are mixed among vegetables. The local products are iron farm tools, and silk cloth is plentiful. The province is vast in size and the land is excellent in quality.

([Mōri] Aki Chūnagon Terumoto holds this province.)

Iwami (Sekishū) Iwami

Middle province rank

There are six districts: Ano, Chikama, Naka, Ōchi, Mino, Kanoashi.

The province is more than two days south to north. Profits from marine plants, linen, and salt are great. Taxes double those of other provinces. The province is average in size and the land is poor in quality.

([Mōri] Aki Chūnagon Terumoto holds this province.)

Oki (Onshū) Oki

Minor province rank

There are four districts: Chiburi, Amabe, Suki, Ochi.

The province is more than two days in each direction. Grains are scarce, but marine plants and honey are plentiful. The province is famous for abalone (J. *awabi*). The province is small in size and the land is poor in quality (K. *sohaguk*).

([Mōri] Aki Chūnagon Terumoto holds this province.)

(It is said that Iwami, Oki, and other provinces along the western coast of Honshu are like the Yŏngdong Ridge in Kangwŏn Province in our country [Chosŏn].)

Sanyōdō: Eight Provinces

This is the sea route from our country for entering and leaving Japan.

Harima (Hanshū) Hoerima

Superior province rank

There are fourteen districts: Akashi, Kako (Higashi-, Nishi-), Kamo, Inami, Shikama, Iiho (Higashi-, Nishi-), Akaho, Sayo, Shiso, Kanzaki (Higashi-, Nishi-), Taka, Mitsubo, Ittō, Issai.

The province is more than three and one-half days in each direction. The land is warm, and one does not see hail. Silk cloth, paper, and cloths are plentiful. Clothing and food abound. The province is vast in size and the land is excellent in quality.

(Several lesser generals who served under the leader of the thieving Japanese hold lands in this province.)

Mimasaka (Sakushū) Mimisaki

Major province rank

There are seven districts: Aida, Katsuta, Tomanishi, Tomahigashi-fu, Kume, Ōba, Mashima.

The province is more than three days east to west. It is surrounded on all four sides by mountains; even when it is cold, there is no wind. Grasses and trees flourish, and clothing and food abound. The province is average in size and the land is excellent in quality.

([Mōri] Aki Chūnagon Terumoto and [Ukita] Bizen Chūnagon Hideie divide this province.)

Bizen (Bishū) Pijyŏn

Major province rank

There are eleven districts: Kojima, Wake, Iwanashi, Oku, Akasaka, Kamimichi, Mino, Chigojima, Shiashi, Tsudaka, Kamagashima.

The province is more than three days in each direction. The province is embraced to the south by the warm air from the sea. [It has] grasses and trees, and grains that ripen early in autumn are sent as taxes early in the season. Sharp long swords, sharp halberds, and cloth are abundant. The province is average in size and the land is excellent in quality.

([Ukita] Bizen Chūnagon Hideie holds this province. He is the son-in-law of the leader of the thieving Japanese [Hideyoshi] through marriage to his adopted daughter.[102] Hideie commanded the Japanese forces in the naval battle near Hansan Island.)

Bitchū (Bishū) Pijyu

Major province rank

There are eleven districts:[103] Tsuu, Kuboya, Kayō, Shimomichi, Asakuchi, Oda (Higashi-, Nishi-), Shizuki, Tetta, Aka (Kami-, Shimo-), Saburōjima, Kishima.

The province is more than three and one-half days east to west. Sharp swords and agricultural tools are plentiful. Grains, marine plants, and linen abound, and every day one can eat lavish food until satiated. The province is vast in size and the land is excellent in quality.

(Ukita Hideie and Mōri Terumoto divide this province.)

Bingo (Bishū) Panggo

Major province rank

There are fourteen districts: Yasu, Fukatsu, Kameshi, Nuka, Numakuma (the [second] character 隅 is also written 隈),[104] Honchi, Ashida-fu, Kōnu, Mikami, Mitani (the [first] character 上 is also written as 三), Mitsugi, Eso, Sera, Mihara (the [second] character 原 is also written as 茨).

To the right is the Chūgoku region.

The province is more than two days east to west. Footpaths between rice fields are long and also extend north–south and east–west. Grains ripen early, and alcohol and vinegar have been produced from ages past. The province is average in size and the land is excellent in quality.

([Mōri] Hidemoto, who is the Aki Saishō and the son of [Mōri] Terumoto, holds this province. Hidemoto is the son-in-law of the leader of the thieving Japanese [Hideyoshi] through marriage to his adopted daughter.)

AKI (GEISHŪ) AGI

Major province rank

There are eight districts: Numata, Takata, Toyota, Sada, Kamo, Saeki, Aki, Takamiya, Itsukushima (not one of the eight districts).

The province is more than two and one-half days south to north. The mountains are high, and timber is plentiful. The sea is close, and salt and seaweed are abundant, but grains are not as abundant. The province is vast in size and the land is excellent in quality.

([Mōri] Terumoto holds this province. The Hiroshima of today is in Aki Province.)

SUŌ (SHŪSHŪ) SUO

Major province rank

There are six districts: Ōshima, Kuka, Kumade (the [second] character 手 is also written as 毛[105]), Tsuno, Saba-fu, Yoshiki.

The province is more than three days east to west. Grasses, honey, and varieties of seafood are plentiful. Local products exceed those of other provinces tenfold. The province is famous for mackerel. The province is average in size and the land is excellent in quality.

([Mōri] Terumoto holds this province.)

NAGATO (CHŌSHŪ) NANGGADO

Middle province rank

There are six districts: Atsusa, Toyora-fu, Mine, Ōtsu, Amu, Mishima.

The province is more than two and one-half days east to west. To the south is the sea, to the north are mountains. The varieties of fish overflow, and miscellaneous grains double those in other provinces. The province is average in size and the land is average in quality.

([Mōri] Terumoto holds this province.)

Nankaidō: Six Provinces

Kii (Kishū) Kii

Major province rank

There are seven districts: Ito, Naka, Nakusa-fu, Ama, Arita, Hidaka, Muro (the [second] character 樓 is also written as 婁).

The province is more than four and one-half days south to north. On three sides are the seas, and the province lacks flat land. Grains do not flourish. The province is limited in size and the land is poor in quality.

(Several lesser generals who served under the leader of the thieving Japanese hold lands in this province.)

Awaji (Tanshū) Iwaji

Minor province rank

There are four districts: Tsuna, Mihara, Mushima, Eshima.[106]

The province is more than one day in each direction. This province is the mother of Japan. (It is said that according to Japanese legend, Awaji is called the mother of Japan because the founders of the Japanese people descended to this island.[107]) The province is called "Futahashira." Cloth, salt, and fish are not scarce, and timber is also plentiful. The province is limited in size and the land is poor in quality.

(Wakisaka Nakatsukasa [no shō Yasuharu] holds this province.[108])

Awa (Ashū) Awa

Major province rank

There are nine districts: Miyoshi, Oe, Naimugashi, Nanishi, Katsura, Naka, Itano, Awa, Mima.

The province is more than two days in each direction. The soil is fertile, and millet and rice are harvested abundantly. The mountains are tall. The varieties of fish and of birds and animals are numerous. The province is average in size and the land is excellent in quality.

(Hachisuka Awa no kami Iemasa holds this province.[109])

Sanuki (Sanshū) Sasuki

Major province rank

There are eleven districts: Ōuchi, Samukawa, Miki, Mino, Yamada, Kanda (the [first] character 神 is also written as 刈.), Ano-fu, Utari, Naka, Tado, Kagawa.

The province is more than three days east to west. Mountains, rivers, and dry fields are in equal balance, and grains are abundant. Fish and shellfish also are numerous. Many famous people have come from this province. The province is vast in size and the land is average in quality.

(Ikoma Uta [no kami Chikamasa][110] and his son [Ikoma] Sanuki no kami Kazumasa divide this province as their holdings.)

Iyo (Yoshū) Iyo

Major province rank

There are fourteen districts: Nii, Sufu, Kuwamura, Ochi, Kazahaya, Noma, Chige,[111] Onsen, Kume, Fuke, Iyo, Kita, Uwa, Uma.

The province is more than days in each direction. Wilderness, wet rice paddies, and fields (burned arable land 火粟田 is written in Japan as *hatake* 畑.) are numerous. Mulberry, hemp, salt, and grasses are abundant. The province is vast in size and the land is average in quality.

(Tōdō Sado no kami [Takatora][112] and Katō Uma no suke [Yoshiaki],[113] and also Ogawa Uma no suke [Suketada],[114] hold lands in this province. [Ikeda] Iyo no kami Hideo died and his lands were transferred to Ogawa.[115])

Tosa (Toshū) Tosa

Middle province rank

There are seven districts: Tosa, Agawa (the [first] character 吾 is also written 五), Takaoka, Hata, Nagaoka, Hatashima, Kagami.

The province is more than two days east to west. The land is fertile and grains flourish well. Timber is plentiful. The province is average in size and the land is excellent in quality.

(Chōsokabe Tosa no kami Morichika holds this province. He died in the *ki-hae* year [1599], and his son succeeded to the proprietorship.[116])

Seikaidō: Nine Provinces

Chikuzen (Chikushū) Chigujyŏn

Major province rank

There are twenty districts: Shima, Kama, Yasu (Kami-, Shimo-), Shikanoshima, Mikasa, Munakata, Onga, Mushiroda, Honami, Sera, Naka, Shaka, Mushima, Kasuya, Ido, Mushirouchi, Kurate, Nokonoshima,[117] Shimotsuasakura, Kamutsuasakura (Kokufu as well as Dazai[fu]).

The province is more than four days south to north. The province is endowed with rice, chestnuts, treasures, and implements. The province is average in size and the land is excellent in quality.

([Kobayakawa] Chikuzen Chūnagon Kinoshita Kingo [Hideaki] holds this province.[118] He is the nephew of the principal wife of the leader of the thieving Japanese [Hideyoshi]. Shikanoshima is held by Nakagawa Shūri no daibu Hidenari.[119])

CHIKUGO (CHIKUSHŪ) CHIGUNGGU

Major province rank

There are ten districts: Mihara, Mii-fu, Ikuwa (the [second] character 桑 is also written as 葉), Mii, Mike, Kamutsuma, Yamato, Yamashimo, Takeno.[120]

The province is more than five days south to north. Grains and varieties of fish are innumerably abundant. Treasures and implements are also plentiful. The province is vast in size and the land is average in quality.

([Kobayakawa] Kingo [Hideaki] holds this province.)

BUZEN (HŌSHŪ) PUJYŎN

Major province rank

There are eight districts: Tagawa, Kiku, Miyako-fu, Nakatsu, Tsuiki, Kamike,[121] Shimotsumike,[122] Usa.

The province is more than four days south to north. It is close to China and overflows with medicinal plants and implements. Brocades are used for taxes. The province is vast in size and the land is average in quality.

(Kuroda Kai no kami [Nagamasa][123] and Mōri Iki no kami [Katsunobu][124] hold lands in this province.)

BUNGO (HŌSHŪ) PUNGGO

Major province rank

There are eight districts: Hida, Kusu, Naori, Ōno, Amabe, Ōkata, Hayami, Kunisaki.

The province is more than three days in each direction. Mulberry and hemp are plentiful, and people have enough clothes. Grains and imported goods are plentiful. The province is average in size and the land is excellent in quality.

(Fukuhara Uma no suke [Naotaka], Ōta Hida no kami [Kazuyoshi],[125] Mōri Minbu no Daiyū [Takamasa], Nakagawa Shūri no daibu Hidenari, Hayakawa Shuma no suke Nagamasa,[126] and Takenaka Gensuke [Takashige],[127] and others hold lands in this province. The Uma no suke later became a monk; lands were taken from the family.)

Hizen (Hōshū) Hijyŏn

Major province rank

There are twelve districts: Kii, Yabu, Mine, Ogi-fu, Kanzaki, Saga, Matsura, Kishima, Fujitsu, Sonoki, Katsuragi, Takaku.

The province is more than five days south to north. The soil is fertile, and sown seeds will yield one hundredfold. As mulberry and *yamaguwa* are grown, there is sufficient clothing for agricultural work. Fish and fowl supplement the diet.[128] The province is average in size and the land is excellent in quality.

(The Ryūzō[ji] are a great family and hold the province. Trade ships from China, Ryukyu, the Nanban, Luzon, and elsewhere arrive and leave without cease. Because Karatsu, Nagoya, and other places are held by Terazawa Shima no kami Masanari,[129] he serves as the commissioner of the sea lanes [J. *suiro bugyō*]. He supervises the arrival and reception of people from our country. The island of Hirado is held by Matsura Hōin [Shigenobu]. Yanagawa Tachibana Une [Muneshige] holds an area of Hizen Province as his domain. His proprietorship is small, but it is said that his army is strong.)

Higo (Hishū) Hinggo

Superior province rank

There are fourteen districts: Tamana, Yamaka, Yamamoto, Kikuchi, Aso, Kafushi, Takuma, Kuma, Akita-fu, Mashiki, Udo, Yatsushiro, Amakusa, Ashikita.

The province is more than five days in each direction. Timber, brush, and firewood are abundant, and grains, varieties of fish, paper, and cotton are plentiful. The province is vast in size and the land is average in quality.

(Katō Kazue [no kami Kiyomasa][130] and Konishi Settsu no kami [Yukinaga][131] divide this province.)

Hyūga (Nisshū) Hiungga

Middle province rank

There are five districts: Usuki, Koyu-fu, Naka, Miyazaki, Morokata.

The province is more than three days in each direction. Mulberry, hemp, and grains are available in balance, and famine and cold weather are not known. The province is average in size and the land is average in quality.

(Shimazu Hyōgo [no kami Yoshihiro] holds this province.[132])

Ōsumi (Gushū) Usumi

Middle province rank

There are eight districts: Ōsumi, Hishikari, Kuwabara, Soo-fu, Ahira (the [first] character 始 is also written as 姑), Kimotsuki, Komaji, Kumage.

The province is more than two days east to west. It is a small province (J. *shōkoku*), but there is an abundant variety of foods and the varieties of fish are numerous. Paper and cloth, in particular, are abundant. The province is average in size and the land is exceptional in quality (K. *chungdaeguk*).

([Shimazu] Yoshihiro holds this province.)

Satsuma (Gushū) Sajuma

Middle province rank

There are fourteen districts: Izumi, Takaki, Satsuma, Heki, Isa, Ata, Kawanobe, Eno, Ibusuki, Kirei, Taniyama, Shikinokojima, Kagoshima, Koshikijima.

The province is more than two days in each direction. It is a small province, but because it is near China, it is rich in military items and other objects. However, there is no mulberry or hemp clothing. The province is average in size and the land is exceptional in quality.

([Shimazu] Yoshihiro holds this province.)

Iki (Isshū) Igi

Minor province rank

There are two districts: Iki, Ishida.

The province is more than one day in each direction. This province and Tsushima are called the two islands. Because the western barbarians invaded, [Katō] Kiyomasa was forced to protect this province and assist in provisioning it. The items presented for taxes are unusual items.

(Matsura Hōin [Shigenobu] holds this province. He also holds Hirado Island, in Hizen Province, together with Iki Island.)

Tsushima (Taishū) Chusima

Minor province rank

There are two districts: Kamiagata, Shimoagata.

The province is as much as one day in each direction. Because this province is distant from the Japanese main islands, it is called "*shima*." There are unusual items here. [Translators' note: The sentence in the text that would be translated here is unclear.¹³³] For that reason, the post of deputy (J. *tandai*) was placed here. The province is small in size and the land is poor in quality.

([Sō] Hashiba Tsushima no kami Yoshitoshi holds this province.¹³⁴)

Hashiba is the surname of Hideyoshi. Because he made Sō Yoshitoshi guide the attack of our country, Hideyoshi bestowed his surname upon Yoshitoshi and rewarded him for his merit.

Taira Shigenobu is an elder official under Yoshitoshi. Japanese call him Yanagawa Shimotsuke no kami [Shigenobu].¹³⁵ He oversees the defense of Tsushima.

The monk [Keitetsu] Genso is an adviser to Yoshitoshi. Japanese call him Ankokuji Saidō. He oversees the writing of various types of documents sent to our country.

The island's capital is called Yoshizu. Even though the mountains and flatlands in that area are good, the castles are not at all the same [as castles elsewhere in Japan]. They are at the base of large mountains or next to the sea, and there are no tall towers or deep ponds that must be defended. On all four sides of the island are mountains, and hills, grass, and trees grow luxuriantly. When something happens suddenly, all that the people can do is flee and hide.

From Yoshizu, to the east is Iki Island. One must always wait during the day for a good wind; then one can cross to that island. To the south is Hirado Island. It is slightly closer than Iki, but the wind and waves are fiercer. To the west is Toyosaki. It is two days away overland. If going by ship, Toyosaki is one day away with a good wind. If by rowed boat, then the passage takes two days. To the west from Toyosaki are our country and the sea; the passage takes half a day.

Tsushima's mountains are long from east to west, and short from south to north. The land is strewn with rocks, and there are no wet rice paddies whatsoever. Because vegetables and barley are sewn atop sand and stones in shallow soil, even when they do grow they reach no more than a few inches.

During peaceful times, islanders sailed to our country for trade and supported themselves in that way. Black horns, pepper, and other goods come from Southeast Asia. Because otter pelts and fox pelts are not used in Japan, the islanders buy these at low prices in their own country and sell them at high prices in our country. But they cannot resell gossamer, thin silk gauze, twill, damask, woolen goods (J. *kei*), other cloths, and coins in our country because these are valued in Japan. Women in Tsushima often wear clothing of our country. And almost all of the men understand Korean. When Tsushima islanders point to a foreign country, they sometimes call it "Nihon," and when they point to our country, they sometimes call it "Chōsen."[136] They do not very much regard themselves as from Japan.

During peaceful times, they gained much profit in our country and little profit in Japan. Thus, from the island's generals to the soldiers, their desire to live under our country is even stronger than their sense of belonging to Japan. As Hideyoshi conquered the sixty-six provinces of Japan, [Sō] Yoshitoshi always feared the accusation of misconduct, and in the end sold out our country, flattered Hideyoshi, and came to stand in the vanguard of the invasion. Hideyoshi rewarded Yoshitoshi for his merit with land in Hakata, in Chikuzen Province,[137] and thus the Tsushima generals for the first time became able to eat (their own) rice. Before then, they ate only rice that had been bestowed by our country.

However, it is said that Yoshitoshi still is unable to own a house and its lot (J. *ieyashiki*) in the Japanese capital. He chose a city near where the father of his wife, [Konishi] Yukinaga, lives and for a time rented a residence there. But having to move from that residence, like other generals, he could not find another house.

Japanese living on the main islands truly are violent, but they are not extremely cunning. Regarding our country, they do not know even east and west, and even eight years after the war began they do not know the names of our military leaders.

The Japanese in Tsushima are not violent, but they are cunning enough to craft numerous clever schemes. And there is nothing about our country that they do not know in detail. From when times were peaceful, they have selected bright children from among the islanders and taught them our language. Further, the islanders teach the fine points of our many types of written texts. When suddenly asked, even our countrymen with discerning eyes cannot recognize a document as one that Japanese composed.

When there is no distance with our country, this means that the Tsushima islanders seek to completely attach themselves. When the Japanese slaves are powerful, the Tsushima islanders betray our country, purchase the duty of guiding the Japanese through our country, and invade. That cunning trick and deception has extraordinary features. If the assistance to and administration by our military officers assigned to provincial posts are not adequate, then undoubtedly, we will be deceived by those people again.

(If we were to execute morning and night a policy of constraint against the Japanese, it would be good if that policy followed the example of banquets in the northern provinces for Jurchens. The Governor of Kyŏngsang Province and the Kyŏngsang Province Army Commander would meet at the port of Pusan, in Tongnae County, prior to the arrival of Japanese during the predetermined period of time. No matter what, state revenues should not be used for escorting Japanese through the provinces to the capital, and the Japanese should not be allowed to learn what is false and what is true about the capital. It would be good to follow the example of bestowing gifts upon the Jurchens in the northern provinces and give simple local products that are appropriate for the items brought by the Japanese. We will not transport the rice of Yŏngnam delivered as taxes and provide it as foodstuffs to the thieves. It will be fine if the Governor and the Army Commander strictly warn the Navy Deputy Commander to set exchange rates for the black horns of water buffaloes, cinnabar, pepper, sulphur, fox pelts, and otter pelts that the Japanese bring according to the three categories of superior quality, average quality, and lesser quality, and also if the Japanese are made to trade in Pusan and then sent home.[138] There will be no exhausting people and horses by transporting Japanese to the capital, permitting residents in the capital to purchase items brought by Japanese at low prices, and fomenting feelings of resentment and bitterness among the Japanese. The period when the Japanese come to present tribute will be set for the beginning of the month, and this will eliminate the abuse of Japanese arriving whenever they want. Regarding the ships, the number will be decided beforehand and the ships will sail as a group. This will eliminate suffering from suspicion of the Japanese. Regarding the Japan House, the entry and exit of people will be strictly prohibited, the building will be guarded, spies will not be able to learn what is false and what is true about the defense of the local area, and other Japanese will not learn about forts and ponds. The rules will already have been established, and the matters to be forbidden will be made clear. Moreover, should we interact with them courteously and show compassion through conferring favor and showing faith, the Japanese truly will fear our dignity and be filled with awe at our virtue. Japanese are not to be invited to the capital and are not to be bestowed annual rice grants, but is there a reason for them to be resentful?

However, only when Japanese of the main islands are plotting invasion will visits to the capital and annual rice grants be permitted. And if Tsushima islanders are allowed to come and report outside the predetermined periods and to not adhere to the predetermined months for presenting tribute goods, they without fail will come prior to the visiting period and report, and probably will warn our country to raise defenses in advance, because they will gain our trust for trying to make amends for the crime of having previously betrayed our country. In handling the Japanese slaves, the question of how to handle Tsushima must be decided first. In handling Tsushima, there is no other policy than this.)

Also, there are [the islands of] Erabu, Hirado Island, Gotō, Shichijima, Takeshima, Isshōjima,[139] Koshikijima, and Hachijōjima. In those areas are islands larger than Iki and Tsushima.

Appendix 2

Japanese Government Offices

Translators' note: Kang Hang provided two types of information for each entry in his list of Japanese government offices, posts, and terms. First is the Japanese word, which is printed in the text's regular font size. Second is an explanatory term or the office's or post's equivalent in Tang China's bureaucracy, which the Japanese government introduced and adapted from the seventh century. The latter information is printed in a smaller font size. In translating Kang's list, we have arranged the text as follows in almost all instances. In the main text are an English translation of the Japanese office, post, or term, and an English translation of the Chinese equivalent. The latter term is in brackets. In the endnotes are the English translations, the romanization of the Japanese term, and Chinese, Japanese, and Korean romanizations of the Chinese term.

Emperor [Son of Heaven][1]
That is, this is the emperor of Japan. He does not cut his hair and does not leave his palace. Before the full moon, on the fourteenth day of each month, he eats vegetables. After the full moon, on the sixteenth day of each month, he eats fish.
In earlier generations, emperors [ignored] the Regent, the Imperial Regent, the Major Counselor, and other officials and ruled themselves. Since the middle period, the regents and other officials have governed as they wished, and the commands of the so-called emperors have not extended beyond the capital. The emperor appointed a Commissioner (J. *bugyō*) for the capital, and that official administered both the capi-

tal and the nearby area. In Hideyoshi's time, Tokuzenin [Maeda] Gen'i became the Kyoto Commissioner.[2] *Bugyō* is the Japanese term for the Chinese term *dianshou*.

Regent [court][3]
Imperial Regent [court][4]
Shogun [*bakufu*][5]
Prime Minister [Grand Pillar of State][6]
Senior Counselor [Grand Councilor of the Right][7]
Middle Counselor [Chancellery][8]
Junior Counselor [Supervising Secretary][9]
Imperial Adviser [Participant in Deliberations on Court Policy][10]
Second Rank [Lord Specially Advanced][11]
Third Rank [Third Grade][12]
Left Senior Controller and Right Senior Controller [Minister][13]
Left Middle Controller and Right Middle Controller [Director][14]
Left Junior Controller and Right Junior Controller [Vice Director][15]
Chamberlain [Reminder][16]
Left [Palace Guard] Commander and Right [Palace Guard] Commander[17]
Captain [Palace Guard Vice Commander][18]
Lieutenant [Palace Guard Third Commander][19]
Office of Imperial Police [Court of Judicial Review][20]
Ministry of Court Affairs [Secretariat][21]
Adjutant [Chamberlain for Law Enforcement][22]
Council Secretariat [External Secretary][23]
Secretariat [Secretariat Director][24]
Bureau of the Wardrobe[25]
Ministry of Ceremonial [Ministry of Personnel][26]
State Academy [Chancellor][27]
Ministry of Civil Affairs [Ministry of Rites][28]
Ministry of Military Affairs [Ministry of Defense][29]
Ministry of Justice [Ministry of Justice][30]
Ministry of Popular Affairs [Ministry of Revenue][31]
Ministry of the Imperial Household [Court of the National Granaries][32]
Bureau of Housekeeping [(Unclear)][33]
Bureau of Music [Imperial Music Office][34]
Agency for Foreign Affairs [Court of State Ceremonial][35]

Ministry of the Treasury [Court of the Treasury]³⁶
Office of Weaving [Weaving and Dyeing Office]³⁷
Office of the Palace Table Master [Chief Minister, Court of Imperial Entertainments]³⁸
Bureau of Carpentry [Directorate for the Palace Buildings]³⁹
Bureau of the Palace Kitchen [Imperial Granaries Office]⁴⁰
Bureau of Palace Equipment [Accommodations Service]⁴¹
Bureau of Medicine [Imperial Medical Office]⁴²
Office of Palace Women [Office of Palace Women]⁴³
Board of Censors [Censorate]⁴⁴
Left Capital Office and Right Capital Office [Metropolitan Prefecture]⁴⁵
Office of the Stables [Stables Office]⁴⁶
Left [Palace Guard] and Right [Palace Guard] [Guard]⁴⁷
Assistant Inspector [Palace Guard]⁴⁸
Left Royal Gate Guard and Right Royal Gate Guard [Imperial Insignia Guard]⁴⁹
Left Bureau of the Imperial Stables and Right Bureau of the Imperial Stables [Office of the Imperial Stables]⁵⁰
Bureau of Military Storehouses [Armory]⁵¹
Left Watch Guard and Right Watch Guard [Militant Guard]⁵²
Office of Palace Repair [Directorate for the Palace Buildings]⁵³
Audit Officers [Unclear]⁵⁴ (I do not know what the first character is. For the time being, I will use the character in the Japanese text.)
Dazaifu Governor-General [Commander-in-Chief]⁵⁵
Senior Assistant Governor-General [Chief Minister]⁵⁶
Guards of the Prince [(Unclear)]⁵⁷
Bureau of Books and Drawings [(Unclear)]⁵⁸
Hayato Office [(Unclear)]⁵⁹
Bureau of Statistics [Bureau of General Accounts]⁶⁰
Bureau of Taxation Commissioner [Two-Thousand-Bushel Official]⁶¹
Acting Senior Governor [Supervisor]⁶²
Senior Inspector [Gentleman of the Capital Gates]⁶³
Office of Water [Office of Imperial Parks]⁶⁴
Bureau of Attendants [Gatekeeper]⁶⁵

In previous times, the men who held these posts had been appointed to perform their duties. From the middle period, though, the government distributed land to men who held government offices. Even when the post was in name only, officials did not perform its duties. In recent times, men have converted post names and province names into their public names, and even retainers of generals and men of lower status have come to hold titles of high-ranking offices and provincial governorships.

Notes

INTRODUCTION

1. Naitō Shunpo estimates the number of captives to have been between 20,000 and 30,000 (*Bunroku Keichō eki ni okeru hiryonin no kenkyū*, 777), while Yi Ch'aeyŏn argues for about 100,000 (*Imjin waeran p'oro silgi yŏn'gu*, 34).
2. In 1604, the monk Yujŏng (1544–1610; also known as Song'un Taesa) was sent as a special envoy to Japan, and when he returned in 1605 he brought more than 3,000 Korean captives back with him (*Sŏnjo sujŏng sillok*, 39:3a [1605.4.1]). And the Korean embassies of 1607 and 1617 brought back 1,418 and 120 people, respectively (Kyŏng Sŏm, *Haesarok*, 2:236; O Yun'gyŏm, *Tongsasang illok*, 2:343). The total number of repatriated captives recorded in the Korean veritable records is 7,500 (Naitō, *Bunroku Keichō ni okeru hiryonin no kenkyū*, 7–11).
3. *Sŏnjo sujŏng sillok*, 25:3a–b [1591.3.1]; de Bary et al., eds., *Sources of Japanese Tradition*, 2nd ed., 1:465–67. Also, Berry, *Hideyoshi*, 208.
4. The three Korean kingdoms (Silla, Paekche, and Koguryŏ), Japan, and Tang China fought in the peninsula in the 660s and 670s while the states on the Korean peninsula were being reconfigured.
5. Swope, "Bestowing the Double-edged Sword," 61–115; Swope, *A Dragon's Head and Serpent's Tail*.
6. Much has been written on this issue. One of the more influential works is Linda Colley's *Britons: Forging the Nation, 1707–1837*.
7. Abe, *Nihon shushigaku to Chōsen*, 62–210.
8. Fujiwara, *Fujiwara Seika shū*, 2:369–370.
9. *Sŏnjo sillok*, 111:9b–11b [1599.4.15].

10. *Sŏnjo sillok*, 115:14b–15a [1599.7.19].
11. Yun Sŏn'gŏ, "Nyŏnbo."
12. Yu Kye signed his postscript as Fifth Counselor in the Office of the Special Counselors (K. *Hongmun'gwan Kyori*; senior fifth grade). Appointed to that post on the twenty-eighth day of the eighth month of 1649, he was later banished to Onsŏng County, in frigid northeast Hamgyŏng Province, for issues related to the temple name of the recently deceased King Injo (*Hyojong sillok*, 1:45b–46a [1649.8.28]).
13. "Ŭpchae sŏnsaeng," in *Yŏnggwang ŭpchi*, 12:344. Yun Sun'gŏ was the second son of Yun Hwang but became the adopted first son of Hwang's older brother Su (*P'ap'yŏng Yun ssi Nojongp'a po*, 13–29).
14. *P'ap'yŏng Yun ssi Nojongp'a po*, 32.
15. Yi Pyŏngdo, *Han'guk yuhaksa*, 258; *P'ap'yŏng Yun ssi*, 24–25; *Ch'angnyŏng Sŏng ssi chokpo*, 3:27b–28a.
16. Yi Haejun, *Chosŏn hugi munjung*, 166–67.
17. "Sau," in *Yŏnggwang ŭpchi*, 12:335.
18. Pyŏn Tongmyŏng, "Kang Hang ŭi p'ilsabon," 243–44.
19. Im Ch'igyun, "*Kanyangnok* yŏngu," 111–12; *Sŏnjo sillok*, 185:1a [1605.3.1].
20. *Sŏnjo sillok*, 188:15b [1605.6.20], 188:16a–b [1605.6.23].
21. Pyŏn Tongmyŏng, "Kang Hang ŭi p'ilsabon," 243–44; Im Ch'igyun, "*Kanyangnok* yŏngu," 112–13; Kang Hang, *Suŭn chip*, "Mokch'a," 6; Kang Hang, *Kanyangnok*, passim.
22. Song Ilgi and An Hyŏnju, "Suŭn Kang Hang," 5–30.
23. Yi Sugwang, *Chibong yusŏl*, 44–47.
24. Yi Chihang, *P'yojurok*, 3:69; Kang Hang, *Kanyangnok*, 38a.
25. Sin Yuhan, *Haeyurok*, 1:76.
26. Kim Sŏng'ae, *Suŭn chip*.
27. Im Ch'igyun, "*Kanyangnok* yŏngu," 113–14; Kang Hang, *Kanyangnok*, Changsŏgak collection.
28. Kang Hang, *Kanyangnok*, in Kang Hang, *Suŭn chip* (1868 printing), Harvard-Yenching Library, Harvard University.
29. Unno Kazutaka, *Chizu ni miru Nihon*, 26.
30. Maeda ikueikai Sonkeikaku bunko, ed., *Shūgaishō*, 80–87.
31. See Andrew Edmund Goble, "*Shokugenshō*," in *Dictionary of Sources of Classical Japan*, 371, for an introduction to *Shokugenshō*.
32. See "Nansenbushū Dai Nihon-koku shōtōzu," in *Tōshōdaiji*, "(2) Kodai Nihon chizu."
33. Kang Hang, *Kanyangnok*, 3b.

34. Kang Hang, *Kanyangnok*, 30a–b.
35. Kang Hang, *Kanyangnok*, 30a, 8a.
36. Unno, *Chizu ni miru Nihon*, 26–27.
37. Kang Hang, *Kanyangnok*, 46a.
38. Kang Hang, *Kanyangnok*, 32b–33a. To the bottom right of "Fuji-san" is a circular mark with designlike lines drawn inside. Its purpose and meaning are unclear.
39. Kang Hang, *Kanyangnok*, 32b.
40. "Waeguk chido," in No In, *Kŭmgyerok*, vol. 6, in No In, *Kŭmgye sŏnsaeng munjip*, 238–39.
41. *Sŏnjo sillok*, 120:12b–13b [1599.12.25].
42. "Waeguk chido," in No In, *Kŭmgyerok*, 6:3a–11b.
43. "Waeguk chido," in *Haedong chido*, 1:6.
44. "Ilbon chŏndo," in "Ko chido ch'ŏp," in *Yŏngnam Tae Pangmulgwan sojang Hanguk ŭi yet chido*, 180.

1. Encounters with the Adversities of War

1. Kang Hang had been promoted to Assistant Section Chief in the Board of Punishments (K. *Hyŏngjo Chwarang*) forty-six days earlier (*Sŏnjo sillok*, 83:27a–b [1596.12.22]). Here, Kang used a Chinese style, *Qiuguan*, in referring to this Chosŏn government post. See Hucker, 177 entry 1324.
2. Yubong was a small village in Yŏnggwang County, Chŏlla Province.
3. Commander Yang Yuan (d. 1598) was a Chinese general who suffered repeated defeats in Chosŏn. During the first invasion, leading the Army of the Center, he fought under Li Rusong (1549–98). Yang returned in the second campaign; King Sŏnjo (1552–1608, r. 1567–1608) went to his camp to greet him (*Sŏnjo sillok*, 88:16b–18a [1597.5.13]). Eschewing the advice of Korean officials to establish positions in mountain forts in 1597, Yang strengthened the city fortress at Namwŏn, in the open land of Chŏlla Province. Defeat there opened the road northward toward Seoul for the Japanese armies. The Ming government later executed Yang outside Seoul's city wall for this defeat (Hawley, *The Imjin War*, 449–52, 468–72, 476).
4. Namwŏn, in Chŏlla Province, was designated as a special county (Town; K. *Tohobu*), the third highest level of county, early in the Chosŏn period, in 1413. The county's center was not attacked during the first Japanese invasion, but it fell in the second invasion, in 1597. See *Sinjŭng Tongguk yŏji sŭngnam* 39:1a–b; Turnbull, *Samurai Invasion*, 190–97.
5. Yi Kwangjŏng (1552–1627) was known for his activities dealing with Ming China

during the Imjin War. He had an illustrious career, reaching the post of Board of Personnel Minister (K. *Ijo P'ansŏ*, senior second grade). He passed the higher civil service examination (K. *munkwa*) in 1590, and held this post of Second Minister in the Board of Taxation (K. *Pun Hojo Ch'amp'an*, junior second grade) by the sixth month of 1597 (*Sŏnjo sillok*, 88:35b–36a [1597.5.25]). These were two of the Six Boards (K. *Yukcho*), similar to ministries in today's governments, and were below the State Council (K. *Ŭijŏngbu*), whose officials advised the king. The Board of Taxation administered the census and the compilation of population records, and oversaw the collection of levies and the performance of corvée labor.

6. Yun Sŏn (1559–1637) was known for his devotion to the royal house during the Imjin War, and he spent much of his official career serving King Kwanghae (1575–1641, r. 1608–23). The Board of Rites (K. *Yejo*) post mentioned here, Assistant Section Chief (K. *Yejo Chwarang*), was at the senior sixth grade. However, Yun's name was printed incorrectly as Yun Sŏnjin in *The Record of a Shepherd*. Of the P'ap'yŏng Yun descent group, Yun passed the higher civil service examination in 1588.

7. Samga County was in Kyŏngsang Province.

8. Open letters of exhortation were missives sent out in times of crisis to rally the people to specific causes. During the first invasion, many such letters were sent out. See Haboush, ed., *Epistolary Korea*, 121–40.

9. Regional Navy Commander Wŏn Kyun (1540–97) was Yi Sunsin's (1545–98) rival. Though Wŏn, helped by Yi's ships, won several battles in 1592, the Korean navy under his command suffered a complete defeat early in the second invasion in 1597. He earned a reputation for his rivalry with and alleged slander of Yi Sunsin. He was of the Wŏnju Wŏn descent group.

10. This reference to Hansan Island is to the naval battle in the Ch'ilch'ŏn Straits in the seventh month of 1597, during which the Japanese naval forces decimated the Korean navy. Wŏn Kyun and several other navy officers died there. Because the navy was the strongest element in the Korean military, this defeat negatively affected Korean defense strategy and opened the southern coastal waters to transit toward Haenam, where the coastline bends northward. For more on this battle, see Yu Sŏngnyong, *The Book of Corrections*, 201–4; Turnbull, *Samurai Invasion*, 184–85.

11. In Chŏlla Province, Hamp'yŏng County bordered Yŏnggwang County to the south, and several counties separated Sunch'ang County from Yŏnggwang. That is, Kang is emphasizing how widely he searched for his superior.

12. These events must have occurred after 1597.7.11, for Kim Sangjun (1561–1635) was

still the Yŏnggwang County magistrate (Great County Magistrate; K. *Kunsu*, junior fourth grade) on that date. He served as the magistrate there from mid-1595 into the ninth or tenth month of 1597 (*Sŏnjo sillok*, 90:7a–b [1597.7.11]; "Ŭpchae sŏnsaeng," in *Yŏnggwang ŭpchi*, 12:344). He was known for his calligraphy. Of the Andong Kim descent group, he passed the higher civil service examination in 1590.

13. The Noryŏng mountain range separated Chŏlla Province into northern and southern halves.
14. The parent here would be Kang's father, for his mother had passed away in 1580. She was born to Kim Sŏnson, of the Yŏngsan Kim descent group. More specifically, her father was of that group's Yŏnggwang branch and was buried in Pulgap District, Yŏnggwang County, the same district where Kang was born and buried. In a pattern common in the Chosŏn period, the marriage of his father and mother linked two descent groups living near each other. See *Chinju Kang ssi sebo: Suŭn-gong p'abo*, 1:19b–20a; *Yŏngsan (P'albong) Kim ssi taedongbo*, 1:103a–105b; *Yŏngsan Kim ssi sebo*, 10:1b–3a.
15. Nonjap Port was located at Yŏnsan, in Yŏnggwang County, in southern Chŏlla Province.
16. Hwang Sin (1560–1617) led the Korean delegation that followed the Chinese embassy to meet Toyotomi Hideyoshi (1537–98) in Kyoto in 1596. Appointed Governor of Chŏlla Province in the seventh month of 1597, he contributed to the reconstruction of Namwŏn after the war (*Sŏnjo sillok*, 90:18b [1597.7.3]). Hwang passed the higher civil service examination in 1588.
17. Kang's father was Kang Kŭkkŏm (1529–1615). He entered government service through a protective appointment (K. *ŭm*). That is, Kŭkkŏm did not pass the higher civil service examination but gained appointment based instead upon the examination success and career of a descent group member of an earlier generation (*Chinju Kang ssi sebo*, 1:19b–20a).
18. Kang had seventeen male and four female cousins (that we can confirm) on his father's side. The text is unclear about how many cousins were present on the beach. Information below suggests that two cousins there were Hyŏp (1563–1607) and Hong (d.u.). Hyŏp was the first son of Kŭkch'ung, who was the sixth son of Obok. Hang's father, Kŭkkŏm, was the fourth son of Obok, who also had entered government service through a protective appointment. Obok's father, Hyangsu, too had entered government service in this manner. Hyŏp passed the military examination. Hong was the second son of Kŭngnyang, who was the second son of Obok. He too passed the military examination (*Chinju Kang ssi sebo*, 1:22b–23a, 1:19a; *Yŏnggwang soksu yŏji sŭngnam*, 3:18b, 3:19a).

19. This brother, Hae (1554–91), studied under Yi I and passed the literary licentiate examination (K. *chinsa*) in 1588. His wife was from the Yŏnggwang Chŏng descent group (*Chinju Kang ssi sebo*, 1:19b–20a), suggesting another local marriage.
20. This wife was Kang's second wife. She was of the Hamp'yŏng Yi descent group, and was born to a secondary wife of Yi Changyŏng (1521–89). The Chosŏn government recognized her as a virtuous wife (K. *chŏngnyŏ*) and erected a gate for her (*Chinju Kang ssi sebo*, 1:20b–21b, "Suŭn Kang Hang sŏnsaeng pusil Hamp'yŏng Yi ssi yŏllyŏmun," in *Chinju Kang ssi sebo*; *Hamp'yŏng Yi ssi chokpo*, 2:3b–5b).
21. The brother-in-law referred to here is Sim Umin. The second son of Sim Anp'yŏng, he married Kang's sister (*Chinju Kang ssi sebo*, 1:22a; *Ch'ŏngsong Sim ssi taedong sebo*, 1920, 1:20a).
22. Myodu and Piroch'o were on the west coast of Chŏlla Province.
23. Yi Sunsin was a Chosŏn navy commander who repeatedly led the navy to victories during the Imjin War. His building of "turtle ships," his strategies based upon knowledge of the waters and straits of Chosŏn's southern coast, his demotion from the post of Regional Navy Commander, his vanquishing of enemy ships, and his death at the close of the war became the stuff of legend. Despite his victories, he was arrested in 1597 and demoted to common soldier. Reappointed as Regional Navy Commander, Yi was killed in a sea battle late in the war, in 1598. He is the supreme hero in the South Korean historical imagination. He was of the Tŏksu Yi descent group and passed the military examination in 1576.
24. Hŭksan Island was in Naju County, which was south of Yŏnggwang County and off the coast of southern Chŏlla Province.
25. Ŏŭi Island was in Yŏnggwang County. The text's printing of "Ŏŭi Island" as 於矣島 may be an error for 於義島. See the map of Yŏnggwang County in the postwar state gazetteer *Haedong chido* for the latter place name (*Haedong chido*, 2:23).
26. Chinwŏl Island was in Yŏnggwang County (*Sinjŭng Tongguk yŏji sŭngnam*, 36:2a–b).
27. Tangdu was at the opening of the salt fields.
28. Kang's second elder brother, Chun (1563–1628), studied under Yi I. He was captured on the same day as Kang. Chun passed the literary licentiate examination in 1591 (*Chinju Kang ssi sebo*, 1:20a). His wife was of the Haeju Ch'oe descent group (*Chinju Kang ssi sebo*, 1:20a; *Haeju Ch'oe ssi sebo*, 2:13–15).
29. Muan County was in southern Chŏlla Province, on the west coast.
30. The white-and-red flag on Japanese ships may have been what is today called the Hinomaru flag, the national flag of Japan that has a red sun in the middle of

1. ENCOUNTERS WITH THE ADVERSITIES OF WAR   139

a white background. This design was used in Japan in the late sixteenth century and earlier. Examples include a helmet worn by Katō Kiyomasa (1562–1611) and a battlefield jacket (J. *jinbaori*) worn by Hideyoshi (*Sengoku fasshon*, 12 item 4 and 41 item 41).

31. T'aean County was in southern Ch'ungch'ŏng Province, along the west coast. "Nanhaeng" means "difficult passage."
32. Kunsan Port was in northern Chŏlla Province, along the west coast.
33. Sado no kami, or Governor of Sado Province, was a title given to Tōdō Takatora (1556–1630).
34. Lu Zhonglian was a person of Qi during China's Warring States period (403–221 B.C.E.). He was greatly disturbed by the ascendancy of Qin, which unified China in 221 B.C.E., and declared that when the ruler of Qin called himself emperor, he would throw himself into the Eastern Sea. See Sima Qian, "Lu Zhunglian," in Sima Qian, *Shiji*, 3:2459–69.
35. Bo Yi was a minister of the Shang dynasty. Although the Shang came to an end due to its tyrannical last king, he remained loyal to his state. Refusing to eat even weeds that belonged to the new dynasty, he starved to death on Mount Shouyang. Bo Yi is a symbol of absolute loyalty, a minister who would not serve two lords. See Sima Qian, "Bo Yi," in Sima Qian, *Shiji*, 3:2121–29.
36. A government storehouse in Naju County, Yŏngsan-ch'ang was combined with Pŏpsŏng-ch'ang, in Yŏnggwang County, in 1512. Prior to this decision, tax goods from seventeen counties were collected at a Yŏngsan storehouse and then conveyed by ship northward to Seoul. Pŏpsŏng-ch'ang collected tax goods from fifteen counties. See *Chungjong sillok*, 16:69b–70a [1512.9.27]; *Sinjŭng Tongguk yŏji sŭngnam*, 35:7a–b, 36:4b.
37. There were two naval commandery headquarters in Chŏlla Province. The Right Naval Commandery was in Haenam County.
38. Sunch'ŏn County, on the southern coast of Chŏlla Province, was the home port for the Chosŏn government's Left Naval Commandery. Waegyo was what Koreans called the base that Konishi Yukinaga (d. 1600) built in Sunch'ŏn in the second half of 1597. "Left" and "Right" indicate left and right as seen by the King of Chosŏn when sitting on the throne. The throne was placed so that north was directly behind the monarch and he faced south. The Left Naval Commandery thus was in eastern Chŏlla Province and eastern Kyŏngsang Province, and the Right Naval Commandery was in western Chŏlla Province and western Kyŏngsang Province.
39. Kang's second sister-in-law was the wife of his second elder brother, Chun. She was of the Haeju Ch'oe descent group (*Chinju Kang ssi sebo*, 1:20a).

40. The Herd Boy and the Weaving Maiden are legendary star-crossed lovers expelled from the celestial world for their love. They are allowed to meet once a year, on the seventh day of the seventh month; hence, rain symbolizes their tears on parting.
41. The two brothers are Chun and Hwan. The father-in-law may be Kim Pong (d.u.), who was the father of Kang's first wife. Kang mentions Pong by name in "A Memorial Sent from Captivity." See chapter 4, note 10.
42. Kang's collected writings, *Suŭn chip*, includes three undated poems sent to Hong Kunok (Kang, *Suŭn chip*, in *Han'guk munjip ch'onggan*, vol. 73, 1:30b–31a, 1:35b, and 1:38b). Hong Kunok lived in Kŭmsan, in Chŏlla Province (Yi U, "Che Ssanggyejŏng," in Yi U, *Oksan sigo*, in *Han'guk munjip ch'onggan*, vol. 53, 22:27b–28a).
43. Toyotomi Hideyoshi (1537–98) unified Japan in 1590 and launched the invasion of Chosŏn in the fourth month of 1592. Following his death in the eighth month of 1598, the Japanese army retreated from Chosŏn. For Hideyoshi's biography in English, see Berry, *Hideyoshi*.
44. The Japanese word translated here as Retired Imperial Regent is *taikō*.
45. One Korean (and Chinese) *ri* was approximately .31 mile.
46. The year 1598 was the twenty-sixth year of the Wanli Emperor's reign (1563–1620, r. 1572–1620). In this period, time was inscribed in the public space in Chosŏn according to Ming reign names. This Chinese ruler is also known as Emperor Shenzong.
47. *The Annual Festivities and Celebrations of the Chu* describes the annual festivities of the mid–Yangzi River region that had belonged to the state of Chu during the Spring and Autumn period (770–476 B.C.E.). The book, originally compiled by Zong Lin, was expanded with commentaries by Du Gongzhan in the early seventh century. The state of Chu was regarded as a place of decorum and refinement, and here Kang is using this to contrast appearance and meaning.
48. Kang Hwan (1565–1638) was Hang's third elder brother. The *Chinju Kang ssi sebo* lists three sons but no daughters for him. He too studied under Yi I (1:20a–b). His wife was from the Kwangsan Kim descent group (*Kwangsan Kim ssi chokpo*, 1:23a–b).
49. It is not clear who Sandu was. He seems to have been someone familiar to Kang.
50. Sō Yoshitoshi (1568–1615) led Tsushima from 1579, when he succeeded to the family headship. He, Konishi Yukinaga, and Shimai Sōshitsu (1539–1615) were deeply involved in the communication between Hideyoshi and King Sŏnjo from 1586 until the eve of invasion. He served in the First Division under Yukinaga. Together with the monk Keitetsu Genso (1537–1611), who had visited Chosŏn

three times as an envoy, he guided the First Division from Pusan to the capital. After the war, he promoted the restoration of diplomatic relations between the new government in Edo and the Chosŏn court.
51. Shussekiji, said to have been founded in the early eighth century, is a Shingon temple in today's Ehime Prefecture. Tōdō Takatora was a devout follower of this form of Buddhism. A Koryŏ-period Korean bell there is said to have been brought from Chosŏn by Takatora (*Ehime-ken shi*, 519–20). "Kinzan" was the mountain name for this temple.
52. The text identifies the title as *Danjō*, or Censor. This term refers to an office in the Board of Censors (J. *Danjōdai*) and may indicate that the monk, prior to taking the tonsure, had been a samurai and had received this Board of Censors title.
53. The place name Itajima was changed to Uwajima after Takatora received lands on the island of Shikoku in 1595.
54. The Temple of Royal Ancestors (K. *Chongmyo*), a state ritual site, was (and is) located east of Kyŏngbok Palace. Japanese soldiers destroyed much of this structure where the spirit tablets of Chosŏn's kings were kept. The facility was rebuilt after the war. Kang mentions the destruction of royal tombs again in chapter 4.
55. Hakuun Kōsetsu was the Buddhist name of Tōdō Torataka (d. 1599).
56. This refers to a man of China's Han dynasty (202 B.C.E.–220) who was taken captive but transformed himself into a crane by relying on Daoist magic. After returning to his hometown, he perched on a signpost on a road and declared that he had returned home after 1,000 years.
57. Kosŏng County was in southern Kyŏngsang Province. Many sea battles were waged off its coast during the Imjin War.
58. In this allusion, Kang refers to Japan.
59. The Yellow Emperor was one of the legendary rulers of China. He carried out a war as a punitive attack on several cruel men.
60. The reference is to an episode during the reign of the First Emperor of Qin (Shi Huangdi; r. 221–209 B.C.E.) in which the master of Daoist methods Xu Fu, with 500 each of young virgin males and females, sailed toward an island in the Eastern Sea.
61. This refers to a feast in which Yue Fei (1104–42), a patriotic general of Southern Song China, drank heavily. The feast occurred when he was about to capture Kaifeng, the old capital of Northern Song China, which had been taken by the Jurchen. He swore that he would capture the capital and bring back the Song emperor, who had been taken by the Jurchen as a captive. Because of the machinations of Qin Kuai, this did not happen. Here, then, "drink heavily" (K.

t'ongŭm) refers to the resolve to reclaim what one has lost, especially the hope of seeing your old ruler.

62. This may be a reference to one of the two Korean navy ships Japanese put on display in Osaka. See Hawley, *The Imjin War*, 546.
63. A wooden figure refers to a wanderer in a foreign land.
64. Kang Sajun (d.u.), identified as a student (K. *kyosaeng*), returned to Chosŏn in 1601, as did Yŏ Suhŭi (d.u.), Kang Ch'ŏnch'u (d.u.), and others (*Sŏnjo sillok*, 136:21b–23b [1601.4.25], 138:10b–11a [1601.6.11]).
65. Chŏng Ch'angse (d.u.) had been taken to Japan sometime prior to the arrival of the Korean officials who accompanied the Chinese embassy to the Kyoto area in the summer of 1596. He met Vice Envoy Pak Hongjang (1558–1598) in Sakai in the autumn of that year (Pak Hongjang, *Tongsarok*, 198 [1596.9.5]).
66. In a letter to the Korean captive Chŏng Hŭidŭk (d.u.), the captive Im Tŭkche (d.u.) wrote that Sŏ Kyŏngbong (d.u.) and Sŏ Kyŏngch'un (d.u.) (as well as Kang Hang and Kim Pong) were living in the Japanese capital. As Sŏ Kyŏngbong and Sŏ Kyŏngch'un share the same first character (K. *kyŏng* 慶) in their given names, they may have been brothers (Chŏng Hŭidŭk, *Haesangnok*, 8:20a).
67. This allusion refers to Lu Zhonglian (see note 33).
68. This allusion refers to Bo Yi (see note 34).
69. The original text has "arctic land," which refers to an area where no plants or trees grow. This is where Su Wu, captured by the Xiongnu, spent years tending sheep. Kang is comparing himself to Su Wu here.
70. "Green Hills" (K. *Ch'ŏnggu*) refers to Chosŏn.
71. Tansoksa, a Sŏn (Zen) temple no longer standing, was on Mount Chiri, in Chinju County, Kyŏngsang Province (*Sejong sillok chiriji*, 150:28b; *Sinjŭng Tongguk yŏji sŭngnam*, 30:15a–b).
72. T'ongjŏng was the pen name of Kang Hoebaek (1357–1402). He served in several posts in the Koryŏ and Chosŏn governments. He is said to have planted a tree at Tansoksa while studying for the Koryŏ government's higher civil service examination there. The tree probably was named after Kang received appointment in 1391 as Assistant Executive in Letters (*Chŏngdang munhak*) (Boku Shōmei, *Kanyōroku*, 276, n. 2; *Chinju Kang ssi sebo*, 1:4a–5a; *T'aejong sillok*, 4:24b [1402.11.19]).
73. Kim Hŭngdal (d.u.) and Kim Hŭngmae (d.u.) were great-grandsons of Kim Sik (1482–1520). They were the second and third sons of Kim Ch'u, who was a younger brother of Kim Kwŏn (1549–1622). In the eighth month of 1596, Hŭngmae met Korean officials in Sakai who had followed the Chinese embassy to Japan. He told them that his younger brother Hŭngdal was living in

Aki Province, in western Honshu. It is not clear whether Hŭngmae returned to Chosŏn with these officials, but, beyond their parentage, the genealogy cited here presents no further biographical information for either son (*Ch'ŏngp'ung Kim ssi sebo*, 2B:24a; Hwang Sin, *Ilbon wanghwan ilgi*, 8:47).

74. Headmaster (K. *Taesasŏng*) was the third ranking post in the State Academy (K. *Sŏnggyun'gwan*), where those who had passed the Chosŏn government's classics licentiate examination and the literary licentiate examination (together called *sama*, separately *saengwŏn* and *chinsa*, respectively) studied for the higher civil service examination. This post was at the senior third grade.

75. Kim Sik gained a reputation for consummate scholarship. A member of the Ch'ŏngp'ung Kim descent group, he passed the higher civil service examination in 1519. That is, he passed the controversial recommendation examination. The purge referred to here also occurred in 1519. Many young, ideological scholar-officials who had gained King Chungjong's confidence, including Cho Kwangjo (1482–1519) and Kim Sik, were purged. In Korean history, this is viewed as a classic case of a struggle between newly rising, ideologically oriented scholars and meritorious officials with their entrenched power. Cho Kwangjo and other officials were to gain lasting fame as the embodiment of principled Confucian scholars. See Wagner, *The Literati Purges*, for more on the purge and Kim Sik.

76. Kim Kwŏn was one of the officials who assisted Kwanghae, then the Crown Prince, during the Imjin War, for which he was rewarded with ennoblement as Lord of Ch'ŏngp'ung. He passed the higher civil service examination in 1580 (*Ch'ŏngp'ung Kim ssi sebo*, 2B:23b–24a).

77. Chu and Yan were states during the Warring States period in China.

78. This allusion refers to an improbable turn of events, such as the growth of a horn on a horse's head. In other words, there will be no miracle that will enable the captives to return home.

79. Tonsured Prince Kōi (1576–1620) was not the uncle of Emperor Go-Yōzei (1571–1617, r. 1586–1611). Rather, he was a younger brother of Go-Yōzei (Boku Shōmei, *Kanyōroku*, 226, n. 9). The *hosshinnō*, or tonsured prince, system, in which sons of the emperor were sent to temples to serve as monks, began in 1099. Kōi's grandfather was an emperor, but his father did not become emperor, suggesting that this system had expanded to accept additional candidates. This temple was known as the Daibutsu temple because Hideyoshi had ordered that a large statue of the Buddha be built there, but its name is Hōkōji.

80. The location of the "northern suburb" is unclear. Kang, living in Fushimi at this time, may have thought that Hideyoshi was buried in the northern part of the city. However, Hideyoshi was not buried in the northern part of Kyoto proper;

the mausoleum in which he was interred in the fourth month of 1599 was in the city's southeast.

81. Nanka Genkō (1538–1604) became a Rinzai Zen monk. He was an adviser to Oda Nobunaga (1534–82), and in 1590 he accepted Hideyoshi's conversion to the Buddhist faith. The next year he became the first abbot of Shōunji temple, which Hideyoshi established in Kyoto in 1591 as the memorial temple for his recently deceased son Tsurumatsu (1589–91). Genkō also served as the founding abbot for two temples established at Myōshinji, in Kyoto, by veterans of the war in Chosŏn. Further, he wrote the commemoration for a portrait of Hideyoshi as the Toyokuni Daimyōjin (Magnificent Deity of the Land of Plenty) seated in the Toyokuni Shrine. This portrait was placed in the shrine after Hideyoshi's death.

82. "Myōsuin Chief Seat [Sō]shun" refers to Fujiwara Seika (1561–1619), with whom Kang spent much time while held in Fushimi. Myōsuin and Sōshun were Buddhist names by which Kang knew him. Seika studied Zen Buddhism at Shōkokuji, the fourth-ranking of the eleven Gozan (Five Mountains) Rinzai Zen temples in Kyoto, but left around 1590. Chief Seat (J. *shuso*) was a high-ranking position in the Gozan temples.

83. Sakai was an important trade port in the Hyōgo area, south of Kyoto and near Osaka. Merchants there handled much of the international trade conducted from central Japan. Kang is incorrect regarding Mao Guoke's reason for being in Japan. Mao had been captured during the Chinese army's attack on Shimazu Yoshihiro's (1535–1619) fort at Sach'ŏn in 1598. In 1600, Tokugawa Ieyasu ordered Yoshihiro to repatriate Mao to China and to send a letter to the Ming China government "proposing that official trade between Japan and China be restarted." A former Korean captive in Japan reported seeing Mao in Karatsu, in northwest Kyushu, in the sixth month of 1599 (Watanabe, "An International Maritime Trader—Torihara Sōan"; Chŏng Hŭidŭk, *Haesangnok*, 48b–49a; *Sŏnjo sillok*, 124:5a–b [1600.4.10]; *Sŏnjo sillok*, 123:6b–7a [1600.3.10]).

84. Tokugawa Ieyasu (1543–1616) established a new government in Edo in 1603, after victory at the Battle of Sekigahara in 1600. Based in eastern Japan in the 1590s, he was one of the most powerful men in Japan, and he did not send troops to Chosŏn. Hideyoshi selected Ieyasu as one of the five elders (J. *go tairō*) to serve as the guardians of his young son, Hideyori.

85. Kako Sōryū was from the same area as Fujiwara Seika and Akamatsu Hiromichi (1562–1600), and maintained a good relationship with Seika (Abe Yoshio, *Nihon shushigaku to Chōsen*, 88). A written conversation (K. *p'ildam*, J. *hitsudan*) in literary Chinese between Kang and Seika, dated to 1598, is extant in a handwrit-

ten reproduction. This conversation is also recorded in Seika's collected works ("Fujiwara Seika—Kang Hang hitsudan," in Tenri daigaku fuzoku Tenri toshokan, ed., *Chōsen tsūshinshi to Edo jidai no hitobito*, photograph 1; Fujiwara Seika, *Fujiwara Seika shū*, 2:369–70).

2. An Exhortation to Koreans Still Held Prisoner in Japan

1. *The Record of a Shepherd* has "Zou and Lu" 鄒魯. Zou refers to the home state of Mencius; Lu was the home state of Confucius.
2. Kings Yu, Tang, Wen, and Wu, and the Duke of Zhou are all sage-kings revered in the Confucian tradition.
3. "Pervasive abundance" refers to *feng* 豊, the fifty-fifth hexagram in *Book of Changes* (*Yijing*). See *Zhouyi zhengyi*, 67c–68b. For a translation into English, see Baynes, *The I Ching; or Book of Changes*, 227–30. "Great joy" refers to *yu* 豫, the sixteenth hexagram. See *Zhouyi zhengyi*, 31b–32b; *The I Ching*, 70–74. "Peace and harmony" refers to *tai* 泰, the eleventh hexagram. See *Zhouyi zhengyi*, 28a–29a; *The I Ching*, 49–54. "Stagnation and obstruction" refers to *pi* 否, the twelfth hexagram. See *Zhouyi zhengyi*, 29a–29b; *The I Ching*, 54–58.
4. Yan Shigu (581–645) served as an official in the Sui government but resigned from that post and moved to Chang'an. In the early Tang period he again held a government post, and from 630 he was engaged in scholarship at imperial command.
5. Liu Zongyuan (773–819) passed the Tang civil service examination in 793. During his career he was active as a government official and a scholar.
6. The reference here is to a pigeon that tumbles over and over backward in flight.
7. The phrase here, which symbolizes an ignorantly futile audacity in resisting a huge force, is from *Zhuangzi*. See *Zhuangzi jiao quan*, 1:439. For an English translation, see Watson, *The Complete Works of Chuang Tzu*, 133.
8. This phrase appears in "Huangyi" in the Daya section of *Book of Poetry* (*Shijing*). The entry states that the people of Mi were arrogant and thus dared to resist a great state by attacking Yuan, to advance to Gong. King Wen became angry and attacked and destroyed the Mi. See *Mao shi zhengyi*, 519a–521b. This refers to the Japanese attacking Chosŏn in order to invade Ming China.
9. This phrase appears in the "Xi gong" chapter of *Zuo zhuan*. The state of Yu was located between the states of Jin and Guo. Saying that it wanted to attack Guo and only borrow from Yu the path there, Jin took Guo, but on the way back also destroyed Yu. See "Xi gong," in *Chunqiu zhengyi*, 1791b. This also refers to the

Japanese plan of conquering Ming China by going through Chosŏn, but also destroying Chosŏn.

10. The Temple of Grain: *Sajikdan*. This state ritual site was (and is) west of Kyŏngbok Palace.

11. Xuanhe was the reign title of Emperor Huizong (1082–1135, r. 1100–26), the last emperor of Northern Song China. He was captured by the Jurchen in 1127 and spent his last years as their prisoner in northern Manchuria. This phrase refers to an anecdote about his exile: he met someone who still wore the clothes of the era when he was emperor as a sign of loyalty to him.

12. King Che of Wei was confined in the state of Wu for a time. Upon being released and returning home, he spoke in the dialect of Wu.

13. Zhongyong was a son of King Tai of Zhou. He and his brother Taibai refused the throne and went to the state of Wu, adopting its customs of cutting the hair and tattooing the body.

14. The Chu prisoner refers to Zhou Yi of Chu, who spent long years as a captive in Jin. Zhou Yi thought that it was not right just to talk about being a former captive. He tried to kill his captor but was unsuccessful. See "Zhou Yi zhuan," in *Jinshu*, 3:1850–53.

15. This refers to Weizi's statement in *Book of History* (*Shujing*): "Even if Shang is destroyed, I cannot become someone else's official or servant" (*Shangshu zhengyi*, 178a).

16. Li Ling (d. 74 B.C.E.), a famous Han general, was defeated by the Xiongnu and accepted their offer of wealth and glory for his transfer of loyalty. For details, see "Li Guang Su Jian zhuan," *juan* 54 of *Hanshu*, 3:2459–70.

17. Kang passed the higher civil service examination in 1593.

18. Kang is freely quoting from a famous phrase of Mencius: "Fish is what I want; the bear's palm is also what I want. If I cannot have both, I would rather take the bear's palm than the fish. Life is what I want; dutifulness is also what I want. If I cannot have both, I would rather take dutifulness than life" (Gaoji I:10:1, in *Mengzi zhushu*, 2752a). For an English translation, see Lau, *Mencius*, 166.

19. This refers to Zu Ti of Jin, who, beating the boat on which he was crossing a river, swore that he would not cross again until the enemy was vanquished. See "Zu Ti zhuan," in *Jinshu*, 2:1693–1702, esp. 1695.

20. This refers to a well-known failed assassin. Yu Rang was well treated by Zhi Bo, but Zhi Bo was killed by Zhao Meng (Zhao Xiangzi). Yu Rang wanted to take revenge but was discovered and killed by Zhao. See "Cige liezhuan," in Sima Qian, *Shiji*, 2519–22.

21. This refers to Zhang Liang's failed attempt to assassinate Shi Huangdi, the First

Emperor of Qin. Zhang, however, assisted Liu Bang to found Han China ("Liu hou shi jia," in *Shiji*, 2033–35).

22. Zhu Xu of Jin (the governor of Xiangyang) was captured by an invading army, but when he shouted that his captor's army was already defeated, it lowered morale, and he was able to return home. See his biography in *Jinshu*, 2132–36.

23. The only reference to the Xia army found in *Book of History* is in connection with its defeat by the Tang. The meaning of the reference in this context is unclear. See *Shangshu zhengyi*, 160a.

24. This refers to the jewel of Zhao. The King of Qin wanted this jewel, and he pledged fifteen towns that belonged to him in exchange for it. Worried that he would not deliver on his promise, the King of Zhao consulted Lian Polin. Lian replied that if the King of Qin did not give up the fifteen towns, he would bring back the jewel intact ("Lian Polin Xiangru liezhuan," in Sima Qian, *Shiji*, 2439–52).

25. This is a reference to Su Wu, who, captured by the Xiongnu, remained faithful to the Han ("Li Guang Su Jian zhuan," *juan* 54 of *Hanshu*, 3:2459–70).

26. The Xiongnu told Su Wu that only if a ram were to give birth would he be released ("Li Guang Su Jian zhuan," *juan* 54 of *Hanshu*, 3:2459–70).

27. Wei Lu was a Han official who, upon capture by the Xiongnu, pledged loyalty to them and therefore was showered with riches. He was sent to Su Wu to ask him to do the same, but Su reprimanded him ("Li Guang Su Jian zhuan," *juan* 54 of *Hanshu*, 3:2459–70).

28. This is an allusion to an edict that the Tang China emperor Dezong (742–805, r. 779–805) issued in 784. When Zhu Ci rebelled, Dezong took refuge at Fengtian, and Zhu put Fengtian under siege for months. Dezong sent out an edict in which he blamed himself and pardoned those who had surrendered to Zhu Ci. This turned the people around to Dezong (*Jiu Tangshu*, 339–40). What Kang is in fact referring to is King Sŏnjo's edicts in which the king blamed himself for the troubles of Chosŏn (O Hŭimun, *Swaemirok*, 1:20–21).

29. This is an allusion to the Tang China emperor Taizong (599–649, r. 626–649), but it refers to King Sŏnjo.

30. This refers to an event concerning the Lu family of Han. After Empress Lu died, her brothers, hoping to continue the family's power, wanted to rebel against the Han. A Han general asked those who supported the Lu family to bare their right shoulder and those who supported the Liu house to bare their left shoulder. All bared their left shoulder, and so the army could kill everyone in the Lu family. See "Lu Tai hou benji," in Sima Qian, *Shiji*, 393–412.

31. This statement is from *Lunyu* 14.17. The full passage reads, "If it weren't for him,

we'd still let our hair hang loose and button our robes to the left like barbarians" (Confucius, *The Analects*, 158).
32. Bo Yi was a famous loyalist of Shang ("Bo Yi liezhuan," in Sima Qian, *Shiji*, 2121–30).
33. The suicide attempt was a protest against the Qin emperor ("Lu Zhonglian liezhuan," in Sima Qian, *Shiji*, 2459–80).

3. A Report to the Royal Secretariat on Japanese Social Practices

1. For Kobayakawa Hideaki (1582–1602), see note 68 in chapter 4, appendix 1.
2. For Maeda Toshinaga (1562–1614), see note 11 in chapter 4, appendix 3.
3. For Ukita Hideie (1572–1655), see note 32 in chapter 4, appendix 1.
4. Yūki Hideyasu (1574–1607) was the second son of Ieyasu. For more information, see note 4 in chapter 4, appendix 3.
5. Kang reached Pusan on 1600.5.19. He then sent a document addressed to the Royal Secretariat. The Chosŏn court treated it as a "memorial submitted as a secret document." Much of his discussion about the possibility of another invasion from Japan is quoted in the *Veritable Records* (*Sŏnjo sillok*, 126:4a–b [1600.6.9]). For Rian, see note 83 in chapter 4, appendix 3.
6. For Hosokawa Tadaoki (1563–1645), see note 38 in chapter 4, appendix 1.
7. Kinoshita Katsutoshi (1569–1649) and Kobayakawa Hideaki (1582–1602) were brothers, Katsutoshi being the eldest son and Hideaki the fifth son of Kinoshita Iesada (1543–1608). Their father was the elder brother of Hideyoshi's wife, the Kita no mandokoro Nene (1547–1624). For more regarding Katsutoshi, see note 23 in chapter 4, appendix 3.
8. Hideyoshi is reported to have said that he should divide Japan into five regions and entrust four of them to Toyotomi Hidetsugu (1568–95), who was the Imperial Regent (J. *Kanpaku*) at this time (Yamashina, *Tokitsune-kyō ki*, 5:367).
9. Sagain Yoichi was Suminokura Soan (1571–1632). He was the first son of Suminokura Ryōi (1554–1614), who was the elder brother of the doctor Yoshida Ian. Soan studied under Fujiwara Seika and was deeply involved in the printing industry in Kyoto in the late sixteenth and early seventeenth centuries. "Soan" and "Ryōi" were Buddhist names of these two men; "Saga" referred to the area in Kyoto where Soan lived. (Boku Shōmei, *Kanyōroku*, 210, n. 5; "Uda Minamotoshi Yoshida," in *Kanei shoka keizu den*, 15:158; Morikawa, "Shoki kokatsuji-ban no inkōsha ni tsuite," 148–75). Portions of Sagain Yoichi's comments about the possibility of another Japanese invasion of Chosŏn were also included in the *Veritable Records* entry discussed in note 5.

10. For Mōri Terumoto (1553–1625), see note 30 in chapter 4, appendix 1.
11. For Ankokuji Ekei (1539?–1600), see note 81 in chapter 4, appendix 1.
12. Portions of Kang's comments about Ankokuji Ekei and his closing comment were also included in the *Veritable Records* entry discussed in note 5.
13. Yanagawa Shigenobu (1539–1605) was a high-ranking official in Tsushima.
14. For Sō Yoshitoshi (1568–1615), see note 52 in chapter 4, appendix 3.
15. Yanagawa Shigenobu's statement that Japanese pirates did not attack sites in Kyŏngsang Province two centuries earlier is inaccurate. Japanese, including Tsushima islanders, frequently raided villages, storehouses, and other sites there from 1350 into the early fifteenth century.
16. The Board of Rites oversaw aspects of interaction with Japanese contacts, including documents, reception, entertainment, and trade. It required Japanese contacts to address their letters (K. *sŏgye*, J. *shokei*) to a specified official based upon administrative hierarchies in Japan and in the Board of Rites, as well as other factors. The Governor of Tsushima addressed his communications to and received communications from the Third Minister, whose post was at the senior third grade (*Sejo sillok*, 17:15b–18a [1459.8.23]).
17. "Hotta Oribe" is a mistake for Furuta Oribe (1543?–1615) (Boku Shōmei, *Kanyōroku*, 220, n. 1). Furuta was a retainer of Hideyoshi and became the leader of Japan's tea world after the death in 1591 of the famous tea master Sen no Rikyū (1522–91). He studied under Rikyū and developed the so-called daimyō tea. He also introduced Oribe ware, a type of pottery favoring imperfect shapes, for the tea ceremony.
18. *Book of Changes* is one of the Chinese classics. Kang assisted Seika in punctuating *Book of Changes* for Japanese readers (Ng, *The I ching in Tokugawa Thought and Culture*, 34).
19. Perhaps Kang inquired about Ian's knowledge of mathematics and astronomy in order to gather military-related data in Japan (Shimoura, *Yoshida—Suminokura-ke no kenkyū*, 36–38).
20. Huang Youxian may refer to Mōri Shigeyoshi (d.u.), a famous mathematician in Japan in the early seventeenth century. Some scholars believe rather that Mōri was born in Japan (Tamura and Shimoura, "Tenri-bon *Sanyōki* ni tsuite," 43–45; Smith and Mikami, *A History of Japanese Mathematics*, 32–36, 60).
21. The seven Chinese texts that form *Seven Military Classics* were brought together around 1078. In addition to becoming "the official textual foundation" for questions and answers relating to military issues on government examinations, these texts were read for military strategy and tactics (Sawyer and Sawyer, *The Seven Military Classics of Ancient China*, 1–2).
22. The characters for *yokomon*, or possibly *ōmon*, are 橫門. Considering the men-

tion of the placement of bamboo and a fan in the tearoom, this word may be an error for *tokonoma* 床の間, an alcove where such objects would be set. For a more detailed description of tea culture in the late sixteenth century, see Cooper, *João Rodrigues's Account of Sixteenth-Century Japan*, 155–58, 272–308.

23. This door may be the *nijiriguchi*, or the low, narrow entrance that Sen no Rikyū introduced into tea practice.
24. Ankokuji Ekei is an example of someone being known by a surname derived from a religious institution, in his case, Ankokuji temple.
25. For discussion of these temple posts see Collcutt, *Five Mountains*, 221–47.
26. Kong Anguo (d.u.) was a twelfth-generation descendant of Kongzi, or Confucius (Loewe, *A Biographical Dictionary of the Qin, Former Han, and Xin Periods [221 B.C.–A.D. 24]*, 206).
27. Zheng Xuan (127–200) wrote a commentary on *Rites of Zhou* (C. *Zhou li*), and "also produced major commentaries and editorial work for the *Ritual*, for *Analects*, *Mencius*, the *Book of Changes*, the *Classic of Poetry* and the *Classic of History*" (de Crespigny, *A Biographical Dictionary of Later Han to the Three Kingdoms [23–220 A.D.]*, 1126–28).
28. Huian was the pen name (C. *hao*) of Zhu Xi (1130–1200).
29. For Shōkōin Tonsured Prince Kōi, see note 77 in chapter 1. This reference to Kōi includes the term "Shōkōin," which was a Buddhist name for the monk and which was not included in the first reference to Kōi.
30. Seishō Shōtai (1548–1608) was a Rinzai Zen monk. He served as Abbot of Shōkokuji temple from 1584 and as manager of the construction of the Daibutsu (The Great Buddha) statue at Hōkōji temple in Kyoto. Hideyoshi entrusted him with writing state letters to Ming China and other diplomatic duties during the war in Chosŏn (Kitajima, "Toyotomi seiken no Chōsen shinryaku to Gozan sō," 182–96).
31. Sanchōrō Hayashi Razan (1583–1657) was a young scholar at this time (Boku Shōmei, *Kanyōroku*, 226, n. 11). The moniker "*Sanchōrō*" would have been a public recognition of Razan's abilities, for he was only eighteen years old in 1600. Razan studied as a teenager at Kenninji temple, another Rinzai Zen temple in Kyoto, but he left before taking the tonsure and becoming a monk. He subsequently became interested in the writings of Zhu Xi, and in 1600 he gave a public lecture. He met Seika in 1604, and Seika introduced him to Ieyasu the following year. Razan worked for the Edo government for much of his career. For the public lecture, see "Hayashi Razan shū furoku," in Kyōto shisekikai, *Hayashi Razan shishū*, 2:3–4.
32. Tetchōrō Ikyō Eitetsu (d. 1603) was a Rinzai Zen monk and abbot of Tōfukuji temple, a Gozan temple in Kyoto. Together with Seishō Shōtai and a third Rinzai

Zen monk from Kyoto (Genho Raisan), he arrived at the invasion headquarters in Nagoya on 1592.4.23. They assisted Hideyoshi with diplomatic matters there (Kitajima, "Toyotomi seiken no Chōsen shinryaku to Gozan sō," 182–96). He painted a portrait of the late Hideyoshi as the Toyokuni Daimyōjin, that is, as a Shinto deity.

33. Kanshitsu Sanyō (1548–1612) was more commonly known as Kanshitsu Genkitsu. Kanshitsu was a Rinzai Zen monk who studied at the Ashikaga Gakkō, an academy in the Kantō area, in the mid-1570s. He became the academy's director in 1587. This school taught Confucian texts and, especially in the sixteenth century, divination. Kanshitsu returned to Kyoto upon the invitation of Toyotomi Hidetsugu and, after Hidetsugu's death in 1595, served Ieyasu. As a practitioner of military divination, "his specialty was the field of battle." See Boku Shōmei, *Kanyōroku*, 226, n. 13; Kawase, *Zōho shintei Ashikaga Gakkō no kenkyū*, 103–18; Butler, "The Way of Yin and Yang," 199–201; Butler, *Emperor and Aristocracy in Japan, 1467–1680*, 144.
34. A copy of *Confucius's Family Teachings* that was printed in Fushimi in 1599 bears a postscript by Kanshitsu Genkitsu (Kawase, *Zōho shintei Ashikaga Gakkō no kenkyū*, 107).
35. The Amaterasu Shrine is the Inner Shrine, or the Naikū, at Ise Shrine, in today's Mie Prefecture.
36. The Kasuga *Daimyōjin* was a syncretic deity, combining associations of five Shinto *kami* deities from Kasuga Shrine and five Buddhist gods from Kōfukuji temple, both in Nara. It protected the Yamato Province area, which included Kyoto and Nara.
37. The character 御 is read most commonly in Japanese as *o, on, go, gyo*, and *mi*. It may be translated as "honorable."
38. Boku Shōmei suggests that Kang is being derisive here, as his description does not fit Japanese customs (*Kanyōroku*, 227, n. 20).
39. For Shimazu Yoshihiro (1535–1619), see note 41 in chapter 4, appendix 1, and chapter 4, appendix 3.
40. This punishment was called *hwan'gwae* in Korean.
41. "Ch'ŏnch'uk," here in the Korean reading, is an ancient Buddhist term for India.
42. Having taken Nagasaki away from the Jesuits after conquering Kyushu in 1587 and claiming Nagasaki as state land, Hideyoshi appointed Nabeshima Naoshige as Deputy (J. *daikan*) for the city. One of the duties of this central government post was to manage trade. The Nabeshima were retainers of the Ryūzōji family.
43. Terazawa Masanari (1563–1633) was more commonly known as Terazawa Hirotaka, and also as Terazawa Sadamasa. Hideyoshi appointed him Nagasaki Commissioner (J. *Nagasaki bugyō*) in 1588. Historians disagree whether Terazawa

continued in that position until 1602 or became Nagasaki Deputy in 1592. How the Nagasaki Commissioner (and/or the Nagasaki Deputy) was involved in Japanese trade with the Chosŏn government is unclear. Regardless, holding lands north of the city and assigned duties related to the war in Chosŏn, Terazawa did not reside in Nagasaki. He remained in Nagoya in northern Kyushu during the first invasion (*Sengoku bushō kassen jiten*, 490–91; Suzuki, *Nagasaki bugyō no kenkyū*, 4–8). Also see note 66 in chapter 4, appendix 1.

44. Hideyoshi received an elephant in 1597 from a Spanish ambassador sent from Manila (Cooper, *They Came to Japan*, 113–14). A camel, other animals, and a peacock may be seen in the folding screen preserved at the National Museum of Ancient Art (Museu Nacional de Art e Antiga) in Lisbon (Sakamoto et al., *Nanban byōbu shūsei*, 72–73).

45. "Yŏngnam" is a traditional reference to Kyŏngsang Province.

46. To be specific, this Nagoya was in Hizen Province (today, in Saga Prefecture) in Kyushu. The larger city also called Nagoya but written with different characters is east of Kyoto and was founded in 1610.

47. In the middle of the intercalary seventh month in 1596, Kyoto residents found hairlike objects that had fallen from the sky. The Buddhist monk Gien (1558–1626) and the Shinto priest Bonshun thought they resembled horse hair. Gien noted that most were white or black, and some were red. Ōtsuki Takasuke found blue hair too, and commented that these objects "weigh less than white human hair." Their sightings followed the devastating earthquake in the intercalary seventh month of 1596 (Boku Shōmei, *Kanyōroku*, 233, n. 1; Gien, *Gien jugō nikki*, 1:62 [1596 (Bunroku 5).intercalary 7.14); Bonshun, *Shun kyūki*, 1:52 (1596 [Bunroku 5].intercalary 7.15); Ōtsuki, *Sadaishi Takasuke ki*, 727 (1596 [Bunroku 5].intercalary 7.16).

48. Ōta Kazuyoshi (d. 1613) supported Hideyoshi and fought in Chosŏn.

49. For Mashita Nagamori, see note 35 in chapter 4, appendix 1.

50. For the locations of mansions damaged in this fire, see Yamada Kunikazu's mapping of Fushimi Castle and the daimyō residences in Fushimi in "Fushimi-jō to sono jōkamachi no fukugen."

51. For Miyabe Nagahiro (1581–1635), see note 54 in chapter 4, appendix 1.

4. A Memorial Sent from Captivity

1. King Sŏnjo received an honorary title consisting of two pairs of two characters each in 1590 (*Sŏnjo sillok*, 24:2b [1590.2.11]). During the Chosŏn period, kings and queens received various honorary titles. The titles were presented posthu-

mously, but from the sixteenth century on they were presented while the monarchs were still alive. Kang's court title, Sŏnmurang, was of the junior sixth rank.
2. This was Commander Yang Yuan of the Ming army.
3. The Japanese army took Namwŏn on the eighteenth day of the eighth month in 1597. Namwŏn escaped being taken by the Japanese during the first invasion, but the eventual Japanese capture of the city is viewed as one of the most brutal of the war. Yang Yuan escaped Namwŏn, but only ten of his several thousand soldiers survived (Sŏnjo sillok, 91:22a–b [1597.8.18]; Sŏnjo sillok, 91:22b–23b [1597.8.18]; Yu Sŏngnyong, The Book of Corrections, 209–12).
4. Kim Sangjun (1561–1635), a government official, was also known for his calligraphy. Of the Andong Kim descent group, he passed the higher civil service examination in 1590.
5. The "Righteous Army" arose in great numbers in 1592, soon after the Japanese army invaded Chosŏn in the fourth month, but its activities were much curtailed after the Chinese army arrived in late 1592.
6. During the second invasion, the Righteous Army's actions were, relatively speaking, insignificant.
7. During the Imjin War, as a way of collecting food for the army, the government sold "empty official appointments" (K. kongmyŏngch'ŏp) in exchange for a certain amount of grain. Those who received the appointment had no real duty or power but enjoyed the prestige of an official appointment for one generation.
8. Muan County was in southwestern Chŏlla Province.
9. Sunch'ŏn County was in southern Chŏlla Province. The Left Province Navy Commander (K. Sugun chŏltosa, senior third grade) and his headquarters were located there.
10. Kim Pong (d.u.) was the father of Hang's first wife, who died in 1587. He belonged to the Chinju Kim descent group. According to a genealogy of this descent group, after being captured and taken to Japan, he returned to Chosŏn on 1600.4.8 (Chinju Kang ssi sebo, 1:20b–21b; Chinju Kim ssi taedongbo, 1:29).
11. An'gol Port was in Ungch'ŏn County, on the southern coast of Kyŏngsang Province. When the area was controlled by the Chosŏn government, a Navy Sub-area Commander (K. Manho, junior fourth grade) and navy ships and sailors assigned to the port guarded it and the nearby coast (Sinjŭng Tongguk yŏji sŭngnam, 32:50a).
12. Akamagaseki is an earlier name for present-day Shimonoseki.
13. Iyo Province, one of the four provinces in Shikoku, was on the island's west coast.
14. Here, "three castle towns" refers to the three districts in Iyo Province that

Hideyoshi granted to Takatora in 1595 (Ueno-shi kobunken kankōkai, *Kōzan-kō jitsuroku*, 1:79).

15. Bungo Province, one of the nine provinces in Kyushu, was in the northern half of the island, on the east coast. It thus faced Shikoku to the west.
16. This refers to an anecdote about a person who, on his deathbed, asked his son not to place his body in the main hall but in a side room, for his sin of not having been able to remonstrate with his king about a wrongful appointment. Upon hearing this, his lord apparently corrected the improper appointment and employed the right person.
17. Ulsan is a port city on the southeast coast of today's South Kyŏngsang Province. The Korean government permitted Japanese to trade and to reside at the nearby port of Yŏm from 1426 to 1510. Yŏm was also the site of a navy base administered by a Navy Sub-area Commander. At the time of the 1592 invasion, the headquarters of the Left Province Army Commander (K. *Ch'wado Pyŏngma chŏltosa*) was in Ulsan County (*Sinjŭng Tongguk yŏji sŭngnam*, 22:3b–4a).
18. Kwŏn Yul (1537–99), of the Andong Kwŏn descent group, was a civil official who won many battles against the Japanese during the Imjin War. The Battle of Haengju in which he, leading 2,800 soldiers, defeated a Japanese army of 30,000 on 1593.2.2 is particularly famous. There, Kwŏn repeated his preferred strategy of fighting the Japanese from within forts rather than in open fields. He became Supreme Field Commander (K. *Towŏnsu*), the head of the Korean military, in the sixth month of 1596. Kwŏn passed the higher civil service examination in 1582. After his death, he was honored as a Merit Subject of the First Class (Hawley, *The Imjin War*, 323–27; *Sŏnjo sillok*, 39:12b [1598.6.7]; *Andong Kwŏn ssi sebo*, 7:25a–28a).
19. In the Japanese calendar, which differed from the Korean calendar, Hideyoshi passed away on the eighteenth day of the eighth month of 1598.
20. The Portuguese cleric João Rodrigues, who lived in Japan for more than thirty years in the late sixteenth century and early seventeenth century, wrote, "Fushimi is two leagues from Miyako [Kyoto], and the intervening distance is completely taken up by the houses of the Miyako people, so that the two cities are just like one" (Cooper, *João Rodrigues's Account of Sixteenth-Century Japan*, 167).
21. Lu Zhonglian was a person of Qi during China's Warring States period (403–221 B.C.E.). He was so disturbed by the way Qin achieved ascendancy and unified China in 221 B.C.E. that he expressed a desire to go to the Eastern Sea to drown himself. See his biography, "Lu Zhonglian," in Sima Qian, *Shiji*, 3:2459–69).
22. This refers to the dynastic change from Shang to Zhou in 1122 B.C.E. It exempli-

fied the concept of the Mandate of Heaven (C. *tianming*, K. *ch'ŏnmyŏng*), showing that the lack of virtue would lead to loss of the Mandate, which would be transferred to a virtuous person who would begin a new dynasty. King Zhou of Shang and King Wu of Zhou exemplified, respectively, the bad last king who lost the Mandate and the virtuous founder of a new dynasty who received the Mandate. See "Great Declaration," in Waltham, *Shu Ching, Book of History*, 113–18. King Wu reigned from 1122 to 1115 B.C.E.

23. *Sŏnjo sillok*, 83:27a–b [1596.12.22]. The Chosŏn government appointed three officials to the senior sixth grade post of Assistant Section Chief (K. *Chwarang*). Kang had served earlier as Reference Consultant in the Office of Editorial Review, a post at the senior seventh grade (K. *Kyosŏgwan Paksa*) (*Sŏnjo sillok*, 66:13b–14a [1595.8.24]).

24. Wen Tianxiang (1236–83) was a scholar in Southern Song China. When the Mongols invaded China in 1275, he joined the army. He served as a high minister and led many battles, but eventually was captured and taken by the Mongols. Wen was imprisoned for three years, but he refused to work for the Mongols and was executed. Zhu Xu (d. 393) was a general in the Jin dynasty. This was a time of constant military strife, and he was captured and taken to a competing state. Through his steadfast loyalty, however, he helped his state win a battle and was able to return home. See his biography, "Zhu Xu," in *Jinshu*, 15:2132–36.

25. Japanese desecrated several tombs of Chosŏn kings, including Sŏnnŭng, the tomb of Sŏngjong (1457–94, r. 1469–94) and his queen, and Chŏngnŭng, the tomb of Chungjong (1488–1544, r. 1506–44) and his queen. These desecrations were regarded as the worst acts of humiliation inflicted upon the Chosŏn monarchy (*Sŏnjo sillok*, 37:17b [1593.4.13]). The Temple of Royal Ancestors (K. *Chongmyo*) was burned when the Japanese occupied Seoul on 1592.5.3. Angry Koreans, including slaves, burned many government buildings in Seoul after King Sŏnjo and his officials evacuated the capital the day before. It is not clear whether the Temple of Royal Ancestors, the symbol of the Chosŏn monarchy, was burned before the Japanese arrived or after, or by what process (*Sŏnjo sillok*, 26:4b–5a [1592.5.3]).

CHAPTER 4, APPENDIX 1. JAPANESE DAIMYO IN THE INVASION OF CHOSŎN AND OTHER INFORMATION

1. In Japanese mythology, Fukiaezu no mikoto is the grandson of Ninigi, who was the grandson of the Sun Goddess, Amaterasu Ōmikami (Aston, *Nihongi*, 95). Fukiaezu's youngest child was Jinmu, the mythological first Emperor of Japan.

2. *Tenson* is a Daoist term meaning "god of the heavens."
3. Tokugawa Ieyasu held a large swath of land in the Kantō area, in eastern Honshu.
4. For a discussion of Hideyoshi's land survey, see Berry, *Hideyoshi*, 111–26.
5. This statement that the Regent (J. *Sesshō*) was selected from among the Fujiwara, Tachibana, Minamoto, and Taira descent groups is incorrect. The Regent and the Imperial Regent were selected from the Fujiwara descent group. Kang likely gleaned this reference to the Fujiwara, Tachibana, Minamoto, and Taira descent groups from Song Lian's *Luoshan ji*. The order of the four surnames matches in both texts, as does the writing of "Fujiwara" with only the first character. Further, the reference to "the four great descent groups" appears in *Luoshan ji* (Song Lian, *Luoshan ji*, 4:13b).
6. Akechi Mitsuhide (1528–82) had supported Oda Nobunaga for several years, but he and his soldiers attacked Nobunaga at Honnōji temple in Kyoto early in the morning of 1582.6.2. Nobunaga fought back, but seeing that the intruders could not be repelled, committed suicide by *seppuku* as a fire raged around him. The current location of Honnōji is not where the temple was located in 1582.
7. The Chosŏn government called the individual in Japan who engaged in diplomatic relations with the King of Chosŏn the King of Japan. Both the Korean government and the Muromachi *bakufu* had entered into tributary relationships with the government of Ming China. As part of the investiture process by which the Emperor of Ming China recognized the ruler of a foreign country in this diplomatic relationship, he bestowed a seal upon his foreign counterpart. To the retired shogun Ashikaga Yoshimitsu he sent a seal bearing the text "seal of the King of Japan" (C. *Riben guowang zhi yin*, J. *Nihon kokuō no in*). The Ming emperor similarly recognized the ruler of Chosŏn as the King of Chosŏn (C. *Chaoxian guowang*, K. *Chosŏn kugwang*). The term "King of Japan" designated that individual, who was not the Emperor of Japan, as hierarchically inferior to the Emperor of Ming China.
8. Hideyoshi was referred to as "Taira no ason" in 1585 (Berry, *Hideyoshi*, 178). In the seventh month of that year he was appointed Imperial Regent by Emperor Ōgimachi (1517–93, r. 1557–86). He subsequently received the surname Toyotomi from this emperor in 1586.
9. Toyotomi Hidetsugu (1568–95) was born to Hideyoshi's sister Tomo (1534–1625) and Miyoshi Yoshifusa (1522–1600). Following his adoption by Hideyoshi and his recognition as heir, Hidetsugu received the title Imperial Regent in 1591. Subsequently, Hideyoshi became the Retired Imperial Regent (J. *Taikō*). Suspected of plotting against Japan's ruler, Hidetsugu killed himself in the seventh

month of 1595 upon Hideyoshi's command (Berry, *Hideyoshi*, 218–19; *Nihonshi jiten*, 849, 1324). For the secret report to Hideyoshi, see Fujita Tsuneharu, *Toyotomi Hidetsugu no kenkyū*, 170–75.

10. The arrival of Xu Fu at Kumano is one of many such legends of this Chinese man's appearance in Japan.
11. "Qin" and "Hata" are written with the same Chinese character.
12. "Hongwu" refers to the reign name for the first Emperor of Ming China, Taizu. The Hongwu period continued from his enthronement in 1368 until his death in 1398.
13. Zekkai Chūshin (1336–1405) was a Buddhist monk of the Rinzai Zen sect. He traveled to Ming China in 1368. However, his Buddhist name is incorrect in *The Record of a Shepherd*. The first character in the name given in the text is rather the fourth character in his full Buddhist name. And the third character, *chū*, is missing.
14. This translation is slightly modified from Keene, *Seeds in the Heart*, 1074.
15. Murai, "Poetry in Chinese as a Diplomatic Art in Premodern East Asia," 59.
16. Kōbō Daishi is the monk Kūkai (774–835). He studied in Tang China from 804 to 806. Upon returning to Japan, Kūkai founded the Shingon sect. In 921 he received the posthumous name Kōbō Daishi.
17. Sanuki Province was one of the four provinces in Shikoku.
18. There is no evidence that Kūkai visited India, the birthplace of Buddhism. Such a statement may be found, though, in the map of Japan entitled "Nansenbushū Dai Nippon-koku shōtōzu," a version of which may have been Kang's model for his own map of Japan. Written text accompanying the map states that Kūkai visited "Tenjiku," that is, India. See map 5, "Nansembushu Dainihon Shotozu," in Cortazzi, *Isles of Gold*, 70.
19. The word *ŏnmun* refers to the Korean alphabet, which King Sejong (1397–1450, r. 1418–50) introduced in 1443. That term was replaced by "*han'gŭl*" in the twentieth century.
20. *Idu* was a means of expressing Korean grammar while writing in literary Chinese. *Idu* phrases were written in Chinese characters, but those delivered the Korean sounds rather than meaning.
21. The unit of length called *ken* was "a little more than two yards." It was the basic measurement used in land surveys. See Brown, *Central Authority and Local Autonomy in the Formation of Early Modern Japan*, 16.
22. In the manuscript map of Japan entitled "Nansenbushū Dai Nihon Shōtōzu" is written text attributed to Kūkai (identified as Kōbō Daishi). That text states that in Japan there are 66 provinces; 2 islands; 601 districts (J. *gun*); 98,000 districts

(J. *kōri*); 909,858 villages (J. *mura*); 405,374 villages (J. *ri*); 809,815 *chō*, 2 *dan*, 3 *shō* of wet rice fields (J. *den*); 117,146 *chō*, 23 *shō* of dry fields (J. *hatake*); 2,958 Buddhist temples; 21,712 Shinto shrines; 1,994,828 males; and 2,904,820 females. (The text also provides figures for two other categories of Shinto shrines. Kang did not include those two categories in *The Record of a Shepherd*.) In this text, Kūkai explained population change thusly: "Because of the cycle of birth and death, the number of human beings will not increase and will not decrease." See plate 54 (2), "Kodai Nihon chizu (denshō Gyōki chizu)," in *Tōshōdaiji*, 54, map 5.

23. The island here called Ezo is today known as Hokkaidō.
24. Yoshida Sōjun (1558–1610) practiced medicine under the name Ian 意庵, which he inherited from his father, Yoshida Sōkei (1512–72). During his medical career, Ian attended to Hideyoshi, Toyotomi Hidetsugu, and Tokugawa Ieyasu. After receiving treatment from Ian in 1600, Emperor Go-Yōzei presented him with a new medical name, 意安, which is also read in Japanese as "Ian." As *The Record of a Shepherd* has the second medical name, its presentation may have occurred before Kang escaped from the Osaka area in the fourth month of 1600. See "Uda Genji—Yoshida," in *Kanei shoka keizu den*, 15:159–61; "Uda Genji Sasaki shōryū Yoshida," in *Shintei Kansei chōshū shokafu*, 7:228; Shinmura, *Nihon iryō shakaishi no kenkyū*, 319–20.
25. Ian's father, Yoshida Sōkei, participated in the tribute mission that Sakugen Shūryō (1501–79) led to Ming China from 1537 to 1540 and in the next, and last, tribute mission of 1547 to 1549. It is said that during the earlier mission, the Emperor of Ming China, Shizong (1507–66, r. 1521–66) greeted Sōkei and presented him with two names. One was Yian 意庵, or Ian in Japanese ("Udawara-shi Sasaki shōryū Yoshida," in *Shintei Kansei chōshū shokafu* 7:227; Shinmura, *Nihon iryō shakaishi no kenkyū*, 319–20).
26. Shimoura Yasukuni suggests that Kang's description of Ian's instrument for measuring time fits with Ian's discussion in his text *Rōkokusan* (Calculating from a Water Clock). Moreover, he speculates that the device for measuring time and the clock mentioned elsewhere in *The Record of a Shepherd* were the same object. He also suggests that Kang's comment that Ian measured distance reflects another text written by Ian (Shimoura, *Yoshida—Suminokura-ke no kenkyū*, 36–38, 49–59).
27. Illa (J. Nichira; d. 583) was not from Silla. Rather, he went to Japan from Paekche on a diplomatic mission in 583 (*Nihon shoki, kōhen*, 108–11). He was born in Paekche to a Japanese father whom a powerful official in the Japanese government had sent there. In Japan, the Paekche envoys killed him for, among other

reasons, disclosing their country's plans to attack northern Kyushu (*Nihonshi daijiten*, 888, 161). Kang's description of Illa treats him as a Korean remembered in Japan.

28. *Tarōbō* is a term for the protective deity of a shrine.
29. *Gongen*, a general Japanese term for deities invested with both Shinto and Buddhist identities, referred to Shinto *kami* who also were considered to be Buddhist bodhisattvas. *Gongen* such as Illa protected mountains.
30. Mōri Terumoto (1553–1625) lived in Aki Province, in western Honshu. He led forces in the Hideyoshi armies that subjugated Shikoku and Kyushu, and later was commanded to contribute 30,000 troops to the Seventh Division in the 1592 invasion. In the period between the evacuation to Pusan in mid-1593 and the launch of the second invasion in mid-1597, Mōri commanded the forts at Pusan and Tongdan. Army assignment and troop numbers here and in the following are from Miki Seiichirō, "Chōsen eki ni okeru guneki taikei ni tsuite," 8–9.
31. Mōri Hidemoto (1579–1650) was the adopted son of Terumoto. He led troops in the Right Army in the second invasion. He married the adopted daughter of Hideyoshi. (The adopted daughter's father was Hideyoshi's uterine younger brother Toyotomi Hidenaga.) His title, Imperial Adviser (J. *Saishō*), was of high rank.
32. Ukita Hideie (1572–1655) gained Hideyoshi's support to succeed as family head after the death of his father, who had supported Nobunaga. Hideie married the daughter that Hideyoshi had adopted from Maeda Toshie. In his early twenties, he led 10,000 troops in the Eighth Division in 1592. In Chosŏn, he served as commander of the Japanese armies and governed the Korean capital, Hansŏng, until the evacuation in mid-1593. In the second invasion, he was Commander of the Left Army. He served as one of the five advisers to Hideyori following Hideyoshi's death in 1598. His title was Middle Counselor (J. *Chūnagon*; junior third rank) (*Nihonshi jiten*, 103; *Sengoku bushō kassen jiten*, 557–59).
33. Ukita Hideie attacked the Southern Detached Palace (K. *Nambyŏlgung*) almost immediately after reaching the capital. The Korean prince Ŭiangun (d. 1588) had resided in this palace until his death in 1588. He was King Sŏnjo's third son and the first son of the monarch's second consort (*Sŏnjo sillok*, 26:4b–5a [1597.5.3]; *Sŏnjo sillok*, 22:8b [1588.3.26]; *Sŏnwŏn kyebo*, 26b [361]).
34. Kobayakawa Takakage (1533–97) was the third son of Mōri Motonari. In 1544 he became the family head of a branch of the Kobayakawa family in Aki Province. In 1549 he became the family head of another branch of the Kobayakawa family, and later unified the two. Kobayakawa led 10,000 troops in the Sixth Division in the 1592 invasion, and he contributed to the defeat of the Chinese-Korean forces

at Pyŏkchegwan, north of Seoul, on 1593.1.27. This victory slowed the advancing army but did not enable the Japanese army to push them farther away from Hansŏng. He returned to Japan in the ninth intercalary month of 1593 because of illness. After adopting the adopted son of Hideyoshi, Hashiba Hidetoshi, whose name then became Kobayakawa Hideaki, Takakage retired in 1595. His title was raised in the eighth month of 1595 to Acting Middle Counselor (J. *Gon Chūnagon*; junior third rank). "Kingo" was the Tang China equivalent for "Emon-fu" (Royal Gate Guard). In Heian, the Royal Gate Guard was responsible for guarding the city gates and was staffed by military men. Kobayakawa had received the title Left Royal Gate Guard Colonel (J. *Saemon no suke*; junior fifth rank upper) in or after 1550 (*Sengoku bushō kassen jiten*, 284–85; "Honke Hagi Mōri-ke," 8).

35. Mashita Nagamori (1545–1615) served as an administrator (J. *bugyō*) in Hideyoshi's government from the mid-1580s and as a commissioner in Hideyoshi's five-man council (J. *go bugyō*). He was commanded to lead 1,000 troops in the Seventh Division in 1592. The final character in the title printed in *The Record of a Shepherd* is an error; Nagamori held the title Right Royal Gate Guard Captain (J. *Uemon no jō*; junior fifth rank lower). See *Nihonshi jiten*, 1069; *Sengoku bushō kassen jiten*, 412–13; Miki, "Chōsen eki ni okeru guneki taikei ni tsuite," 8–9.

36. Date Masamune (1567–1636), who lived in northeastern Japan, came to support Hideyoshi in 1590 when he chose not to assist the Hōjō against Hideyoshi's army at Odawara. His army entered Chosŏn in the fourth month of 1593. After fighting at Yangsan, Ulsan, Kimhae, and Chinju, he was permitted to withdraw from Chosŏn in the ninth month of that year. The title Middle Captain (J. [*Konoe*] *Chūjō*) reported in *The Record of a Shepherd* may be an error. In 1597, Masamune received the title Right Royal Gate Guard Provisional Junior Captain (J. *U Konoe Gon no shōshō*), at the junior fourth rank lower and below Middle Captain (Kobayashi, *Date Masamune*, 91–95; *Nihonshi jiten*, 735; *Sengoku bushō kassen jiten*, 501–4).

37. Wakisaka Yasuharu (1554–1626) commanded naval units in both invasions. In the period between the evacuation to Pusan in mid-1593 and the launch of the second invasion in the summer of 1597, he commanded the fort at An'gol Port, west of Pusan. The second character in the title printed in *The Record of a Shepherd* is an error. Wakisaka received the title Ministry of Court Affairs Assistant Vice Minister (J. *Nakatsukasa no shō*; junior fifth rank lower) in 1585 (*Sengoku bushō kassen jiten*, 464–65).

38. Hosokawa Tadaoki (1563–1645) participated in the Ninth Division in the 1592 invasion. He was raised to the title Governor of Etchū Province (J. *Etchū no*

kami) in 1596, during the visit of the envoy of the Emperor of Ming China (*Nihonshi jiten*, 1053; *Sengoku bushō kassen jiten*, 533–36).

39. Toda Katsutaka (d. 1594) served in the 1592 invasion. He was originally stationed at Kaesŏng, north of Seoul, but, his unit being deemed too small should the Chinese-Korean army capture P'yŏngyang and advance toward Hansŏng, he was transferred to Sangju, in Kyŏngsang Province, and replaced at Kaesŏng by Kobayakawa Takakage's unit (Turnbull, *Samurai Invasion*, 136). He held the title Ministry of Popular Affairs Assistant Vice Minister (J. *Minbu no shō*; junior fifth rank lower). The lands in Shikoku that Tōdō Takatora received from Hideyoshi in 1595 had previously belonged to Toda. He died of illness in Japan in 1594.

40. Ishida Mitsunari (1560–1600) received the title Ministry of Civil Affairs Assistant Vice Minister (J. *Jibu no shō*; junior fifth rank lower) in 1585. During the 1592 invasion, Mitsunari served as one of the several Nagoya ship commissioners (J. *fune bugyō*). They oversaw the departure of the troop ships and supply ships from Nagoya, in Hizen Province, which was the staging base for the invasion and the site of the war headquarters. He went to Chosŏn in the sixth month with other ship commissioners to deliver updates to the generals there. As the war turned against the Japanese in early 1593, Mitsunari participated in planning the negotiations with Chinese generals and the retreat to Pusan. After the death of Hideyoshi, Mitsunari served in the five-man council intended to support Hideyori and govern the country. They were involved in coordinating the withdrawal from Chosŏn (Imai, *Ishida Mitsunari*, 43–64; *Nihonshi jiten*, 59; *Sengoku bushō kassen jiten*, 310–12).

41. Shimazu Yoshihiro (1535–1619) served in the Fourth Division in the first invasion. In the period between the evacuation to Pusan in mid-1593 and the launch of the second invasion in the summer of 1597, he commanded the fort at Yŏngdŭng Port, Kŏje Island. Following Hideyoshi's death, Shimazu's forces provided cover for other Japanese armies as they abandoned the invasion and returned to Japan. His was the last army to leave Chosŏn (*Sengoku bushō kassen jiten*, 433–34).

42. Ryūzōji Masaie (1556–1607) held lands in northwestern Kyushu. Hideyoshi ordered him to step away from political matters in 1590 and exempted him from military duties (*Sengoku bushō kassen jiten*, 345, 429–31). The term *"jinushi,"* or landholder, may refer to Masaie's lack of status as a daimyō.

43. Asano Nagamasa (1547–1611) oversaw supplies and led troops in the 1592 invasion. He later served in Hideyoshi's five-man council (*Nihonshi jiten*, 16).

44. Asano Yukinaga (1576–1613) was the first son of Nagamasa. He was assigned to the Eighth Division for the invasion in 1592. Yukinaga entered Chosŏn in 1593

and served as commander of Sŏsaeng Port, in southeastern Kyŏngsang Province, from the seventh month of 1597 (*Nihonshi jiten*, 16; *Sengoku bushō kassen jiten*, 386–88).

45. Ikoma Chikamasa (1526–1603) received the title Bureau of Music Director (J. *Uta no kami*; junior fifth rank lower) in 1585. He fought in the Fifth Division in the first invasion (*Nihonshi jiten*, 55; *Sengoku bushō kassen jiten*, 322–23).

46. Ikoma Kazumasa (1555–1610) received the title Governor of Sanuki Province (J. *Sanuki no kami*; junior fifth rank lower) in 1591. In the second invasion he was a general in the Left Army and fought at Ulsan (*Sengoku bushō kassen jiten*, 356).

47. Chōsokabe Morichika (1575–1615) was the fourth son of Motochika. He participated in both invasions of Chosŏn (*Sengoku bushō kassen jiten*, 411–12).

48. Hachisuka Iemasa (1558–1639) received the title Governor of Awa Province (J. *Awa no kami*; junior fifth rank lower) in 1586. He served in the Fifth Division in the first invasion. Hideyoshi assigned him supervision of Ch'ungch'ŏng Province. During the period between the evacuation to Pusan in mid-1593 and the launch of the second invasion in the summer of 1597, Iemasa commanded the fort at Changmun Port, Kŏje Island. In the second invasion, he was a general in the Left Army (*Nihonshi jiten*, 940; *Sengoku bushō kassen jiten*, 515–16).

49. Ikeda Hideo (d. 1597 or 1598) joined Hideyoshi's service after the death of Nobunaga and the defeat of Akechi Mitsuhide. Then known as Ikeda Akio, he received the given name Hideo for his role in Hideyoshi's successful Odawara campaign in 1590. (The character *hide* in "Hideo" is that in "Hideyoshi.") He died in Chosŏn.

50. Tōdō Takatora served as an Iki Ship Commissioner during the first invasion. In the second invasion, he served in the Left Army in the campaign to take Chŏlla and Ch'ungch'ŏng provinces. After the fall of Namwŏn to the combined Left Army and Right Army on 1597.8.15, Takatora and Katō Yoshiaki separated from the Left Army and headed west toward the coast. Takatora's naval forces captured Kang and his immediate family members at Yŏnggwang in the tenth month of 1597 (*Nihonshi jiten*, 824).

51. Ōtani Yoshitsugu (1559–1600) received the title Ministry of Justice Assistant Vice Minister (J. *Gyōbu no shō*; junior fifth rank lower) in 1585. He served as a Nagoya Ship Commissioner in 1592 and also participated in the second invasion (*Nihonshi jiten*, 159; *Sengoku bushō kassen jiten*, 305–6; Miki, "Chōsen eki ni okeru guneki taikei ni tsuite," 8–9).

52. Katō Yoshiaki (1563–1631) served as an Iki Ship Commissioner in the first invasion. He later held command duties at the fort at An'gol Port in the period

between the evacuation to Pusan in mid-1593 and the launch of the second invasion in mid-1597. During the second invasion, he served in the Left Army and fought at Sunch'ŏn and Ulsan (*Sengoku bushō kassen jiten*, 480–82).

53. Ogawa Suketada (1549–1601) fought alongside Asano Nagamasa at Kimhae during the 1592 invasion.
54. Miyabe Nagahiro (1581–1635) received the title Ministry of Military Affairs Assistant Vice Minister (J. *Hyōbu no shō*; junior fifth rank lower) in 1586. Serving in the first invasion, he withdrew from Chosŏn in the second half of 1593, and did not serve in the second invasion (*Sengoku bushō kassen jiten*, 498). He was also known as Miyabe Nagafusa.
55. Fukuhara Naotaka (d. 1600) joined the fighting in Chosŏn in 1593 together with Kumagai Naomori. He also served in the second invasion (*Sengoku bushō kassen jiten*, 315). The first two characters in this entry are the first character of Fukuhara Naotaka's surname and the second character of his adult given name, thus rendering his name as "Fukutaka." Naotaka is identified by the correct surname of Fukuhara in the Bungo Province entry in the gazetteer of Japan in appendix 1.
56. Nakagawa Hidenari was the younger brother of Nakagawa Hidemasa (1569–92 or 1593), who died in Kangwŏn Province. Hidenari was permitted to return to Japan in the second half of 1593 (*Sengoku bushō kassen jiten*, 269; Miki, "Chōsen eki ni okeru guneki taikei ni tsuite," 8–9).
57. Katō Kiyomasa (1562–1611) led the Second Division in the first invasion. From Seoul, he proceeded to Hamgyŏng Province, which he administered from Anbyŏn, the province's southernmost county. In the period between the evacuation to Pusan in mid-1593 and the launch of the second invasion in 1597, Katō commanded the fort at Sŏsaeng, east of Pusan. During the second invasion, he served in the Right Army.
58. Konishi Yukinaga (ca. 1558–1600), was born in Sakai and raised in the capital area. A Christian, he is thought to have been baptized as a child. He led the First Division into Chosŏn in 1592, entering the Korean capital first and subsequently proceeding to P'yŏngan Province. His army never reached China, though. In the period between the evacuation to Pusan and the launch of the second invasion in 1597, he commanded the forts at Ungch'ŏn and Tongdan, in Kyŏngsang Province. He served in the Left Army in the second invasion (*Nihonshi jiten*, 455; *Nihon Kirisutokyō rekishi daijiten*, 531, 803).
59. Kuroda Nagamasa (1568–1623) received the title Governor of Kai Province (J. *Kai no kami*; junior fifth rank lower). A Christian, he served in the Third Division in the first invasion. Hideyoshi assigned him supervision of Hwanghae

Province. In the period between the evacuation to Pusan in mid-1593 and the launch of the second invasion in mid-1597, Kuroda commanded the fort at Kijang, east of Pusan. During the second invasion he was a general in the Right Army (*Nihonshi jiten*, 359; *Sengoku bushō kassen jiten*, 451–52).

60. Mōri Katsunobu (d. 1611), also known as Yoshinari, served in the Fourth Division in the first invasion and was assigned to administer Kangwŏn Province (Turnbull, *Samurai Invasion*, 75–76, 187).

61. Mōri Takamasa (1559–1628) was not born into the Mōri family. Rather, Hideyoshi sent him as a hostage to Mōri Terumoto after Terumoto had accepted peace following Nobunaga's death in 1582. Takamasa's surname subsequently became Mōri. He served in the Ninth Division in the first invasion and as a Chosŏn Ship Commissioner (*Sengoku bushō kassen jiten*, 472–73).

62. Matsura Shigenobu (1549–1614) lived in Hirado, a port town in Hizen Province in northwest Kyushu. In the first invasion, his army fought in the First Division. In the period between the evacuation to Pusan in mid-1593 and the launch of the second invasion in mid-1597, Matsura and Sō Yoshitoshi assisted Konishi Yukinaga in commanding the forts at Ungch'ŏn and Tongdan. He led troops in the Left Army in the second invasion (*Sengoku bushō kassen jiten*, 395–96).

63. Takenaka Takashige (1562–1615) was also known as Takenaka Shigetoshi. He served in the Eighth Division in the first invasion. In the second invasion, he served as a Military Inspector (J. *Gun metsuke*) in the Left Army. Hideyoshi may have introduced the six military inspectors for coordinating and overseeing the fighting, thinking that it would be possible to so conduct the war. The deployment of military inspectors may indicate that, unlike as in 1592, Hideyoshi had no intention of entering Chosŏn; the second invasion aimed first at securing and controlling the southern half of the country (Nakano, *Bunroku—Keichō no eki*, 191–92).

64. In the first invasion, Hayakawa Nagamasa (d.u.) served as a Chosŏn Ship Commissioner (J. *Kōrai fune bugyō*) and in the Ninth Division. In the second invasion, he served as a Military Inspector in the Right Army.

65. Tachibana Muneshige (d. 1643) lived in Chikugo Province, in northern Kyushu. He was commanded to provide 2,500 troops to the army and fought in the Sixth Division. His forces reached Paekch'ŏn and Ubong counties in Hwanghae Province before returning to Hansŏng as the Chinese-Korean army advanced southward. Tachibana's army contributed to the defeat of the Chinese-Korean army at Pyŏkchegwan (*Sengoku bushō kassen jiten*, 523–25; Nakano, *Tachibana Muneshige*, 61–112). The surname Yanagawa and the surname Tachibana are

printed incorrectly in this entry. Here, Yanagawa appears as 楊川; the appropriate rendering is 柳川. Tachibana here is 立橘; the appropriate rendering is 立花. Muneshige was also known as Tachibana Munetora.

66. Terazawa Hirotaka (1563–1633) received the title Governor of Shima Province (J. *Shima no kami*; junior fifth rank lower) in 1589. He served in Chosŏn as Ship Commissioner (*Nihonshi jiten*, 795; *Sengoku bushō kassen jiten*, 490–91). In chapter 3 he is identified as Terazawa Masanari. See note 43 in chapter 3.

67. Sō Yoshitoshi controlled Namhae Island, in western Kyŏngsang Province, during the second invasion.

68. Kobayakawa Hideaki (1582–1602) was the son of Kinoshita Iesada, who was the elder brother of Hideyoshi's wife, the Kita no mandokoro Nene. He was adopted by Hideyoshi at the age of three and named Hashiba Hidetoshi. In the eighth month of 1593, following the birth of Hideyoshi's son Hideyori, Hidetoshi became the adopted son of Kobayakawa Takakage. His adult given name became Hideaki after Takakage's death in Japan in the sixth month of 1597. Hideaki, while still a teenager, was the Supreme Commander (J. *Sōtaishō*) of the second invasion and was based at Pusan (*Nihonshi jiten*, 457; *Sengoku bushō kassen jiten*, 321–22, 350–51; Wada, *Kanshoku yōkai*, 139–40).

69. The term "Hizen Ryūzōji" refers to Ryūzōji Masaie. "Hizen" is an abbreviation of his title *Hizen no kami*, or Governor of Hizen Province.

70. "Nabeshima Kaga no kami" refers to Ryūzōji Masaie's retainer and maternal uncle Nabeshima Naoshige (1538–1618). In the first invasion, he served in the Second Division. He was based at Kimhae, west of Pusan, during the second invasion. After the capture of Seoul in 1592, he accompanied Katō Kiyomasa into Hamgyŏng Province. In the period between the evacuation to Pusan in mid-1593 and the launch of the second invasion in mid-1597, Naoshige commanded the fort at Chukto. His son Katsushige (1580–1657) participated in both invasions (*Sengoku bushō kassen jiten*, 345, 429–31; *Nihonshi jiten*, 871–72).

71. During the second invasion, Katō Kiyomasa was based at Ulsan, on the east coast of Kyŏngsang Province. There he and his forces outlasted a Chinese-Korean siege over the winter of 1597–98.

72. Kuroda Nagamasa fought in the Right Army during the second invasion, and held the fort at Sŏsaeng Port.

73. Mōri Katsunobu fought in the Left Army in the second invasion, and was based at Pusan Port.

74. Mōri Takamasa (d. 1597) was a military inspector in the second invasion. He died in the ninth month of 1597 during the naval battle in the Noryang Straits, in Chŏlla Province. See chapter 4, appendix 2.

75. Tachibana Muneshige commanded the base at Kosŏng, in Kyŏngsang Province, during the second invasion. He also commanded the fort at An'gol Port.
76. Terazawa Masanari (1563–1633) served as commissioner on Kŏje Island in the eighth month of 1593 (Kitajima, *Chōsen nichinichi ki—Kōrai nikki*, 258).
77. Kakimi Kazunao (d. 1600) entered Chosŏn in the eleventh month of 1592 and, with Kumagai Naomori, delivered commands from Hideyoshi. He was a military inspector in the second invasion (*Sengoku bushō kassen jiten*, 307).
78. The second character in the adult given name of Kumagai, which renders the name as Naoshige, likely is an error for the second character in the name of Kumagai Naomori, who died in 1600. Naomori served as the lodgings supervisor for the invasion force gathering in Nagoya. In Chosŏn, he was often paired in duties with Kakimi Kazunao. Naomori served as a military inspector of the Right Army in the second invasion. In the eighth month of 1597, he attacked the fort on Mount Hwangsŏk, in Anŭm County in western Kyŏngsang Province, and in the third month of 1598 he aided Katō Kiyomasa during the Ulsan siege (*Sengoku bushō kassen jiten*, 306–7; *Sinjŭng Tongguk yŏji sŭngnam*, 31:37a).
79. Kurushima Michifusa (1561–97), based in Shikoku and a pirate leader active in the Inland Sea in Japan, served Hideyoshi from at least 1582 and participated in several campaigns in Japan. He served in the second invasion and died in the naval battle in the Noryang Straits in the ninth month of 1597. The phrase "Kurushima no kami" is an error. As Michifusa had received the title Governor of Izumo Province (J. *Izumo no kami*; junior fifth rank lower) in 1595, this entry may lack the province name Izumo (*Sengoku bushō kassen jiten*, 289).
80. Yi Sunsin commanded the Korean naval forces as Regional Navy Commander (K. *Sugun T'ongjesa*) at the battle in the Noryang Straits in the ninth month of 1597.
81. Ankokuji Ekei (d. 1600) entered Ankokuji, a Rinzai Zen temple in Aki Province, as a child. In 1569, he became abbot (J. *jūji*) of the temple, which was a subtemple of Tōfukuji, in Kyoto. Ekei supported the Mōri family, in particular as an adviser and as their representative in meetings with other military leaders. The negotiations described here are those between Hideyoshi and Mōri Terumoto following the death of Oda Nobunaga in 1582. He participated in both invasions and contributed to the construction of Kiyomasa's fort in Ulsan. See Kawai, *Ankokuji Ekei*.
82. *Gakumon ki* is an error for *Gakumonsho ki* (Records from the Study Hall). ("Gakumonsho" refers to the study hall built in Fushimi Castle, though it was also used for tea gatherings.) The Buddhist monk Saishō Shūtai (1548–1608) wrote

this text in 1597. In it, he discusses Hideyoshi's foreign policy ("the names of the brave soldiers will be heard across the four seas"), the construction of Fushimi Castle, the view inside the castle, and Hideyoshi's virtue (Saishō Shūtai, *Gakumonsho ki*, 1045–47; Shimofusa, "Saishō Shūtai").

83. Shen Weijing (fl. 1540–97), appointed Mobile Corps Commander (C. *Youji Jiangzhun*), which was a "tactical duty assignment" in Ming China's government, led the Chinese negotiations with Konishi Yukinaga in 1592 and 1593 that resulted in talks with Hideyoshi in Nagoya in 1593. He returned to China with the Japanese demands and subsequently met Hideyoshi in Osaka in 1596. The negotiations resulted in failure, and Hideyoshi invaded Chosŏn again in mid-1597 (Hucker, *A Dictionary of Official Titles in Imperial China*, 584, item 8037; Swope, "Deceit, Disguise, and Dependence").

84. "Ankokuji Saidō" and "Genso" refer to Keitetsu Genso. This Buddhist monk was the abbot of a temple in Tsushima, and through his previous visits to Seoul he was familiar with the geography from Pusan to the capital (*Nihonshi jiten*, 374).

85. Ikeda Hideo's (d. 1598) "son Magoshirō" may refer to Ikeda Hideuji (d.u.), who accompanied his father to Chosŏn in 1597. If it does, "Magoshirō" is an error for "Magojirō" (http://ja.wikipedia.org/wiki/%E6%B1%A0%E7%94%B0%E7%A7%80%E6%B0%8F; accessed March 4, 2012).

Chapter 4, Appendix 2. Suggestions for Military Reform and War Strategies

1. Mobile Inspector (K. *Sunch'alsa*) was a military post that provincial governors held as a temporary concurrent appointment. Because military officials could not serve as governor of a province, only civil officials held appointments to this military post. The military post of Army Commander (K. *Pyŏngma chŏltosa*, junior second grade) was often held by civil officials. The text here has only "*Chŏltosa*," but context identifies this as the Army Commander rather than the Navy Commander (K. *Sugun chŏltosa*, senior third grade).

2. The military post of Supreme Field Commander was held by an official sent from the capital.

3. Zhang Liang (d. 189 B.C.E.) was a famous military policy strategist who helped Liu Bang found the Han dynasty. Han Shin (d. 196 B.C.E.) was a strategist who helped Liu Bang to reunify China. Liu Bei (161–223) was the founding emperor of Shu Han. He was made famous in popular culture by the novel *Romance of the*

Three Kingdoms. Yue Fei (1103–42) was a famous general-strategist in Southern Song China. He defeated the Jurchen but was killed as a consequence of slander against him.

4. Yi Pongnam (1555–97) was Chŏlla Province Army Commander at the time of the Battle of Namwŏn. He was killed at this battle on 1597.8.16. Yi had passed the military examination (K. *mukwa*). See *Sŏnjo sujŏng sillok*, 31:6a [1597.9.1]; *Ugye Yi ssi taedongbo*, 172–73.

5. The magistrate of Namwŏn County was the Town Magistrate (K. *Tohobusa*, junior third grade); the magistrate of Naju County was the City Magistrate (K. *Moksa*, senior third grade). Defense Commander (K. *Pang'ŏsa*) was a province-level military appointment. Yi Pongnam was serving as the Chŏlla Province Defense Commander by 1593.7.5. As for Army Commander, two men held this appointment in Chŏlla Province. One was the Governor of Chŏlla Province, for whom this was a concurrent appointment. King Sŏnjo had appointed Yi as magistrate of Namwŏn County by 1594.10.20; he subsequently appointed Yi as magistrate of Naju County on 1596.3.7. On 1597.1.27, Yi became the Chŏlla Province Army Commander and Navy Commander (*Sŏnjo sillok*, 40:5a–b [1593.7.5], 56:47b–48a [1594.10.20], 73:7b–8b [1596.3.7], 84:27a–31a [1597.1.27]).

6. Wŏn Kyun, because of his conflict with Yi Sunsin and his defeat in the Battle of the Ch'ilch'ŏn Straits, acquired notoriety as a schemer who failed his country.

7. This refers to the Battle of the Ch'ilch'ŏn Straits, which was fought along the southeast coast of Kyŏngsang Province and near Kŏje Island and resulted in the largest defeat that the Korean navy suffered during the Imjin War. Of a fleet of 160 ships, all but 12 were lost, as were hundreds of sailors and soldiers. Wŏn Kyun also died in this battle. His forces had already suffered severe losses in a failed attempt to attack the Japanese naval forces at Pusan on the eighth day of the seventh month. Retreating, the Korean ships stopped in the Ch'ilch'ŏn Straits. See Turnbull, *Samurai Invasion*, 183–85; Hawley, *The Imjin War*, 455–62.

8. Hansan Island, near T'ongyŏng, in Kyŏngsang Province, functioned as a crucial defense post for Chŏlla and Kyŏngsang provinces. The Battle of Hansan Island, fought on 1592.7.8, is said to have been a turning point in the first invasion. Triumphant, the Korean navy came to dominate the sea and thus blocked the Japanese military's maritime supply line along the coast and north to Seoul. See Turnbull, *Samurai Invasion*, 100–105.

9. The Right Naval Headquarters was in Haenam County, in the southwest corner of Chŏlla Province.

10. This was the Battle of Myŏngnyang, fought on 1597.9.16. It is famous because with a fleet of only 13 ships, 12 of which were remnants from the Battle of the

Ch'ilch'ŏn Straits, Yi Sunsin defeated the Japanese fleet of 133 ships, destroying 31 of them. See Turnbull, *Samurai Invasion*, 201–2.

11. Kurushima Michifusa's death in this battle is thought to have lowered the Japanese navy's morale.

12. Pak Hongno (1552–1624) served as Mobile Inspector while Governor of Chŏlla Province. He was demoted after this naval defeat. Of the Chuksan Pak descent group, he passed the higher civil service examination in 1582 (*Sŏnjo sillok*, 89:5b–6a [1597.6.3], 89:9a [1597.6.6], 89:27a [1597.6.15], 89:42b [1597.6.26], 90:9a [1597.7.13]; Han'guk inmyŏng taesajŏn p'yŏnch'ansil, ed., *Han'guk inmyŏng taesajŏn*, 307). King Sŏnjo appointed Hwang Sin (1562–1617) as Governor of Chŏlla Province in the seventh month of 1597 (*Sŏnjo sillok*, 90:18b [1597.7.3]). Hwang followed the Chinese embassy that visited Hideyoshi in Osaka in 1596. (The meeting ended in failure when Hideyoshi realized that the Emperor of Ming China had not accepted a relationship of hierarchical inferiority with the Japanese ruler.) Of the Ch'angwŏn Hwang descent group, he passed the higher civil service examination in 1588.

13. Kang seems to be stating that there were fifty-three counties in Chŏlla Province at the time he wrote. The state gazetteer *Sinjŭng Tongguk yŏji sŭngnam*, which was printed in 1531, has fifty-seven counties. In 1594, the court merged Nŭngsŏng County and Hwasun County, and in 1597 it merged Koksŏng County and Namwŏn County. The specific date of the second change is not clear, but as of the beginning of 1598, there may have been fifty-five counties in Chŏlla Province.

14. The loss of the defense post at Hansan Island made Chŏlla Province much more vulnerable. The Japanese army of 56,000 troops led by generals including Konishi Yukinaga attacked Namwŏn. The Chinese army of 3,000 troops and the Korean army of 1,000 troops defended the fort. The battle, fought from the thirteenth to the sixteenth of the eighth month, was fierce, and the Japanese won in the end.

15. Chŏlla Province was spared during the first invasion but suffered great damage during the second invasion.

16. O Ŭngt'ae (b. 1542) was a general in Chosŏn. He was serving as the magistrate of Kyŏngwŏn County, in northeastern Hamgyŏng Province, when the Japanese invaded in 1592. He was appointed Chŏlla Province Defense Commander before the ninth month of 1597 (*Sŏnjo sillok*, 92:2a–b [1597.9.25]).

17. Kim Kyŏngno (1567–1597), who was from Namwŏn County, hurried to Namwŏn upon learning in Chŏnju, to the south, that Japanese armies were approaching the city. He died in the Battle of Namwŏn (Kim Sŏkchu, "Agan

Kunsu chŭng Hyŏngjo P'ansŏ Sin-gong sijang," in Kim Sŏkchu, *Sigam sŏnsaeng yugo*, 22:60a–63a; *Sŏnjo sujŏng sillok*, 31:6a [1597.9.1]). He had passed the military examination, had later been appointed magistrate of Kimhae County, and was serving as Chŏlla Province Auxiliary Defense Officer (K. *Chobangjang*) by late 1596 (*Sŏnjo sillok*, 27:26b [1592.6.29]; *Sŏnjo sillok*, 82:58b–66a [1596.11.26]; *Han'guk inmyŏng taesajŏn*, 73). The Chosŏn government issued the military post of Auxiliary Defense Officer to county magistrates who had passed the military examination. Kim had served as Town Magistrate of Kimhae County, on the southern coast of Kyŏngsang Province, and thus was eligible for this appointment (*Sŏnjo sillok*, 27:26b [1592.6.29]).

18. Tamyang County was in central Chŏlla Province.
19. Guo Ziyi (697–781) was a great general of Tang China. He became famous for his quelling of the An Lushan Rebellion from 755 to 763. Guo has been deified in Chinese popular religion.
20. Weisheng was a person who would keep his word at the risk of his life. Xiaoji kept constant filial devotion despite being persecuted by his parents.
21. In China, these surnames were of the most prestigious and powerful families during the period of division and the subsequent Sui and Tang dynasties.
22. This Emperor Taizu (927–976, r. 960–976) was the founding emperor of Song China. The passage refers to the way he founded and consolidated Song China by placing good people in appropriate posts for many years.
23. King Sŏnjo sent this mission to Japan in 1590. The first Korean embassy to reach the Japanese capital area since 1443, its ostensible objective was to determine whether Hideyoshi was in fact planning to invade Chosŏn as he had intimated in his messages to King Sŏnjo. Hwang Yun'gil (b. 1536) and Kim Sŏng'il (1538–93) led the mission as Envoy and Vice Envoy, respectively. The assessments they presented to the king differed. Hwang believed that an invasion was imminent, but Kim disagreed. This mission has acquired notoriety in history, in part because factional politics at the Korean court informed the conflicting reports (Yi Sangbaek, *Han'guksa*, 601–2).
24. Konishi Yukinaga led the First Division in the 1592 invasion and entered Seoul first. His daughter, baptized as Maria, was married to Sō Yoshitoshi around 1590. Yoshitoshi was baptized in 1591 by Alexandro Valignano (1539–1606), a Jesuit missionary who visited Japan three times in the late sixteenth century. Yoshitoshi's Christian name was Dario. He separated from his wife and left the church after the invasion (*Nihon Kirisutokyō rekishi daijiten*, 803).
25. Katō Kiyomasa (1562–1611) raced against Yukinaga to be the first general to enter

Seoul. He was famous for his physical prowess and cruelty, and was Yukinaga's rival in war and in politics.
26. One *jō* was 10 *shaku*; one *shaku* was one-third of a meter. One *jō*, then, was 3.3 meters, or 10.82 feet. However, this Japanese measurement changed over time and was used differently depending on the situation.
27. The depth of this moat was approximately 86.61 feet.
28. The Kŭmsŏng in Tamyang County was a walled fort built during the Koryŏ period. Maintained until 1894, it was one of the best-constructed and largest forts in Korea (*Sinjŭng Tongguk yŏji sŭngnam*, 39:13b–14a).
29. The Kŭmsŏng in Naju County, in southern Chŏlla Province, is one of the oldest forts in the Korean peninsula, believed to have been constructed during the Three Kingdoms period. This fort is also the best constructed—it never fell to an attacking army (*Sinjŭng Tongguk yŏji sŭngnam*, 35:2b–4a).
30. Here, "army commanders" refers to the multiple army commanders who were assigned to each province.
31. Chŏngŭp and Changsŏng were counties in central Chŏlla Province. Imam was a mountain fort in central Chŏlla Province that dated from the Koryŏ period (*Sinjŭng Tongguk yŏji sŭngnam*, 36:15a–b).
32. Tongbok and Ch'angp'yŏng were counties in southern Chŏlla Province. During the Koryŏ period, Tongbok was sometimes called Ongsŏng because it was a walled fort. Kang is probably referring to the town of Tongbok that grew near the walled fort called Ongsŏng.
33. Yŏng'am and Haenam were counties in southwest Chŏlla Province.
34. Posŏng and Sunch'ŏn were counties in south-central Chŏlla Province.
35. "Regents" is from the text's "*sekkan*." This Japanese term combined into one word the names of two powerful government positions in the Heian government, *Sesshō* (regent for an emperor in his minority) and *Kanpaku* (regent for an adult emperor, or Imperial Regent). His comment about the "regents" not living until old age is not entirely accurate. Nobunaga did not take either post before his death at forty-nine years of age in 1582. Hideyoshi became the Imperial Regent in the seventh month of 1585 and lived to be sixty-three. Hideyoshi passed the title of Imperial Regent to his heir Hidetsugu in the twelfth month of 1591 and then became the Retired Imperial Regent. Forced to commit suicide in the seventh month of 1595, Hidetsugu passed away at twenty-eight years of age.
36. This allusion refers to an anecdote that tells how Bian Zhuangzi took advantage of a situation in which two tigers fought over a cow. Instead of attacking the two tigers, he waited until one was killed and the other exhausted. He then killed the

surviving tiger. This denotes a strategy of watching two of your nemeses fight and then overwhelming the exhausted winner.

37. In Japan, 10 *shō* equaled one *to*, and 10 *to* equaled one *koku*. In Chosŏn, 10 *toe* equaled one *mal*, and 15 or 20 *mal* equaled one *sŏk*.

38. One *to* was approximately 16.37 quarts, and one *koku* was approximately 163.46 quarts, but there was no standard amount for these measures in Japan at this time (Tonomura, *Community and Commerce in Late Medieval Japan*, xiv). A Korean *mal* was approximately 5.44 quarts, and one *sŏk* was approximately 81.72 (small *sŏk*) quarts or 108.97 (large *sŏk*) quarts. A Japanese *koku* at 163.46 quarts contained 30 Korean *mal*.

39. The masks worn by Japanese soldiers may have been *menbamu*, or face guards. Japanese soldiers wore such masks at the Battle of Haengju, north of Seoul, in the second month of 1593 (Hawley, *The Imjin War*, 324–27).

40. Current scholarship seems to concur in this assessment. See Swope, "Crouching Tigers, Secret Weapons," 27–28. Practitioners of Korean traditional archery place their targets at a distance of approximately 475 feet.

41. This explanation was inserted into the edition of *The Record of a Shepherd* included in Kang's collected writings.

42. If the reference here is to Toyotomi Hideyori, then the age is incorrect. Born in 1593, Hideyori would have been six years of age in 1598. If the reference is to Hideyoshi's first son, Tsurumatsu, he would have been ten years of age in 1598. However, Tsurumatsu, who was born in 1589, died in 1591.

43. The Japanese term *masu* was a measure for volume. In Kyoto in the late sixteenth century, one "capital *masu*" (J. *kyō masu*) was approximately 61 ounces ("Masu," in Takayanagi and Takeuchi, eds., *Nihonshi jiten*, 891).

44. The military post held by Yi Yŏp may have been Chŏlla Province Army Inspector (K. *Pyŏngma uhu*, junior third grade). See Chŏng Hŭidŭk, *Haesangnok*, 21a–b.

45. Natsuka Masaie was one of the commissioners in Hideyoshi's five-man council. During the war in Chosŏn, he supervised delivery of military supplies (*Nihonshi jiten*, 870).

46. The text has the place name as 土毛, but this is probably a mistake for Habu 土生, the second character in the text seeming to be a mistake (Boku Shōmei, *Kanyōroku*, 81, n. 3).

47. In chapter 1 Nagauemon is identified as Konishi Yukinaga's older brother. The only confirmed older brother of Yukinaga is Jōsei (d.u.), who was baptized in 1579. See Matsuda, *Kinsei shoki Nihon kankei Nanban shiryō no kenkyū*, 756–88; *Konishi Yukinaga—Don Agostinho*, 107.

48. Paek Suhoe (1574–1642), of the Yangsan Paek descent group, was from Yangsan

County, in southeast Kyŏngsang Province. He was captured and taken to Japan in 1592, at the age of nineteen, returning to Chosŏn in 1600. Paek was admired for his unwavering loyalty to Chosŏn during his long years as a captive (*Han'guk inmyŏng taesajŏn*, 320). His poems in both Chinese and Korean on themes of longing for the homeland are famous.

49. This refers to the repatriation of Korean captives from Japan.
50. There is an inaccuracy in what Kang writes here. His reference is actually to Naitō Joan (1550?–1626). As Naitō Hida no kami Joan, he served under Konishi Yukinaga from around 1585. Like Yukinaga, he was a Christian, and Yukinaga permitted him to use the surname Konishi in public. However, there is no evidence that Joan was Yukinaga's cousin. Naitō's adult name was Naitō Tadatoshi. He was in Beijing in 1594 and 1595 to deliver to the Emperor of Ming China Hideyoshi's letter presenting his demands. Yukinaga and a Chinese official had rewritten Hideyoshi's letter, however, softening his demands and placing Hideyoshi, and thus Japan, under the Emperor and Ming China in the language and the diplomacy of hierarchy (Matsuda, "Tanba Yagi-jō to Naitō Joan ni tsuite," 1–24).
51. The Japan House (K. *Waegwan*, J. *Wakan*) was a compound near the port of Pusan, in Tongnae County, where the Chosŏn government permitted Japanese to lodge while in Chosŏn for diplomacy or trade. Although the government opened three compounds in the fifteenth century—in the port of Che (Ungch'ŏn County), the port of Yŏm (Ulsan County), and the port of Pusan—after the Riot of the Three Ports in 1510, the court permitted trade only at Pusan from 1512 and again from 1547 (after a large pirate attack in 1544). As the invasion became inevitable, the Tsushima government gradually emptied the Pusan compound. The Chosŏn government did not permit other foreigners to trade there. The Korean government reopened the Japan House in Pusan in 1609. See Lewis, *Frontier Contact Between Chosŏn Korea and Tokugawa Japan*.
52. Wang Jiangong (d.u.), a Battalion Squad Leader (C. *Qianbazong*) in the Ming military, arrived in Chosŏn early in the fourth month of 1600, having sailed on a Japanese ship with a Japanese general sent by the Governor of Tsushima Sō Yoshitoshi (*Sŏnjo sillok*, 124:5a–b [1600.4.10]).
53. Yi Tŏkhyŏng (1561–1613) was one of the most renowned and active ministers of King Sŏnjo's reign. Of the Kwangju Yi descent group, he passed the higher civil service examination in 1580. During the Imjin War, he contributed greatly to negotiations with Japan and China. He reached the third-highest post at court, Third State Councilor (*Uŭijŏng*, senior first grade) in 1598, at age thirty-eight, and later served as Chief State Councilor (K. *Yŏngŭijŏng*, senior first grade). Yi also argued after the war for attacking Tsushima, but the court chose a differ-

ent policy. He led an embassy to China in 1608, following the enthronement of Kwanghae (*Han'guk inmyŏng taesajŏn*, 618).

Chapter 4, Appendix 3. Japanese Generals Who Participated in the Imjin and Chŏngyu Invasions

1. *Daifu* was the Tang China equivalent of the Japanese bureaucratic post of Palace Minister (J. *Naidaijin*; junior second rank). Ieyasu received the title Palace Minister in 1596.
2. Fuji[wara] Minamoto Yoshisada, printed here as 藤源義定, was Nitta Yoshisada 新田義貞 (1301–38) (Boku Shōmei, 137–38, n. 3). A samurai based in eastern Japan, Nitta, responding to Emperor Go-Daigo (1288–1339, r. 1318–39), defeated the Kamakura bakufu in 1333 and supported Go-Daigo and the Southern Court in the War of the Southern and Northern Courts (1333–36). Yoshisada did not serve as Imperial Regent in the Southern Court, for those emperors did not fill that position between 1333.6.29 and 1352.1.15. He rather would have received an honorary appointment.
3. This discussion of warfare may refer to the battles fought between Ieyasu's forces and Hideyoshi's forces at Komaki and at Nagakute in Owari Province, and in Ise Province in 1584. Hideyoshi failed to defeat Ieyasu at Komaki and Nagakute. However, he did succeed in bringing Ieyasu under his administrative purview (*Sengoku bushō kassen jiten*, 848–51; Berry, *Hideyoshi*, 78–79; Totman, *Tokugawa Ieyasu*, 47–48).
4. Yūki Hideyasu (1574–1607) was the second son of Tokugawa Ieyasu. In 1584, he became the adopted son of Hideyoshi, whose surname was still Hashiba at that time, but his presence in Hideyoshi's family was also as a hostage sent by Ieyasu. In 1590, Hideyasu married the daughter of Yūki Harutomo (1534–1614) and succeeded his father-in-law. He received the title Governor of Mikawa Province (J. *Mikawa no kami*) (*Sengoku bushō kassen jiten*, 343–344). However, Hideyasu was not Ieyasu's first son. Nobuyasu, Ieyasu's first son, was born in 1559 and died in 1579. Kang, perhaps not aware of Nobuyasu, is referring here to Hideyasu, who was born in 1574 and died in 1607. The further identity of the Iki no kami has not yet been confirmed.
5. Tokugawa Hidetada (1579–1632) was Ieyasu's third son. The moniker "Edo Chūnagon" derived from his receiving the title Acting Middle Counselor in 1592 (*Sengoku jinmei jiten*, 688–89). He succeeded Ieyasu as Shogun in 1605.
6. The title Iki no kami, or Governor of Iki Province, may perhaps be an inaccurate reference to Matsudaira Tadateru (1592–1683), who was Ieyasu's sixth son.

Born in 1592, he was nine years old in 1600. In 1599 he became the head of the Nagasawa branch of the Matsudaira family. However, he did not receive the title Governor of Iki Province. Rather, he received the title Governor of Kazusa Province (J. *Kazusa no kami*). Ieyasu's seventh son, Yoshinao, was born in the eleventh month of 1600, or after Kang had returned to Chosŏn.

7. Calculated from his birth in 1542, Ieyasu was sixty-three years old in 1604.
8. Mōri Terumoto was commander of the Seventh Division in the 1592 invasion, and served as one of the five elders from 1597.
9. Another Japanese word that is written with the characters for "*ōuchi*," 大内, but pronounced differently means "palace."
10. Calculated from his birth in 1553, Terumoto was forty-eight years old in 1600.
11. Maeda Toshinaga (1582–1614) was a son of Maeda Toshiie. Together with his father he served Oda Nobunaga, and he married a daughter of Nobunaga. Subsequently serving Hideyoshi, Toshinaga did not fight in Chosŏn. He succeeded Toshiie as a member of the five elders that supported Hideyori. Governor of Hizen Province (J. *Hizen no kami*) was the first title that he received (*Nihon kodai chūsei jinmei jiten*, 913).
12. Maeda Toshiie (1538–99) was one of the five elders. He gained the northern half of Kaga Province in a grant from Hideyoshi in 1584 and held all but two districts in 1598. For the activities of Toshiie and Toshinaga in Kaga and nearby provinces in the sixteenth century, see Brown, *Central Authority and Local Autonomy in the Formation of Early Modern Japan*, 39–50. His title here is Senior Counselor.
13. Toyotomi Hideyori (1593–1615) was born to Hideyoshi and his secondary wife, Yodo-dono, in 1593. He became Hideyoshi's heir after Toyotomi Hidetsugu committed suicide following their father's command in the seventh month of 1595. Hideyori participated in the coming-of-age ceremony (J. *genpuku*) in the ninth month of 1597 at the age of five. On Hideyori from his birth until his father's death, see Fukuda, "Toyotomi Hideyori kenkyū josetsu," 123–46.
14. Maeda Toshiie died in 1599, the Korean *kihae* year, and not in 1598, the Korean *musul* year. See Boku Shōmei, *Kanyōroku*, 141, n. 1.
15. Hideyoshi began the construction of Osaka Castle in the ninth month of 1583. In addition to residences in Fushimi, daimyō and other elites also maintained residences near Osaka Castle.
16. Satake Yoshinobu (1570–1633) feigned support for Tokugawa Ieyasu at the Battle of Sekigahara and instead aided Ishida Mitsunari and Uesugi Kagekatsu (*Sengoku bushō kassen jiten*, 492–93).
17. Hideyoshi removed Uesugi Kagekatsu from Echigo Province in early 1598 and sent him to Aizu, in Mutsu Province. The reference "Echigo Nagon" here is in-

correct in that it reflects Kagekatsu's former base and abbreviates his title, *Gon Chūnagon*, or Acting Middle Counselor (*Sengoku bushō kassen jiten*, 447–50).
18. Hori Hideharu received Echigo Province after Hideyoshi moved Kagekatsu to Aizu in early 1598 (*Sengoku bushō kassen jiten*, 340–41).
19. Date Masamune killed his younger brother Kojirō (Masamichi, b. 1568?) in 1590, in response to a plot to kill him, behind which Mogami Yoshiaki (1546–1614) "was pulling the strings." Yoshiaki was the elder brother of the mother of Masamune and Kojirō. Masamune explained that he could not permit his mother to be so besmirched by Yoshiaki (Kobayashi, *Date Masamune*, 60).
20. Satake Yoshishige (1547–1612) followed Yoshishige as family head in 1587 or 1588 (*Sengoku jinmei jiten*, 462–63).
21. The Satake family had held Hitachi Province since 1335.
22. Mogami Yoshiaki did not participate in the war in Chosŏn.
23. Kinoshita Katsutoshi was the eldest of these four brothers. He held lands in Wakasa Province valued at 62,000 *koku*, and his castle was in Obama. He received the title Palace Guard Lieutenant after 1588 ("Toyotomi-shi: Kinoshita," in *Shintei Kansei chōshū shokafu* 18:137–38).
24. Kinoshita Nobutoshi (1577–1642) was the third of these four brothers ("Toyotomi-shi: Kinoshita," in *Shintei Kansei chōshū shokafu*, 18:138). He married the daughter of Hosokawa Yūsai, which made him the younger brother-in-law of Hosokawa Tadaoki. Like his brothers Katsutoshi and Toshifusa, he supported Hideyoshi.
25. Kinoshita Toshifusa (1573–1637) was the second of these four brothers ("Toyotomi-shi: Kinoshita," in *Shintei Kansei chōshū shokafu*, 18:138; *Sengoku bushō kassen jiten*, 508–9).
26. Ukita Hideie's wife, Gō (1574–1634), was born to Maeda Toshiie and later adopted by Hideyoshi. Hideie and Gō were married in 1585. After Hideie was exiled in 1606, Gō returned to her biological family in Kaga. There she met Naitō Joan and Takayama Ukon (1552–1615), both of whom were Christians. She was baptized in 1606 or 1607. See Kitagawa, "The Conversion of Hideyoshi's Daughter Gō."
27. Akamatsu Hiromichi (1562–1600) was also known as Saimura Masahiro. His father was of the Saimura family and his mother of the Akamatsu family. He married the sister of Ukita Hideie. Hiromichi received instruction from Fujiwara Seika and befriended Kang.
28. One such person was Kim Yŏch'ŏl, a young boy in the Kwangsan Kim descent group when taken in 1592. Ukita Hideie is said to have entrusted Yŏch'ŏl to his wife, Gō, for care, and she then sent the boy to her mother in Kaga. This boy's

name became Wakita Kyūbei Naokata, and he grew up to become a samurai serving the Maeda in the Kaga domain, an official who became Town Magistrate, an expert in *The Tale of Genji*, a recognized *renga* poet, and the author of "Admonitions for Town Magistrates" ("Machibugyō kokoroesho"). In retirement, he became a Buddhist monk. Jōtetsu, which is the Japanese reading of his Korean given name, was part of his Buddhist name. See Nelson, "Law and Order in the Making of Early Modern Japan," 53–81.

29. This incident involving Ukita Hideie and some of his retainers, which historians call the Ukita Rebellion, may have occurred not in Fushimi but in Osaka. It probably began in the fall of 1599 and ended in early 1600 rather than beginning in the second month of 1600 (Ōnishi, "Hideyoshi shigo no Ukita-shi," 17–19).

30. This reference to the Hyōgo no kami describes its function in the Heian government, not its function as a title for samurai elites in the late sixteenth century.

31. This is a reference to Hideyoshi's invasion of Kyushu in 1587 and his defeat of Shimazu Yoshihiro, who had taken control of the lower six of the island's nine provinces, but not the entire island.

32. This disturbance in Shimazu territory was the Shōnai Rebellion (J. *Shōnai no ran*). Shimazu Tadatsune's murder of Ijūin Tadamune in Kyoto in 1599 prompted this violence. Tadamune's son Tadamasa (1576–1602) led the fight against Tadatsune, who had returned to Satsuma Province. The twelve forts mentioned by Kang probably refer to the twelve forts that supported the main fort, where Tadamasa was based. The rebellion ended in early 1600.

33. The first character in "Horio" in *The Record of a Shepherd*, 崛, is incorrect. The correct character is 堀. Both characters are read as *kul* in Korean.

34. The character 崛 in "Hori" in *The Record of a Shepherd* is incorrect. The correct character is 堀.

35. The second character in "Ryūzōji" in *The Record of a Shepherd*, 蔵, is incorrect. The correct character is 造. In Korean, the former character is read as *chang*, the latter as *cho*.

36. Hideyoshi's year of birth is more commonly given today as 1537. Nakamura District is now in the city of Nagoya, and his birthplace is now part of the grounds of Toyokuni Shrine. This Nagoya site is marked and commemorated by a stone pillar. Oda Nobunaga, Katō Kiyomasa, Maeda Toshiie, and Asano Nagakatsu (the father of Asano Nagamasa) also were born in what is now Nagoya.

37. The Jesuit priest Luis Frois (1532–97) wrote that Hideyoshi had "six fingers on one hand" (Ruis Furoisu, *Furoisu Nihonshi 4: Toyotomi Hideyoshi-hen 1—Hideyoshi no tenka tōitsu to Takayama Ukon no tsuihō*, 203).

38. Nobunaga did not gain appointment as Imperial Regent. Rather, in 1577 he

received a title of lesser status, Minister of the Right (J. *Udaijin*). This was the third-ranking position in the court's bureaucracy at the time.

39. These "rebels" may have participated in the Ikkō *ikki* revolt that Nobunaga suppressed in Echizen Province in 1575. Members of this revolt belonged to the Jōdo Shinshū Honganji sect of Buddhism and believed that worship of the Amida Buddha would lead one to salvation and rebirth in the Pure Land (J. *Jōdo*). Hideyoshi and Akechi Mitsuhide fought in Nobunaga's forces.

40. Hideyoshi received the title Governor of Chikuzen Province (J. *Chikuzen no kami*) in 1575. He took control of Himeji Castle in 1580.

41. Hideyoshi's given name was Tōkichirō 藤吉郎.

42. Hideyoshi is seen using the surname Hashiba from 1573.

43. This paragraph and the three that follow relate to the battle at Miki Castle, in Harima Province, fought between Bessho Nagaharu (d. 1580) and Hideyoshi, on the command of Nobunaga. The battle began in 1578 and continued for almost two years, until Nagaharu's suicide in the first month of 1580 ("Miki-jō no tatakai," in Rekishi to bungaku no kai and Shimura, *Kassen sōdō jiten*, 409–10).

44. Shimizu Muneharu (1537–82) was Mōri Terumoto's lieutenant at Takamatsu Castle, in Bitchū Province (Boku Shōmei, *Kanyōroku*, 151–52, n. 2).

45. Akechi Mitsuhide attacked Oda Nobunaga at Honnōji temple in Kyoto in 1582.

46. This report may be that which Mitsuhide had sent to Mōri Terumoto, but which fell into Hideyoshi's possession before reaching Terumoto. See Berry, *Hideyoshi*, 76.

47. Hideyoshi laid siege to Takamatsu Castle from the fourth month into the sixth month of 1582. Nobunaga was preparing to join Hideyoshi there when he was killed. Shimizu Muneharu committed suicide in the river a few days after receiving Hideyoshi's demand. See "Yamazaki no tatakai," in Rekishi to bungaku no kai and Shimura, *Kassen sōdō jiten*, 440–41.

48. Hideyoshi did not kill Akechi Mitsuhide. Rather, Mitsuhide fled from the battleground and was killed by peasants in Ogurusu, a village near Fushimi. Mary Elizabeth Berry writes, "Hideyoshi collected Mitsuhide's head and body and carried them back to Honnōji for the approval of Nobunaga's spirit" (Berry, *Hideyoshi*, 72).

49. Hideyoshi did not personally conduct a service for Nobunaga for thirty-seven days. While Mitsuhide and his forces attacked Nobunaga at Honnōji temple, in Kyoto, Nobunaga committed seppuku as fire raged through the temple. Whether he died due to the self-inflicted wounds or due to the fire, the fire burned his corpse. Hideyoshi held a funeral for Nobunaga several months later. See Lamers, *Japonius Tyrannus*, 224–27, for a discussion of the funeral and the politics surrounding it.

50. Boku Shōmei suggests that this was the Negoro and the Saiga *ikki* of 1585. The former group was led by Shingon Buddhist monks, the latter by Jōdo Shinshū Buddhist monks (Boku Shōmei, *Kanyōroku*, 153, n. 4; Berry, *Hideyoshi*, 85–86).
51. See Elisonas, "Christianity and the Daimyo," 346–59.
52. Sō Yoshitoshi (1568–1615) became the governor of Tsushima in 1579, at the age of twelve. The governor oversaw the islanders' trade with Chosŏn. Hideyoshi had Yoshitoshi communicate with King Sŏnjo in the years before the invasion, and in the course of those discussions Yoshitoshi became the first governor of Tsushima to visit Chosŏn. He led troops in the first division, which was commanded by Konishi Yukinaga.
53. For Xu Yihou's communications with the government of Ming China, see Masuda, "Satsuma, Ming China, and the Invasion of Korea," in Masuda, *Japan and China*, 180, 182–83. Xu Yihou wrote:

> In the *xinwei* year [Longqing 5; Genki 2; 1571], my ship was passing through Guangdong and was captured. Fortunately, the lord of Satsuma in Japan liked to use unorthodox methods and thus saved our lives. Every time it was [Chinese] villainous sorts who drew the *wakō* pirates into wreaking havoc on our great [Ming] state. They took prisoners of merchants and fishermen and turned around and sold their wares. It was all very sad. In the *yiyou* year [Wanli 13; Tenshō 13; 1585], I [Xu Yihou] and the others fearfully reported to the lord of Satsuma on the murders of Chen Hewu, Qian Shaofeng, and some ten or more others, that their wives and children were dead, and that the remaining bandits had gone off to Cambodia, Siam, Luzon, and elsewhere. A small number of pirate vessels awaited them there. In the *dinghua* year [Wanli 15; Tenshō 15; 1587], Hideyoshi brought down Satsuma, Hizen, and Higo, and the pirate ships stealthily set out to sea. I accompanied the lord of Satsuma to an audience [with Hideyoshi]. He risked death in an appeal to Hideyoshi, and as a result the order to have [the pirates] executed was rescinded. There were still two pirate leaders who had not been captured. From that time forward till the present day, there has been peace on the high seas.
>
> . . . Those Chinese who lived for a long period of time in Japan all belonged to bands of pirates. Not one of them, I believe, ever dared speak the truth [about Hideyoshi's expedition]. Furthermore, all the villagers who operated shops were not well versed in national affairs, and not one of them either ever spoke the truth about this.

This text was written in 1591 and reached Ming China in 1592. Masuda did not translate Xu's full text here (Masuda, "Satsuma, Ming China, and the Invasion of

Korea," 182; Xu Yihou, "Wanli ershinian eryue ershiliuri Xu Junwang jidao Xu Yihou Chen Jimi shiqing," 1a–3a).

54. Yŏngnam refers to Kyŏngsang Province.
55. Honam refers to Chŏlla Province.
56. Hideyoshi's mother was the Ōmandokoro Naka (1513–92).
57. This structure was Fushimi Castle. The earthquake struck in the early morning darkness of the thirteenth day of the intercalary seventh month of 1596. Fushimi and the southern part of Kyoto sustained great damage. Nara, Osaka, Sakai, Kobe, and areas in Shikoku too incurred damage. The earthquake toppled the *donjon* (J. *tenshu*) of Fushimi Castle. See Sangawa, *Hideyoshi o osotta daijishin*.
58. The character for "*shō*" in "*shōjō*" in Mashita Nagamori's title is printed as 正 in *The Record of a Shepherd*. That may be an error, for there was no such post in the Royal Gate Guard. In 1585 Hideyoshi issued Nagamori the title of Right Royal Gate Guard Captain (*Sengoku bushō kassen jiten*, 412–13).
59. For Maeda Gen'i (1539–1602), see note 2 in appendix 2.
60. Ōno Harunaga (d. 1615) was the son of the wet nurse (Ōkura-kyō no tsubone, d. 1615) of Yodo-dono (1567–1614). This is significant because Yodo-dono was the first of Hideyoshi's secondary wives. Trusted by Hideyori and Yodo-dono, Harunaga followed Hideyori in death in 1615 after Hideyori's defeat at Osaka Castle by Tokugawa Hidetada's (1579–1632) forces. The title Office of Palace Repairs Master (J. *Shuri no daibu*) was at the junior fourth rank lower (*Sengoku bushō kassen jiten*, 409–10).
61. For a detailed description of Japanese construction methods, see Cooper, *João Rodrigues's Account of Sixteenth-Century Japan*, 137–58.
62. Rumors circulated that Yodo-dono was having an affair with Ōno Harunaga (Kuwata, *Yodo-gimi*, 115).
63. One *masu* may have been approximately 1.63 quarts.
64. Daibutsuji was the popular name for Hōkōji, a Tendai sect temple in Kyoto that Hideyoshi founded and constructed in the 1580s and 1590s. "*Daibutsu*" (The Great Buddha) refers to a large statue of the Buddha that Hideyoshi had ordered built in 1586, and "*ji*" identifies the place as a temple. When finished, the Buddha statue, at more than 19 meters, was taller than the eighth-century Daibutsu at Tōdaiji temple in Nara. In 1595, the image, made of wood and layered with gold, was placed in the Hall of the Great Buddha (J. *Daibutsuden*) at Hōkōji. However, the earthquake in the intercalary seventh month of 1596 destroyed the Daibutsu. In 1599, Hideyori ordered the construction of a replacement. A fire in 1602 destroyed that image and the hall.
65. This small mound is Mimizuka (Ear Mound) in Kyoto. Hideyoshi constructed it for the burial of the noses and the repose of the victims' souls. Mimizuka is

near to Hōkōji temple and Toyokuni Shrine. For a history of Mimizuka, see Kin Heidō, *Mimizuka*.

66. Cao Cao (155–220) was a general in Later Han China.

67. Senhime (1597–1666) was the first daughter of Tokugawa Hidetada and his principal wife. She was married to Hideyori in 1603. He was eleven years old; she was seven. After Hideyori's death in 1615, she was remarried the following year (*Tokugawa shoka keifu*, 1:40). Kang's information suggests that her first marriage had already been agreed upon.

68. This shrine is not the present-day Toyokuni Shrine in Kyoto. After Hideyoshi's death, Maeda Gen'i supervised the construction of a mausoleum, to be named Hōkoku-byō, atop Mount Amidagamine, which is behind Hōkōji. On the seventeenth day of the fourth month of 1599, Emperor Go-Yōzei (1572–1617, r. 1586–1611), reading text thought to have been written by Yoshida Kanemi (1535–1610), whose family had been extremely powerful in Shinto since the late fifteenth century, proclaimed that Hideyoshi had been promoted to a god and announced his divine name, Toyokuni Daimyōjin. On the eighteenth day of the fourth month, Hideyoshi was placed in the mausoleum. The next day, he received the senior first rank title *Toyokuni Daimyōjin*. Hideyoshi's birth family did not have a household deity (J. *ujigami*), unlike the imperial family, aristocratic families, and many samurai families.

In having himself deified, Hideyoshi is thought to have sought an additional way to support his young son Hideyori's succession as head of the government. A second mausoleum was built at the base of Mount Amidagamine "in order that it might serve as the protector shrine for Hōkōji there." The Yoshida family managed Toyokuni Shrine, and Shinryūin Bonshun (1553–1632), who was Kanemi's younger brother, served as the chief priest. After defeating the Toyotomi family in 1615, the Edo government confiscated the shrine's land and revoked its permission to function as a Shinto shrine. The Toyokuni Shrine next to Hōkōji fell into disrepair; it was rebuilt in 1880. The Meiji government constructed a new Hōkoku Shrine on Mount Amidagamine in 1897 (Bitō, "Thought and Religion: 1550–1700," 393–94; Boot, "The Death of a Shogun," 156–57).

69. This report of a disturbance in Kumano may not be accurate (Boku Shōmei, *Kanyōroku*, 167, n. 2).

70. These hostages included Mao Guoke and Wang Jiangong, who appear elsewhere in *The Record of a Shepherd* (Boku Shōmei, *Kanyōroku*, 169, n. 2). See chapter 1, note 83.

71. Fukuhara Naotaka married the younger sister of Ishida Mitsunari (*Sengoku bushō kassen jiten*, 315).

72. Hideyori departed Fushimi Castle on the tenth day of the first month of 1599

(*Tokitsune-kyō ki*, 136; Gien, *Gien jugō nikki*, 10–11). Ieyasu moved into Fushimi Castle on the thirteenth day of the intercalary third month of 1599 (*Tokitsune-kyō ki*, 194).

73. In 1599 the intercalary third month fell between the third month and the fourth month in the Japanese calendar. In China and Chosŏn that year, there was an intercalary fourth month between the fourth month and the fifth month.
74. Hijikata Katsuhisa (1553–1608) later served under Ieyasu in the Battle of Sekigahara.
75. There is no evidence that Ōno Harunaga conceived a child with Yodo-dono after Hideyoshi's death (Kuwata, *Yodo-gimi*, 115).
76. This explanation of Ōno Harunaga's death is not accurate. He died fighting for Hideyori and against Ieyasu at Osaka Castle in 1615.
77. See note 4 above for Hideyasu's genealogy.
78. Ikuta Sanzaemon is Ikeda Terumasa (Boku Shōmei, *Kanyōroku*, 176).
79. Tian Heng (d. 202 B.C.E.) was the ruler of the reconstituted Qi in ancient China after the fall of the Qin empire. In contest with Liu Bang, he committed suicide rather than submit to Liu Bang, who had proclaimed himself the emperor of Han China. Tian's 500 soldiers, upon learning of their leader's passing, followed him in death (Boku Shōmei, *Kanyōroku*, 177, n. 1).
80. The military post of Army Aide was *Pyŏngma p'yŏngsa*, at the senior sixth grade.
81. There is debate regarding whether guns reached Japan in 1543 together with Portuguese who landed at Tanegashima in southern Kyushu, at earlier dates from Southeast Asia aboard pirate ships, or in 1542 together with Portuguese aboard a ship belonging to the Chinese trader-pirate Wang Chih (d. 1559). For a discussion of Japanese use of guns in maritime contexts in Japan in the sixteenth century, see Fujita Tatsuo, *Hideyoshi to kaizoku daimyō*, 24–31.
82. Boku Shōmei notes that where *The Record of a Shepherd* has the two-character phrase 西夷 (western barbarians), the original Chinese text has 四夷 (barbarians of the four directions). Our translation follows Pak's correction (*Kanyōroku*, 80, n. 4).
83. Rian was a student of Ian (Yoshida Sōjun) (Kang Hang, "*Rekidai meii denryaku* jo," dated 1598.12).
84. Kang mentions a visit by Rian and a visit by Ian in his preface to *Rekidai meii denryaku* (Famous Physicians of the Past, abridged). Ian had already obtained a preface, dated the first month of 1597, from another before approaching the Korean captive. Kang's preface appears first in the printed volume ("*Rekidai meii denryaku* jo," 2a–b).
85. Fujiwara no Sadaie (1162–1241), also known as Fujiwara no Teika, is famous for

his literary accomplishments. "*Kōmon*" likely refers to his having served as Acting Middle Counselor in 1232.
86. As Emperor Kanmu (r. 781–806) lived from 737 to 806, it would seem unlikely that Akamatsu Hiromichi was a ninth-generation descendant.
87. The title *Kunhak sŏkch'ae ŭimok* may be an error for *Kunhak sŏkchŏn ŭimok*, or *Regulations for the Rites for Confucius at Local Schools*. The latter title is seen in Cho Kyŏngnam, *Nanjung chamnok*, 190. Cho was working closely from Kang's writings in this section of *Nanjung chamnok*.
88. Abe Yoshio speculates that Keian may be the doctor who was imprisoned in 1618 for being a Christian, but having successfully treated Emperor Go-Mizunoo (1596–1680, r. 1611–29), he was permitted to teach students while incarcerated (Abe, *Nihon shushigaku to Chōsen*, 88).
89. This Japanese deckhand may be the individual who sailed with Kang and the other Koreans as far as Iki Island and there left the Koreans to return home (Kang Hang, *Kanyangnok*, in Yi Ŭrho, *Suŭn Kanyangnok*, 255). As Kang writes elsewhere in *The Record of a Shepherd*, they decided to sail past Tsushima.

5. Postscript

1. The phrase "black-toothed ones" refers to the Japanese and to the practice from ancient times of dyeing the teeth black.
2. Lord Su is Su Wu (140–60 B.C.E.), an official of the Han dynasty. He headed a diplomatic mission to the Xiongnu. Through a complex series of events, he and his fellow Chinese envoys were ordered to surrender to the Xiongnu under threat of death. Su Wu alone refused. After many trials and tortures, he was sent to a faraway place to tend sheep. Though he was constantly urged to surrender, he persevered. In 81 B.C.E., a Han envoy who was informed that Su was alive used a ploy to trick the Xiongnu into admitting Su's existence. Su was repatriated to China, where he was honored and given high office. Su and shepherding sheep have since then become synonyms for faithfulness in prisoners of war. For details, see "Li Guang Su Jian zhuan," *Hanshu*, 3:2459–70. The Chosŏn government too compared Kang to Su (*Hyŏnjong kaesu sillok*, 19:5a–b [1668.4.13]).
3. Kang Hang, *Kanyangnok*, in Kang Hang, *Suŭn chip*, 85b–86a.
4. This is one of the poems eulogizing Yi Yŏp (Kang Hang, *Kanyangnok*, in Kang Hang, *Suŭn chip*, 87a).
5. Sŏkchu was the pen name of Kwŏn P'il (1569–1612), who was a famous poet in the late sixteenth century and the early seventeenth century. His writings are collected in *Sŏkchu sŏnsaeng munjip*. (*Andong Kwŏn ssi sebo*, 8:42a–43a.)

6. This phrase in five-character regular verse is titled "In the Evening of the Fifteenth Day of the Seventh Month, Facing the Moon, I Had a Longing for Yi Chamin" (Kwŏn P'il, "Ch'ilwŏl sibo ya taewŏl hoe Yi Chamin," in Kwŏn P'il, *Sŏkchu sŏnsaeng munjip*, 3:7a). Kang and Kwŏn met on at least one occasion, after which Kang sent a note thanking Kwŏn for the visit (Kang Hang, "Sa Sŏkchu Kwŏn P'il yŏjang naebang," in Kang Hang, *Suŭn chip*, 1:18b). For a poem to Kwŏn, see "Hwa Kwŏn Sŏkchu," in Kang Hang, *Suŭn chip*, 1:43a. Further, Kwŏn wrote a celebration of Kang's return from Japan. He mentions first meeting Kang when the latter came to Chinwŏn County on official duty (Kwŏn P'il, "Kang T'aech'o so ja chŏkchung nae: Kam i sŏng si pyŏng sŏ," in Kang Hang, *Suŭn chip, purok*, 1a–b). This encounter may have occurred during the invasion. The last line, "A letter is transmitted by a goose," refers to the ploy that the Han envoy used in order to make the Xiongnu admit that Su Wu was still alive (see note 2). The Han emperor went on a hunting expedition and shot a goose, which had a letter from Su Wu tied to one of its feet ("Li Guang Su Jian zhuan," *Hanshu*, 3:2466).
7. Yun Sun'gŏ (1596–1688) was a well-known stylist and calligrapher. He studied poetry under Kang, and Confucian texts and rites under other teachers. Of the P'ap'yŏng Yun descent group, Yun passed the classics licentiate examination (K. *saengwŏn*) in 1633. He served in government posts from the mid-1640s, but did not reach a high position (*Han'guk inmyŏng taesajŏn*, 559, 355, 162–63; *P'ap'yŏng Yun Ssi Nojongp'a po*, 1:13). His father, Yun Hwang, served as the Yŏnggwang County magistrate (K. *Kunsu*, junior fourth grade) from 1609 into the second half of 1613. In 1667, Sun'gŏ wrote the preface for Kang's edition of the Song-period Chinese text *Gangjian huiyao* (Yun Sun'gŏ, "Kanggam hoeyong sŏ," in Kang Hang, *Kanggam hoeyong*).
8. In the Chosŏn period, P'ap'yŏng was in P'aju County, which was in Kyŏnggi Province and northwest of Seoul. This postscript is also in Yun Sun'gŏ's collected writings ("Suŭn Kang-gong *Kanyangnok* pal," in Yun Sun'gŏ, *Tongt'o chip*, 5:22b–23b). In addition, Yun wrote a posthumous biography (K. *haengjang*) of Kang. Much of the information came from *The Record of a Shepherd* (Yun Sun'gŏ, "Suŭn Kang-gong haengjang," in Yun Sun'gŏ, *Tongt'o chip*, 6:14a–28b).

Appendix 1. The Eight Circuits and Sixty-six Provinces of Japan

1. Emperor Yōmei (d. 587) reigned from 585 to 587.
2. Emperor Monmu (683–707) reigned from 697 to 707.

APPENDIX 1. THE EIGHT CIRCUITS AND SIXTY-SIX PROVINCES OF JAPAN   185

3. From ancient times, Japanese governments divided provinces into four hierarchical categories, based on the province's population and importance. The ranking of the provinces and of their governors varied accordingly. The post of governor of a superior province (J. *taikoku*) was at the junior fifth grade upper; of governor of a major province (J. *jōkoku*) at the junior fifth grade lower; of governor of a middle province (J. *chūgoku*) at the senior sixth grade lower; and of governor of a minor province (J. *gekoku*) at the junior sixth grade lower.

4. All references to *Setsuyōshū* below will be to the 1597 text, which is commonly called the Ekirin text after the Buddhist monk who compiled it. We have used it because it is the newest confirmed edition in Japan while Kang was there. If Kang used *Setsuyōshū*, he may have seen an earlier edition. Regarding the entry for Atagi, the 1597 *Setsuyōshū* also has "Atago" (Ekirin, *Setsuyōshū*, 556).

5. The ranks assigned to each province in *The Record of a Shepherd* match those in *Shokugenshō* in all but two instances, noted separately below.

6. The 1597 *Setsuyōshū* also has "Heigun" (Ekirin, *Setsuyōshū*, 557).

7. *The Record of a Shepherd* has the districts Shikinoagata and Shikinoshimo in a different order than the 1597 *Setsuyōshū*. The "upper" district (Shikinoagata) appears before the "lower" district (Shikinoshimo) in *The Record of a Shepherd*.

8. The 1597 *Setsuyōshū* also has "[Ta]ke[chi]" (Ekirin, *Setsuyōshū*, 557).

9. Emperor Wu ruled Liang from 502 to 549.

10. This province entry has the province name "Yamato" twice incorrectly as 太和. However, the province name Yamato and the country name Yamato were written with the same characters, as 大和. Also in this entry, a reference to a name for Japan appears as 和國. This rendering almost certainly lacks the first character, 大. For "Yamatai," this province entry has 野馬臺, or "Yamadae" in Korean. However, "Yamatai" was 邪馬臺. This form is read in Korean as "Samadae."

11. Mashita Nagamori was one of the five commissioners who served Hideyoshi from around 1595, and who after Hideyoshi's death were to govern the country below the five elders. The other four commissioners were Ishida Mitsunari, Natsuka Masaie, Maeda Gen'i, and Asano Nagamasa. From around 1597, Mashita held lands totaling 200,000 *koku* (*Nihonshi jiten*, 1552; Berry, *Hideyoshi*, 139–41; "Taikō-sama ondai gohaibunchō [Keichō ninen koro]," 630).

12. Shinjō Naoyori (1538–1612) received 13,000 *koku* of lands from Hideyoshi (*Sengoku bushō kassen jiten*, 381–82).

13. The 1597 *Setsuyōshū* has "Yasukabe-shuku" (Ekirin, *Setsuyōshū*, 557).

14. The 1597 *Setsuyōshū* has "Sara" and "Sakara" (Ekirin, *Setsuyōshū*, 557).

15. *The Record of a Shepherd* does not provide a *han'gŭl* transliteration of "Izumi."

16. Koide Hidemasa (1540–1604) received 30,000 *koku* of lands in 1585. Around

1597, his land holdings totaled 30,000 *koku*. He attended to Hideyoshi's wife, the Kita no mandokoro Nene, at a flower-viewing event in the third month of 1598 and was dispatched to guard Osaka Castle just before Hideyoshi's death in the eighth month of 1598 ("Taikō-sama ondai gohaibunchō [Keichō ninen koro]," 633; *Sengoku bushō kassen jiten*, 329).

17. Ishida Masazumi received 15,000 *koku* in Ōmi Province and held 25,000 *koku* there from 1595 (*Nihonshi jiten*, 1552).
18. The 1597 *Setsuyōshū* has "Higashinari" and "Nishinari-fu." The difference between the place names in *The Record of a Shepherd* and in the 1597 *Setsuyōshū* is the second character in each place name. The 1597 *Setsuyōshū* has 成, but *The Record of a Shepherd* has 城. Both characters are read in Korean as "*sŏng*" (Ekirin, *Setsuyōshū*, 557).
19. The 1597 *Setsuyōshū* has "Yatabe" and "Yabe" (Ekirin, *Setsuyōshū*, 557).
20. The 1597 *Setsuyōshū* has "Toyo" on the left side of "Teshima" (Ekirin, *Setsuyōshū*, 557). That is, "Toyo" would indicate "Toyoshima" as the place name.
21. "The emperor's capital" (K. *hwangsŏng*) refers to Kyoto and also to Yamashiro Province, which bordered Settsu Province to the west.
22. The 1597 *Setsuyōshū* has "Abe-bu" (Ekirin, *Setsuyōshū*, 557).
23. Tsutsui Junkei (1549–84) was the governor (J. *shugo*) of Yamato Province from 1576 into 1584, and in 1580 succeeded in gaining control of the entire province (*Sengoku bushō kassen jiten*, 217–19).
24. Junkei's son was Tsutsui Sadatsugu (1562–1615). Sadatsugu's birth father was Jimyōji Junkoku (d.u.), but he was adopted by Junkei in 1572 and succeeded him in 1584. After Junkei's death, Hideyoshi ordered Sadatsugu to relocate to Iga Province in 1585; he held 200,000 *koku* there. That same year, Sadatsugu received the title Governor of Iga Province (J. *Iga no kami*, junior fifth rank lower). At the time of the 1592 invasion, he was stationed at the Nagoya headquarters. In 1598, he possessed land holdings totaling 60,000 *koku* (*Nihonshi jiten*, 1552; *Sengoku bushō kassen jiten*, 402; "Keichō sannen daimyōchō," 123).
25. Natsuka Masaie (d. 1600) was one of the five commissioners. He received the title Ministry of the Treasury Vice Minister (J. *Ōkura no daibu*, senior fifth rank lower). Around 1597, Natsuka held lands totaling 50,000 *koku* (*Sengoku bushō kassen jiten*, 312–13; "Taikō-sama ondai gohaibunchō [Keichō ninen koro]," 630).
26. *The Record of a Shepherd* has three districts.
27. Kuki Yoshitaka (1542–1600) received 35,000 *koku* in Shima and Ise provinces in 1584. He received the title Governor of Ōsumi Province (J. *Ōsumi no kami*, junior fifth rank lower) in 1585 or 1586 (*Nihonshi jiten*, 1552; *Sengoku bushō kas-*

sen jiten, 313–15). Kuki Moritaka (1573–1632) succeeded as family head in 1597 (*Sengoku bushō kassen jiten*, 313–15, 487–88).

28. Owari Province was of major province rank (Wada, *Kanshoku yōkai*, 172–73).
29. The 1597 *Setsuyōshū* has "Echi" and "Aichi" (Ekirin, *Setsuyōshū*, 558).
30. Fukushima Masanori (1561–1624) received the title Left Royal Gate Guard Master (J. *Emon-fu Saemon no taifu*) in 1585. He received holdings of 200,000 *koku* in Owari Province in 1595 (*Sengoku bushō kassen jiten*, 456–58; *Nihonshi jiten*, 1551; Nakabe, *Kinsei toshi no seiritsu to kōzō*, 282; "Taikō-sama ondai gohaibunchō [Keichō ninen koro]," 631).
31. The 1597 *Setsuyōshū* has "Akumi" and "Ai[mi]" (Ekirin, *Setsuyōshū*, 558).
32. "Ikuta Sanzaemon" refers to Ikeda Terumasa (1564–1613), who received lands assessed at 152,000 *koku* in Mikawa Province in 1590 (Boku Shōmei, *Kanyōroku*, 103; *Nihonshi jiten*, 1551; *Sengoku bushō kassen jiten*, 382–84).
33. Tanaka Yoshimasa (1548–1609) received lands assessed at 57,400 *koku* in 1590 and lands assessed at 30,000 *koku* in 1595. Around 1597, his holdings totaled 100,000 *koku* ("Taikō-sama ondai gohaibunchō [Keichō ninen koro]," 631; *Nihonshi jiten*, 1551; *Sengoku bushō kassen jiten*, 351–53; Nakabe, *Kinsei toshi no seiritsu to kōzō*, 282).
34. The 1597 *Setsuyōshū* states that Tōtōmi Province had fourteen districts. The fourteenth district was Toyoda.
35. The 1597 *Setsuyōshū* has "Ifusa" and "Inasa" (Ekirin, *Setsuyōshū*, 558).
36. The 1597 *Setsuyōshū* has "Nakakami" and "Nakami" (Ekirin, *Setsuyōshū*, 558).
37. Horio Yoshiharu (1543–1611) received lands valued at 112,000 *koku* in 1590 and held lands totaling 112,000 *koku* around 1597 (*Nihonshi jiten*, 1551; *Sengoku bushō kassen jiten*, 370–71; "Taikō-sama ondai gohaibunchō [Keichō ninen koro]," 631). In the Japanese government, "*Tatewaki*" was a shortened term for "*Tatewaki toneri*," meaning soldiers skilled at the military arts who were selected to guard the Imperial Palace and the prince (Wada, *Kanshoku yōkai*, 258–60).
38. The 1597 *Setsuyōshū* has "Rohara" and "Io[hara]" (Ekirin, *Setsuyōshū*, 558).
39. Nakamura Kazuuji (d. 1600) received lands assessed at 140,000 *koku* in 1590, as well as lands assessed at 5,000 *koku* in Tōtōmi Province in 1595. In 1585, he received the title Ministry of Ceremonial Assistant Vice Minister (J. *Shikibu no shō*, junior fifth rank lower). In 1598, his holdings totaled 145,000 *koku* ("Keichō sannen daimyōchō," 123; *Nihonshi jiten*, 1550; *Sengoku bushō kassen jiten*, 303; Nakabe, *Kinsei toshi seiritsu to kōzō*, 282).
40. Jinglian was the courtesy name (C. *zi*) of Song Lian (1310–80), an official in the Ming China government. In mid-1374, Song compiled the *Great Ming Calendar* (C. *Da Ming rili*). His writings were of interest in Japan. One reason may have

been that he wrote about Buddhist temples and monks in that country (F. W. Mote, "Sung Lien," in *Dictionary of Ming Biography, 1368–1644*, 2:1225–1231; Wang, *Official Relations between China and Japan, 1368–1549*, 100; Song Lian, *Hanlin beiji*, 3:13a–16a, 7:1a–b, 10:11a–3b; Wang Hongxu, *Mingshi gao*, vol. 3, 18:8a–11b). Korean scholars knew of Song Lian by 1544 at the latest. Yi Hwang, the most influential Confucian scholar in the early Chosŏn period, mentioned Song in his writings (*Chungjong sillok*, 103:2a [1544.5.2]; Yi Hwang, "Udok Song sangye unun," *Munjip kodŭng* 1:40a–b (286).

41. A poem about Mount Fuji is found in a collection of Song Lian's writings called *Luoshan ji*. The poem in *The Record of a Shepherd* and the poem in *Luoshan ji* vary in each of their four lines. A note accompanying the latter identifies the three provinces as Izu, Suruga, and Sagami. See Song Lian, *Luoshan ji*, 4:13b.
42. "Ise Province" is a mistake for "Owari Province."
43. The 1597 *Setsuyōshū* has Kai Province before Izu Province (Ekirin, *Setsuyōshū*, 558).
44. For a discussion of Ieyasu's holdings around 1593, see Sippel, "Mapping the Tokugawa Domain from 1590 through the Early Nineteenth Century," 55–57, 66–67.
45. The 1597 *Setsuyōshū* has Tsuru as a fifth district, although the province entries state that there are "four districts." Tsuru is the last district in the list (Ekirin, *Setsuyōshū*, 558).
46. Asano Nagamasa received the title Board of Censors Assistant Vice Minister (J. *Danjō no shōhitsu*, junior fifth rank lower) in 1588. He gained lands assessed at 55,000 *koku* in 1593, and in 1598 held lands totaling 217,000 *koku* (*Sengoku bushō kassen jiten*, 367–69; Nakabe, *Kinsei toshi seiritsu to kōzō*, 281; "Keichō sannen daimyōchō," 123). Asano Yukinaga received lands assessed at 160,000 *koku* on the same day as his father Nagamasa in 1593 (Nakabe, *Kinsei toshi seiritsu to kōzō*, 281).
47. The 1597 *Setsuyōshū* has "Takaza" and "[Taka]kura" (Ekirin, *Setsuyōshū*, 558).
48. Ogasawara, *Nihon tō*, 70, 219–20.
49. Satomi Yoshiyasu (1573–1604) succeeded to the family headship in 1587. His base was in Awa Province, but his failure to support Hideyoshi appropriately in 1590 resulted in the reduction of his holdings to only lands in that province. He did not fight in Chosŏn, but he traveled to the Nagoya headquarters in Kyushu in 1593 with Ieyasu (*Sengoku bushō kassen jiten*, 325–26).
50. Satake Yoshinobu received lands in Hitachi Province in 1590 and additional lands in 1599 (*Nihonshi jiten*, 1550).
51. The 1597 *Setsuyōshū* has "Ikako" and "Ikō" (Ekirin, *Setsuyōshū*, 559).

APPENDIX 1. THE EIGHT CIRCUITS AND SIXTY-SIX PROVINCES OF JAPAN   189

52. Kyōgoku Takatsugu (1563–1609) received the title Ministry of Court Affairs Chamberlain (J. *Nakatsukasa no shō jijū*, junior fifth rank lower) in 1585, and apparently was subsequently raised to titles of higher rank. Takatsugu received lands in Ōmi Province in 1595 and 1598, and on at least one other occasion. In the 1592 invasion, he served at the Nagoya headquarters in Kyushu (*Sengoku bushō kassen jiten*, 352–53; Nakabe, *Kinsei toshi seiritsu to kōzō*, 283).

53. Ishida Mitsunari received lands assessed at 194,000 *koku* in 1595 (Nakabe, *Kinsei toshi seiritsu to kōzō*, 282).

54. Natsuka Masaie received lands assessed at 50,000 *koku* in 1595 and subsequently received an additional 12,000 *koku* of lands (*Nihonshi jiten*, 870; Nakabe, *Kinsei toshi seiritsu to kōzō*, 281; "Taikō-sama ondai gohaibunchō [Keichō ninen koro]," 631).

55. Oda Hidenobu (1580–1605) was the first son of Oda Nobutada, a Christian who was the first son of Oda Nobunaga and who also died at Honnōji temple. Hidenobu was baptized in 1595 and received the title Acting Middle Counselor in 1596. Around 1597, his holdings totaled 180,000 *koku*. "Keichō sannen daimyōchō" states that Hidenobu held 130,000 *koku* in 1598 (*Sengoku bushō kassen jiten*, 331–32; "Taikō-sama ondai gohaibunchō [Keichō ninen koro]," 628; "Keichō sannen daimyōchō," 122; *Nihon Kirisutokyō rekishi daijiten*, 260).

56. This note matches that in the 1597 *Setsuyōshū* (Ekirin, *Setsuyōshū*, 560).

57. The first adult given name of Kanamori Nagachika (1524–1608) was Yoshichika. Oda Nobunaga bestowed upon him the character *"naga"* from his own name; thus Kanamori became known as Nagachika. In 1586, Hideyoshi endowed him with lands in Hida Province. In 1598, Nagachika held lands totaling 33,000 *koku* (*Sengoku bushō kassen jiten*, 350; "Taikō-sama ondai gohaibunchō [Keichō ninen koro]," 630).

58. Kanamori Yoshishige (1558–1615) was adopted by Kanamori Nagachika. He received the title Governor of Izumo Province (J. *Izumo no kami*, junior fifth rank lower) and 10,000 *koku* of land in Hida Province in 1585 (*Sengoku bushō kassen jiten*, 416).

59. Sengoku Hidehisa (1551–1614) began serving under Hideyoshi when the latter was known as Kinoshita. He received the title Governor of Echizen Province (J. *Echizen no kami*, junior fifth rank lower) in 1592. Around 1597, his holdings totaled 57,000 *koku*. In *The Record of a Shepherd*, the surname Sengoku is printed as 千刻. This may be read in Japanese as *"sengoku,"* but the accurate rendering of Hidehisa's surname is 仙石 (*Sengoku bushō kassen jiten*, 392–93; "Taikō-sama ondai gohaibunchō [Keichō ninen koro]," 632).

60. The 1597 *Setsuyōshū* has "Jōshū" rather than "Yashū" (Ekirin, *Setsuyōshū*, 560).

61. To speculate, the *han'gŭl* spelling of this province name as "Kamijugye" suggests that the rendering may have been based upon someone's pronunciation of the province name as "Kamizuke" rather than as "Kōzuke."
62. This likely is a reference to Sano Nobuyoshi (1566–1622). Nobuyoshi was born to Tomita Ippaku (Tomonobu; d. 1599), who was a retainer of Hideyoshi. He was adopted by Tentokuji Hōen, who may also have been known as Sano Fusatsuna. Hōen joined with Hideyoshi in 1582. In 1590, Hideyoshi recognized him as the head of the Sano family. Hōen adopted Tomita Nobutane in 1592 and made this new son his successor. Nobutane soon changed his name to Nobuyoshi, and in 1592 he received from Hideyoshi possession of Sano family land valued at 39,000 *koku*. Around 1597, "Sano," which is almost certainly a reference to Nobuyoshi, possessed land holdings totaling 39,000 *koku* (*Sengoku bushō kassen jiten*, 317–18; "Taikō-sama ondai gohaibunchō [Keichō ninen koro]," 632; "Fujiwara-shi Hidesato-ryū Sano," in *Shintei Kansei chōshū shokafu*, 14:14–15; "Uda Genji Sasaki shoryū Tomita," in *Shintei Kansei chōshū shokafu*, 19:370).
63. "Mujunoogu" likely is a rendering of the Japanese term "Mutsu no Oku."
64. The 1597 *Setsuyōshū* has "fifty-four" districts (Ekirin, *Setsuyōshū*, 560).
65. In the 1597 *Setsuyōshū*, this note is as 又田. *The Record of a Shepherd* has 又作菊田 (Ekirin, *Setsuyōshū*, 560).
66. The 1597 *Setsuyōshū* has 阿曽沼 and glosses it as "Asonuma" (Ekirin, *Setsuyōshū*, 560).
67. The 1597 *Setsuyōshū* has "Mohara" and "Monohara" (Ekirin, *Setsuyōshū*, 560).
68. Date Masamune held lands totaling 614,000 *koku* around 1579 and 609,000 *koku* in 1598 ("Taikō-sama ondai gohaibunchō [Keichō ninen koro]," 628; "Keichō sannen daimyōchō," 122).
69. Uesugi Kagekatsu (1556–1623) was lord of the Aizu-Wakamatsu Castle and also held other lands in Mutsu Province. In 1592, he went to the Nagoya headquarters. He deployed troops in Chosŏn at Ungch'ŏn in the sixth month of 1593, and returned to Japan in the ninth month. In 1594, Kagekatsu received the title Acting Middle Counselor. He gained holdings assessed at 1,200,000 *koku* in Aizu in early 1598 (*Sengoku bushō kassen jiten*, 447–50; Nakabe, *Kinsei toshi seiritsu to kōzō*, 283; "Taikō-sama ondai gohaibunchō [Keichō ninen koro]," 628; "Keichō sannen daimyōchō," 122; Berry, *Hideyoshi*, 127–28). The term "*nagon*" in *The Record of a Shepherd* almost certainly is a mistake for *Gon Chūnagon* (Acting Middle Counselor).
70. Nanbu Nobunao (1546–99) succeeded to lands in Mutsu Province. He entered Chosŏn in 1593 and returned to Japan the following year (*Sengoku jinmei jiten*, 301–2).

APPENDIX 1. THE EIGHT CIRCUITS AND SIXTY-SIX PROVINCES OF JAPAN 191

71. The 1597 *Setsuyōshū* has twelve districts for Dewa Province (Ekirin, *Setsuyōshū*, 560).
72. Mogami Yoshiaki held lands totaling 130,000 *koku* around 1597 (*Sengoku bushō kassen jiten*, 390–91; "Taikō-sama ondai gohaibunchō [Keichō ninen koro]," 629).
73. Akita Sanesue (1576–1660) established his base in Akita District in the late 1580s and early 1590s, and received lands from Hideyoshi in 1591 (*Sengoku bushō kassen jiten*, 566).
74. Kinoshita Katsutoshi (1569–1649) was the first son of Kinoshita Iesada (1542–1608) and received lands in Obama, in Wakasa Province, from Hideyoshi. He participated in the Odawara campaign and the invasion of Chosŏn (*Sengoku bushō kassen jiten*, 546, 645–46). His title was Palace Guard Lieutenant (J. *Konoe-fu Shōshō*, senior fifth rank lower). Kinoshita Toshifusa, also born to Kinoshita Iesada, held lands in Takahama, in Wakasa Province (*Sengoku bushō kassen jiten*, 508–9). He bore the title Ministry of Imperial Household Assistant Vice Minister (J. *Kunai no shō*, junior fifth rank lower).
75. The order of the next six provinces from Kaga Province in *The Record of a Shepherd* does not match that in the 1597 *Setsuyōshū*. In the latter text, the order of provinces is Echizen, Kaga, Noto, Etchū, Echigo, and Sado. In *The Record of a Shepherd*, the order is Kaga, Echizen, Etchū, Echigo, Noto, and Sado.
76. The 1597 *Setsuyōshū* identifies Kaga Province as of major province rank (Ekirin, *Setsuyōshū*, 561).
77. The districts in Kaga Province are not listed in *The Record of a Shepherd*. The place in the column where the names of the districts would be listed is blackened, and no characters are visible. The 1597 *Setsuyōshū* lists five districts: Yone, Nomi, Ishikawa, Kaga-fu, and Kahoku (Ekirin, *Setsuyōshū*, 561).
78. Judging from the layout of information in the entries for other provinces, the district names seem to have been blacked out.
79. The place in the entry's second column where information regarding Kaga Province's economy likely would have been written is similarly blackened. A column of full-size characters in *The Record of a Shepherd*'s geography section totals twenty characters; the blackened portion in this column is equal to thirteen full-size characters. The description of Kaga Province's economy in the 1597 *Setsuyōshū* totals thirteen characters (Ekirin, *Setsuyōshū*, 561).
80. Maeda Toshiie (1538–99) was known as the Kaga Dainagon, not the Chikuzen Dainagon as reported in *The Record of a Shepherd*. His title from 1596 was Senior Counselor. Around 1597, Maeda possessed land holdings totaling 235,000 *koku*. "Keichō sannen daimyōchō" gives the figure of 230,000 *koku* in 1598 ("Suga-

wara-shi Maeda," in *Shintei Kansei chōshū shokafu* 17:269–72; "Taikō-sama ondai gohaibunchō [Keichō ninen koro]," 628; "Keichō sannen daimyōchō," 122).

81. Maeda Toshinaga (1562–1614), the first son of Toshiie, married a daughter of Oda Nobunaga. He received the title Governor of Hizen Province (J. *Hizen no kami*, junior fifth rank lower) in 1585, and succeeded to the family headship in 1598 (*Sengoku bushō kassen jiten*, 393–95).

82. The childhood name Magoshirō likely refers to Toshiie's second son, Toshimasa (d. 1633). Toshimasa received lands in Noto Province from his father in 1598 ("Sugawara-shi Maeda," in *Shintei Kansei chōshū shokafu* 17:274).

83. The 1597 *Setsuyōshū* identifies Echizen Province as of the major province rank (Ekirin, *Setsuyōshū*, 561).

84. Oda Nobuo (1558–1630), also known as Oda Nobukatsu, was the second son of Oda Nobunaga. He spent time at the Nagoya headquarters in 1592. Nobuo's first son Hideo (1583–1610) received lands in Echizen Province (*Sengoku bushō kassen jiten*, 474–76).

85. Ōtani Yoshitsugu (1559–1600) received lands assessed at 50,000 *koku* in Echizen Province following service to Hideyoshi in the invasion of Kyushu in 1587 (*Sengoku bushō kassen jiten*, 305–6).

86. Uoji likely is Uonuma. See "Kuni-gun-ken hyō," in Uno Shunichi et al., *Nihonshi jiten*, 1162.

87. Hori Hideharu (1576–1606) held Echigo Province. He possessed land holdings totaling 550,000 *koku* around 1597. Of that total, 150,000 *koku* were held by two retainers in Echigo Province (the Murakami family at 90,000 *koku* and the Mizoguchi family at 60,000 *koku*). See *Sengoku bushō kassen jiten*, 340–41; "Taikō-sama ondai gohaibunchō [Keichō ninen koro]," 629; Nagashima, "Keichō sannen Toyotomi Hideyoshi no Hori Kyūtarō ate Echigo-kuni chigyōgata mokuroku ni tsuite," 133. The printing of Hidemasa's surname as 堀里 is incorrect. His surname was 堀.

88. Echigo linen met high demand in the Kyoto market. Hideyoshi's holding of lands in Echigo Province valued at 5,000 *koku* may have been due to his interest in having direct access to this linen (Nagashima, "Keichō sannen Toyotomi Hideyoshi no Hori Kyūtarō ate Echigo-kuni chigyōgata mokuroku ni tsuite," 129).

89. Uesugi Kagekatsu took Sado Island by force in 1588 (*Sengoku bushō kassen jiten*, 447–50).

90. Around 1597, Maeda Gen'i possessed land holdings totaling 50,000 *koku* (*Sengoku bushō kassen jiten*, 319–20; "Taikō-sama ondai gohaibunchō [Keichō ninen koro]," 629). Maeda Sui (1576–1601) was the first son of Gen'i. He was baptized in 1595 and took the name Paolo.

91. The 1597 Setsuyōshū identifies Yosa as "Yosa-fu" (Ekirin, *Setsuyōshū*, 561).
92. Katano may be "Takeno." See "Kuni-gun-ken hyō," in *Nihonshi jiten*, 1163.
93. Hosokawa Yūsai Fujitaka (1534–1610) participated in the Kyushu and Odawara campaigns and also spent time at the Nagoya headquarters. Following Oda Nobunaga's death in the sixth month of 1582, he took the tonsure and moved to a castle in Tango Province. Yūsai, the name by which he is best known, principally for his cultural activities, was the first half of his Buddhist name (J. *hōmyō*). See *Sengoku bushō kassen jiten*, 358–59. Hosokawa Tadaoki was Yūsai's first son. He possessed land holdings totaling 110,000 *koku* around 1597 ("Seiwa Genji Yoshiie-ryū Ashikaga shōryū Hosokawa," in *Shintei Kansei chōshū shokafu* 2:301–8; "Taikō-sama ondai gohaibunshō [Keichō ninen koro]," 628).
94. Koide Yoshimasa (1565–1613) was a cousin of Hideyoshi, born to Hideyoshi's aunt. In 1595, he received lands assessed at 53,200 *koku* in Tajima Province. He had gained the title Governor of Yamato Province (J. *Yamato no kami*, junior fifth rank lower) before this. Around 1597, he possessed lands totaling 53,000 *koku* (*Sengoku bushō kassen jiten*, 385; "Taikō-sama ondai gohaibunchō [Keichō ninen koro]," 632).
95. Bessho Yoshiharu (1579–1654) succeeded his father Shigemune (1529–91) and held lands in Tajima Province. Shigemune had received 15,000 *koku* of land in Tajima from Hideyoshi in 1585. Around 1597, Yoshiharu possessed holdings totaling 15,000 *koku* ("Yagi-han," in *Sanbyakuhan hanshu jinmei jiten*, 3:418–19; "Taikō-sama ondai gohaibunchō [Keichō ninen koro]," 636).
96. Miyabe Nagahiro possessed land holdings totaling 50,000 *koku* around 1597. He received the title Ministry of Military Affairs Assistant Vice Minister in 1586 ("Taikō-sama ondai gohaibunchō [Keichō ninen koro]," 632; *Sengoku bushō kassen jiten*, 498).
97. "Ue no taifu" may refer to Kinoshita Nobutoshi. Nobutoshi was the younger brother of Kinoshita Toshifusa. His title, to which he was appointed in 1592, was Right Royal Gate Guard Master (J. *Emon-fu Uemon no taifu*, junior fifth rank lower). Nobutoshi was appointed lord of Himeji Castle during the tenure of his father Iesada as the administrator of Osaka Castle, which began before the Battle of Sekigahara. Iesada had been appointed lord of Himeji Castle in 1595, apparently (Boku Shōmei, *Kanyōroku*, 120, n. 3; *Sengoku bushō kassen jiten*, 645–46, 350–51). It would seem that Nobutoshi succeeded Iesada as the Himeji Castle lord before Kang left Fushimi.
98. Around 1597, Kobayakawa Hideaki held lands totaling 300,000 *koku*. See "Taikō-sama ondai gohaibunchō (Keichō ninen koro)," 628; "Keichō sannen daimyōchō," 122. The latter document cited here, dated in the title to 1598, states 336,140 *koku*.

99. In 1598, Mōri Terumoto held lands totaling 1,205,000 *koku* ("Taikō-sama ondai gohaibunchō [Keichō ninen koro]," 628; "Keichō sannen daimyōchō," 122).
100. The 1597 *Setsuyōshū* has "ten" districts (Ekirin, *Setsuyōshū*, 562).
101. The 1597 *Setsuyōshū* has "Tatenui" (Ekirin, *Setsuyōshū*, 562).
102. In a common practice among samurai, Ukita Hideie received the character "*hide*" in his adult given name from Hideyoshi. He was ten years old at the time. His wife, whom Hideyoshi had adopted as a daughter, was born to Maeda Toshie. Hideyoshi promoted Hideie to the title Middle Counselor. Hideie held Bizen Province as a domain. In 1598, his land holdings totaled 474,000 *koku*. His year of birth is also given as 1573 (*Sengoku bushō kassen jiten*, 557–59; "Taikō-sama ondai gohaibunchō [Keichō ninen koro]," 628; "Keichō sannen daimyōchō," 122).
103. The 1597 *Setsuyōshū* has "nine" districts and lists eleven place names (Ekirin, *Setsuyōshū*, 563).
104. The 1597 *Setsuyōshū* has "Numakuma" and "Numazumi" (Ekirin, *Setsuyōshū*, 563).
105. Kumade 熊出 may be a mistake for Kumage 熊毛. See "Kuni-gun-ken hyō," in *Nihonshi jiten*, 1165.
106. The 1597 *Setsuyōshū* has "two" districts, but lists four place names. Those four names also appear in *The Record of a Shepherd* (Ekirin, *Setsuyōshū*, 563).
107. This legend is the land creation myth in *Kojiki* and *Nihon shoki* in which Izanagi and Izanami create the island of Onogoro. See Philippi, *Kojiki*, 49–50; Aston, *Nihongi*, 6–12.
108. Wakisaka Yasuharu held lands totaling 30,000 *koku* in 1598 ("Keichō sannen daimyōchō," 125).
109. Hachisuka Iemasa held lands totaling 173,000 *koku* around 1597 ("Taikō-sama ondai gohaibunchō [Keichō ninen koro]," 630).
110. Ikoma Chikamasa and his son Ikoma Kazumasa together held lands totaling 122,000 *koku* around 1597. In 1598, Chikamasa's lands totaled 61,000 *koku* ("Taikō-sama ondai gohaibunchō [Keichō ninen koro]," 630; "Keichō sannen daimyōchō," 124).
111. The 1597 *Setsuyōshū* has "Chige" and "Chiki" (Ekirin, *Setsuyōshū*, 564).
112. Tōdō Takatora received lands assessed at 70,000 *koku* in the seventh month of 1595 and increases in 1598 and again in 1600. In 1598, he held lands totaling 70,000 *koku*. He received the title Governor of Sado Province (J. *Sado no kami*, senior sixth rank lower) in 1585 (*Nihonshi jiten*, 1553; *Sengoku bushō kassen jiten*, 476–77; "Keichō sannen daimyōchō," 124).
113. Katō Yoshiaki received lands assessed at 60,000 *koku* in the seventh month of 1595 and saw his holdings increased in 1596, in 1598, and after the war in Chosŏn.

APPENDIX 1. THE EIGHT CIRCUITS AND SIXTY-SIX PROVINCES OF JAPAN 195

Around 1597, his lands totaled 100,000 *koku*; in 1598, they totaled 60,000 *koku* (*Nihonshi jiten*, 1553; "Taikō-sama ondai gohaibunchō [Keichō ninen koro]," 631; "Keichō sannen daimyōchō," 124).

114. Ogawa Suketada received lands assessed at 20,000 *koku* in 1595 (*Nihonshi jiten*, 1553). He remained at the Nagoya headquarters as an administrator during 1592, and fought in Chosŏn in 1593.

115. Ikeda Hideo received lands assessed at 20,000 *koku* in 1595 (*Nihonshi jiten*, 1553).

116. It was Chōsokabe Motochika and not Chōsokabe Morichika who died in 1599. Morichika (1575–1615) succeeded Motochika (1539–99) (Boku Shōmei, *Kanyōroku*, 126, n. 7). Father and son both bore the title Governor of Tosa Province (J. *Tosa no kami*, junior fifth rank lower).

117. The 1597 *Setsuyōshū* does not provide a gloss of the place name "Nokonoshima." This gloss is from *Nihon chimei daijiten 40: Fukuoka-ken*, 1050.

118. Kobayakawa Hideaki received this province in 1594.

119. Nakagawa Hidenari held lands totaling 70,000 *koku* around 1597. In 1598, his holdings were 66,000 *koku* ("Taikō-sama ondai gohaibunchō [Keichō ninen koro]," 631; "Keichō sannen daimyōchō," 124).

120. The 1597 *Setsuyōshū* has "Takeno" and "Takano" (Ekirin, *Setsuyōshū*, 564).

121. The 1597 *Setsuyōshū* has "Kamitsuke" and "Kamisumeki" (Ekirin, *Setsuyōshū*, 564).

122. The 1597 *Setsuyōshū* has "Shimotsuke" and "Shimosumeki" (Ekirin, *Setsuyōshū*, 564).

123. Kuroda Nagamasa held lands totaling 130,000 *koku* around 1597 ("Taikō-sama ondai gohaibunchō [Keichō ninen koro]," 631).

124. Mōri Katsunobu held lands totaling 60,000 *koku* around 1597 ("Taikō-sama ondai gohaibunchō [Keichō ninen koro]," 631).

125. Ōta Kazuyoshi (d. 1617) held lands totaling 35,000 *koku* around 1597 ("Taikō-sama ondai gohaibunchō [Keichō ninen koro]," 633).

126. Hayakawa Nagamasa (d.u.) received lands assessed at 57,929 *koku* in 1593 (Nakabe, *Kinsei toshi seiritsu to kōzō*, 281).

127. Takenaka Takashige held lands totaling 13,000 *koku* around 1597 ("Taikō-sama ondai gohaibunchō [Keichō ninen koro]," 637).

128. *Yamaguwa* (*Morus bombycis*) is a type of mulberry.

129. Terazawa Masanari held lands totaling 30,300 *koku* in 1598 ("Keichō sannen daimyōchō," 124).

130. Katō Kiyomasa held lands totaling 195,000 *koku* around 1597 ("Taikō-sama ondai gohaibunchō [Keichō ninen koro]," 631). The Bureau of Statistics (J. *Kazue*) was in the Ministry of Popular Affairs (J. *Minbu*).

131. Konishi Yukinaga held lands totaling 146,000 *koku* around 1597, and 146,300 *koku* in 1598 ("Taikō-sama ondai gohaibunchō [Keichō ninen koro]," 631; "Keichō sannen daimyōchō," 123).
132. Shimazu Yoshihiro held lands totaling 559,530 *koku* around 1597. His holdings totaled 630,000 *koku* in 1598 ("Taikō-sama ondai gohaibunchō ([Keichō ninen koro]," 629; "Keichō sannen daimyōchō," 122).
133. Boku Shōmei, *Kanyōroku*, 134, n. 8.
134. Sō Yoshitoshi held lands totaling 10,000 *koku* around 1597 ("Taikō-sama ondai gohaibunchō [Keichō ninen koro]," 630).
135. In *The Record of a Shepherd* the first character in "Yanagawa" is printed as 楊, which is read in Korean as *"yang."* The correct character for this Japanese surname is 柳, which is read in Korean as *"yu."*
136. Of course, as Kang has just written that many men in Tsushima understand Korean, we cannot know whether islanders said the name of the peninsula country in the Japanese reading, "Chōsen," or in the Korean reading, "Chosŏn." Similarly, perhaps they said "Nippon" rather than "Nihon."
137. Sō Yoshitoshi received lands in Tashiro, in Hizen Province, after the war in Chosŏn ended, in exchange for lands in Satsuma Province that he had received from Hideyoshi in 1595 (*Sengoku bushō kassen jiten*, 399–401). The Tsushima daimyō held the Tashiro lands throughout the Edo period.
138. In Kyŏngsang Province, the Navy Deputy Commander (K. *Sugun ch'ŏmjŏlchesa*, junior third grade) was stationed at the ports of Pusan and Che.
139. The island of Isshōjima has not been confirmed.

Appendix 2. Japanese Government Offices

1. Emperor (J. *teiō*) [Son of Heaven (C. *tianzi*, J. *tenshi*, K. *ch' ŏnja*)]. "Imperial King" may be a more precise translation of the term *teiō*.
2. Oda Nobuo appointed Maeda Gen'i as Kyōto Commissioner (J. *Kyōto bugyō*) in 1583. Gen'i served until 1600, and also was Hideyoshi's conduit to the imperial court. Gen'i was his Buddhist name; he received the name Tokuzenin from the court in 1596 (*Nihon kodai chūsei jinmei jiten*, 911–12).
3. Regent (J. *Sesshō*) [court (J. *Denka*)]. The Regent post was introduced in 866, and the holder served for a child emperor. The child emperor became an adult upon the coming-of-age ceremony conducted in the year when he turned eleven.
4. Imperial Regent (J. *Kanpaku*) [court (J. *Denka*)]. The Imperial Regent served as the regent for an emperor in his majority.

5. Shogun (J. *Shōgun*) [tent government (C. *mufu*, J. *bakufu*, K. *makpu*)]. An abbreviation of *Seii taishōgun*, or Barbarian-Conquering General.
6. Prime Minister (J. *Dajō Daijin*) [Grand Pillar of State (C. *Daxiangguo*, J. *Daishōkoku*, K. *Taesangguk*)]. Another Tang Chinese name in addition to *Daxiangguo*, and with the same meaning, was *Dazhuguo* 大柱國, "a common unofficial reference to paramount executive officials such as Counselors-in-chief (C. *Ch'eng-hsiang* [*Chengxiang*]), Grand Councilors (C. *Tsai-hsiang* [*Zaixiang*]), and Grand Secretaries (C. *Ta hsüeh-shih* [*Da xueshi*])." In other words, the Prime Minister was the equivalent of the Director of the Department of State Affairs (C. *Shangshu*[*sheng*] *ling*). See Hucker, 126–27 entry 483, 412 entry 5049, and 464 entry 5916. Here and below, when quoting Hucker, his Wade-Giles romanization of Chinese terms will be followed by the pinyin romanization in brackets. Also, as here, references below to Hucker's *A Dictionary of Official Titles in Imperial China* will not include the book title.

    In Japan, there were three *daijin*, the Prime Minister, the Left Minister (J. *Sadaijin*), and the Right Minister (J. *Udaijin*). Kang does not include the latter two officials in this list. Prime Minister in the State Council (J. *Dajōkan*) was the highest appointed position in the Yōrō Code of 718. However, this post was rarely filled, and was later superseded by the two regent positions. The consistent absence of a Prime Minister resembled trends in Tang China. See *Shokugenshō*, 604; Wada, *Kanshoku yōkai*, 51, 386; *Xin Tangshu*, 1184–86; Borgen, *Sugawara no Michizane and the Early Heian Court*, 64.
7. Senior Counselor (J. *Dainagon*) [Grand Councilor of the Right (C. *Yaxiang*, J. *Ashō*, K. *Asang*)]. In Japan, the Senior Counselor was at the senior third grade. The Chinese term *Yaxiang*, which is the Tang Chinese equivalent in Kitabatake Chikafusa's *Shokugenshō*, is an "unofficial reference to a Grand Councilor of the Right" (C. *Yu ch'eng-hsiang* [*You chengxiang*]) in the Song period and to a lesser official in the Han period. In the Tang period, the post name *Chengxiang* (Vice Director of the Department of State Affairs) replaced the earlier post name. See *Shokugenshō*, 607; Hucker, 575 entry 7854, 126–27 entry 483, and 412 entry 5053.
8. Middle Counselor (J. *Chūnagon*) [Chancellery (C. *Huangmen* [*shilang*], J. *Kōmon* [*jirō*], K. *Hwangmun* [*sinang*])]. In Japan, Middle Counselor was established at the senior fourth grade upper in 705 and raised to the junior third grade in 733. The Chinese term in *The Record of a Shepherd* identifies the office, the Chancellery, but does not specify the equivalent post. In *Shokugenshō* are three equivalents, *Huangmen* being the third. That is, *Shokugenshō* also does not include the full post name.

    Huangmensheng was an "alternate official designation of the Chancellery (C.

Men-hsia sheng [*Menxiasheng*])." Therefore, the equivalence *Huangmen shilang*, or Vice Director of the Chancellery, is not the primary official reference to this Tang post. The official reference was *Menxia shilang*, or again, Vice Director of the Chancellery. The post of *Shilang* in the Chancellery was at the senior third grade in *Xin Tangshu*; Tonami Mamoru places it at the senior fourth grade upper. See *Ryō no gige*, 6, n. 1; *Shokugenshō*, 607; Hucker, 262 entry 2846, 262 entry 2847, and 329 entry 3942; *Xin Tangshu*, 1205–9; Tonami, "Tō-dai hyakkanhyō," in *Tōdai seiji shakaishi kenkyū*.

9. Junior Counselor (J. *Shōnagon*) [Supervising Secretary (C. *Jishi*[*zhong*], J. *Kyūji*[*chū*], K. *Kŭpsa*[*chung*])]. *Shokugenshō* provides the three-character post name *Iishizhong* (Supervising Secretary) as the equivalent. *The Record of a Shepherd* has only the first two characters, or the office name. This Chinese post was at the senior fifth grade upper in the Chancellery. Both the Junior Counselor in Japan and the Supervising Secretary in Tang China performed duties relating to official documents moving through the bureaucracy. See *Shokugenshō*, 608; Sansom, "Early Japanese Law and Administration (Part I)," 76; Hucker, 133 entry 587; *Xin Tangshu*, 1205–9; Tonami, "Tō-dai hyakkanhyō."

10. Imperial Adviser (J. *Saishō*) [Participant in Deliberations on Court Policy (C. *Canyi*; J. *Sangi*; K. *Ch'amŭi*)]. For the first character in the Chinese equivalent, *The Record of a Shepherd* provides 三 (J. *san*, K. *sam*) rather than 参 (J. *san*, K. *ch'am*). See Boku Shōmei, *Kanyōroku*, 94, n. 4. In Japan, Imperial Adviser, an extracodal post, was at the senior fourth grade lower. This official served on the Council of State.

In Tang China, Participant in Deliberations About Court Policy (C. *Canyi chaozheng*) was a "supplementary title conferred on eminent officials entitling them to participate in policy discussions in the Administration Chamber (C. *Cheng-shih t'ang* [*Zhengshitang*]) as members of the group known collectively by the quasi-official term Grand Councilors (C. *Tsai-hsiang* [*Zaixiang*])." See Hucker, 518 entry 6882. The Japanese term in Kang's entry, *Saishō*, is written with the same characters as the Chinese term for Grand Councilor.

11. Second Rank (J. *nii*) [Lord Specially Advanced (C. *Tejin*; J. *Tokushin*; K. *T'ŭkchin*)]. The Chinese term *tejin* was "a supplementary (C. *chia* [*jia*]) title, in early use apparently only as an honorific but in Tang and Liao [China] probably involving added responsibilities. At least in Tang, [it was] perhaps increased rank to 2a." See Hucker, 490 entry 6335. Hucker's term "2a" here means senior second rank.

12. Third Grade (J. *sanmi*) [Third Grade (C. *sanpin*, J. *sanpin*, K. *samp'um*)]. This entry title refers to the titles of the senior third grade. There were five posts of

the senior third grade and higher: Prime Minister at the senior first grade, Minister of the Left at the senior second grade, Minister of the Right at the junior second grade, Senior Counselor at the senior third grade, and Daizaifu Governor-General (J. *Sotsu*) at the senior third grade. From the fourth grade down, all senior and junior grades were divided into upper and lower. For example, at the senior fourth grade were the senior fourth grade upper and the senior fourth grade lower.

In Tang China, these were the civil prestige title of Grand Master of the Palace with Golden Seal and Purple Ribbon (C. *Jinzi guanglu tafu*) and the military prestige title of General-in-chief Commanding the Troops (C. *Guanjun ta jiangjun*). See Hucker, 168 entry 1159 and 284 entry 3291; "Kani sōtōhyō," in *Nihonshi jiten*, 1422–23.

13. Left Senior Controller and Right Senior Controller (J. *Sau Daiben*) [Minister (C. *Shangyin*; J. *Shōin*; K. *Sangyun*)]. The Senior Controller (J. *Daiben*) was at the junior fourth grade upper. The Left Senior Controller oversaw the four ministries of Court Affairs, Ceremonial, Civil Administration, and Popular Affairs (J. *Nakatsukasa, Shikibu, Jibu*, and *Minbu*), and the Right Senior Controller oversaw the four ministries of Military Affairs, Justice, Treasury, and Imperial Household (J. *Hyōbu, Gyōbu, Ōkura*, and *Kunai*). Posts of the Left were superior to posts of the Right in the Chinese, Korean, and Japanese bureaucracies.

In the Tang bureaucracy, *Shangshu* (Minister) referred to the head of each of the six ministries, at the senior third grade. In *Shokugenshō*, however, the Tang Chinese equivalent is the Left Senior Director of the Department of State Affairs and the Right Senior Director of the Department of State Affairs (C. *Shangshu zuoyou tacheng*). See Sansom, "Early Japanese Law and Administration (Part I)," 76; Wada, *Kanshoku yōkai*, 394; Hucker, 411 entry 5044; *Shokugenshō*, 608.

14. Left Middle Controller and Right Middle Controller (J. *Sau Chūben*) [Director (C. *Langzhong*, J. *Rōchū*, K. *Nangjung*)]. The Left Middle Controller and the Right Middle Controller were at the senior fifth grade upper.

In the Tang bureaucracy, the Director (C. *Langzhong*) was the third-ranking official in the ministries. At the senior fifth grade upper, the Director was below the Vice Minister (C. *Shilang*), at the senior fourth grade upper. However, this name for the Tang equivalent does not appear in *Shokugenshō*. In that Japanese text, the Tang equivalent is the Left Middle Director of the Department of State Affairs and the Right Middle Director of the Department of State Affairs (C. *Shangshu zuoyou zhongcheng*). See Sansom, "Early Japanese Law and Administration (Part I)," 76; Wada, *Kanshoku yōkai*, 394; Hucker, 301 entry 3565; *Xin Tangshu*, 1186–1202; *Shokugenshō*, 608.

15. Left Junior Controller and Right Junior Controller (J. *Sau Shōben*) [Vice Director (C. *Yuanwai lang*, J. *Ingai rō*, K. *Wŏnoe nang*)]. The Left Junior Controller and Right Junior Controller posts were at the senior fifth grade lower. In the Tang bureaucracy, the Vice Director (C. *Yuanwai lang*) managed a bureau within the ministry to which he was appointed. His post was at the junior sixth grade upper. *Shokugenshō* does not report "Vice Director" as an equivalent, and Hucker does not report the equivalent (C. *Shangshu zuoyou silang*) recorded in *Shokugenshō*. See Hucker, 597 entry 8251; Tonami, "Tō-dai hyakkanhyō"; *Xin Tangshu*, 1186–1202; *Shokugenshō*, 608.

16. Chamberlain (J. *Jijū*) [Reminder (C. *Shiyi*, J. *Shūi*, K. *Sŭbyu*)]. The Chamberlain served in the Ministry of Court Affairs. This post was at the junior fifth grade lower (Sansom, "Early Japanese Law and Administration [Part I]," 77; *Ryō no gige*, 8–9). *Shokugenshō* lists two posts as equivalents. The first is that cited as the equivalent in *The Record of a Shepherd*, Reminder (C. *Shiyi*). The second is Rectifier of Omissions (C. *Puque*). Both officials were remonstrance officials in China. See *Shokugenshō*, 610; Hucker, 425 entry 5256 and 391–92 entry 4777.

17. Left [Palace Guard] Commander and Right [Palace Guard] Commander (J. *Sau Taishō*) [Palace Guard Commander (C. *Muxia*, J. *Makuka*, K. *Makha*)]. The court divided the Palace Guard (J. *Konoefu*), an extracodal office established in 807, into the Left Palace Guard and the Right Palace Guard. The Left Palace Guard Commander (J. *Sadaishō*) and the Right Palace Guard Commander (J. *Udaishō*) were the commanding officers in the Palace Guard. In *Shokugenshō*, *Muxia*, the Tang equivalent in *The Record of a Shepherd* is third among the five Chinese terms for the Left Commander and the Right Commander.

    The first Tang term in *Shokugenshō* is Great General in the Forest of Plumes Army (C. *Yulinjun dajiangjun*). This post was at the senior third grade. There were two armies "prefixed Left and Right in the Northern Command" (C. *pei-ya* [*beiya*]) and, from 662, stationed in the Tang capital. Another possible equivalent is the Army of the Celestial Water Bearer, which was "one of the Twelve Armies (C. *shih-erh chün* [*shierjun*]) stationed at the capital." Troops from outside the capital were rotated through for service. The Tang government seems to have eliminated this unit in 636. See Hucker, 591 entry 8151; *Shokugenshō*, 633; *Xin Tangshu*, 1289–90.

18. Captain (J. *Chūjō*) [Palace Guard Vice Commander (C. *Yulin*, J. *Urin*, K. *Uim*)]. Captain was a post in the Palace Guard. *Shokugenshō* provides [Forest of Plumes Army] Palace Guard Vice Commandant (C. *Yulin zhonglangjiang*) as the first Tang equivalent. See *Shokugenshō*, 633–34; Hucker, 591 entry 8153 and 301 entry 3564.

19. Lieutenant (J. *Shōshō*) [Palace Guard Third Commander (C. *Yulin*, J. *Urin*, K. *Uim*)]. This too was a post in the Palace Guard. *Shokugenshō* provides [Forest of Plumes Army] Palace Guard Third Commandant (C. *Yulin cijiang*) as the Tang equivalent. See *Shokugenshō*, 634; Hucker, 591 entry 8153.
20. Office of Imperial Police (J. *Kebiishi*[*chō*]) [Court of Judicial Review (C. *Dali*, J. *Dairi*, K. *Taeri*)]. The Office of Imperial Police was established around 810, and gradually became the most important policing unit in the capital of Kyoto. *Shokugenshō* identifies the Tang equivalent as the Court of Judicial Review (C. *Dali*). This later became the Court of Judicial Review (C. *Dalisi*). However, the earlier *Dali* (Chamberlain for Law Enforcement) had already by the Tang period transformed into the Court of Judicial Review, which oversaw judicial proceedings. See *Shokugenshō*, 625–26; Hucker, 468 entry 5984 and 468 entry 5986; Friday, *Hired Swords*, 128–36, 222–23.
21. Ministry of Court Affairs (J. *Nakatsukasa*[*shō*]) [Secretariat (C. *Chungyi*, J. *Chūi*, K. *Chungyun*)]. *Shokugenshō* provides two equivalents for the Ministry of Court Affairs. One is the Secretariat (C. *Zhongshusheng*); the other is the Phoenix Hall (C. *Fengge*), which was "the official variant designation" for the Secretariat (Hucker, 214 entry 1998). The Secretariat was one of the three departments (C. *sansheng*), together with the Chancellery (mentioned above) and the Department of State Affairs (described above), that were the most important offices in the Tang government. However, the equivalent in *The Record of a Shepherd* is not provided in *Shokugenshō*. See *Shokugenshō*, 609; Hucker, 194 entry 1619.
22. Adjutant (J. *Hōgan*) [Chamberlain for Law Enforcement (C. *Tingwei*, J. *Teii*, K. *Chŏngwi*)]. This Japanese term may perhaps be understood in two ways. In the first reading, in the Heian period the pronunciation was "*hōgan*" when used with reference to men serving in the Office of Imperial Police, and "*hangan*" when referring to men in the Audit Board and in other offices who held this post.

    In the second reading, in the administrative structure, ministries, bureaus, and other administrative offices were staffed at the highest levels by four layers of officials. Here, *hangan* refers to the third of these four levels. Men assigned to these posts typically were born to fathers eligible for posts of the fifth grade. Officials appointed to the fourth and lowest post were born to fathers of a lower status rank. The *hangan* held decision-making powers, but men in the lower post did not. *Hangan* represented an important divide in the bureaucratic and status rank hierarchies that informed appointment and promotion. See Satō Masatoshi, "Kodai Nihon no shitōkansei," 25–28.

    The Chinese equivalent in *The Record of a Shepherd* does not appear to have been a Tang post. That term, Chamberlain for Law Enforcement (C. *Tingwei*), has an earlier history but seems not to have been in use by the Tang period. The "Kanshoku Wa–Kanmei taishōhyō: Wamei–Kanmei" table of Japanese-Chinese equivalencies and Boku Shōmei both show that Chinese post as equivalent to two lesser positions for imperial police, Vice Director (J. *Suke*) and Secretary. See Hucker, 512 entry 6767 and 512–13 entry 6776; "Hōgan," in *Heian jidaishi jiten*, 2:2278; "Kanshoku Wa–Kanmei taishōhyō: Wamei–Kanmei," in *Iwanami Nihonshi jiten*, 1419–21; Boku Shōmei, *Kanyōroku*, 94, n. 15.

23. Council Secretariat (J. *Geki*[*chō*]) [External Secretary (C. *Waishi*, J. *Gaishi*, K. *Oesa*)]. The Council Secretariat (J. *Gekichō*) was attached to the Council of State and assisted with documents. Two posts are noted in the *Shokugenshō* entry for *Geki*, Senior Secretary (J. *Daigeki*) and Junior Secretary (J. *Shōgeki*). A Tang equivalent, *Waishi*, or that in *The Record of a Shepherd*, is provided for "Junior Secretary." See Hucker, 561 entry 7604; *Shokugenshō*, 608.

24. Secretariat (J. *Naiki*[*kyoku*]) [Secretariat Director (C. *Zhuxia*[*shi*] and *Neishi*, J. *Chūha* and *Naishi*, K. *Chuha* and *Naesa*)]. *Shokugenshō* reports the *Naikikyoku*, or the Secretariat. This office's Tang equivalent was the Secretariat (C. *Neishizhu*), as recorded in *Shokugenshō*. The Chinese post name *Neishi* (Secretariat Director) was used from 618 to 620 and from 684 to 705. See *Shokugenshō*, 610; Hucker, 181 entry 1385 and 350 entry 4236.

25. Bureau of the Wardrobe (J. *Nuidono*[*ryō*]). The Bureau of the Wardrobe was attached to the Ministry of Court Affairs. *The Record of a Shepherd* does not provide a Tang equivalent for this office. In *Shokugenshō*, the Tang equivalent is the Clothing Service (C. *Shangyizhu*). In the Tang period, the Clothing Service was one of the six services attached to the Palace Administration (C. *Dianzhongsheng*). Its highest post was at the senior fifth grade. See Boku Shōmei, *Kanyōroku*, 94, n. 16; Hucker, 408 entry 5004; "Kanshoku Wa–Kanmei taishōhyō: Wamei–Kanmei," 1421; *Shokugenshō*, 612.

26. Ministry of Ceremonial (J. *Shikibu*[*shō*]) [Ministry of Personnel (C. *Libu*, J. *Ribu*, K. *Ibu*)]. The Tang equivalent in *The Record of a Shepherd*, the Ministry of Personnel (C. *Libu*), matches that in *Shokugenshō*. See Hucker, 306 entry 3630; *Shokugenshō*, 612.

27. State Academy (J. *Daigaku*) [Chancellor (C. *Jijiu*, J. *Saishū*, K. *Cheju*)]. The State Academy was attached to the Ministry of Ceremonial. In Tang China, Chancellor (C. *Jijiu*), at the junior third grade, was the highest-ranking post in the Directorate of Education (C. *Guozijian*). In this instance, Kang provided a post rather than the office as the equivalent. The full term in *Shokugenshō* for the equivalent, Chancellor, is Directorate of Education Chancellor (C. *Guozi*

jijiu). See Hucker, 130 entry 542 and 299 entry 3541; *Xin Tangshu*, 1265–66; *Shokugenshō*, 613.

28. Ministry of Civil Affairs (J. *Jibu*[*shō*]) [Ministry of Rites (J. *Reibu*, K. *Yebu*, C. *Libu*)]. In Tang China, Minister of the Ministry of Rites (C. *Libu*) was a senior third grade post. This equivalent matches in *The Record of a Shepherd* and in *Shokugenshō*. Also, in *Shokugenshō* the Ministry of Popular Affairs (J. *Minbushō*) precedes the Ministry of Civil Affairs. In *The Record of a Shepherd*, the Ministry of Civil Affairs precedes the Ministry of Popular Affairs. See Hucker, 306–7 entry 3631; *Shokugenshō*, 616.

29. Ministry of Military Affairs (J. *Hyōbu*[*shō*]) [Ministry of Defense (C. *Pingbu*, J. *Heibu*, K. *P'yŏngbu*)]. The Tang equivalent in *Shokugenshō* is Ministry of Defense (C. *Bingbu* 兵部). The Tang equivalent in *The Record of a Shepherd* is printed inaccurately as 平部. Both the first character in 兵部 and the first character in 平部 may be read in Japanese as *hei*. In Korean, the first character in 兵部 is read as *pyŏng* and the first character in 平部 is read as *p'yŏng*. See *Shokugenshō*, 616; Hucker, 384–85 entry 4691; "Kanshoku Wa–Kanmei taishōhyō: Wamei–Kanmei," 1421.

30. Ministry of Justice (J. *Gyōbu*[*shō*]) [Ministry of Justice (C. *Taobu*, J. *Tōbu*, K. *T'obu*)]. In *Shokugenshō*, the equivalent Tang office is the Ministry of Justice (C. *Xingbu*). In *The Record of a Shepherd*, *Taobu* 討部 as the equivalent Tang office is a mistake for *Xingbu* 刑部. See Hucker, 245–46 entry 2590; *Shokugenshō*, 617.

31. Ministry of Popular Affairs (J. *Minbu*[*shō*]) [Ministry of Revenue (C. *Hubu*, J. *Kobu*, K. *Hobu*)]. The Tang equivalents match in *The Record of a Shepherd* and in *Shokugenshō*. See Hucker, 258 entry 2789; *Shokugenshō*, 615.

32. Ministry of the Imperial Household (J. *Kunai*[*shō*]) [Court of the National Granaries (C. *Sinong*[*si*], J. *Shinō*[*ji*], K. *Sanong*[*si*])]. *Shokugenshō* has two equivalents for the Ministry of the Imperial Household. The first is Ministry of Works (C. *Gongbu*). The second is that in *The Record of a Shepherd*, the Court of the National Granaries (C. *Sinong*), but only the first two of the three characters in the court's name are recorded. The full Chinese name for Court of the National Granaries is *Sinongsi*. In Tang China, the Court of the National Granaries supervised "receipts and disbursements of the central government's grain revenues." See Hucker, 453–54 entry 5371 and 294 entry 3462; *Shokugenshō*, 618.

33. Bureau of Housekeeping (J. *Kamon*[*ryō*]) [(Unclear) (C. *Sasao*[*shu*], J. *Saisō*, K. *Saso*)]. The Bureau of Housekeeping was attached to the Ministry of the Treasury. *Shokugenshō* has *Sasaoshu* 洒掃署 as the Tang equivalent; *The Record of a Shepherd* provides only the first two characters of "*Sasaoshu*." Following the "Kanshoku Wa–Kanmei taishōhyō: Wamei–Kanmei" table, the Chinese

equivalent would be the Canopies Office (C. *Shougongshu*) in the Court of the Imperial Regalia. See *Shokugenshō*, 620; "Kanshoku Wa–Kanmei taishōhyō: Wamei–Kanmei," 1421; Hucker, 433 entry 5384.

34. Bureau of Music (J. *Uta[ryō]*) [Imperial Music Office (C. *Dayue[shu]*, J. *Daigaku*, K. *Taeak*)]. In Japan, the Bureau of Music was attached to the Ministry of Civil Affairs. The Tang equivalent, Imperial Music Office (C. *Dayue*), matches in *The Record of a Shepherd* and in *Shokugenshō*. Both texts have the first character printed as C. *da* 大, whereas *Xin Tangshu* has C. *tai* 太. In *Xin Tangshu*, this office is called *Taiyueshu*, which also may be translated as "Imperial Music Office." It was subordinate to the Court of Imperial Sacrifices (C. *Taichangsi*). See *Shokugenshō*, 616; *Xin Tangshu*, 1243–44; Hucker, 486 entry 6269.

35. Agency for Foreign Affairs (J. *Genba[ryō]*) [Court of State Ceremonial (C. *Honglu[si]*, J. *Kōro[ji]*, K. *Hŭngno[si]*)]. In Japan, the Agency for Foreign Affairs was attached to the Ministry of Civil Administration. In Tang China, the Court of State Ceremonial was in the Ministry of Rites. *Shokugenshō* presents the full, three-character title of the Court of State Ceremonial, *Honglusi*. See Hucker, 264 entry 2906; *Xin Tangshu*, 1257–58; *Shokugenshō*, 616.

36. Ministry of the Treasury (J. *Ōkura[shō]*) [Court of the Treasury (C. *Dafu*, J. *Daifu*, K. *Taebu*)]. The Chinese equivalent is shortened in *The Record of a Shepherd* to the first two characters. In full, it is *Dafusi* (Court of the Treasury), as recorded in *Shokugenshō*. See Hucker, 465 entry 5940; *Ryō no gige*, 46–47; *Shokugenshō*, 618.

37. Office of Weaving (J. *Oribe [no tsukasa]*) [Weaving and Dyeing Office (C. *jian Zhiranshu*, J. *ken Shokusensho*, K. *kyŏm Chingnyangsŏ*)]. In Japan, the Office of Weaving was attached to the Ministry of the Treasury. In Tang China, the Weaving and Dyeing Office was subordinate to the Directorate of Imperial Manufactories (C. *Shaofujian*); its highest post was at the senior eighth grade. Both *The Record of a Shepherd* and *Shokugenshō* present the full name of the Tang equivalent office. See Hucker, 159 entry 1005; *Xin Tangshu*, 1271; Sansom, "Early Japanese Law and Administration (Part I)," 92; Boku Shōmei, *Kanyōroku*, 95, n. 28; *Shokugenshō*, 618.

38. Office of the Palace Table Master (J. *Daizen[shiki] Daibu*) [Chief Minister, Court of Imperial Entertainments (C. *Guanglu*, J. *Kōroku*, K. *Kwangnok*)]. The Japanese phrase in *The Record of a Shepherd* combines an office in the Japanese government, *Daizen*, and the highest post in that office, *daibu*. In Japan, the Office of the Palace Table was attached to the Ministry of the Imperial Household.

The Tang equivalent in *Shokugenshō* does not match the equivalent in *The Record of a Shepherd*. In *Shokugenshō* is the Banquets Office (C. *Daguanshu*).

APPENDIX 2. JAPANESE GOVERNMENT OFFICES   205

The equivalent in *The Record of a Shepherd* is printed as *Guanglu*. This may be an abbreviation of *Guanglusi* (Court of Imperial Entertainments). See Boku Shōmei, *Kanyōroku*, 95, n. 29; Wada, *Kanshoku yōkai*, 113–15; Hucker, 467 entry 5973 and 288 entry 3348; Sansom, "Early Japanese Law and Administration (Part I)," 93; *Shokugenshō*, 619.

39. Bureau of Carpentry (J. *Moku*[*ryō*]) [Directorate for the Palace Buildings (C. *Jiangzuo*, J. *Shōsaku*, K. *Changjak*)]. In Japan, the Bureau of Carpentry was attached to the Ministry of the Imperial Household. The Tang equivalent was the Directorate for the Palace Buildings (C. *Jiangzuojian*), subordinate to the Ministry of Works.

    The first character in the Chinese term in *The Record of a Shepherd* differs from that in *Shokugenshō*. In *The Record of a Shepherd*, the name is printed as 匠作; *Shokugenshō* has 将作監. The first characters in both terms are read as *shō* in Japanese and as *chang* in Korean. See *Shokugenshō*, 619; Hucker, 140 entry 708; *Xin Tangshu*, 1272–73.

40. Bureau of the Palace Kitchen (J. *Ōi*[*ryō*]) [Imperial Granaries Office (C. *Dacang*, J. *Ōkura*, K. *Taech'ang*)]. In Japan, the Bureau of the Palace Kitchen was attached to the Ministry of the Imperial Household. In *The Record of a Shepherd*, the equivalent Tang office name is written as *Dacang* 大倉. In *Xin Tangshu*, the first character is *tai* 太, thus *Taicang*. This is the Imperial Granaries Office (C. *Taicangshu*). It was subordinate to the Court for the National Granaries. In *Shokugenshō*, the first character is that in *The Record of a Shepherd*, thus rendering the romanization as *Dacangshu*. See Hucker, 483 entry 6232; *Shokugenshō*, 619.

41. Bureau of Palace Equipment (J. *Tonomo*[*ryō*]) [Accommodations Service (C. *Shangcang*, J. *Shōsō*, K. *Sangch'ang*)]. In Japan, the Bureau of Palace Equipment was attached to the Ministry of the Imperial Household. For the Chinese post, the second character in the term in *The Record of a Shepherd* seems to be in error. Rather than 尚倉 as in *The Record of a Shepherd*, the Tang equivalent is 尚舍局 (Accommodations Service; *Shangshezhu*), which was one of the six services attached to the Palace Administration. See *Shokugenshō*, 619; Hucker, 410 entry 5035.

42. Bureau of Medicine (J. *Tenyaku*[*ryō*]) [Imperial Medical Office (C. *Dai*, J. *Daii*, K. *Taeŭi*)]. In Japan, the Bureau of Medicine was attached to the Ministry of the Imperial Household. Similar to the Imperial Granaries Office discussed above, in the name of the equivalent Tang office, *The Record of a Shepherd* and *Shokugenshō* have the character 大, and *Xin Tangshu* has 太. Further, where *The Record of a Shepherd* provides the first two characters in the office name,

Shokugenshō has the full three-character name, *Daishu*. In *Xin Tangshu*, the office name is *Taiishu*. *Shokugenshō* also provides a second equivalent, Palace Medical Services (C. *Shangiyaoju*). See Hucker, 479 entry 6183; *Xin Tangshu*, 1244–45; *Shokugenshō*, 620.

43. Office of Palace Women (J. *Uneme* [*no tsukasa*]) [Office of Palace Women (C. *Cainu*, J. *Uneme*, K. *Ch'aeyŏ*)]. The Office of Palace Women was attached to the Ministry of the Imperial Household. In China, the term *Cainu* referred to imperial concubines of lower rank, at the senior eighth grade in the Tang period. *The Record of a Shepherd* has the first two characters, and *Shokugenshō* has the full three-character office name. In *Shokugenshō*, the equivalent is *Cainushu* (Office of Palace Women). See Hucker, 515 entry 6839 and 413 entry 5076; *Shokugenshō*, 621.

44. Board of Censors (J. *Danjō*[*dai*]) [Censorate (C. *Shuangtai*, J. *Sōdai*, K. *Sangdae*)]. The Board of Censors was not attached to a ministry in the Japanese government. *Shuangtai*, the Tang equivalent in *The Record of a Shepherd*, was an "unofficial reference to the Censorate." The official Chinese name for the Censorate was *Yushitai*. *Shokugenshō* provides three equivalents: *Yushitai*, *Xiantai*, and *Shuangtai*. The second term too was an "unofficial" reference. See Hucker, 593–94 entry 8184, 438 entry 5488, and 243 entry 2540; *Shokugenshō*, 621; *Xin Tangshu*, 1235–40.

45. Left Capital Office and Right Capital Office (J. *Saukyō*[*shiki*]) [Metropolitan Prefecture (C. *Jingzhao*[*fu*], J. *Keichō*[*fu*], K. *Kyŏngjo*[*bu*])]. *The Record of a Shepherd* combines into one title and one entry what are presented in two entries under separate titles in *Shokugenshō*. *The Record of a Shepherd* has *Saukyō* (Left Capital Office and Right Capital Office) where *Shokugenshō* has *Sakyōshiki* (Left Capital Office) and *Ukyōshiki* (Right Capital Office). *Shokugenshō* presents two Tang equivalents in the first entry. The first term is Metropolitan Prefecture (C. *Jingzhao*), but the second term, C. *Pingi*, is not in Hucker. The full name of the Tang equivalent office is *Jingzhaofu*. This term applied to Chang'an, which was the capital of Tang China, and the surrounding area. See Hucker, 170 entry 1191; *Shokugenshō*, 622.

46. Office of the Stables (J. *Shume*[*sho*]) [Stables Office (C. *Jiushu*, J. *Kyūsho*, K. *Kuso*)]. In Japan, the Office of the Stables was called *Shumesho*. The Chinese term in *The Record of a Shepherd* is incomplete, providing only the first and third characters. The full Chinese term is *Jiumushu*. This office was attached to the heir apparent's household. See Hucker, 176–77 entry 1312; *Shokugenshō*, 623; Wada, *Kanshoku yōkai*, 33.

47. Left [Palace Guard] and Right [Palace Guard] (J. *Sau*) [Guard (C. *Weifu*, J. *Efu*, K. *Wibu*)]. Boku Shōmei suggests that the Japanese term *Sau* refers to the *Sau Konoefu*. The *Konoefu* (Palace Guard) was established in 807 and divided into the Left Palace Guard and the Right Palace Guard. The court subsequently reduced the guards in the capital; the Palace Guard was one of the new Six Guards (J. *rokefu*).

   The Chinese equivalent in *The Record of a Shepherd* does not match that in *Shokugenshō*. In the latter text are two terms: *Yulin*, or Palace Guard; and *Qinwei*, which may also be glossed as Palace Guard. See the next entry for further discussion of *Qinwei*. See Boku Shōmei, *Kanyōroku*, 95, n. 38; Hucker, 564 entry 7664; Friday, *Hired Swords*, 61–65; *Shokugenshō*, 633; Tyler, *The Tale of Genji*, 2:1166.

48. Assistant Inspector (J. *Shōgen*) [Palace Guard (C. *Qinwei*, J. *Shinei*, K. *Ch'inwi*)]. The Tang equivalent in *The Record of a Shepherd* and the Tang equivalent in *Shokugenshō* differ in the first character, but both terms may be read in Japanese as "*Shinei*." The first character in *The Record of a Shepherd*, 新, is in error. The appropriate character is that in *Shokugenshō*, 親. Rewritten with the character in *Shokugenshō*, the two-character equivalent in *The Record of a Shepherd* is Palace Guard (C. *Qinwei*; in full as C. *Qinweifu*). Each of these Chinese terms was an "unofficial reference to the Imperial Bodyguard or other special military units." However, *Shokugenshō* has a four-character term as the equivalent for Assistant Inspector. That term is Palace Guard Commandant (C. *Qinwei Xiaowei*). See Hucker, 170 entry 1187 and 238–39 entry 2456; *Shokugenshō*, 634; Sansom, "Early Japanese Law and Administration (Part II)," 120.

49. Left Royal Gate Guard and Right Royal Gate Guard (J. *Sau Emon*[*fu*]) [Imperial Insignia Guard (C. *Jinwu*[*wei*], J. *Kingo*[*ei*], K. *Kŭmo*[*wi*])]. The Royal Gate Guard (J. *Emonfu*) originally was one of the Five Guards stationed in the Japanese capital. The office included men from provincial regiments who guarded the outer and middle gates to the palace and the gates to the emperor's residence. The guards also performed other duties relating to protection and policing. The office name *Emonfu* was not used for a period of time but was restored in 811 when two existing guard units were renamed *Sau Emonfu* (Left Royal Gate Guard and Right Royal Gate Guard).

    Shokugenshō provides two Tang equivalents. The first is Imperial Insignia Guard (C. *Jinwu*[*wei*]); the second is Gate Guard (C. *Jianmen*). If the Chinese term *wei* is added to the characters in the second equivalent term, Gate Guard, that equivalent becomes Palace Gate Guard (C. *Jianmenwei*). The Palace Gate Guard was composed of Left and Right units in the capital. *The Record of a Shep-*

herd provides Imperial Insignia Guard as the Tang equivalent. See Hucker, 168 entries 1162 and 1166, and 149 entries 843 and 847; Friday, *Hired Swords*, 27–30, 64; *Shokugenshō*, 634.

50. Left Bureau of the Imperial Stables and Right Bureau of the Imperial Stables (J. *Sau Ma*[*ryō*]) [Office of the Imperial Stables (C. *Dianzuojiu*, J. *Tensakukyū*, K. *Chŏnjakku*)]. The Japanese name of the Bureau of the Imperial Stables may also be read as *Meryō*. The Chinese equivalent in *The Record of a Shepherd* does not match that in *Shokugenshō*. The term in *The Record of a Shepherd* is printed in three characters, as *Dianzuojiu*. This Chinese term is not in Hucker. The *Shokugenshō* equivalent has the first and third characters in "*Dianzuojiu*." With the suffix C. *shu*, this is the Office of the Imperial Stables, which was attached to the Court of the Imperial Stud (C. *Taipusi*). See Hucker, 501 entry 6551; *Shokugenshō*, 635.

51. Bureau of Military Storehouses (J. *Hyōgo*[*ryō*]) [Armory (C. *Wuku*, J. *Buko*, K. *Mugo*)]. The Tang equivalent for the Bureau of Military Storehouses is the Armory (C. *Wukushu*). The Armory was attached to the Court of the Imperial Regalia (C. *Weiweisi*). See Hucker, 571 entry 7782; *Xin Tangshu*, 1249; *Shokugenshō*, 635.

52. Left Watch Guard and Right Watch Guard (J. *Sau Hyōe*[*fu*]) [Militant Guard (C. *Wuwei*, J. *Buei*, K. *Muwi*)]. The Watch Guard (J. *Hyōefu*) was established with left and right guards. The Japanese government drew the men in these units from "among the provincial and lower central nobility." They were to become government officials, but first they guarded the gates deep inside the imperial palace. The Tang equivalent was Militant Guard (C. *Wuwei*). See Hucker, 574 entry 7834; Friday, *Hired Swords*, 27–30; *Shokugenshō*, 635; Tyler, *The Tale of Genji* 2:1167–68.

53. Office of Palace Repair (J. *Shuri*[*shiki*]) [Directorate for the Palace Buildings (C. *Kuangzuo*, J. *Shōsaku*, K. *Changjak*)]. The Office of Palace Repair was an extracodal office. The Chinese term in *The Record of a Shepherd*, *Kuangzuo*, matches that in *Shokugenshō* but does not appear in the *Xin Tangshu* entry. Following the "Kanshoku Wa–Kanmei taishōhyō: Wamei–Kanmei" table, the equivalent office in the Tang bureaucracy is the Directorate for the Palace Buildings (C. *Jiangzuojian*), which was subordinate to the Ministry of Works. See *Shokugenshō*, 624; *Xin Tangshu*, 1272–73; "Kanshoku Wa–Kanmei taishōhyō: Wamei–Kanmei," 1421; Hucker, 140 entry 708.

54. Audit Officers (J. *Xgeyu*) [(Unclear) (C. *XiangX*, J. *KōX*, K. *HyangX*)]. The character represented here as *X* is illegible. In the Chōsen Kenkyūkai's 1911

translation of *The Record of a Shepherd* is the character J. *ka* 勘 and the three-character term 勘解使, or J. *Kageshi* (Audit Officer). Boku Shōmei suggests that this entry represents the four-character term 勘解由使, or J. *Kageyushi* (Audit Officer). Following these two renderings, the text in *The Record of a Shepherd* would become J. *Kageyu* 勘解由. And the Chinese equivalent in *The Record of a Shepherd* would become 向勘, or C. *Xiangkan*. However, this two-character combination is not found in *Dai kanwa jiten*.

The Japanese court originally attached the suffix J. *kyoku* 局 to "*Kageyushi*." *Shokugenshō* states that the post of "*Kageyushi*" "is called *Gōgan* [勾勘]. This term is not necessarily a Chinese name." Neither C. *Xiangkan* nor 勾勘 (C. *Goukan*) is in *Dai Kanwa jiten* or Hucker. See *Kanyōroku*, in Ōmura, *Kakukan sensei jikki—Kanyōroku—Tōkyō zakki*, 38; Boku Shōmei, *Kanyōroku*, 96, n. 45; *Shokugenshō*, 624; Wada, *Kanshoku yōkai*, 195.

55. Dazaifu Governor-General (J. *Sotsu*) [Commander-in-Chief (C. *Dudu*, J. *Totoku*, K. *Todok*)]. Assigned to the Kyushu Government-General (J. *Dazaifu*), which was in Chikuzen Province, in northern Kyushu, were the Governor-General at the junior third grade, the Senior Assistant Governor-General (J. *Daini*) at the senior fifth grade upper, and two men as Junior Assistant Governor-General (J. *Shōni*) at the junior fifth grade lower. In *Ryō no gige*, *Dudu* is the Chinese equivalent. See Batten, "Cross-border Traffic on the Kyushu Coast, 794–1086," 382, n. 24; Sansom, "Early Japanese Law and Administration (Part II)," 118–20; *Ryō no gige* 6, 7–8, 8–9, 5; Hucker, 544 entry 7311; *Shokugenshō*, 632.

56. Senior Assistant Governor-General (J. *Daibu*) [Chief Minister (C. *Daqing*, J. *Daikyō*, K. *Taegyŏng*)]. In *The Record of a Shepherd*, the Japanese term *daibu* is written as 大武. Another Japanese administrative term read as "*daibu*," 大夫, is equivalent to the Chinese equivalent *Daqing*, or Chief Minister. This Chinese post referred to the official who headed an agency such as those that comprised the Nine Courts in the Tang government, or an office such as the Court of State Ceremonial (C. *Honglusi*) or the Court of the Imperial Clan (C. *Zongzhengsi*). In Japan, the Master (J. *Daibu* 大夫) headed the Office of the Empress's Household in the Ministry of Court Affairs, the Office of the Palace Kitchen in the Ministry of the Imperial Household, and the Capital Offices (J. *Kyōshiki*). See Boku Shōmei, *Kanyōroku*, 96, n. 47; Hucker, 173 entry 1255 and 177 entry 1317.

57. Guards of the Prince (J. *Tatewaki*) [(Unclear) (C. *Yuefa*, J. *Geppō*, K. *Wŏlbŏp*)]. Men with military skills were selected from among *toneri*, or retainers of the ruling family, and assigned to guard and protect the prince. This unit was established in 776, and the number of men increased over time from ten to thirty in

210   APPENDIX 2. JAPANESE GOVERNMENT OFFICES

857. The Chinese equivalent, 月法, is unclear. The term is not in *Shokugenshō*, *Dai Kanwa jiten*, or Hucker. See Wada, *Kanshoku yōkai*, 258–60; Farris, *Heavenly Warriors*, 27–28.

58. Bureau of Books and Drawings (J. *Zusho*[*ryō*]) [(Unclear) (C. *Diyin*, J. *Teiin*, K. *Chŏyun*)]. In Japan, the Bureau of Books and Drawings was attached to the Ministry of Court Affairs. The Chinese equivalent in *The Record of a Shepherd*, 抵尹, is not in *Dai Kanwa jiten*. In *Shokugenshō*, the Tang equivalent is the Palace Library (C. *Bishusheng*). See *Shokugenshō*, 611; Hucker, 376–77 entry 4588 and 378 entry 4598; *Ryō no gige*, 8–9.

59. Hayato Office (J. *Hayato* [*no tsukasa*]) [(Unclear) (C. *Puyifan*, J. *Fugihan*, K. *Puŭiban*)]. The Japanese term printed in *The Record of a Shepherd*, 準人, is an error for 隼人. The full Japanese term is *Hayato no tsukasa* 隼人司. The Hayato Office was attached to the Royal Gate Guard. The Tang equivalent in *The Record of a Shepherd* is *Puhufan* 布護反. In *Shokugenshō*, though, the Tang equivalent is *Puhushu* 布護署. However, "*Puhushu*" is not in Hucker. See *Shokugenshō*, 617; Morohashi, *Dai Kanwa jiten*, vol. 4, 406; Boku Shōmei, *Kanyōroku*, 96, n. 50.

60. Bureau of Statistics (J. *Kazue*[*ryō*]) [Bureau of General Accounts (C. *Duzhi*, J. *Toshi*, K. *Toji*)]. Tyler has "*Kazoe*" in his translation of *The Tale of Genji*. In Japan, the Bureau of Statistics was attached to the Ministry of Popular Affairs. The name of this bureau may also be read as *Shukeiryō*. The Tang equivalent in *The Record of a Shepherd*, *Duzhi*, is the second term in *Shokugenshō*; the first term is Treasury Bureau (C. *Jinbu*[*si*]), one of the four bureaus in the Ministry of Revenue. The Bureau of General Accounts (C. *Duzhisi*) was under the Ministry of Revenue (C. *Duzhi*), which was attached to the Department of State Affairs (C. *Shangshusheng*). See Hucker, 537 entry 7194 and 167 entry 1142; *Xin Tangshu*, 1192–93; *Shokugenshō*, 615; Tyler, *The Tale of Genji*, 2:1163.

61. Bureau of Taxation Commissioner (J. *Chikara*[*ryō*] *taishi*) [Two-Thousand-Bushel Official (C. *Erqianshi*, J. *Nisenkoku*, K. *Ich'ŏnsŏk*)]. The Bureau of Taxation was attached to the Ministry of Popular Affairs. This bureau's name may also be read as *Shuzeiryō*. The Japanese word *taishi* does not appear as a post in the Bureau of Taxation. Hucker notes that from the Yuan period into the Qing period, this term, as *dashi* in Chinese, was a "common designation of the head of an agency, usually of low status." See Hucker, 470 entry 6017.

The second term in this pair, Two-Thousand-Bushel Official, was from the Han period to the period of north-south division (206 B.C.E.–589) a "generic reference to the highest-ranking officials of government below the Three Dukes, notably including Commandery Governors because in Han they received annual salaries in money and various commodities reckoned to approximate the value of 2,000 bushels of grain." See Hucker, 205 entry 1828.

In *Shokugenshō* are two Tang equivalents. The first is Granaries Bureau (C. *Cangbu*[*si*]), which was in the Ministry of Revenue. The second is State Farms Bureau (C. *Tuntian*[*si*]), which was in the Ministry of Works. See Boku Shōmei, *Kanyōroku*, 96, n. 52; Hucker, 519 entry 6907, 550 entry 7409, and 550 entry 7414; Sansom, "Early Japanese Law and Administration (Part I)," 88; *Shokugenshō*, 615.

62. Acting Senior Governor (J. *Gon Kami*) [Supervisor (C. *Panguandai*, J. *Hōgandai*, K. *P'angwandae*)]. This post was at the junior fifth grade upper. Ancient Japanese governments placed this official in provinces ranked as "great" (J. *dai*) (thirteen provinces) and as "large" (J. *jō*) (thirty-five provinces)—forty-eight of the sixty-six provinces. He served as the top official in the provincial administration office when the appointed governor remained in the capital. See Wada, *Kanshoku yōkai*, 164.

The second term in this entry seems not to be a Chinese term. In Japanese, *Hōgandai* refers to officials in supervisory positions. A likely reference here is to a local provincial official (J. *zaichō kanjin*) who served in the provincial headquarters (J. *kokuga*) as *Hōgandai*.

63. Senior Inspector (J. *Kenmotsu*) [Gentleman of the Capital Gates (C. *Chengmenlang*, J. *Jōmonrō*, K. *Sŏngmunnang*)]. In Japan, the Senior Inspector was assigned to the Ministry of Court Affairs. In China, the Gentleman of the Capital Gates was posted to the Chancellery. See *Shokugenshō*, 610; Hucker, 128 entry 505; Sansom, "Early Japanese Law and Administration [Part I]," 78.

64. Office of Water (J. *Moitori* [*no tsukasa*]) [Office of Imperial Parks (C. *Shanglinshu*, J. *Jōrinchō*, K. *Sanginso*)]. In Japan, the Office of Water was attached to the Ministry of the Imperial Household. The Tang equivalent in *The Record of a Shepherd* is the Office of Imperial Parks (C. *Shanglinshu*). This office was attached to the Court of the Imperial Granaries (C. *Sinongsi*). See *Shokugenshō*, 621; Hucker, 409 entry 5022 and 405 entry 4959.

65. Bureau of Attendants (J. *Ōtone*[*riryō*]) [Gatekeeper (C. *Menpu*, J. *Monboku*, K. *Munbok*)]. In Japan, the Bureau of Attendants was attached to the Ministry of Court Affairs. It was composed of left and right bureaus and staffed with attendants selected from appropriate sons in families of the sixth, seventh, and eighth court ranks. Their duties included "waiting upon the great people at court, carrying messages, and acting as escorts."

In Tang China, Gatekeeper (C. *Menpu*), the equivalent post provided in

The Record of a Shepherd, was attached to the Office for the National Altars (C. *Jiaosheshu*) but was unranked. This term does not appear as an equivalent in *Shokugenshō*, however. That Japanese text has an office, Palace Gates Service (C. *Gongweizhu*), that was one of six attached to the Palace Domestic Service (C. *Neishisheng*) and staffed by eunuchs. The Palace Gates Service was "responsible primarily for keeping the keys for entrance into the inner quarters of the imperial palace and for opening and closing the gates at proper times." See *Shokugenshō*, 611; "Kanshoku Wa–Kanmei taishōhyō: Wamei–Kanmei," 1421; Hucker, 329 entry 3949 and 296 entry 3495; Sansom, "Early Japanese Law and Administration (Part I)," 78–80; *Ryō no gige*, 8.

Bibliography

Abe Yoshio. *Nihon shushigaku to Chōsen*. Tokyo: Tōkyō daigaku shuppankai, 1965.
Akioka Takejirō, ed. *Nihon kochizu shūsei*. Tokyo: Kajima kenkyūjo shuppankai, 1971.
Andong Kwŏn ssi sebo. 1907.
Aston, W. G., trans. *Nihongi: Chronicles of Japan from the Earliest Times to A.D. 697*. Rutland, Vt.: Charles E. Tuttle, 1972.
Batten, Bruce L. "Cross-border Traffic on the Kyushu Coast, 794–1086." In *Heian Japan, Centers and Peripheries*, ed. Mikael Adolphson, Edward Kamens, and Stacie Matsumoto, 357–83. Honolulu: University of Hawai'i Press, 2007.
Baynes, Cary F. *The I Ching; or Book of Changes: The Richard Wilhelm Translation Rendered Into English*. New York: Pantheon, 1961.
Berry, Mary Elizabeth. *Hideyoshi*. Cambridge, Mass.: Harvard University Press, 1982.
Bitō, Masahide. "Thought and Religion: 1550–1700." In *The Cambridge History of Japan*, vol. 4, *Early Modern Japan*, ed. John Whitney Hall, 373–424. Cambridge: Cambridge University Press, 1991.
Bonshun. *Shun kyūki*. 8 vols. Tokyo: Zoku gunsho ruijū kanseikai, 1970–1999.
Boot, W. J. "The Death of a Shogun: Deification in Early Modern Japan." In *Shinto in History: Ways of the Kami*, ed. John Breen and Mark Teeuwen, 144–66. Richmond, UK: Curzon Press, 2000.
Borgen, Robert. *Sugawara no Michizane and the Early Heian Court*. Cambridge, Mass.: Council on East Asian Studies, Harvard University, 1986.
Brown, Philip C. *Central Authority and Local Autonomy in the Formation of Early Modern Japan: The Case of Kaga Domain*. Stanford: Stanford University Press, 1993.

Butler, Lee. *Emperor and Aristocracy in Japan, 1467–1680*. Cambridge, Mass.: Harvard University Asia Center, 2002.

Butler, Lee A. "The Way of Yin and Yang: A Tradition Revived, Sold, Adopted." *Monumenta Nipponica* 51, no. 2 (1996): 189–217.

Ch'angnyŏng Sŏng ssi chokpo. Tōkyō daigaku Tōyō bunka kenkyūjo toshoshitsu collection.

Chinju Kang-ssi seboso, ed. *Chinju Kang ssi sebo: Suŭn-gong p'abo*. N.p.: Chinju Kang ssi seboso, 1963.

Chinju Kim ssi taedongbo. Taejŏn, Republic of Korea: Hoesangsa, 2006.

Cho Kyŏngnam. *Nanjung chamnok*. In *Taedong yasŭng*, vol. 6. Kyŏngsŏng: Chōsen kosho kankōkai, 1910.

Ch'oe Hyeju. "Han-mal ilche-ha chaejo Ilbonin ŭi Chosŏn kosŏ kanhaeng saŏp." *Taedong munhwa yŏngu* 66 (2009): 417–47.

Chŏng Hŭidŭk. *Haesangnok*. In *Haehaeng ch'ongjae*, 8:59–140. Seoul: Minjok munhwa ch'ujinhoe, 1974.

Ch'ŏngp'ung Kim ssi sebo.

Ch'ŏngsong Sim ssi taedong sebo, 1920.

Chunqiu zhengyi. In *Shisanjing zhushu*. Beijing: Zhonghua shuju, 1980.

Collcutt, Martin. *Five Mountains: The Rinzai Zen Monastic Institution in Medieval Japan*. Cambridge, Mass.: Council on East Asian Studies, Harvard University, 1981.

Colley, Linda. *Britons: Forging the Nation, 1707–1837*. New Haven: Yale University Press, 1992.

Confucius. *The Analects*. Trans. David Hinton. Washington, D.C.: Counterpoint, 1998.

Cooper, Michael. *They Came to Japan: An Anthology of European Reports on Japan, 1543–1640*. Berkeley: University of California Press, 1965.

———, ed. *João Rodrigues's Account of Sixteenth-Century Japan*. London: Hakluyt Society, 2001.

Cortazzi, Hugh. *Isles of Gold: Antique Maps of Japan*. New York: Weatherhill, 1983.

Dai Nihon shiryō. Tokyo: Tōkyō daigaku Shiryō hensanjo, 1901–2011.

de Bary, Wm. Theodore, Carol Gluck, and Arthur E. Tiedemann, eds. *Sources of Japanese Tradition*, 2nd ed., Vol. 1: *From Earliest Times to 1600*. New York: Columbia University Press, 2002.

de Crespigny, Rafe. *A Biographical Dictionary of Later Han to the Three Kingdoms (23–220 A.D.)*. Leiden: Brill, 2007.

Dictionary of Sources of Classical Japan. Paris: De Boccard, 2006.

Ehime-ken shi: Gakumon, shūkyō. Matsuyama, Japan: Ehime-ken, 1985.
Ekirin. *Setsuyōshū.* In *Kohon Setsuyōshū rokushū kenkyū narabi ni sōgō sakuin,* vol. 1. Tokyo: Benseisha, 1979.
Elisonas, Jurgis. "Christianity and the Daimyo." In *The Cambridge History of Japan,* vol. 4, *Early Modern Japan,* ed. John Whitney Hall, 235–300. Cambridge: Cambridge University Press, 1991.
Farris, William Wayne. *Heavenly Warriors: The Evolution of Japan's Military, 500–1300.* Cambridge, Mass.: Council on East Asian Studies, Harvard University, 1992.
Friday, Karl. *Hired Swords: The Rise of Private Warrior Bands in Early Japan.* Stanford: Stanford University Press, 1992.
Fujita Tatsuo. *Hideyoshi to kaizoku daimyō: Umi kara mita sengoku shūen.* Tokyo: Chūō kōron shinsha, 2012.
Fujita Tsuneharu. *Toyotomi Hidetsugu no kenkyū.* Tokyo: Meicho shuppan, 2003.
Fujiwara Seika. *Fujiwara Seika shū.* 2 vols. Tokyo: Kokumin seishin bunka kenkyūjo, 1938–1939.
Fukuda Chizuru. "Toyotomi Hideyori kenkyū josetsu." In *Shokuho no seiji kōzō,* ed. Miki Seiichirō. Tokyo: Yoshikawa kōbunkan, 2000.
Furoisu, Ruis [Luis Frois]. *Furoisu Nihonshi 4: Toyotomi Hideyoshi-hen 1—Hideyoshi no tenka tōitsu to Takayama Ukon no tsuihō.* Trans. Matsuda Kiichi and Kawasaki Momota. Tokyo: Chūō kōronsha, 2000.
Haehaeng ch'ongjae. 12 vols. Seoul: Minjok munhwa ch'ujinhoe, 1974.
Gerhart, Karen M. *The Material Culture of Death in Japan.* Honolulu: University of Hawai'i Press, 2009.
Gien. *Gien jugō nikki.* In *Shiryō sanshū,* vol. 2. Tokyo: Zoku gunsho ruijū kanseikai, 1976–1986.
Goodrich, L. Carrington and Chaoying Fang, eds. *Dictionary of Ming Biography, 1368–1644.* 2 vols. New York: Columbia University Press, 1976.
Haboush, JaHyun Kim. "Contesting Chinese Time, Nationalizing Temporal Space: Temporal Inscription in Late Chosŏn Korea." In *Time, Temporality, and Imperial Transition: East Asia from Ming to Qing,* ed. Lynn A. Struve, 115–41. Honolulu: Association for Asian Studies and University of Hawai'i Press, 2005.
——, ed. *Epistolary Korea: Letters in the Communicative Space of the Chosŏn, 1392–1910.* New York: Columbia University Press, 2009.
Haedong chido. Seoul: Sŏul taehakkyo Kyujanggak, 1995.
Haeju Ch'oe ssi sebo. Taejŏn, Republic of Korea: Hoesangsa, 2000.
Han'guk inmyŏng taesajŏn p'yŏnch'ansil, ed. *Han'guk inmyŏng taesajŏn.* Seoul: Singu munhwasa, 1976.

Hanshu. In *Ershisi shi*. Beijing: Zhonghua shuju, 1995.

Hawley, Samuel. *The Imjin War: Japan's Sixteenth-Century Invasion of Korea and Attempt to Conquer China*. Seoul: Royal Asiatic Society, Korea Branch, 2005.

Hazelton, Keith. *A Synchronic Chinese-Western Daily Calendar 1341–1661* A.D. Minneapolis: Ming Studies, 1985, 2nd printing, rev.

Hirano Kunio and Seno Seiichirō, eds. *Nihon kodai chūsei jinmei jiten*. Tokyo: Yoshikawa kōbunkan, 2006.

Hiraoka Jōkai. "Toyokuni Daimyōjin no seiritsu: Hōkōji Daibutsu-den no zōritsu." In *Gongen shinkō*, ed. Hiraoka Jōkai, 195–221. Tokyo: Yūzankaku, 1991.

"Honke Hagi Mōri-ke." In *Kinsei Bōchō shoke keizu sōran fu shinsen Ōuchi-shi keizu*, ed. Misaka Keiji, 1–17. Yamaguchi, Japan: Matsuno shoten, 1966.

Hucker, Charles O. *A Dictionary of Official Titles in Imperial China*. Stanford: Stanford University Press, 1985.

Hwang Sin. *Ilbon wanghwan ilgi*. In *Haehaeng ch'ongjae*, 8:41–58. Seoul: Minjok munhwa ch'ujinhoe, 1974.

Hyojong sillok. In *Chosŏn wangjo sillok*, vols. 35–36. Seoul: Kuksa p'yŏnch'an wiwŏnhoe, 1955–1963.

Hyŏnjong kaesu sillok. In *Chosŏn wangjo sillok*, vols. 37–38. Seoul: Kuksa p'yŏnch'an wiwŏnhoe, 1955–1963.

Im Ch'igyun. "*Kanyangnok* yŏngu: Sasil, chesi wa ch'ehŏm ŭi hyŏngsŏnghwa." *Chŏngsin munhwa yŏn'gu* 24, no. 2 (2001): 105–28.

Imai Rintarō. *Ishida Mitsunari*. Tokyo: Yoshikawa kōbunkan, 1961.

Japan Memory Project Online Glossary of Japanese Historical Terms. University of Tokyo Historiographical Institute, http://wwwap.hi.u-tokyo.ac.jp/ships/shipscontroller?cfname=W26/26.ctl&pfid=out001&session=01922182425182A8238FEFFECEFD96CFC6EAF926AEA1&screen=indx (accessed May 7, 2011).

Jinshu. In *Ershisi shi*. Beijing: Zhonghua shuju, 1995.

Jiu Tangshu. Beijing: Zhonghua shuju, 1975.

Kanei shoka keizu den. Tokyo: Zoku gunsho ruijū kanseikai, 1980–1994.

Kang Hang. *Kanyangnok*. Changsŏgak, Hangukhak Chung'ang Yŏn'guwŏn.

———. *Kanyangnok*. In Yi Ŭrho, trans., *Suŭn Kanyangnok*. Seoul: Yangyŏnggak, 1984.

———. *Kanyangnok*. In Boku Shōmei (Pak Chongmyŏng), trans., *Kanyōroku: Chōsen jusha no Nihon yokuryūki*. Tokyo: Heibonsha, 1984.

———. "Rekidai meii denryaku jo." In *Rekidai meii denryaku*, by Yoshida Sōjun. Tōyō bunko collection.

———. *Kanyangnok*. In Kang Hang, *Suŭn chip*. In *Han'guk munjip ch'onggan*, vol. 73. Seoul: Minjok munhwa ch'ujinhoe, 1991.

Kawai Masaharu. *Ankokuji Ekei*. Tokyo: Yoshikawa kōbunkan, 1959.
Kawase Kazuma. *Zōho shintei Ashikaga Gakkō no kenkyū*. Tokyo: Kōdansha, 1974.
Keene, Donald. *Seeds in the Heart: Japanese Literature from Earliest Times to the Late Sixteenth Century*. New York: Henry Holt, 1993.
"Keichō sannen daimyōchō." In *Zoku gunsho ruijū*, vol. 25, part 1, *Buke-bu*. Tokyo: Zoku gunsho ruijū kanseikai, 1924.
Kim Sŏkchu. *Sigam sŏnsaeng yugo*. In *Han'guk munjip ch'onggan*, vol. 145. Seoul: Minjok munhwa ch'ujinhoe, 1995.
Kim Sŏng'ae. *Suŭn chip*. http://db.itkc.or.kr/index.jsp?bizName=MH&url=/itkcdb/text/nodeViewIframe.jsp?bizName=MH&seojId=kc_mh_a287&gunchaId=&muncheId=&finId=&NodeId=&setid=1284630&Pos=0&TotalCount=1&searchUrl=ok (accessed December 11, 2009).
Kin Heidō (Kŭm Pyŏngdong). *Mimizuka: Hideyoshi no hanagiri—Mimigiri o megutte*. Tokyo: Sōwasha, 1978.
Kitagawa, Tomoko. "The Conversion of Hideyoshi's Daughter Gō." *Japanese Journal of Religious Studies* 34, no. 1 (2007): 9–25.
Kitajima Manji. *Chōsen nichinichi ki—Kōrai nikki: Hideyoshi no Chōsen shinryaku to sono rekishi-teki kokuhatsu*. Tokyo: Soshiete, 1982.
———. "Toyotomi seiken no Chōsen shinryaku to Gozan sō." In *Bakuhansei kokka to iiki—Ikoku*, ed. Katō Eiichi, Kitajima Manji, and Fukaya Katsumi, 179–217. Tokyo: Azekura shobō, 1989.
———. "Nitchō kankei no shiseki o tazunete." *Nihon rekishi* 716 (2008): 43–45.
Kobayashi Seiji. *Date Masamune*. Tokyo: Yoshikawa kōbunkan, 1959.
Kodaigaku kyōkai and Kodaigaku kenkyūjo, eds. *Heian jidaishi jiten*, 3 vols. Tokyo: Kadokawa shoten, 1994.
Konishi Yukinaga—Don Agostinho. Yatsushiro: Yatsushiro shiritsu hakubutsukan Mirai no mori myūjiamu, 2007. [Exhibition catalogue.]
Kuwata Tadachika. *Yodo-gimi*. Tokyo: Yoshikawa kōbunkan, 1958.
Kwangsan Kim ssi chokpo.
Kwŏn P'il. *Sŏkchu sŏnsaeng munjip*. Seoul: Kyŏng'in munhwasa, 1993.
Kyŏng Sŏm. *Haesarok*. In *Haehaeng ch'ongjae*, 2:233–340. Seoul: Minjok munhwa ch'ujinhoe, 1974.
Kyōto shisekikai, ed. *Hayashi Razan shishū*. Reprint, Kyoto: Perikansha, 1979.
Lamers, Jeroen. *Japonius Tyrranus: The Japanese Warlord Oda Nobunaga Reconsidered*. Leiden: Hotei Publishing, 2000.
Lewis, James B. *Frontier Contact Between Chosŏn Korea and Tokugawa Japan*. London: RoutledgeCurzon, 2003.

Loewe, Michael. *A Biographical Dictionary of the Qin, Former Han, and Xin Periods (221 B.C.–A.D. 24)*. Leiden: Brill, 2000.

Maeda ikueikai Sonkeikaku bunko, ed. *Shūgaishō*. Tokyo: Yagi shoten, 1998.

Mao shi zhengyi. In *Shisanjing zhushu*. Beijing: Zhonghua shuju, 1980.

Masuda, Wataru. *Japan and China: Mutual Representations in the Modern Era*. Trans. Joshua A. Fogel. Richmond, UK: Curzon, 2000.

Matsuda Kiichi. *Kinsei shoki Nihon kankei Nanban shiryō no kenkyū*. Tokyo: Kazama shobō, 1967.

———. "Tanba Yagi-jō to Naitō Joan ni tsuite." [*Kyōto gaikokugo daigaku*] *Cosmica* 7 (1977): 1–24.

"Matsuke Chōfu Mōri-ke." In *Kinsei Bōchō shoke keizu sōran fu shinsen Ōuchi-shi keizu*, ed. Misaka Keiji, 18–24. Yamaguchi, Japan: Matsuno shoten, 1966.

Mencius. Trans. D. C. Lau. Harmondsworth, England: Penguin, 1970.

Mengzi zhushu. In *Shisanjing zhushu*. Beijing: Zhonghua shuju, 1980.

Miki Seiichirō. "Chōsen eki ni okeru guneki taikei ni tsuite." *Shigaku zasshi* 75, no. 2 (1966): 1–26. (Reprinted in Fujiki Hisashi and Kitajima Manji, eds., *Toyotomi seiken*, 306–23. Tokyo: Yūseidō shuppan, 1974.)

Minegishi Sumio and Katagiri Akihiko, eds. *Sengoku bushō kassen jiten*. Tokyo: Yoshikawa kōbunkan, 2005.

Morikawa Osamu. "Shoki kokatsuji-ban no inkōsha ni tsuite: Saga no Suminokura (Yoshida) Soan o megutte." *Biburia* 100 (1993): 148–75.

Morohashi Tetsuji. *Dai Kanwa jiten*. Tokyo: Daishūkan shoten, 1956.

Murai Shōsuke. "Poetry in Chinese as a Diplomatic Art in Premodern East Asia." In *Tools of Culture: Japan's Cultural, Intellectual, Medical, and Technological Contacts in East Asia, 1000s–1500s*, ed. Andrew Edmund Goble, Kenneth R. Robinson, and Haruko Wakabayashi, 49–69. Ann Arbor, Mich.: Association for Asian Studies, 2009.

Nagahara Keiji, ed. *Iwanami Nihonshi jiten*. Tokyo: Iwanami shoten, 1999.

Nagashima Fukutarō. "Keichō sannen Toyotomi Hideyoshi no Hori Kyūtarō ate Echigo-kuni chigyōgata mokuroku ni tsuite." [*Kansei gakuin daigaku*] *Ronkyū* 17, no. 4 (1967): 126–38.

Naitō Shunpo. *Bunroku Keichō eki ni okeru hiryonin no kenkyū*. Tokyo: Tōkyō daigaku shuppankai, 1976.

Nakabe Toshiko. *Kinsei toshi no seiritsu to kōzō*. Tokyo: Shinseisha, 1967.

Nakano Hitoshi. *Tachibana Muneshige*. Tokyo: Yoshikawa kōbunkan, 2001.

———. *Bunroku—Keichō no eki*. Tokyo: Yoshikawa kōbunkan, 2008.

"Nansenbushū Dai Nippon-koku shōtōzu." Tōkyō daigaku toshokan collection.

Nelson, David Gordon. "Law and Order in the Making of Early Modern Japan: Seventeenth-Century Kanazawa Castle Town Administration." Ph.D. diss., Indiana University, 2007.

Ng, Wai-Ming. *The I ching in Tokugawa Thought and Culture*. Honolulu: University of Hawai'i Press, 2000.

Nihon chimei daijiten 40: Fukuoka-ken. Tokyo: Kadokawa shoten, 1988.

Nihon Kirisutokyō rekishi daijiten. Tokyo: Kyōbunkan, 1988.

Nihon shoki. In *Shintei zōho Kokushi taikei*. Tokyo: Yoshikawa kōbunkan, 2000.

No In. *Kŭmgyerok*. In No In, *Kŭmgye sŏnsaeng munjip*. In *Kŭmgye sŏnsaeng munjip—Maeo sŏnsaeng munjip*. Seoul: Kyŏng'in munhwasa, 1997.

O Hŭimun. *Swaemirok*. Seoul: Kyŏng'in ilbosa, 1990.

O Yun'gyŏm. *Tongsasang illok*. In *Haehaeng ch'ongjae*, 2:340–97. Seoul: Minjok munhwa ch'ujinhoe, 1974.

Ogasawara Nobuo. *Nihon tō: Nihon no waza to bi to tamashii*. Tokyo: Bungei shunju, 2007.

Ōmura Tomonojō, ed. *Kakukan sensei jikki— Kanyōroku—Tōkyō zakki*. Keijō: Chōsen kenkyūkai, 1911.

Ōnishi Yasumasa. "Hideyoshi shigo no Ukita-shi: Iwayuru Ukita sōdō o chūshin ni." *Nihon rekishi* 727 (2008): 16–31.

Ōtsuki Takasuke. *Sadaishi Takasuke ki*. In *Kaitei Shiseki shūran*, vol. 25. Tokyo: Kondō shuppanbu, 1903.

Pak Chongmyŏng, trans. *Kanyōroku: Chōsen jusha no Nihon yokuryŭki*. Tokyo: Heibonsha, 1984.

Pak Hongjang. *Tongsarok*. In *Nong'adang Pak Hongjang ŭi saeng'ae wa Imjin kuguk hwaldong* by Chang Tongik, 1–28. Taegu, Republic of Korea: Kyŏngbuk taehakkyo T'oegye yŏnguso, 2002.

P'ap'yŏng Yun ssi Nojongp'a po. Taejŏn, Republic of Korea: Nong'yŏng ch'ulp'ansa, 1983.

Philippi, Donald L., trans. *Kojiki*. Tokyo: University of Tokyo Press, 1968.

Pyŏn Tongmyŏng. "Kang Hang ŭi p'ilsabon *Kanyangnok* koch'al: Yŏnggwang Naesan Sŏwŏn sojangbon ŭl chungsim ŭro." *Asea yŏngu* 12 (1996): 239–51.

Rekishi to bungaku no kai and Shimura Arihiro, eds. *Kassen sōdō jiten*. Tokyo: Bensei shuppan, 2005.

Ryō no gige. In *Yakuchū Nihon ritsuryō*, ed. Ritsuryō kenkyūkai, vol. 9, *Ryō no gige yakuchū hen ichi*. Tokyo: Tōkyōdō shuppan, 1989.

Saishō Shūtai. *Gakumonsho ki*. In *Nanyōkō*, by Saishō Shūtai. In *Zoku gunsho ruijū*, 13:2. Tokyo: Zoku gunsho ruijū kanseikai, 1907.

Sakamoto Mitsuru et al., eds. *Nanban byōbu shūsei*. Tokyo: Chūō Kōron bijutsu shuppan, 2008.
Sanbyakuhan hanshu jinmei jiten. Tokyo: Shinjinbutsu ōraisha, 1987.
Sangawa Akira. *Hideyoshi o osotta daijishin: Jishin kōkogaku de Sengokushi o yomu*. Tokyo: Heibonsha, 2010.
Sansom, G. B. "Early Japanese Law and Administration (Part I)." *Transactions of the Asiatic Society of Japan* 9 (1932): 67–109.
——. "Early Japanese Law and Administration (Part II)." *Transactions of the Asiatic Society of Japan* 10 (1933): 117–49.
Satō Masatoshi. "Kodai Nihon no shitōkansei." *Shigaku zasshi* 116, no. 8 (2007): 1–38.
Sawyer, Ralph D. with Mei-chün Sawyer, trans. *The Seven Military Classics of Ancient China*. Boulder, Colo.: Westview Press, 1993.
Sengoku fasshon: Bushō no bigaku. Nagoya: Tokugawa bijutsukan, 2009. [Exhibition catalogue.]
Sengoku jinmei jiten. Tokyo: Yoshikawa kōbunkan, 2006.
Shangshu zhengyi. In *Shisanjing zhushu*. Beijing: Zhonghua shuju, 1980.
Shimofusa Toshikazu. "Saishō Shūtai: *Gakumonsho ki* o chūshin ni." *Kokugo kokubun* 41, no. 11 (1972): 47–60.
Shimoura Yasukuni. *Yoshida—Suminokura-ke no kenkyū*. N.p.: Kinki wasan zemināru, 1999.
Shinmura Taku. *Nihon iryō shakaishi no kenkyū: Kodai chūsei no minshū seikatsu to iryō*. Tokyo: Hōsei daigaku shuppankyoku, 1985.
Shintei Kansei chōshū shokafu. Tokyo: Zoku gunsho ruijū kanseikai, 1965.
Shokugenshō. In *Gunsho ruijū*, 5:603–38. Tokyo: Zoku gunsho ruijū kanseikai, 1944.
Sima Qian. *Shiji*. In *Ershisi shi*. Beijing: Zhonghua shuju, 1995.
Sin Yuhan. *Haeyurok*. In *Haehaeng ch'ongjae*, 1:48–76, 2:1–15. Seoul: Minjok munhwa ch'ujinhoe, 1974.
Sinjŭng Tongguk yŏji sŭngnam. Seoul: Myŏngmundang, 1959.
Sippel, Patricia G. "Mapping the Tokugawa Domain from 1590 through the Early Nineteenth Century." [*Kokusai kirisutokyō daigaku Ajia bunka kenkyūjo*] *Ajia bunka kenkyū* 21 (1995): 49–69.
Smith, David Eugene and Yoshio Mikami. *A History of Japanese Mathematics*. 1914; reprint, Mineola, N.Y.: Dover, 2004.
Song Ilgi and An Hyŏnju. "Suŭn Kang Hang p'yŏnch'an *Kanyangnok* ŭi kyogam yŏn'gu." *Sŏji hakpo* 33 (2009): 5–30.
Song Lian. *Hanlin beiji*. In *Song Xueshi wenji*. In *Sibu chonggan jibu*.
——. *Luoshan ji*. In Kokuritsu kōbunshokan Naikaku bunko collection.

Sŏnjo sillok. In *Chosŏn wangjo sillok*, vols. 21–25. Seoul: Kuksa p'yŏnch'an wiwŏnhoe, 1955–1963.
Sŏnjo sujŏng sillok. In *Chosŏn wangjo sillok*, vol. 25. Seoul: Kuksa p'yŏnch'an wiwŏnhoe, 1955–1963.
Sŏnwŏn kyebo. In *Han'guksa*, vol. 7, *Nyŏnp'yo*. Seoul: Ŭryu munhwasa, 1959.
Suzuki Yasuko. *Nagasaki bugyō no kenkyū*. Kyoto: Shibunkaku, 2007.
Swope, Kenneth M. "Deceit, Disguise, and Dependence: China, Japan, and the Future of the Tributary System, 1592–1596." *The International History Review* 24, no. 4 (December 2002): 757–82.
———. "Crouching Tigers, Secret Weapons: Military Technology Employed During the Sino-Japanese Korean War, 1592–1592." *Journal of Military History* 69, no. 1 (January 2005): 11–42.
———. "Bestowing the Double-edged Sword: Wanli as Supreme Military Commander." In *Culture, Courtiers, and Competition: The Ming Court (1368–1644)*, ed. David M. Robinson, 61–115. Cambridge, Mass.: Harvard University Asia Center, 2008.
———. *A Dragon's Head and a Serpent's Tail: Ming China and the First Great East Asian War, 1592–1598*. Norman: University of Oklahoma Press, 2009.
T'aejong sillok. In *Chosŏn wangjo sillok*, vols. 1–2. Seoul: Kuksa p'yŏnch'an wiwŏnhoe, 1955–1963.
"Taikō-sama ondai gohaibunchō (Keichō ninen koro)." In *Hōkō ibun*, ed. Kusaka Hiroshi. Tokyo: Hakubunkan, 1914.
Takayanagi Mitsutoshi and Takeuchi Rizō, eds. *Nihonshi jiten*, 2nd ed. Tokyo: Kadokawa shoten, 1974.
Tamura Saburō and Shimoura Yasukuni. "Tenri-bon *Sanyōki* ni tsuite." *Sūri Kaiseki Kenkyūjo kōkyūroku* 1064 (1998): 41–62; http://www.kurims.kyoto-u.ac.jp/~kyodo/kokyuroku/contents/pdf/1064-5.pdf (accessed August 2, 2009).
Tenri daigaku fuzoku Tenri toshokan, ed. *Chōsen tsūshinshi to Edo jidai no hitobito*. Tokyo: Tenri gyararii, 1989.
Tokugawa shoka keifu. Tokyo: Zoku gunsho ruijū kanseikai, 1970.
Tonami Mamoru. *Tōdai seiji shakaishi kenkyū*. Kyoto: Dōhōsha, 1986.
Tonomura, Hitomi. *Community and Commerce in Late Medieval Japan: The Corporate Villages of Tokuchin-ho*. Stanford: Stanford University Press, 1992.
Tōshōdaiji. Tokyo: Kadokawa shoten, 1955.
Totman, Conrad. *Tokugawa Ieyasu, Shogun: A Biography*. San Francisco: Heian, 1983.
Tsuda Saburō. *Kita no mandokoro: Hideyoshi botsugo no haran no hassei*. Tokyo: Chūō kōronsha, 1994.

Turnbull, Stephen. *Samurai Invasion: Japan's Korean War, 1592–1598*. London: Cassell, 2002.
Tyler, Royall. *The Tale of Genji*. 2 vols. New York: Viking Penguin, 2001.
Ueno-shi kobunken kankōkai, ed. *Kōzan-kō jitsuroku: Tōdō Takatora den*. Osaka: Seibundō, 1998.
Ugye Yi ssi taedongbo. N.p.: Ugye Yi Ssi Taedongbo P'yŏnch'an wiwŏnhoe, 1984.
Unno Kazutaka. *Chizu ni miru Nihon: Wakoku—Jipangu—Dai Nippon*. Tokyo: Daishūkan shoten, 1999.
Uno Shunichi et al., eds. *Nihonshi jiten*. Tokyo: Kadokawa shoten, 1996.
Wada Hidematsu. *Kanshoku yōkai*. Ed. Tokoro Isao. Tokyo: Kōdansha, 1983.
Wagner, Edward Willett. *The Literati Purges: Political Conflict in Early Yi Korea*. Cambridge, Mass.: East Asian Research Center, Harvard University, 1978.
Waltham, Clae. *Shu Ching, Book of History: A Modernized Edition of the Translations of James Legge*. Chicago: Henry Regnery, 1971.
Wang Hongxu. *Mingshi gao*. Tokyo: Kyūko shoin, 1973.
Wang, Yi-t'ung. *Official Relations Between China and Japan, 1368–1549*. Cambridge, Mass.: Harvard University Press, 1953.
Watanabe, Miki. "An International Maritime Trader—Torihara Sōan: The Agent for Tokugawa Ieyasu's First Negotiations with Ming China, 1600." In *The East Asian "Mediterranean": Maritime Crossroads of Culture, Commerce and Human Migration*, ed. Angela Schottenhammer, 169–76. Wiesbaden: Harrassowitz Verlag, 2008.
Watson, Burton. trans. *The Complete Works of Chuang Tzu*. New York: Columbia University Press, 1968.
Xin Tangshu. Beijing: Zhonghua shuju, 1975.
Xu Yihou. "Manli ershinian eryue ershiliuri Xu Junwang jidao Xu Yihou Chen Jimi shiqing." In "Jinbao Wo jing," in *Quan Zhe bingshi kao*. In Kokuritsu kōbunshokan Naikaku bunko collection.
Yamada Kunikazu. "Fushimi-jō to sono jōkamachi no fukugen." In *Toyotomi Hideyoshi to Kyōto: Jurakutei, Odoi to Fushimi-jō*, ed. Nihonshi kenkyūkai, 198–240. Kyoto: Bunrikaku, 2001.
Yamashina Tokitsune. *Tokitsune-kyō ki*. In *Dai Nihon kokiroku*, vol. 9. Tokyo: Iwanami shoten, 1975.
Yi Ch'aeyŏn. *Imjin waeran p'oro silgi yŏn'gu*. Seoul: Pagijŏng, 1995.
Yi Chihang, *P'yojurok*. In *Haehaeng ch'ongjae*, 3:65–69. Seoul: Minjok munhwa ch'ujinhoe, 1974.
Yi Haejun. *Chosŏn hugi munjung sŏwŏn yŏn'gu*. Seoul: Kyŏng'in munhwasa, 2008.

Yi Hwang. *T'oegye chip*. In *Han'guk munjip ch'onggan*, vol. 31. Seoul: Munjip munhwa ch'ujinhoe, 1989.
Yi Hyŏnjong, ed. *Kaejŏng jŭngbop'an Tongyang nyŏnp'yo*. Seoul: T'amgudang, 2005.
Yi Pyŏngdo. *Han'guk yuhaksa*. Seoul: Asea munhwasa, 1987.
Yi Sangbaek. *Han'guksa: Kŭnse chŏn'gi p'yŏn*. Seoul: Ŭryu munhwasa, 1962.
Yi Sugwang. *Chibong yusŏl*. Keijō: Chōsen kosho kankōkai, 1915.
Yi U. *Oksan sigo*. In *Han'guk munjip ch'onggan*, vol. 53. Seoul: Munjip munhwa ch'ujinhoe, 1990.
Yŏji tosŏ. Seoul: T'amgudang, 1973.
Yŏnggwang soksu yŏji sŭngnam. Han'guk kungnip chungang tosŏgwan collection.
Yŏnggwang soksu yŏji sŭngnam. Ed. Kang Yŏnghwan et al. Yŏnggwang, Republic of Korea: Yŏnggwang imwŏn, 1931.
Yŏnggwang ŭpchi. In *Chŏlla-do ŭpchi*, vol. 12. Seoul: Sŏul taehakkyo Kyujanggak, 2005.
Yŏngnam Tae Pangmulgwan sojang Han'guk ŭi yet chido: Top'an p'yŏn. Seoul: Yŏngnam taehakkyo pangmulgwan, 1998.
Yŏngsan Kim ssi sebo.
Yŏngsan (P'albong) Kim ssi taedongbo. Seoul: Han'guk chokpo tosŏgwan, 1990.
Yŏrŭp wŏnu sajŏk. Seoul: Minch'ang munhwasa, 1991.
Yu, Sŏngnyong. *The Book of Corrections: Reflections on the National Crisis During the Japanese Invasion of Korea, 1592–1598*. Trans. Choi Byonghyon. Berkeley: Institute of East Asian Studies, University of California, 2002.
Yun Sŏn'gŏ. "Nyŏnbo." In Yun Sŏn'gŏ, *Nosŏ sŏnsaeng chip*. Han'guk kungnip chungang tosŏgwan collection.
———. "Kanggam hoeyo sŏ." In Kang Hang, *Kanggam hoeyong*. Koryŏ taehakkyo tosŏgwan collection.
———. *Tongt'o chip*. In *Han'guk munjip ch'onggan*, vol. 100. Seoul: Minjok munhwa ch'ujinhoe, 1992.
Zhouyi zhengyi. In *Shisanjing zhushu*. Beijing: Zhonghua shuju, 1980.
Zhuangzi jiao quan. Ed. Wang Shumin. Beijing: Zhonghua shuju, 2007.

Index

Abe Yoshio, xiii, 183n88
Akamatsu Hiromichi (Saimura Masahiro), xix, 76, 95–96, 144n85, 176n27, 183n56, 183n86
Akechi Mitsuhide, 48, 80–81, 156n6, 178n39, 178nn45–46, 178n48
Akita Sanesue, 191n73
Amaterasu Shrine, 36, 151n35
An Hyŏnju, xxiii
An'gol Port, 153n11
Ankokuji Ekei, 31, 33, 53, 80, 89, 149nn11–12, 150n24, 166n81
Annual Festivities and Celebrations of the Chu, 7, 140n47
Asano Nagamasa (Danjō; Shōhitsu Nagamasa), 51, 78, 82–83, 88–90, 161n43, 185n11, 188n46
Asano Yukinaga, 51–52, 78, 161n44, 188n46
Ashikaga Gakkō, 151n33
Ashikaga Yoshimitsu, 156n7
astronomy, 33
Azuma kagami (Mirror of the East), 47

barbarians, xv, 4, 7, 23–27, 39, 50, 84–85, 155n25

Battle of Ch'ilch'ŏn Straits, 136n10
Battle of Sekigahara, xxx, 144n84, 175n16, 182n74, 193n97
Bessho Nagaharu (Bessho Shōzaburō), 79–80, 178n43
Bessho Shigemune, 193n95
Bessho Yoshiharu, 115, 193n95
Bian Zhuangzi, 63, 171n36
Bo Yi, 4, 27, 45, 139n35, 142n68, 148n32
Board of Rites (Chosŏn), 32, 149n16
Bonshun (Shinryūin Bonshun), 152n47, 181n68
Book of Changes (*Zhouyi*), 33, 149n18
Book of History (*Shujing*), 146n15
Book of Poetry (*Shijing*), 145n8
Buddhism, 11, 35, 49, 141n51, 144n82, 151n36, 178n39, 179n50

Cao Cao, 85, 181n66
captives, Korean, 3–5, 34; acculturation of, 25, 42; escape attempts by, xii, xvi, xix, 6, 10–12, 20–22, 42–45; Kang's exhortation to, 23–27; number of, ix–x, 133n1; repatriation of, ix, 133n2. *See also particular names*

Changsŏgak text (*The Record of a Shepherd*), xxiv
Che, 173n51, 196n138
Che, King (Wei), 146n12
Chibong yusŏl (Classified Essays of Chibong), xxiii
China. *See* Ming China
Chinese language, 34, 36, 49, 53, 94, 157n20
Cho Kwangjo, 143n75
Chŏn Sisŭp, 15
Chŏng Ch'angse, 15, 16, 142n65
Chŏng Hŭidŭk, 142n66
Chŏng Yŏnsu, 44
Chŏngyu War. *See* Imjin War
Chōsokabe Morichika, 51, 52, 78, 162n47, 195n116
Chōsokabe Motochika, 78, 92, 195n116
Chungjong, King, 143n75
civilization, exclusive *vs.* inclusive, xi–xvii, xxx, 7, 23–24, 27. *See also* barbarians
Confucianism, xii–xvii, 23, 26, 35, 95–96, 143n75, 151nn33–34, 183n87
Confucius's Family Teachings, 151n34
customs, Japanese, 25, 32–37, 48, 62–63, 86, 92–93, 149n22, 150n23

Daoism, 141n60
Date Chūjō Masamune, 51, 73, 75, 88–89, 92, 160n36, 176n19, 190n68
Date Kojirō, 176n19
Dezong, Emperor, 147n28
Diagram of the Civilized and the Barbarous (Huaidu), 24
diplomacy: Chinese, 69–71, 156n7; envoys of, 37, 58–59, 69–71, 140n50, 156n7; Japanese, 37, 58–59, 69–71, 140n50, 150n30, 151n32, 156n7; and peace negotiations, 59, 67–70, 85–88

divination, xv, 33, 151n33
Dōhei, 43

earthquakes, 39, 83, 152n47, 180n57, 180n64
Edo, xxvii, xxix
espionage, xi–xiii, xvi, 148n5, 149n19

fortifications: Japanese, 59–60; Korean, 57, 60–62, 171nn28–29, 171n31
Fujiwara Minamoto no Yoshisada (Nitta Yoshisada), 72, 174n2
Fujiwara no Sadaie (Fujiwara no Teika), 95, 182n85
Fujiwara Seika (Myōsuin Sōshun), xiii–xv, xix, 19–21, 29, 95–96, 144n82, 144n85, 150n31; students of, 76, 148n9, 176n27
Fukiaezu no mikoto (Tenjin), 47, 155n1
Fukuhara Nagataka, 88–89
Fukuhara Naotaka, 51, 52, 121, 163n55, 181n71
Fukushima Masanori, 77, 88, 105, 187n30
Furuta Oribe (Hotta Oribe), 33, 149n17
Fushimi, xxvii, xxix
Fushimi Castle, 14–15, 34, 44, 83, 180n57

Gakumonsho ki (Records from the Study Hall; Saishō Shūtai), 53, 166n82
Gangjian huiyao, 184n7
generals, Japanese, 51–53, 71–97; alliances and plots among, 88–91; lands of, 91–92. *See also* particular names
generals, Korean, 57–58. *See also* particular names
Genho Raisan, 150n32
Gien (monk), 152n47
Gō (wife of Ukita Hideie), 176n26, 176n28
Go-Mizunoo, Emperor, 183n88

Go-Yōzei, Emperor, 35, 143n79, 158n24, 181n68
Guan Zhong, 27
Guo Jin, 57
Guo Ziyi, 56, 170n20

Ha Taein, 16
Hachisuka (Hasuka) Iemasa, 51–52, 78, 88, 162n48, 194n109
Haedong chido (Atlas of the Eastern Country), xxix
Haehaeng ch'ongjae, xxiii
Hakuun Kōsetsu (Tōdō Torataka), xxvi, 12, 43, 141n55
Han dynasty, xi, 146n21
Han Shin, 55, 167n3
Hashiba Hidetoshi. *See* Kobayakawa Hideaki
Hata family, 48
Hayakawa Nagamasa, 52, 88, 89, 121, 164n64, 195n126
Hayashi Razan, xiv, 35, 150n31
He Yingchao, xvii–xviii
Heian court, xx–xxi
Hijikata Kanpei (Hijikata Katsuhisa), 39, 90–91, 182n74
home, concept of, xi, xiv, xvii, 25, 96
Hong Kunok, 6, 140n42
Hori Hideharu (Hori Kyūtarō), 74, 176n18, 192n87
Hori Hidemasa (Hori Kyūtarō), 74, 77, 92
Horio Yoshiharu (Horikawa Yoshiharu), 77, 92, 105, 177n33, 187n37
Hosokawa Tadaoki, 30, 51, 73, 78, 88–92, 160n38
Hosokawa Yūsai Fujitaka, 114, 193n93
Hotta Oribe (Furuta Oribe), 33, 149n17

Huang Youxian (Mōri Shigeyoshi), 33, 149n20
Huizong, Emperor (Xuanhe), 25, 146n11
Hŭksan Island, 2, 138n24
Hwang Sin, 2, 56, 137n16, 169n12
Hwang Yun'gil, 170n23

Ian. *See* Yoshida Sōjun
Ichimura, 15, 19
identity, Korean, x–xi, xiv, xvii
Ijūin Tadamasa, 177n32
Ijūin Tadamune, 177n32
Ikeda Hideo (Ikeda Akio), 51, 52, 54, 162n49, 167n85, 195n115
Ikeda Hideuji, 167n85
Ikeda Magoshirō, 54
Ikeda Terumasa (Ikuta Sanzaemon), 78, 182n78, 187n32
Iki no kami (son of Ieyasu), 72, 91
Ikoma Chikamasa, 51, 78, 92, 162n45, 194n110
Ikoma Kazumasa, 51–52, 78, 162n46, 194n110
Ikyō Eitetsu, 35, 81, 150n32
Illa (Nichira), 36, 50, 158n27
Im Ch'igyun, xxiv
Im Taehŭng, 20, 69
Im Tŭkche, 142n66
Imjin War (*Imjin Waeran*), ix–xi, xix, 8, 29–31, 71–97, 138n23, 153nn6–7; battles of, 1–2, 55–56, 135nn3–4, 136nn9–10, 144nn83–84, 154n18, 168nn6–10, 169n14; Japanese generals in, 51–53
Imjŏng, Prince (Ōuchi Sakyō no daibu), 73
Ishida Masazumi, 186n17
Ishida Mitsunari, xxx, 82–84, 109, 161n40, 181n71, 185n11, 189n53; military service of, 51, 66, 73–74, 77, 87–90, 175n16

228   INDEX

Japan: administrative districts of, xiii, xvi, xx, xxv–xxx, 43, 49–51, 101–27, 157n22, 185n3, 185n7; administrative offices of, xiii, xx–xxi, 43, 47–48, 129–32, 153n7, 156n5, 171n35; construction in, 34, 39; customs of, 25, 32–37, 48, 62–63, 86, 92–93, 149n22, 150n23; and diplomacy, 37, 58–59, 69–71, 140n50, 150n30, 151n32, 156n7; flag of, 138n30; and foreigners, xv, 37; geography of, 37–38, 50; "King" of, 156n7; maps of, xvi, xxii–xvi, xxv–xxx, xxvi, 43, 157n18, 157n22; and Ming China, xv, 33–34, 82, 145n9; monks in, 35–36, 94–95; natural disasters in, xv, 11, 38–39, 83, 152n47, 180n57, 180n64. *See also* military, Japanese

Japan House (K. *Waegwan*, J. *Wakan*), 71, 126, 173n51

Japanese language, 34, 49

Jimyōji Junkoku, 186n24

Kakimi Kazunao, 53, 166nn77–78
Kako Sōryū, 20, 144n85
Kamakura *bakufu*, xx, 174n2
Kanamori Nagachika (Kanamori Yoshichika), 189nn57–58
Kanamori Yoshishige, 189n58
Kang Aesaeng, 3, 5
Kang Ch'ŏnch'u, 15, 142n64
Kang Chun, 42, 44, 138n28, 139n39, 140n41
Kang family, xxi–xxii, 2–9, 137n14, 137nn17–18, 138nn19–21, 153n10; brothers of Hang, 8, 20, 42, 44, 138n28, 139n39, 140n41, 140n48; capture of, 3–7, 41–42; and return to Chosŏn, 95–96; and Takatora, ix, 13, 19–21, 42, 45, 66, 96
Kang Hae, 138n19

Kang Hang (Suŭn): background of, 146n17, 152n1, 155n23; biography of, 184n8; students of, xiv, xx–xxii, 99–100
Kang Hoebaek (T'ongjŏng), 16, 142n72
Kang Hong, 2, 137n18
Kang Hwan, 42, 44, 140n41, 140n48
Kang Hyangsu, 137n18
Kang Hyŏp, 2, 137n18
Kang Kahŭi, 8
Kang Karyŏn, 6
Kang Kŭkch'ung, 137n18
Kang Kŭkkŏm, 137nn17–18
Kang Kŭngnyang, 137n18
Kang Obok, 137n18
Kang Sajun, 15, 16, 20, 44, 142n64
Kang Uyŏng, 6
Kang Yewŏn, 8
Kang Yong, 3
Kanmu, Emperor, 183n86
Kanshitsu Sanyō (Kanshitsu Genkitsu), 35, 151nn33–34
Kanyangnok. *See Record of a Shepherd, The*
Kasuga Shrine, 36, 151n36
Katō Kiyomasa (Katō Toranosuke), 73, 92, 95; military service of, 15, 30, 51–52, 62, 66–68, 75, 77–78, 84–85, 87–91, 163n57, 165n71; and Yukinaga, 59, 62, 87–88, 170n25
Katō Yoshiaki, 51–52, 78, 162n50, 162n52, 194n113
Keian (monk), 96, 183n88
Keitetsu Genso (Ankokuji Saidō), 53, 140n50, 167n84
Kim Changsaeng, xxi
Kim Ch'u, 142n73
Kim Chuch'ŏn, 3
Kim Hŭngdal, 16, 142n73
Kim Hŭngmae, 16, 142n73

Kim Kwŏn, 16, 142n73, 143n76
Kim Kyŏnghaeng, 29, 96
Kim Kyŏngno, 56, 169n17
Kim Pong, 42, 44, 140n41, 142n66, 153n10
Kim Sangjun, 1–2, 41, 136n12, 153n4
Kim Sik, 16, 142n73, 143n75
Kim Sŏkpok, 44, 71
Kim Sŏng'il, 58, 170n23
Kim Sŏnson, 137n14
Kim Ujŏng, 15, 44
Kim Yŏch'ŏl (Wakita Kyūbei Naokata; Jōtetsu), 176n28
Kinoshita Iesada, 148n7, 165n68, 191n74, 193n97
Kinoshita Katsutoshi, 30, 75, 78, 95, 148n7, 176nn23–24, 191n74
Kinoshita Nobutoshi, 75, 176n24, 193n97
Kinoshita Toshifusa, 75, 176nn24–25, 191n74, 193n97
Kobayakawa Hideaki (Hashiba Hidetoshi), 75–76, 148n7, 159n34, 165n68; lands of, 92, 193n98, 195n118; military service of, 29–30, 52, 77, 88, 90–91
Kobayakawa Takakage, 51, 159n34, 161n39, 165n68
Kōbō Daishi. *See* Kūkai
Kōi, Prince, 16, 35, 143n79, 150n29
Koide Hidemasa, 103, 185n16
Koide Yoshimasa, 115, 193n94
Kōjin, 43
Kong Anguo, 35, 150n26
Konishi, Maria, 170n24
Konishi Jōsei, 172n47
Konishi Nagauemon, 19–20, 69, 172n47
Konishi Yukinaga, 19, 39, 69–70, 140n50, 173n50, 196n131; brothers of, 172n47; and Kiyomasa, 59, 62, 87–88, 170n25; military service of, 51–52, 59, 62, 67, 78,

81–89, 163n58, 164n62, 167n83, 169n14, 170nn24–25
Korean language, 157n20
Kūkai (Kōbō Daishi), xviii, xxvi, 49, 157n16, 157n18, 157n22
Kuki Yoshitaka, 186n27
Kumagai Naomori, 163n55, 166nn77–78
Kumagai Naoshige, 53, 166n78
Kŭmgyerok (The Account of Kŭmgye), xxviii
Kŭmsŏng, 60, 61, 171nn28–29
Kunhak sŏkch'ae ŭimok, 96, 183n87
Kunhak sŏkchŏn ŭimok (Regulations for the Rites of Confucius at Local Schools), 183n87
Kuroda Masanaga, 78
Kuroda Nagamasa, 51–52, 62, 85, 87–89, 163n59, 165n72, 195n123
Kurushima Michifusa, 53–54, 56, 166n79, 169n11
Kwanghae, King, 136n6
Kwŏn P'il (Sŏkchu), 183n5, 184n6
Kwŏn Yul, 154n18
Kyōgoku Takatsugu, 189n52
Kyŏngbok Palace, 141n54, 146n10
Kyoto, xxvii, xxix

land: of Japanese generals, 91–92; salary, xix, 53, 57–58, 92
Li Ling, xi, 25, 146n14
Li Rusong, 135n3
Lian Polin, 147n24
Liu Bang, 146n21, 167n3, 182n79
Liu Bei, 55, 167n3
Liu Zongyuan, 24, 145n5
loyalty, xi–xvii, xx, 11, 23, 26, 46, 68–69, 155n24
Lu family (Han), 27, 147n30

Lu Zhonglian, 4, 27, 45, 139n34, 142n67, 154n21
Luoshan ji (Song Lian), 188n41

Maeda Gen'i (Tokuzenin Gen'i), 83, 88, 114, 130, 181n68, 185n11, 192n90, 196n2
Maeda Sui (Paolo), 192n90
Maeda Toshiie, 73, 86, 159n32, 175nn11–14, 176n26, 191n80, 192nn81–82, 194n102
Maeda Toshimasa (Magoshirō), 192n82
Maeda Toshinaga, 29, 73–75, 84, 86, 89–91, 175n11, 192n81
Manch'un, 3
Mao Guoke, 19, 144n83, 181n70
Mashita Nagamori, 39, 51, 77, 83, 88, 90, 160n35, 185n11
Matsudaira Tadateru, 174n6
Matsura Shigenobu, 52, 53, 122, 123, 164n62
Mencius, 23, 146n18
military, Japanese, xviii–xix, 34, 54–71; fortifications of, 59–60; practices of, 53–54, 63–64, 92–94; weaponry of, 35, 63–64, 70–71, 182n81. *See also* generals, Japanese
military, Korean, xviii–xix, 54–71; appointments of, 56–57; fortifications of, 57, 60–62, 171nn28–29, 171n31; organization of, 55, 57–58, 167nn1–2, 168n5, 169n13; status of, 54–56; and strategy, 43–44, 64–68, 93–94; and training, 24, 62. *See also* generals, Korean
Mimizuka, 66, 84–85, 180–81n65
Minamoto no Yoritomo, xxii–xxiii, 47, 94
Ming China, ix–x, 179n53; and diplomacy, 69–71, 156n7; and Imjin War, 8, 87, 144n83; and Japan, xv, 33–34, 82, 145n9
Miyabe Nagahiro, 39, 51, 77–78, 163n54, 193n96

Miyoshi Yoshifusa, 156n9
Mogami Yoshiaki, 75, 176n19, 176n22, 191n72
Mogami Yoshimitsu, 78, 88, 92
monks, Japanese, 35–36, 94–95. *See also particular names*
Monmu, Emperor, 184n2
Mōri Hidemoto, 51, 52, 118, 159n31
Mōri Iki no kami Katsunobu (Yoshinari), 52, 121, 164n60, 165n73, 195n124
Mōri Minbu no daiu (no taifu, no kami) Takamasa, 52, 56, 164n61, 165n74
Mōri Motonari, 159n34
Mōri Shigeyoshi (Huang Youxian), 33, 149n20
Mōri Terumoto, 72–73, 175n10, 178n46; lands of, 47, 75, 91–92, 194n99; military service of, 51–53, 68, 80–83, 86, 88–92, 159nn30–31, 164n61, 166n81, 175n8
Mun'gi (boatman), 2–3
Muromachi *bakufu*, xx, 49, 156n7
Myōsuin Sōshun. *See* Fujiwara Seika

Nabeshima Katsushige, 165n70
Nabeshima Naoshige, 52, 62, 151n42, 165n70
Naesan Sŏwŏn text (*The Record of a Shepherd*), xxii–xxiii
Nagasaki, 151nn42–43, 152n43
Nagasuka Iemasa, 88
Nagoya (central Honshu), 177n36
Nagoya (Kyushu), 38, 82, 122, 151n32, 152nn43–46, 161n40, 162n51, 166n78, 167n83, 186n24, 188n49, 189n52, 190n69, 192n84, 193n93, 195n114
Naitō Joan (Konishi Joan; Naitō Tadatoshi), 70, 173n50, 176n26
Nakagawa Hidemasa, 163n56

Nakagawa Hidenari, 51, 163n56, 195n119
Nakamura Kazuuji, 187n39
Namwŏn, 1, 41, 55, 56, 135nn3–4, 137n16, 153n3, 162n50, 168nn4–5, 169nn13–14,17
Nanbu Nobunao, 190n70
Nanka Genkō, 19, 144n81
"Nansenbushū Dai Nihon-koku shōtōzu" (Orthodox Map of Great Japan in Jambūdvīpa), xxvi
Natsuka Masaie, 83, 88–89, 172n45, 185n11, 186n25, 189n54
Nene, Kita no mandokoro (wife of Hideyoshi), 30, 148n7, 165n68, 185n16
Neo-Confucianism, xiii–xiv
Nitta Yoshisada (Fujiwara Minamoto Yoshisada), 72, 174n2
No In, xxviii
Nobushichirō, 4

O Ŭngt'ae, 56
Oda Hidenobu, 78, 189n55
Oda Hideo, 192n84
Oda Nobunaga, xviii, 30, 72, 113, 144n81, 159n32, 171n35, 175n11, 177n36, 177n38; death of, 47–48, 77–81, 156n6, 178n45, 178nn47–49; and Hideyoshi, 47–48, 77–81, 166n81, 178n39, 178n43, 178nn47–49; sons of, 189n55, 192n84
Oda Nobuo (Oda Nobukatsu), 113, 192n84, 196n2
Oda Nobutada, 189n55
Ogawa Suketada, 51, 163n53, 195n114
Ōgimachi, Emperor, 156n8
Ōkura-kyō no tsubone, 180n60
Ōmandokoro Naka, 180n56
Ōno Harunaga, 83–84, 90–91, 180n60, 180n62, 182nn75–76
Oryeŭi sŏ (The Five Rites of the State), 96

Osaka, xxvii, xxix
Osaka Castle, 73–74, 175n15
Ōta Kazuyoshi, 39, 152n48, 195n125
Ōtani Yoshitsugu, 51, 76, 78, 162n51, 192n85
Ōtsuki Takasuke, 152n47
Ōzu Castle, 7, 10, 12

Paek Suhoe, 69, 172n48
Pak Chongmyŏng (Boku Shōmei), 179n50
Pak Hongjang, 142n65
Pak Hongno, 56, 169n12
Pak Yŏjip, 15
Pan Mi, 57
pirates, 32–34, 37, 149n15, 166n79, 173n51, 179n53, 182n81
prisoners of war. See captives, Korean
Pusan, xv, xvii, 29, 32, 38, 46, 58, 68, 71, 76, 82, 96, 126, 141n50, 148n5, 159n30, 160n37, 161nn40–41, 162n48, 162n52, 163nn57–59, 165n68, 168n7, 173n51, 196n138

Qin, King of, 147n24
Qin dynasty, 27, 146n21
Qin Kuai, 141n61
Qin Shi Huangdi, 48, 146n21
Qing dynasty, x

Record of a Shepherd, The (*Kanyangnok*; Kang Hang), ix–xiv, xviii, xxi–xxv, xxix–xxx, 99–100
Record of the Various Customs (*Fengtuji*), 24
Rian, 30, 94, 182nn83–84
Righteous Army, 41, 153nn5–6
Ryūzōji Masaie, 37, 51–52, 62, 78, 92, 161n42, 165n69

Saimura Masahiro. *See* Akamatsu Hiromichi
Saishō Shūtai, 35, 53, 81, 150n30, 150n32, 166n82
Sakai, 19, 69, 142nn65–73, 144n83, 163n58, 180n57
Sakugen Shūryō, 158n25
Sanada Masayuki, 77, 92
Sandu, 8, 140n49
Sano Fusatsuna, 190n62
Sano Nobuyoshi, 78, 110, 190n62
Satake family, 75, 176n21
Satake Yoshinobu, 73, 88, 92, 175n16, 188n50
Satake Yoshishige, 176n20
Satomi Yoshiyasu, 188n49
Seishō Shōtai, 35, 150n30, 150n32
Sen no Rikyū, 149n17
Sengoku Hidehisa, 110, 189n59
Setsuyōshū (Collection of Words for Everyday Use; Ekirin text), xxv–xxvii, 185n4
Seven Military Classics (*Wujing qishu*), 34, 149n21
Shen Weijing, 53, 167n83
Shenzong, Emperor, 140n46
shepherding. *See* Su Wu
Shimai Sōshitsu, 140n50
Shimazu Tadatsune, 177n32
Shimazu Yoshihiro, xxiii, 37, 76–77; lands of, 81–83, 92, 196n132; military service of, 51–52, 62, 67, 77, 85, 87–88, 144n83, 161n41, 177n31
Shimizu Muneharu, 178n44, 178n47
Shinjō Naoyori, 185n12
Shintoism, 36, 151n36
Shizong, Emperor, 158n25
Shokugenshō (Treatise on the Origins of Government Offices), xxvi, 185n5

Shōnai Rebellion, 77, 177n32
Shūgaishō (Collection of Oddments), xxvi
Shussekiji, 9, 43, 141n51
Sim Anp'yŏng, 2–3, 138n21
Sim Umin, 138n21
Sin Chŏngnam, 71
Sin Kyeri, 19–20, 69
Sin Tŏkki, 44
Sin Yuhan, xxiv
Sŏ Kuk, 13
Sŏ Kyŏngbong, 142n66
Sŏ Kyŏngch'un, 15, 142n66
Sō Yoshitoshi (Dario), 8, 37, 140n50, 170n24, 173n52, 179n52; lands of, 70, 196n134, 196n137; military service of, 31, 52–53, 59, 62, 67–70, 81, 85, 164n62, 165n67
Sŏng Hon, xxi
Song Ilgi, xxiii
Song Lian (Jinglian), 187n40, 188n41
Sŏng Munjun, xxi
Song Siyŏl, xxi–xxii
Sŏnjo, King, xv–xvi, xxii, 29, 135n3, 147nn28–29, 152n1, 159n33, 170n23
Spring and Autumn Annals (*Chunqiu*), 94
Su Wu, xi–xii, xv, 26, 99–100, 142n69, 147nn24–27, 183n2, 184n6
Suminokura Ryōi, 148n9
Suminokura Soan (Sagain Yoichi), 31, 148n9
Sunjo, King, xxiv
Suŭn chip (The Collected Writings of Suŭn), xxi–xiv, 140n42
swords, Japanese, 35, 63–64, 70–71

Tachibana Muneshige (Tachibana Munetora). *See* Yanagawa Muneshige
Tai, King (Zhou), 146n13
Taizong, Emperor, 147n29

Taizu, Emperor, 57, 170n22
Takayama Ukon, 176n26
Takenaka Shigetaka, 88
Takenaka Takashige (Takenaka Gensuke; Takenaka Shigetaka; Takenaka Shigetoshi), 52, 164n63, 195n127
Tanaka Yoshimasa, 77, 105, 187n33
Tang, King, 23, 145n2
Tansoksa, 16, 17, 142nn71–72
tea culture, Japanese, 34, 149n22, 150n23
Temple of Grain (*Sajikdan*), 24, 146n10
Temple of Royal Ancestors (*Chongmyo*), 24, 67, 141n54, 155n25
Tentokuji Hōen, 190n62
Terazawa Masanari (Terazawa Hirotaka; Terazawa Sadamasa), 37, 52, 96, 151n43, 165n66, 166n76, 195n129
Tetchōrō Ikyō Eitetsu, 35, 81, 150n32
Tian Heng, 182n79
Toda Katsutaka, 51, 161n39
Tōdō Takatora, 95, 139n33, 141n51; and Kang family, ix, 13, 19–21, 42, 45, 66, 96; lands of, 153n14, 161n39, 194n112; military service of, 13, 51–52, 78, 87–88, 162n50
Tōdō Torataka (Hakuun Kōsetsu), xxvi, 12, 43, 141n55
T'oegye school (Zhu Xi Neo-Confucianism), xiii–xiv
Tokugawa Hidetada, 72, 86, 91, 174n5, 181n67
Tokugawa Ieyasu, 39, 83, 95, 144nn83–84, 150n31, 175n7, 175n16; and Hideyoshi, 65–66, 72–73, 81, 85–86, 144n84, 174n3, 181n72; lands of, 47, 72, 91–92, 156n3; military service of, xxx, 19, 29–31, 37, 68–77, 81, 84–85; rulership of, xxx, 72, 86–92, 96; sons of, 72, 86, 91, 174nn4–6

Tokugawa Nobuyasu, 174n4
Tokugawa Senhime, 86, 181n67
Tokugawa shogunate, x, xiv
Tokugawa Yoshinao, 174n6
Tokuzenin Gen'i. *See* Maeda Gen'i
Tomita Ippaku, 190n62
Tongnae, 15, 44, 58, 126, 173n51
Toyotomi Hidenaga, 159n31
Toyotomi Hidetsugu, 48, 84, 90, 148n8, 151n33, 156n9, 171n35, 175n13
Toyotomi Hideyori, xxvii, 73, 85–91, 144n84, 172n42, 175n13, 180n60, 181n68, 181n72
Toyotomi Hideyoshi, ix–x, 15, 72–87, 140n43, 150n30, 167n83, 177n36; and conquest of Japan, 47–48, 62, 148n8, 171n35, 177n31; death of, xix, 11, 18–19, 30, 44, 65–66, 73, 86–87, 143n80, 154n19, 181n68; and Ieyasu, 65–66, 72–73, 81, 85–86, 144n84, 174n3, 181n72; Kang's depiction of, 11, 18, 21, 24; name of, 48, 79, 156n8, 178nn41–42; and Nobunaga, 47–48, 77–81, 166n81, 178n39, 178n43, 178nn47–49; wives of, 30, 84–86, 90, 148n7, 165n68, 175n13, 180n60, 180n62, 182n75, 185n16
Toyotomi Tsurumatsu, 144n81, 172n42
Tsushima, xxv–xxvii, 6, 31–32, 58–59, 70, 95–97, 173nn51–53, 179n52
Tsutsui Junkei, 186nn23–24
Tsutsui Sadatsugu, 77, 92, 186n24

Uesugi Kagekatsu, 73–75, 88, 92, 175nn16–17, 190n69, 192n89
Ŭiangun, Prince, 159n33
Ukita Hideie, 29, 39, 76, 176nn26–28, 177n29, 194n102; and Hideyori, 73, 86, 91; lands of, 92; military service of, 51–52, 73–74, 88–89, 159nn32–33

Ulsan, 8, 44, 67, 154n17, 160n36, 162n46, 165n71, 166n78
Unno Kazutaka, xxvii

Valignano, Alexandro, 170n24
Veritable Records, xviii, 133n2, 148nn5–9

Wakisaka Yasuharu, 51, 160n37, 194n108
Wang Jiangong, 19, 71, 173n52, 181n70
weaponry, Japanese, 35, 63–64, 70–71, 182n81
Wei Lu, 147n27
Weisheng, 56
Weizi, 25
Wen, King (Zhou), 23, 145n2, 145n8
Wen Tianxiang, 45, 155n24
Wŏn Kyun, 1, 55–56, 136nn9–10, 168n6
writing system, Japanese, 34
Wu, Emperor, 39, 185n9
Wu, King (Zhou), 4, 27, 45, 145n2, 154n22

Xiaoji, 56
Xiongnu, xi–xii, 147nn24–27
Xu Fu, 36, 48–49, 141n60, 157n10
Xu Yihou, 82, 179n53
Xuanhe (Emperor Huizong), 25, 146n11

Yamatai, xxvii, xxix
Yan Shigu, 24, 145n4
Yanagawa Muneshige (Yanagawa Tachibana Une; Tachibana Muneshige; Tachibana Munetora), 52, 164n65, 166n75
Yanagawa Shigenobu, 31, 149n13, 149n15
Yanagawa Tachibana Une. *See* Yanagawa Muneshige
Yang Usang, 5

Yang Yuan, 1, 41, 135n3, 153n3
Yi Ch'aeyŏn, 133n1
Yi Changyŏng, 138n20
Yi Chihang, xxiii
Yi Hwang (T'oegye), xiii–xiv
Yi I (Yulgok), xxi, 138n19, 138n28
Yi Kwangjŏng, 1, 41, 135n5
Yi Pongnam, 55, 168nn4–5
Yi Sugwang (Chibong), xxiii
Yi Sunsin, xix, 2, 53, 55–56, 136n9, 138n23, 166n80, 168n6
Yi Tŏkhyŏng, 71, 173n53
Yi Yŏp, 15, 68–69, 172n44, 183n4
Yŏ Suhŭi, 142n64
Yodo-dono, 84–86, 90, 175n13, 180n60, 180n62, 182n75
Yŏm (port), 154n17, 173n51
Yōmei, Emperor, 184n1
Yonggye Shrine, xxi–xxii
Yoshida family, 181n68
Yoshida Kanemi, 181n68
Yoshida Sōjun (Ian), 33, 50, 94, 148n9, 149n19, 158n24, 158n26, 182nn83–84
Yoshida Sōkei, 158nn24–25
Yu, King, 23–24, 145n2
Yu Kye, xxi, 134n12
Yu Rang, 146n20
Yubong Village, xxi, 1, 135n2
Yue Fei, 55, 141n61, 167n3
Yujŏng (Song'un Taesa), 133n2
Yūki Harutomo, 174n4
Yūki Hideyasu, 30, 72, 91, 148n4, 174n4
Yun family, xxi–xxii
Yun Hwang, xxi, 134n13, 184n7
Yun Mun'gŏ, xxi
Yun Sŏn (Yun Sŏnjin), 1, 136n6
Yun Sŏn'gŏ, xxi

Yun Su, 134n13
Yun Sun'gŏ, xxi–xxiii, 100, 134n13, 184nn7–8
Yūsai, 193n93

Zekkai Chūshin, 49, 157n13
Zen Buddhism, 144n82
Zhang Liang, 26, 55, 146n21, 167n3
Zhao, jewel of, 147n24
Zhao, King of, 147n24
Zhao Meng (Zhao Xiangzi), 26, 146n20
Zheng Xuan, 35, 150n27
Zhi Bo, 146n20
Zhongyong, 146n13
Zhou, Duke of, 23, 145n2
Zhou, King (Shang), 154n22
Zhou Yi, 146n14
Zhu Ci, 147n28
Zhu Xi (Huian), xiii–xiv, 35, 150n28, 150n31
Zhu Xu, 45, 147n22, 155n24
Zu Ti, 26, 146n19
Zuo zhuan, 145n9

GPSR Authorized Representative: Easy Access System Europe, Mustamäe tee 50, 10621 Tallinn, Estonia, gpsr.requests@easproject.com